D1685845

THE
CONTEMPORARY
PRINT

THE CONTEMPORARY PRINT

from Pre-Pop to Postmodern

SUSAN TALLMAN

With 334 illustrations, 161 in colour

THAMES AND HUDSON

For N.

© 1996 Thames and Hudson Ltd, London

British Library Cataloguing-in-Publication Data
A catalogue record for this book is available from
the British Library

ISBN 0-500-23684-4

Printed and bound in Singapore by C. S. Graphics

CONTENTS

INTRODUCTION

The contemporary print is simultaneously one of the most successful and one of the most disparaged art forms of our time. Between 1960 and the present the print has moved from the margins of art production to its center. No longer an isolated technical specialty, printmaking is now a standard part of most artistic careers. No longer confined to drawers, boxes, or albums, it has taken over wall spaces formerly occupied by painting. Not only do the best artists of our time make prints, some of the best artworks of our time are prints.

And yet in contrast to the acres of ink that have been spilled on painting, sculpture, photography, or film, there has been remarkably little critical writing about the print. Most art periodicals and newspapers treat prints as a kind of oversized philately, focussing on auction prices and other issues of the market-place. Serious writing on the subject is concentrated in periodicals dedicated to prints, most notably *The Print Collector's Newsletter*, read zealously by print devotees and few others. Print historians such as Pat Gilmour, Riva Castleman, Richard Field, and Alexander Dückers have written insightful and informative works on the subject, but there has been no major international survey for more than a decade. Recent years have seen a profusion of catalogues raisonnés of artists, printshops, and publishers which provide invaluable assistance for the dedicated print follower, but which do not claim to review the linkages and distinctions between artists, shops, movements, and continents. This book has been written to provide a cogent history of the contemporary print, and to assemble in one place basic information about the artists, ideas, techniques, and socioeconomic forces that have brought it to its present paradoxical position.

It should, perhaps, come as no surprise that prints have become so vital a medium, given that the most conspicuous aspect of our visual landscape today is reproduction. The causes and consequences of this fact have been observed by critics, sociologists, and philosophers, and have not been lost on artists, whose business it is to provide our visual lives with meaning. The century's two most important theoretical texts on the print – William Ivins's *Prints and Visual Communication* and Walter Benjamin's *The Work of Art in the Age of Mechanical Reproduction*[1] – are not about artists' prints at all, but rather about the effects of reproduction and multiplicity. Ivins's book, published in 1953, dealt with the history of "exactly repeatable pictorial statements" not as artists' playthings, but as instruments of technological and scientific knowledge whose dispersal made possible the creation of the modern world. Ivins also expressed the critical notion of a visual "syntax" of reproduction – the idea that any given medium has strengths and weaknesses that determine what gets represented and what does not, and that profoundly alter the content of that which it claims to reproduce or represent.[2] Benjamin's famous essay, first published in Germany in 1936 but only generally available from the mid-1950s, is even less concerned with printmaking as an art form, concentrating instead on true mass production. What Benjamin called the "aura" of a work of art – its quality of unique existence – was, he felt, doomed to wither in a world where technology has made it possible for images to proliferate and circulate independently of an original. Photographic reproduction would thus form a cornerstone of a newly politicized aesthetic: "for the first time in world history, mechanical reproduction emancipates the work of art from its parasitical dependence on ritual. To an ever greater degree the work of art reproduced becomes the work of art designed for reproducibility… the instant the criterion of authenticity ceases to be applicable to artistic production, the total function of art is reversed. Instead of being based on ritual, it begins to be based on another practice – politics."[3]

Such ideas about the social impact of reproduction have been critical to much of the art produced since 1960, and not only to prints – they underlie Warhol's and Lichtenstein's painted emulations of cheap printing in the early 1960s, as well as Sherrie Levine's and Barbara Kruger's media-critical art in the late 1980s. Though the convention of the limited edition has become the de facto standard among printmakers, printshops, and print publishers, it is still just a convention – an arbitrary confinement of replication. All editions, of course, are ultimately limited, it is just a question of whether anyone kept track of the numbers: there are "unlimited" editions of ten and "limited" editions of 10,000. Clearly, however, the production of "original" prints by artists and the production of movies, advertisements, and the other truly populist

forms discussed by Ivins and Benjamin, are of radically different orders. But over the course of the last thirty-five years, artists have intentionally manipulated this gap, narrowing it with an embrace of mass communication and something approximating industrial manufacture, or widening it in pursuit of the more traditional pleasures of intimate address and something approximating the handmade.

The edition is just one of the print's specific attributes, and other characteristics have been equally important to its role in contemporary art. First and most obviously, most prints are produced through a distinctive set of procedures that result in distinctive appearances: woodcut displays graphic force, substantiality, and a subtle sense of relief; etching and engraving offer thin and sensitive wires of ink; aquatint and mezzotint deliver soft, furry expanses of tone; lithography, the "flattest" of the standard techniques, can provide crumbly, chalky lines or diaphanous washes. While these properties no longer inspire much that is new in the way of critical discourse, they continue to be essential to the way artists work. Even in the most conceptual of work, particular techniques are chosen for how they look, and many artists continue to be drawn to printmaking by the variety and beauty of the surfaces it can produce, or by some peculiar affinity for the physical and material demands of the medium. Painters, such as Motherwell and Newman, exploited the painterly liquidity of lithography, and the translucent clarity of ink on paper (so different from that of paint on canvas). More draftsmanlike artists, such as Jim Dine, revelled in the linear riches and tactility of etching, while sculptors such as Donald Judd or Joel Shapiro utilized the concrete materiality of woodblocks. The disinterest of many artists in the social ambitions of multiplicity is revealed in edition sizes of less than ten prints.

Another distinguishing feature of the print is its production by means of a separate printing surface or matrix (a lithographic stone, etching plate, woodblock, etc.), interposed between the artist's hand and the final image. Pat Gilmour put it succinctly: "the potential the print has for multiplication is acquired at the expense of direct touch. There is no print process that does not place at one remove from the sheet of paper the hand that seeks to mark it… Once printed, the mark is not intrinsically better or worse than one drawn directly; it is simply different."[4] While a great deal of effort has been spent in this century to deny this difference, and to produce prints that were "indistinguishable from drawings," one of the great achievements of the recent print has been the transformation of this perceived disadvantage into a source of meaning. Artists from Jasper Johns to Bruce Nauman have used the doublings and reversals that occur naturally when transferring images between plates, stones, and paper to articulate essentially philosophical issues of similarity and dissimilarity, identity and non-identity. Abstract artists in search of a scientific, impersonal foundation for art, and Pop artists mimicking the world around them, have both embraced the mechanistic "look" and rationalizing distance that the matrix places between the artist and the viewer. Printerly mechanics also encourage the serial development of images – proofs can be taken of successive stages of development in a way that is not possible in painting, where the successive "states" all overlie previous ones, or plates can be recombined permutationally – an attribute of great importance to artists such as Sol LeWitt for whom the revelation of a process was more critical than the arrival at a "final" image.

But despite the obvious relevance of the print to vital issues of contemporary art, prejudice remains pandemic, even among those most involved in print production. Barnett Newman wrote in the preface to his masterful portfolio of lithographs, *18 Cantos*, "I must explain that I had no plan to make a portfolio of 'prints'. I am not a printmaker…" Tom Phillips, who was elected to the Royal Academy on the basis of his printmaking, said that "To find myself, in court as it were, described as a *printmaker* sends a chill down my spine." What is the cause of this contempt? Certainly there are volumes of technically proficient, visually pointless prints, though the same might be said of painting, drawing, or sculpture. Many people, furthermore, continue to regard prints as a commercially tainted addendum to an artist's "real work." Another problem lies in the perception of printmaking as an isolated discipline. (Note that it was not the medium itself that Newman and Phillips objected to, but the category.) For much of this century, printmaking was a sequestered art form, with its own exhibitions, periodicals, competitions, and collectors, but this has largely changed over the course of the last thirty-five years. What has been described, perhaps rosily, as a "flourishing ecology" of specialist print galleries, exhibitions and publications, has dwindled, while in the institutional mainstream of museums and commercial galleries the prints of non-specialists have become steadily more visible.

A more important obstacle in the way of appreciating the print is what we might call the "neither fish nor fowl" problem. Partly handmade and partly automated, partly populist and partly elitist, the original print has struck many as either a fussy little craft or as posters with pretensions. This notion of an original print – one that did not reproduce drawings or paintings, but that bore an image developed expressly for the medium in which it existed – is historically recent, a by-product of the invention of photography and the subsequent scramble to justify artistic activities and incomes. Historically, the purpose of the print was to provide efficient, economical reproductions that could be widely distributed. Print technologies, like paper-making, were known from ancient times in Asia, but did not reach Europe until the late fourteenth century when the woodcut came into common use, providing religious souvenirs for pilgrims and playing cards for wastrels. The woodcut was followed almost immediately by engraving and etching, and in 1798 by lithography.[5] Artists such as Rembrandt and Goya discovered and exploited the rich formal properties latent in these techniques, and produced masterpieces that could not have been produced in any other way, but the vast bulk of printmaking was of a far more routine and reproductive sort. The arrival of photography and photomechanical print methods profoundly altered the role of traditional printmaking by negating its primary function, which was as a vehicle for reproduction. Print media were now "free" to be reclaimed by artists such as Whistler, who eschewed reproduction in favor of spontaneous, intuitive, irreproducible effect, and who instituted the practice of artificially limiting editions to increase the aura of rarity. A hierarchy of media was established in which etching was deemed the most "artistic" since it was the furthest removed from the stain of commerce, while the more economical lithography was considered less artistic. Subsequent generations were equally concerned with drawing distinctions between commercial printing and artistic or "original" printing.

This attempt to define the original print has done real damage to the cause of prints – accepting originality as a value in itself has placed the print at an impossible disadvantage. A print can never be as "original" as a painting, so whether or not you call it "an original print," it will never be "original" enough.

Even in the 1960s organizations such as the Print Council of America continued to define the original print largely by its exclusion of photomechanical means, even while Pop art was revitalizing printmaking by its energetic and inventive manipulation of those means.[6] Such proscriptions no longer carry much weight, but there remains a lingering distrust of prints that seem to replicate an artist's drawing or painting – despite Jasper Johns's demonstration that such replication can be done with an increase of meaning rather than a diminution of it – and there is a suspicion about works for which the artist did not directly manufacture the matrix from which

the image is printed. This grievance resurfaced as recently as the mid-1980s when Crown Point Press began working with Japanese artisans trained in the Ukiyo-e tradition, who would cut intricate blocks in precise imitation of an artist's preparatory drawing. Though this was exactly how some of the greatest prints in history had been produced, many people refused to consider the Crown Point prints "original."

Increased acceptance of collaboration as a working method has been essential to the rise in print production, but the balance of responsibilities between printers and artists continues to be a topic of controversy. This interaction is usually called collaboration, but the equality implied by the word is misleading: aesthetically the artist is always in charge, and the printer must figure out what the artist wants, and how to achieve it. The publisher puts up the money to produce the edition in exchange for a number of the prints or a percentage of the profits (usually 50 per cent), and often initiates the project, playing matchmaker between artist and printer. Once the printers and the artist have arrived at a proof that all are happy with, the edition can be printed, often by a different set of printers in the same shop. Edition size can be determined by any number of factors: the stability of the plate or stone, a guess at what the market will bear, the artist's favorite number. The edition size of early Universal Limited Art Editions publications was determined by sunset, since they would print only the number that could be done in one day. Once the edition is printed it is curated: all the impressions are inspected, rejected ones are destroyed, and accepted ones are stacked and counted in preparation for the artist's signing them. Lower edition numbers do not indicate better or even earlier impressions, only which sheets ended up on the top of the stack the day the artist came to sign.

This book attempts to chart the forms and uses of the print over a period of some thirty-five years and two continents, but it is far from being all-inclusive, and the terms of inclusion should perhaps be set out. Though the year 1960 is used here as a starting point, the distinction between "modern" and "contemporary" is as much one of character as of chronology. Robert Rauschenberg was producing "contemporary" art in 1950, while plenty of "modern" art is still being produced today. Much modernist art of the 1930s, 1940s, and 1950s stressed a heroic vision of individual identity, an integrity of process and materials, direct physical action, and the expression of subjective emotional states through personal styles. These values tended to encourage technical specialization. Modernist printmakers (of whom S. W. Hayter is the most famous) worked from a combination of subconscious impulse and intense physical involvement with their materials. In contrast to this privileging of the individual, recent thought in many disciplines – art, psychology, linguistics, and even biology – has tended to consider individual identity as a product of larger organisms or economies. Thus one of the major shifts between what strikes us as "modern" and what strikes us as "contemporary" is from an internal to an external view – from analyses of the subconscious to analyses of perception and communication; from the picture of a solitary Jackson Pollock, flinging paint in his studio, to that of Robert Rauschenberg at Gemini GEL, surrounded by technicians and art-making machinery. While modernism had given natural pride of place to painting – that most direct, visceral, and autographic of art forms – the new priorities embraced the collaborative and indirect nature of printmaking.

Instead of a fixed definition of originality or, indeed, of the print itself, I have applied some flexible guidelines. The works herein were all designed by artists, whether by picking up a burin or by picking up a telephone. Most exhibit at least two of the three traditional qualities of a print: membership in an edition; the use of paper as a support; and the presence of an image imprinted by pressing the paper against an image-bearing matrix. And while most are the product of the venerable print technologies – relief printing (woodcut or linocut), intaglio printing (etching, aquatint, etc.), and lithography – there are also watermarks, photostats, handmade papers, and digitally manipulated photographs.

The book is dominated by artists who are printmakers in addition to being painters, sculptors, performance or conceptual artists. This emphasis may disappoint people who feel, rightly, that specialist printmakers are in dire need of critical and public attention. But my concern has been to represent printmaking as an art that intersects and interacts with the critical art ideas of the day. Prints have become a critical form because their modes and procedures can articulate so many of the concerns fundamental to recent art: an interest in the mechanics of meaning and communication; a desire to reveal the processes by which an image arises; a will to expose or manipulate the social and economic contexts of art; and a conviction that understanding the workings of reproduction is essential to understanding life in the late twentieth century. I do not necessarily believe, as some print curators do, that the most important prints are made by artists whose "primary" form of expression is painting, but I think that in the past thirty-five years few important artists have limited themselves to any single art-making technique. Furthermore, it is often difficult to tell what an artist's "primary" expression is: Jasper Johns's prints are accepted as being a critical element of his work, as vital as his paintings and drawings; the importance of Richard Hamilton's prints, it could be argued, outweighs that of his paintings. Several artists commonly thought of as painters were, for some period of time, specialist printmakers – both Jim Dine and Ed Ruscha gave up canvas for several years to concentrate on graphic work; other artists trained as printmakers only to branch out later into other forms. The artists discussed in this book range from "specialist" or "primary" printmakers, deeply involved in the materials and mechanics of the medium, to those who have never set foot in a printshop.

The book is not, primarily, a technical history. Technologies of print production are both ingenious and elaborate, but they are (or should be) merely a means to an end. As master printer Ken Tyler observed, "knowing how one puts the color down with a roller isn't very interesting. It may take five years to know how to do it correctly, but it's not very interesting."[7] That said, it is also true, as Ivins observed, that the aptitudes of any given technology impose their structure on both images and ideas. In the course of this book, print technologies are discussed in terms of their impact on art rather than in any applied, practical sense.

The works discussed here have almost all been made in North America or Europe. This is not because the print activity elsewhere in the world is inconsequential – Latin America, Asia, and Eastern Europe all have long and vital printmaking traditions, and there are inventive printmakers from Africa to the Arctic – but rather because economic and cultural factors have resulted in an exchange of ideas and influences between North America and Europe that has (for better or worse) been largely independent of the rest of the world. The book is, furthermore, weighted somewhat in favor of American art. This may reflect the biases of an American author (though one who lives in Europe), but it is also a reflection of the fact that for two of the three decades under discussion, America was the pre-eminent art "power," exporting far more that it managed to import. This imbalance, which will be noticed in any survey of museum collections, is exacerbated in the world of prints. As the bi-continental publisher Peter Blum observed, "there's no question that the print market is incomparably larger in the United States than in Europe,"[8] and while the size of the market is not a direct measure of

quality, it is representative of the greater number of printshops, the greater number of prints made, and a greater awareness on the part of artists of what prints are and can be.

There is a further demographic imbalance, even within American art, namely a preponderance of East Coast-based white males, reflecting the inescapable force of the market on print production. The market is a force in any art, whether the period under discussion is quattrocento Italy or 1980s New York, but it is more of a force in printmaking for the simple reason that so many prints are not only sold by commercial enterprises, but manufactured by commercial enterprises. And since most commercial enterprises – even in the art world – tend toward conservativism, the people who are invited to make prints are most often already successful artists (which in turn means they are most often white and male). Any artist can, of course, choose to make prints – woodblocks and linocuts can be run up on a kitchen table, and artists who have the technical expertise and the desire can often avail themselves of academic or community-based printshops such as the Printmaking Workshop in New York – but most forms of printmaking are time-consuming, labor intensive, and costly, and they require a network of distribution to reach their audience. Printmaking without some form of institutional framework is extraordinarily difficult. However, even the demographics of print production are showing signs of change. The later chapters of this book offer a slightly more balanced perspective, reflecting changes in the broader art world.

Finally, in attempting to compile the crude data of objects and events into something resembling a narrative, I have sometimes favored the eruption of new ideas rather than the continuation of established ones – new ideas, after all, move the story along. It is important, then, to state the obvious: many of the greatest prints of the period have been produced by mature artists, refining rather than inventing the forms and ideas that have driven their work. I must also offer the usual disclaimer for attempting to write history as it is occurring. Every generation displays oversights and enthusiasms incomprehensible to those who follow. I have tried to balance personal taste by consulting print curators, collectors, dealers, and artists on both continents. Still, readers will doubtless find points of disagreement. Those for whom this book acts as an entry point into the world of contemporary prints will simply have to remind themselves that there exist far more than are contained in this book, and that it may be time to take a look.

10/20   J. Dubuffet 63

I

PAINTERS AND PRINTERS

This narrative begins in 1960 because of a constellation of events that seems to mark out a change in the temperament of art at about this time. In Paris, Yves Klein was imprinting art from life by instructing naked women to press their paint-covered bodies directly onto canvas. In London, Richard Hamilton was arguing that the ever-expanding technologies of reproduction were capable not just of supplying us with novel entertainments, but could provide "knowledge about the subtleties of the human machine, which can, in turn, establish new relationships of that organism to its environment."[1] In Los Angeles, the Tamarind Lithography Workshop was founded to rescue the art of lithography from extinction. And in West Islip, Long Island, Jasper Johns finished his first print: a simple, symmetrical, black and white lithograph of a target. Johns's lithograph, an eloquent and utterly enigmatic statement of the obvious, signalled no great technical advance in printmaking – the tools and methods used to make it were more than 150 years old – but it represented a way of thinking about the printed image, in which its inescapable traits of repetition and mechanical interposition were considered as essential elements of meaning. These scattered events were portents of a set of attitudes, artists and institutions that would make the print a critical part of contemporary art practice.

The momentous triumph of American Abstract Expressionist painting after 1945 had shifted the art world's center of gravity from Paris to New York. While this transformed the world of painting, it had little immediate effect on the world of prints, which occupied a somewhat segregated niche. In Europe, the great Parisian printshops were busy reproducing the drawings of Picasso, Chagall, Dalí, and other eminent painters. In America, printmaking continued to be the province of specialist printmakers such as Louis Schanker, Adja Yunkers, or Leonard Baskin. Most of the great American painters of the 1940s and 1950s associated printmaking with either politics or pretension: Franz Kline felt it concerned "social attitudes...like Mexicans in the 1930s; printing, multiplying, educating," and concluded "I can't think about it; I'm involved in the private image,"[2] while Larry Rivers thought of printmaking as "the dull occupation of pipe-smoking corduroy deep-type artisans."[3] Though there had been great American prints from Winslow Homer to Edward Hopper, these were either not well known or viewed as part of the regionalist, anecdotal canon young painters were attempting to escape. Finally, the infrastructure necessary to broader print activity was missing in America: there were few print galleries, collectors, or printers who had any interest in the most up-to-date art.

1 Jean Dubuffet
L'Enfle-Chique I 1961
Color lithograph
58 × 35 cm (22¾ × 13¾ in.)

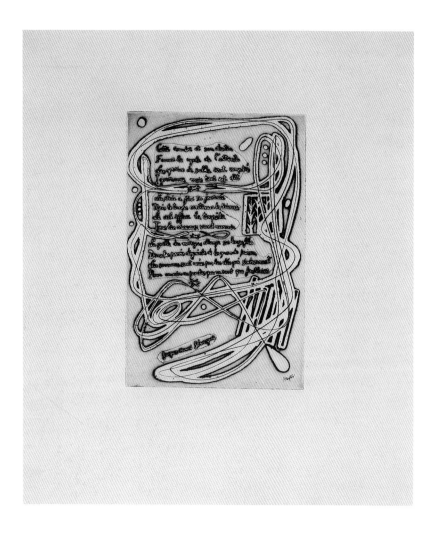

2 Stanley William Hayter
Page from *21 Etchings and Poems*, with
poem by Jacques-Henri Levesque 1960
Engraving
29.1 × 19.3 cm (11⁷⁄₁₆ × 7⁹⁄₁₆ in.)

The main exposure these painters had to the making of prints came from the Works Progress Administration (WPA) workshops of the 1930s, and from the temporary relocation from Paris to New York of Stanley William Hayter's influential Parisian printshop Atelier 17. Hayter was a virtuoso of color intaglio printing and of semi-automatist engraving (while holding the burin he would move the plate about without premeditation, later retrieving and reinforcing biomorphic forms and figures discovered in the loopy lines). But the presence of Atelier 17 in the 1940s was important for more than technical reasons: it was a hub for the exiled European art community – Chagall worked there, as did the Surrealists Masson, Tanguy, and Ernst – and it

was one of the few venues where younger Americans could work alongside eminent Europeans. Robert Motherwell, Jackson Pollock, William Baziotes, and Mark Rothko all tried printmaking with Hayter, though the allure of the burin and press did not hold them. Only Motherwell became seriously involved with the printed image, and then only after a twenty-year hiatus. Pollock's plates were not discovered and editioned until after his death.[4] Nonetheless, Pollock is reported to have said that he had had two masters – Thomas Hart Benton and Stanley William Hayter – and it has been argued that his early engravings, with their "all-over" webs of interlocking lines, were precursors of his later breakthroughs in painting.[5] More generally, Hayter's belief that an image must grow out of an improvisatory collaboration between material and the artist's impulses was clearly absorbed by the American painters. "If you know what it is going to look like," Hayter asked, "why bother making it?"[6]

Hayter's insistence that artists work every stage of their own plates, from drawing to editioning, was in direct contrast to the European printshop tradition of using technicians to translate an artist's drawing into print. In 1956 Una Johnson, print curator of the Brooklyn Museum, wrote that "one of the distinguishing features of prints in the United States is that the majority of them are printed by the artist himself, and not by a professional craftsman-printer as is so often the case in France,"[7] an observation that reflected both the nationwide dearth of "professional craftsman-printers," and the absorption of Hayter's principles by the nation's printmakers. Hayter's approach encouraged dedication to the exploration and development of one particular technique. Two of Hayter's followers, Mauricio Lasansky and Gabor Peterdi, were masterful technicians, who, by virtue of their academic positions – Lasansky at the University of Iowa and Peterdi at Yale – exerted a strong influence on academic printmaking in America, which came to occupy a separate sphere from the urban art world.[8] By the 1960s, intaglio was seen as a technique of academe and of specialist printmakers. Lithography became the technique of professional collaborative printshops and the artists who used them, largely due to the independent establishment of three very different organizations: Pratt Contemporaries (1956), Universal Limited Art Editions (1957), and Tamarind Lithography Workshop (1960).

Pratt Contemporaries (later Pratt Graphics Workshop, then Pratt Graphics Center) was founded to provide professional artists who wished to make prints with facilities, and to train students in the art of lithography. Artists could proof and print themselves, or they could hire printers to assist them (though the artists were expected to draw their own stones). Initially funded by the Rockefeller Foundation and affiliated with the Pratt Institute, it was both a service organization and an educational institution, and it made possible the creation of early, important prints by Jim Dine, David Hockney, Barnett Newman, and Claes Oldenburg.

ULAE was established by Tatyana Grosman as a business, albeit one where, as Robert Motherwell remarked, "it is simply assumed that the world of the spirit exists as concretely as lemon yellow or women's hair."[9] Grosman had originally intended to make silkscreen reproductions of famous paintings, a plan altered by the chance discovery of lithographic stones in a garden pathway of her Long Island cottage.[10] She located a small second hand press, a skilled lithographic printer, Robert Blackburn, and was given the valuable advice by William Lieberman that reproducing existing artworks was not nearly as fascinating as producing new ones. Recognizing the printerly potential of younger artists, Grosman induced Jasper Johns and Robert Rauschenberg to begin two of the most important printmaking careers of the century.

Tamarind Lithographic Workshop was neither a business nor a school, but an institution dedicated to the revival of a single print medium, lithography. Also a beneficiary of corporate largesse, it was supported by the Ford Foundation.[11] Tamarind conducted research on lithographic techniques and materials, offered residencies to artists, educated art professionals, and established models of documentation. In 1971 it published *The Tamarind Book of Lithography: Art and Techniques*, which remains the standard technical reference. Most importantly, it established a training program for master printers who spread out across the country like apostles of lithography, founding printshops, training more printers, and soliciting more artists.[12] Since one function of the artists' residencies was to expose printer-trainees to a wide variety of aesthetic convictions and demands, the range of artists was very broad. Important Abstract Expressionist painters were invited (Sam Francis made nearly a hundred lithographs during a single residency in 1963), as were professional printmakers such as Adja Yunkers, who had previously concentrated on woodcut. Not surprisingly, fewer great prints came off Tamarind presses than off those of ULAE, whose only task was the production of images. But the network advanced by Tamarind made possible the upcoming print "boom," and fundamentally altered perceptions of the field. Within five years of Tamarind's founding, lithography seemed a perfectly reasonable thing for serious artists to pursue.

June Wayne, the artist who founded Tamarind, observed in her initial funding request that a "handful of creative people is all that is needed for a renaissance in an art, if that handful comes together at the right time, in the right place."[13] But more important than the simple proliferation of lithographic technique was a profound change in the attitudes of artists toward the machine, and toward more indirect and collaborative ways of working. Tatyana Grosman had felt that the reason that the Abstract Expressionists did not make prints was that there were no shops for them to work in and no publishers to pester them to do so, but there were other

3 Willem de Kooning
Landscape at Stanton Street 1971
Lithograph
75.9 × 56.5 cm (29⅞ × 22¼ in.)

4 Grace Hartigan
The Hero Leaves His Ship I 1960
Lithograph
75.5 × 53.5 cm (29¼ × 21⅛ in.)

impediments, too. First, there was the problem of size: the painters of the New York School had developed their work on a physically grand scale, and prints were usually small. Secondly, these were painters for whom direct physical contact between the artist and his product was fundamental to both their method and their ideology, and prints are always indirect, with a manufactured matrix standing between artist and object. Grosman was legendary for her persistence when courting artists, but Willem de Kooning, Franz Kline, and David Smith all steadfastly refused her invitations. "To most Abstract Expressionists," Robert Motherwell said, "printmaking – whatever their dim concept of it was – didn't seem a natural, logical or convenient point of attack for what we were involved in."[14] It was an opinion

which even success did little to alter: in 1960 de Kooning was persuaded by friends into a printshop in Berkeley, California, where by swabbing a large stone with a mop dipped in tusche (a greasy ink used to paint on lithographic stones) he produced *Untitled* (1960), a direct and dramatic application of "action painting" to print.[15] But it seems to have made a greater impression on the viewing public than on de Kooning, who waited another ten years before returning seriously to the medium. The two sets of lithographs done at Hollander's Workshop in 1970–71 were strong and subtle works, but de Kooning was never to become a printmaker in earnest.

One lure that the print did hold was its literary association with poetry, and several important painters made their first published prints as contributions to the *livre d'artiste*[16] *21 Etchings and Poems* (1960).[17] Initially a project of the American remnant of Atelier 17 (Hayter had returned to Paris in 1950), *21 Etchings and Poems* featured an international array of painters, printmakers, and poets including Hayter, the dedicated engraver; Pierre Alechinsky, a *peintre-graveur* in the European tradition; de Kooning; and Franz Kline, who managed to avoid direct printerly involvement by contributing a photo-etching made from one of his drawings.[18] Nonetheless, the presence of two such eminent painters gave, as Lanier Graham has noted, "a new aura of respectability to printmaking in America."[19] Using an arcane intaglio method, the poets were able to write their words without reversing them (normally, anything on a plate or stone appears in reverse when printed), so that the poems appeared on the plates amid the artist's imagery. The result is a remarkable physical synthesis of text and image, though it suggests that the artists were lending themselves to a literary collaboration quite distinct from their habitual artistic concerns.

The literary aura of the print has faded somewhat as prints have come to rival paintings in scale and drama, but it is worth noting that the origins of both Tamarind and ULAE were tied to a love of the *livre d'artiste*: June Wayne's awareness of the artistic potential (and the dire straits) of lithography reached a critical point when she went to Paris to make lithographs to accompany an edition of John Donne's *Songs and Sonnets*; and Tatyana Grosman's early aim was to publish lithographic books that would bring together the best artists and the best writers of the day.

ULAE's first important publication was a collaboration between Larry Rivers and Frank O'Hara. Rivers and O'Hara were intimate friends, and they chose to work on the stones simultaneously, as a kind of improvised duet. The prints have the look of notes exchanged in class behind the teacher's back: a concoction of quick sketches, private jokes, and jerky, unpolished handwriting (O'Hara had to write

backwards so the letters would read from left to right.) Nonetheless, *Stones* (1957–59), like Grace Hartigan's beautiful suite of lithographs to accompany Barbara Guest's poem "The Hero Leaves His Ship," represents a watershed in American printmaking – prints that were neither precious nor political, and that reflected an intense engagement with both materials and ideas. As the market for American prints developed through the 1960s, the formal, bound *livre d'artiste* remained an oddity – later books, like Robert Motherwell's *A la pintura*

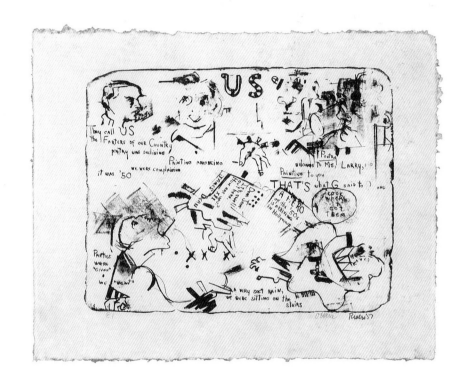

(1968), were important exceptions to a rule that favored works for the wall over works on the shelf.

Grosman was drawn to Motherwell by what she called "the word in the painting,"[20] a phrase that encompasses both the calligraphic quality of his forms and the persistently literary character of his work. (The only two first-generation Abstract Expressionists to devote serious attention to prints, Robert Motherwell and Barnett Newman, were also the most

5 Larry Rivers
Stones: US 1957
Lithograph
48.2 × 59 cm (19 × 23¼ in.)

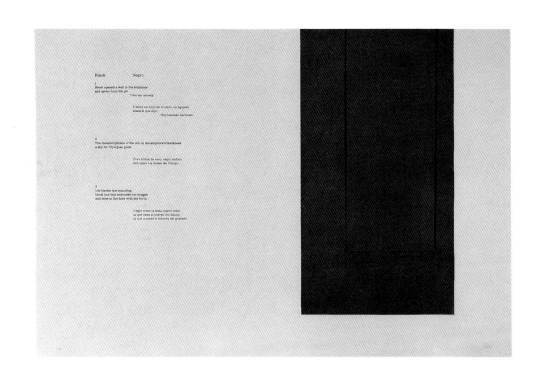

6 Robert Motherwell
A la pintura: Black 1–3 1968
Letterpress, lift-ground etching,
and aquatint
65.5 × 97 cm (25¼ × 38³⁄₁₆ in.)

7 Robert Motherwell
Gauloises Bleues (White) 1970
Aquatint and linecut
57.6 × 39.3 cm (22¾ × 15½ in.)

8 Robert Motherwell
Automatism B 1965–66
Lithograph
76.2 × 52.7 cm (30 × 20¼ in.)

bookish.) Motherwell worked briefly at ULAE in the early 1960s, but the prints that marked his serious return to the medium were the *Automatism* lithographs done in 1965–66 with Irwin Hollander,[21] in which for the first time he successfully adapted the heroic gestures of action painting to the modest housing of a printed sheet of paper. Motherwell, who made collages throughout his career, understood both the emotional tenor of reduced scale and the close intimacy with materials that are vital to works on paper. These were essential attributes of his printmaking, as was his appreciation of the representational ambiguity that erupts when fragments of the real world enter abstraction. His *Gauloises Bleues* series of prints begins with a collage edition – a torn cigarette package sheltered in aquatint – but later prints employ linecut to reproduce the cigarette label design, allowing the artist to alter the design's scale to suit the composition, its presence as flotsam taken as read. The competing and overlapping power of abstraction and representation can be seen as the undercurrent of *A la pintura*. Raphael Alberti's poem cycle about great painting is accompanied by Motherwell's spare, abstract aquatints (he chose the medium, newly available at ULAE, for its chromatic intensity). The pictures are not of the objects that occupy Alberti, but of "essences" those objects invoke. His iconography, Motherwell acknowledged, was best at representing "the bluenesses of blues, light and air and color, walls, perspective, and a general sense of the Mediterranean… solitude, weight, intensities, placing, decisiveness, and ambiguities; it cannot deal with Venus."[22] Motherwell lived three full decades into the American print revival, eventually installing full lithography and etching shops in his studio, and leaving a catalogue of more than 400 prints behind him.

Barnett Newman died just nine years after making his first print, and his ambivalent feelings for the medium can be discerned by his disclaimer in the preface to *18 Cantos* (1964) that he was "not a printmaker."[23] Newman

probably meant to assert that the *Cantos* were the result of artistic impulses that took the form of prints, rather than of print impulses struggling to be art. He had begun making lithographs at the Pratt Graphics Workshop in 1961, partly as therapy for depression following the death of his brother.[24]

In the three untitled lithographs Newman produced at Pratt, and more overtly in the *18 Cantos* (pl. 28), Newman identified one of the most problematic aspects of the print for painters who believed that image and object should be indivisible: the presence of paper margins. On a monochromatic canvas, Newman's "zip" divided the field utterly, but on paper it became a mere stripe, "an internal mullion,"[25] set between two rectangles afloat in a larger field. A Newman painting strove to be a totality, an object that, edge to edge,

9 Barnett Newman
Untitled 1961
Lithograph
76.4 × 56.2 cm (30¹/₁₆ × 22¹/₈ in.)

constructed its own reality, a task that is almost impossible for a print. The printed image is usually surrounded by margins, edged by a matt and encased in a frame, with the result that a print tends to look more like a picture of a thing than like the thing itself.[26] The easy solution to Newman's dilemma was to trim the paper so that the image bled to the edges, as

later resolutions, never can.

Newman's lithographs are an example of how the critical awareness of purely formal properties in painting led to a reconsideration of the specific material qualities of the print. Even the mechanical processes of printmaking benefited from inventive formal analysis. For Sam Francis, a member of Abstract

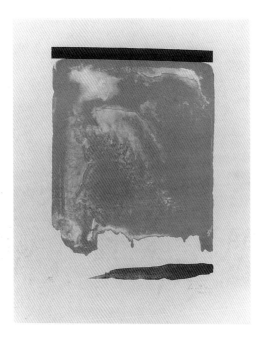

10 Helen Frankenthaler
Persian Garden 1965–66
Color lithograph
65.5 × 51 cm (25¾ × 20 in.)

11 Lee Bontecou
Fifth Stone 1964
Lithograph
105.1 × 75.5 cm (41¼ × 29⅛ in.)

Opposite:
12 Cy Twombly
Untitled II 1967–74
Etching, open bite, and aquatint
69.5 × 102.5 cm (27½ × 40½ in.)

13 Mark Tobey
Ground of Confidence 1972
Drypoint and color aquatint
51 × 33.8 cm (20 × 13¼ in.)

in his paintings, but Newman heeded Grosman's observation that a lithograph is different from a canvas, and worthy of its own solutions.[27] In the end, each of the *18 Cantos* developed "its own personal margins,"[28] whose proportions vary from print to print, as does the paper size and the image size. Newman, furthermore, orchestrated the set as a whole by establishing a distinct rhythm of internal relationships, whose "symphonic mass lends additional clarity to each individual canto," while "each canto adds its song to the full chorus."[29] Together they elucidate the artist's thought and development in a way that a single image, in which all changes of heart and digressions of mind have been covered up by

Expressionism's "Second Generation," the arbitrary and inorganic separations of color printing became a compositional tool. In most forms of printmaking each color requires a separate plate or stone. Thus the artist must draw different elements of the composition on different surfaces, while imagining their synthesis. Furthermore, all the drawing is done in black and white, regardless of the color intended in the print. For many painters, these were almost insurmountable blocks to creative thought. The critic Robert Hughes compared it to "learning to play Ping Pong backwards in a mirror with a time lapse."[30] De Kooning said, "I couldn't work with different colors at different times. I can only work with what's there. If it's not there, I can't experience it."[31] But for Francis, a student of Eastern philosophies who believed that accidents were a form of "divine guidance,"[32] such indirection was fascinating, and the inevitable surprises that erupt from reversals, separations, or simple miscalculations proved to be moments of creation rather than catastrophe. Generating

stone – a remarkable simulation of a painterly aesthetic in inhospitable territory.

The print revival that began in the late 1950s in America was first and foremost a lithographic revival, and the link between lithography and painting was a natural one: the basic implements of lithographic drawing –

new compositions by turning, recombining, or re-inking plates, Francis made neat formal acknowledgment of both the manual and editorial spontaneity that structures his art (pl. 29).

For Helen Frankenthaler, on the other hand, all the discrete stages, indirectness, and strategy of printing disrupted the primal unity of artist, gesture, and mark. Working at ULAE in the early 1960s, she tried to preserve the spontaneity of her canvases by working quickly and impulsively, "discarding stones like typing paper."[33] In *Persian Garden* (1965–66), a broad swathe of lithographic tusche mimics the poured stains of her canvases while revealing the texture and shape of the lithographic

a loaded paint brush or a crayon – would be familiar to any painter; and compared to etching or woodcut, lithography was a facile imitator of painted texture and surface. But there were important exceptions to the dominance of lithography and painting. Some of the most rigorous lithographs produced at ULAE in the 1960s were made by the sculptor Lee Bontecou, whose emphasis on drawing and spacial illusion were entirely removed from the painterly concerns of her contemporaries.

Cy Twombly's ULAE prints were an uncommon example of painterly etching. In his paintings Twombly had retained the gesturalism of Abstract Expressionism, but replaced its heroicism with the more humble and familiar motions of writing. Drawn in reverse and encased in the stiffness of metal etching plates, Twombly's looping lines seem calcified with the accretions of time and process, forming an image at once urgent and rife with history. In later prints Twombly used

lithography, exploiting not its painterly fluidity, but its graphic transparency – each print in the portfolio *Six Latin Writers and Poets* (1976) consists of a single scribbled name, and invokes the grand complexities of cultural memory through the simultaneously expressive and possessive act of writing a name.

Mark Tobey's quiet, meditative abstractions also lay outside the dominant concerns of New York-based Abstract Expressionism, and Tobey only began his intense involvement with printmaking when he moved to Switzerland at the age of seventy. In the last sixteen years of his life Tobey produced more than one hundred etchings, lithographs, screenprints, and monotypes, in both a flung-ink style derived from Sumi calligraphic drawing (which was also an influence on Sam Francis), and his better-known webs of interlacing lines and marks.

One of the most remarkable adaptations of painterly sensibility to intaglio processes occurred in the work of Richard Diebenkorn. It is typical of Diebenkorn's wayward timing that at the height of the American lithographic revival he chose to begin working intensively in etching, just as, at the apex of the critical success of Abstract Expressionism, he returned to the depiction of landscape and the human figure. *41 Etchings Drypoints* (1965) is a collection of small, black-and-white interior scenes, seated women, table-top still lifes, and cityscapes. The mood of quiet observation bordering on melancholy is invoked partly by the nature of the subjects, partly by the sense of time passing that is imbued by the prints' rhythmic sequence, and partly by the etching medium itself. While lithography may capture the nuance of the brush, etching is better at revealing the architecture of the image, the linear tautness that underlies all Diebenkorn's art and makes his moves between figuration and abstraction seem almost superficial.

41 Etchings Drypoints was the first publication of Crown Point Press, founded by Kathan Brown, an etcher who had trained in London and who favored a clean, restrained approach to the medium that was quite different from the elaborate, expressive color intaglio techniques of Hayter and his followers.[34] At the time of the Diebenkorn project Brown said she "was printing for myself and my friends. It didn't occur to me for years that it was a business."[35] Her attitude was typical of the new

American printshops, most of which were founded on an idealized vision of the European model, but developed along quite different lines. In place of the production-oriented ethos that actually governed many of the most famous French shops, where editions were large, decisions were based on economy, and artists had to adhere to a schedule whereby often proofs could be viewed just once a week, Grosman and Wayne promoted an almost mystical respect for the artist and for materials. And while French shops employed *chromistes* whose job was to translate artists' drawings into prints, Brown maintained that "the best work does not come from studying a drawing and matching the look of it. What we want to do is match something else, the artist's idea…"[36]

ULAE, Crown Point, and other American shops both printed and published, developing long-standing relationships with artists who,

as a group, were seen to represent the aesthetic interests of the organization, European shops, on the other hand, often succeeded by serving the public taste rather than attempting to structure it. The same shop that printed Picasso printed Bernard Buffet.

Europe in 1960 enjoyed both a plethora of craftsmen and a tradition of printmaking within the context of painterly careers. After the war, the print business, like the art business generally, had resettled in Paris, which still boasted a singular array of galleries, collectors, master printers, and distinguished artists. Pre-eminent among these was Picasso, endlessly inventive and almost impossibly prolific (the catalogue raisonné of his prints runs to more than two thousand entries). Picasso epitomized the European ideal of the *peintre-graveur*, an artist who could exchange brush for burin as the mood took him or as

15 Pablo Picasso
1.6.68 from the "347" engravings 1968
Aquatint
53.5 × 65.5 cm (21 × 25¾ in.)

Opposite:
14 Richard Diebenkorn
11 from *41 Etchings Drypoints* 1965
Etching and aquatint
45 × 37.5 cm (17¾ × 14¼ in.)

16 Ben Nicholson
Tesserete 1966
Etching and india ink
19 × 23 cm (7½ × 9 in.)

the image required. In the 1940s and 1950s, Picasso had enjoyed a fruitful liaison with the celebrated Parisian printshop Mourlot, the results of which contributed to the development and popularity of lithography worldwide. Riva Castleman observed that for many collectors in the 1950s, "the only prints worth owning came from the School of Paris in general, and Picasso in particular."[37]

In the 1960s, however, Picasso turned away from the lithographic finesse of Mourlot and returned to etching, the medium he had used for his great prints of the 1930s, and to linocut, a crude relief process using linoleum-covered blocks. Picasso was able to exploit linocut's capacity for bold and curvaceous pattern, while elevating its simple technique into one of astonishing complexity in "reduction" linocuts, produced not with the multiple blocks usually required for color printing, but with a single block that was cut away in stages, each stage

printed over the last. It is a method that requires a precise combination of spontaneity and strategy (since an element once cut away can never be reprinted) and the results were both clever and compelling. But Picasso's best known, and most influential, prints of the 1960s were the 347 etchings and engravings executed in a seven-month flurry of activity in 1968. These gained a quick notoriety for their graphic sexuality: rapacious Spanish grandees chase naked women, and naked women expose themselves with professional nonchalance to artists and admirers who occasionally get to bed them, while the repeated figure of a short, stout and remarkably Picasso-like homunculus is reduced to peeking through curtains, a perennial voyeur. The dramas of aging and loss, vision and desire, sex and power, are acted out in scratchy drypoints and extraordinary, blotchy lift-ground aquatints, at once elegant and scabrous.

Picasso's example as an artist, and as a market phenomenon, encouraged a cascade of prints by the masters of Modernism. Some, like Ben Nicholson's late etchings, were carefully considered works, created for the specific linear and dimensional properties of print. A great many other artists, however, were content with highly polished replications of works created for another situation entirely. Few of the eminent pre-war painters shared Picasso's fascination with the awkwardnesses and peculiarities of print processes, and many were content to see their drawings or paintings translated into print by technicians.[38] This practice is as old as printmaking itself: for centuries, artists have relied on the skilled hands of engravers, blockcutters, and lithographers to render their designs in reproducible form. As long as design was deemed more critical than the autographic peculiarities of the artist's hand, there was no problem. However, when autographic peculiarities did matter, when they were in fact a large part of what the collector was paying for, the distinction became significant. Deceptive sales practices and the indiscriminate use of the word "original" by publishers and galleries further confused matters. In one notorious incident, French border police seized a truck loaded with sheets of blank paper signed by Dalí on their way to be printed with a reproduction of a Dalí drawing. Since in theory the function of the artist's signature was to say "I saw this and approved it," if not exactly "I made it," the Dalí exposure was shocking, and confirmed the hunch of many artists and collectors that lithography was less an art medium than a marketing device.

Among many younger painters, however, the idealized model of the *peintre-graveur* continued to hold sway. In Europe, as in America, painters had moved toward a form of expressive abstraction, rooted in Surrealist automatism, and aspiring to spiritual self-awareness. Few of these European painters, who are often grouped under the labels "Informel" or "Tachism,"[39] shared the American aversion to printmaking. After the technological and ideological monstrosities of two world wars, the meditative intimacy of the print, and its connection to the benign, bookish stream of European humanism, were seen as positive, redemptive qualities. And because of a wealth of masterful technicians, European prints exhibited a chromatic range and technical variety absent from the monochrome lithography that dominated serious prints in America.

Though the market for abstract prints was negligible in the 1950s, Hans Hartung, Pierre Soulages, Emil Schumacher, and K. R. H. Sonderborg were among many artists who became active and innovative printmakers. Unlike the more polished productions of the School of Paris, the prints of these artists did not mimic the appearance of drawings, but exploited the distinct materiality of etching, woodcut, and lithography. Soulages, for example, would allow acid to eat away the plate around his broad strokes and architectonic forms, liberating them from the tidy rectangle of the plate mark; blank paper does not simply surround the image but erupts through it in sudden surges of brightness (pl. 31). "I don't work with oils or inks or copper plates," Soulages explained. "I work with light."[40] The distinction between the print as imitation and the print as investigation can be seen clearly in the work of the Dutch painter Bram van Velde, whose first prints are accomplished, even uncanny, recreations of gouaches, but whose later prints, no longer concerned with replication, erupt with light and an acrobatic balance of color and form.

The marriage of material specificity to immaterial transcendence can also be found in the prints of so-called "Matter Painters" such as Antoni Tàpies or Alberto Burri. Tàpies incorporated sand, mud, coarse sacking, and other detritus into his paintings, not for textural novelty, but to invoke the scarred surfaces of the world, elegiac traces of human life that carry a mystical promise of spiritual renewal. In his prints, the paper is frequently

17 Antoni Tàpies
Untitled 1962
Lithograph and collagraph with flocking
56 × 76.2 cm (22¹⁄₁₆ × 30 in.)

18 Antoni Tàpies
Plate 2 from the *Suite Catalana* 1972
Intaglio
76.2 × 101.5 cm (30 × 39¹¹⁄₁₆ in.)

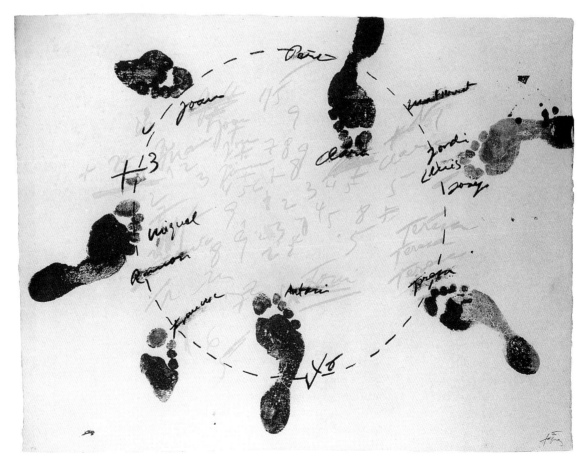

flocked, embossed, torn, layered, or covered
with sawdust, straw, horsehair, or varnish, as
in his *Untitled* of 1962. In other works, such as
Ditades damunt diari (Fingerprints on newspaper,
pl. 30), direct conscription of the tactile world
is replaced by metaphor or metanym. In an
image from *Suite Catalana* (1972), footprints
record the steps of the Sardana, the Catalan
national dance, and thus constitute a political
statement of ethnic identity. At the same time,
the footprints' status as the relics of real
people – of individual identity – is reinforced
by the handwritten names that surround them.
Finally, Tàpies considers feet to be among
those ignoble parts of the body that
"communicate a sort of fundamental human
solidarity" – an identity that transcends
boundaries.[41]

European postwar painters are sometimes
criticized for having lacked the radical
imagination of Pollock and de Kooning, an
opinion that might seem to be bolstered by the
ease and elegance with which they took to the
small scale and technical mysteries of print.
But the prominence of printing could also be
seen as an indication of the broader cultural
sophistication and integration of European
artists. The ongoing discourse of painters,
sculptors, philosophers, and poets in Europe
found natural expression in a profusion of
poem-and-print portfolios, small magazines,
and illustrated books. The *livre d'artiste* was
a vital form for many artists, including
Alechinsky, Baj, Burri, Dubuffet, Jorn, and
Tàpies. The graphic duality of the written word
and the drawn mark was a persistent source
of fascination. The prominent Surrealist poet
Henri Michaux made etchings, such as those
in the 1965 portfolio *Parcours* (Wanderings), in
which a tight, twittering line wraps back and
forth across the page, realizing the rhythms
of language, without its specific and limiting
content. Alechinsky often used his nimble line
to suggest scratchy script or to divide his
compositions into multiple frames, giving his
prints the appearance of slightly deranged
comics, or storyboards for the subconscious.

Jorn and Alechinsky, along with Karel
Appel, Corneille, and the poet Pierre
Dotrement, were early members of CoBrA, an
officially short-lived but stylistically long-lasting
movement that attempted to reach a
spontaneous core of imagination and emotion
within the human psyche. CoBrA (from
Copenhagen, Brussels, and Amsterdam, homes
of artist members) represented an expressive
alternative to abstraction; it abhorred
pomposity and gave full rein to irrational
narrative impulses and whimsical illustrative
quirks of a kind that thrived in print. In the
1970s Appel guessed that he had made "four

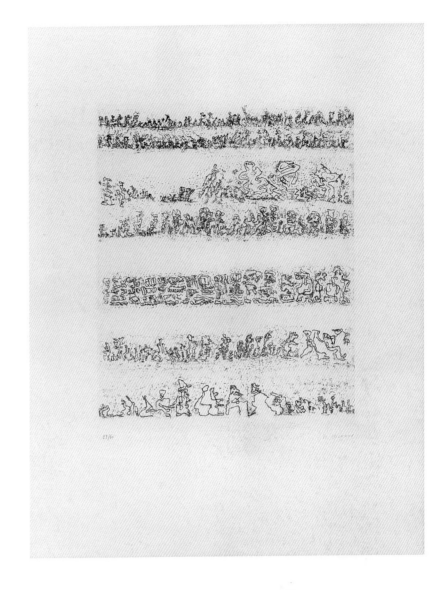

19 Henri Michaux
Plate 2 from the portfolio *Parcours*
(Wanderings) 1965
Etching
52.8 × 40.8 cm (20¼ × 16 in.)

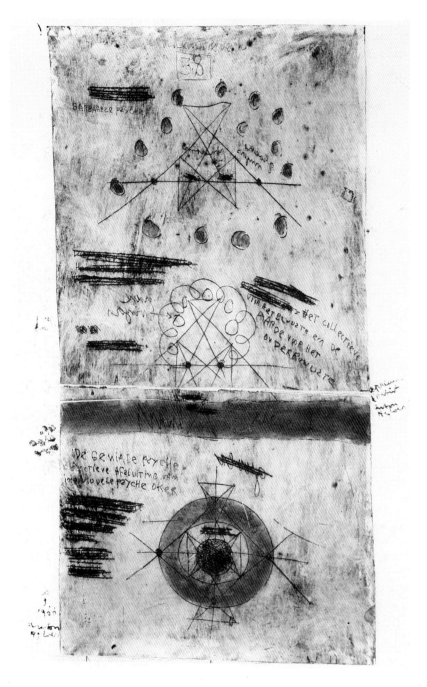

20 Anton Heyboer
de Geniale Psyche 1966
Color etching
100 × 65 cm (39½ × 25½ in.)

hundred lithographs at the very least;"[42] Corneille had trained as a printmaker; and Alechinsky had studied typography and book illustration before working extensively with Hayter. Alechinsky's characteristic fusion of quick-witted calligraphic gestures, representational drawing and automatist doodling has appeared in almost every print medium, but most trenchantly in radiant color etchings (pl. 32).

The expressionist Dutch printmaker Anton Heyboer was not personally associated with CoBrA (or any other group of artists), but he also made art by responding to the impulses of the subconscious – perhaps with greater urgency than any of his compatriots. Heyboer, who led a peripatetic and traumatizing child-hood, began etching while institutionalized, and his enigmatic, rough-hewn etchings are as much an attempt to organize thought as to touch upon primitive emotion.

For Jorn, CoBrA was one in a long series of ideological and stylistic associations. He had worked with Leger and Le Corbusier in the 1930s, joined CoBrA in the late 1940s, and in the 1950s became involved with the Situationist critique of capitalism and the passive consumers of spectacle it produced. Throughout these changes, he made woodcuts, etchings, and lithographs, moving between figuration and abstraction, but always main-taining the sense of mythopoeic narrative that is visible in both his proto-Pop lithographs of photographic clippings encumbered with Rorschach-like ink blots, and in his late abstract lithographs, where gestures seem to float on a sequence of distinct planes and yet to be carrying on a coherent conversation.

This Expressionist engagement with the condition of society also motivated many younger artists in 1950s who took up more clearly figurative modes. In Germany, the prints of Horst Antes, Horst Janssen and Paul Wunderlich conveyed familiar aspects of the human condition: crises of sexuality, emotional anguish, political idiocy. In Spain, the prints of Antonio Saura often used historically specific events and personages to comment on more general issues, portraying the great and powerful as impotent, pathetic, and deranged. All these prints participate in the long and honorable tradition of the European print: a tradition that assimilates replication and popularization, but that in this century has given precedence to the expressiveness and nuance of the artist's hand.

Jean Dubuffet's *Phénomènes* (1958–62), "one of the most extraordinary works in the history of lithography,"[43] represents a radical departure from this reverence for manual touch. Dubuffet felt that "manual dexterity, special aptitudes, whether innate or acquired, have always seemed dull and quite useless for artistic creation,"[44] and the 300 lithographs of *Les Phénomènes* can be seen as a direct result of Dubuffet's avoidance of painterly finesse: they are images pulled directly from the lithographic process, without reference to painterly models and without recourse to crayon or brush. To make them, Dubuffet took impressions from "earth, walls, stones, old suitcases,…a friend's bare back, threads, crumbs, torn shreds of paper," or developed them from the essential chemistry of lithography, "mixtures such as water and turpentine, the oxidization of zinc exposed to sunlight, the crackling of varnish, resin powder heated on a match flame."

"I had the impression," Dubuffet wrote, "most satisfying for me, that in approaching lithography with bare hands, using no tool other than the roller, I espoused its own methods, that I entered more wholly into its discipline." Dubuffet recognized that, in addition to visual qualities that an artist might find attractive, printmaking had certain distinct procedural qualities that could be turned to advantage – most importantly, the possibility of breaking the act of creation into discrete, preservable stages. He began the lithographs with the idea of producing a catalogue of textures and surfaces which could serve as the raw material for subsequent work – combined into richly modulated color prints, or torn into

shapes and employed in assemblages – but he became increasingly fascinated with the enigmatic, suggestive properties of the basic images themselves.

His work on *Les Phénomènes* convinced Dubuffet of two points: that "the artist's function consists of naming things as much as creating pictures," and that "fruitful discoveries are made, not through the production of images, but from the interpretation made of them." These ideas, born of print rather than painting, were to be of fundamental importance to the art of the following decades.

21 Jean Dubuffet
Scintillement from *Géographie*, the fourth color album of *Les Phénomènes* 1959–60
Color lithograph
63.5 × 45 cm (25 × 17¾ in.)

2

JOHNS AND RAUSCHENBERG

Robert Rauschenberg and Jasper Johns are widely accepted as two of the greatest printmakers of our century. In the late 1950s, when most artists and critics believed, along with Harold Rosenberg, that art was "inseparable from the biography of the artist,"[1] the art of Rauschenberg and Johns proposed a radical alternative: an art that was not focussed on the subjective, emotional life of the artist, but that incorporated the external world and examined its apperception by the human mind. In the 1960s, their involvement in lithography (and later, in other print media) legitimized printmaking, not only as an eloquent vehicle for painterly expression, but as a field of ideas.

Rauschenberg had, early in his career, made several informal forays into print: in 1950 he and Susan Weil had produced life-sized photograms by placing people and things on architectural blueprint paper exposed in the sun; in 1951 he had instructed the composer John Cage to drive his Model A Ford through a puddle of ink and onto a stretch of paper rolled out in a New York City street, producing what is, in effect, a 22-foot-long monoprint.[2] Nonetheless, he had little interest in traditional printmaking when first invited to ULAE in 1960. His now famous comment was that "the second half of the 20th century was no time to start writing on rocks."[3]

When he relented and began working at ULAE in 1962, his first lithographs were fairly simple one or two stone productions in which images of Siamese cats and baseball players shared space with autographic scribbles and splashes of lithographic tusche. The Coke-bottle image in *Merger* (1962) was hand-drawn[4] but Rauschenberg soon began applying tusche-daubed objects directly to the stone. "I don't want a picture to look like something it isn't," Rauschenberg said, "I want it to look like something it is. And I think a picture is more like the real world when it's made out of the real world."[5]

Rauschenberg had long worked in collage and assemblage, and printing offered a rich duality – a way to incorporate the detritus of everyday life without the literalism of discrete objects. He applied an eclectic variety of objects to litho stones: leaves, tools, notebook paper, and old *New York Times* printers "mats" – blocks in which photographic images appear in relief, so they can be printed alongside lead type. The images he chose were not special, poignant, or lovely – "if it is interesting by itself," Rauschenberg said, "it doesn't need me"[6] – and he arranged them without the imposition of any discernible narrative or symbolism. Rauschenberg, like Johns, never wanted his work to be an exposure of personal feeling, and he savored the slight remove, the odd formality, that the printed surface inserted between the artist and the viewer. With the stone acting as an intermediary, the borrowed

22 Robert Rauschenberg
Accident 1963
Lithograph
104.8 × 75 cm (41¼ × 29½ in.)

incorporated the disaster by having the lithograph printed from the two halves of the broken stone, employing the brilliant white fissure as a dramatic element, and coyly adding a second stone to print a pile of "debris" at bottom. *Accident*, for all its jumble of disconnected pictorial references, is also a revelation of its own history.

The adventure into lithography was, Rauschenberg noted, a "big influence on [my] paintings."[9] The same year he began working at ULAE he also began using commercially prepared silkscreens to make paintings on canvas. The screens allowed him to apply, recombine, and overwork photographic images on canvas in much the same way that he did in lithography, but with even greater flexibility, since he was not bound to the physical dimensions of the found objects he chose to print from. Photographic screens could be made any size. Both the prints and the paintings were graphic in demeanor and heavily indebted to the grimy, mass-market imagery of newspapers and magazines, but the scale was often drastically different. The painting *Barge* (1963), for instance, covers eighteen times the area of the related lithographs *Breakthrough I* and *II* (1964). And the mechanical awkwardness of stone lithography and printing blocks gives the printed images a chunky substantiality quite unlike the supple mistiness of the paintings.

In 1964 Rauschenberg and the printers at ULAE found a way to transfer screenprint images onto stone, allowing him the same compositional flexibility he had in painting. From this point onward, photographs took over increasing amounts of surface area from the inky splashes and brushstrokes of the early lithographs. Compositions such as *Drizzle* (1967) or *Landmark* (1968) are almost entirely borrowed images, selected and arranged in Rauschenberg's non-hierarchical, purposeful disorder.

Rauschenberg said that he likes to "put off the final fixing of a work for as long as possible,"[10] and his unfastened compositions preserve that sense of openness and flexibility.

pictures and the artist's loose, painterly addenda coalesced into a pictorial mass in which the stolen and the invented were no longer separable.

Rauschenberg's art had always been improvisatory, and his printmaking thrived on the unpredictability of operating at the brink of mechanical competence. Nowhere is this clearer than in *Accident* (1963), the print that brought international recognition to Rauschenberg and to ULAE.[7] When the first stone cracked during initial proofing, Rauschenberg redrew the image on a second stone, which also cracked after just a few proofs (a piece of cardboard wedged under a roller was discovered as the culprit).[8] He then

His aesthetic had found confirmation, early in his career, in the work of his friend John Cage. Influenced by both the cerebral mischief of Marcel Duchamp and the transcendent detachment of Zen philosophy, Cage sought a form of art that did not perpetually refer to the "self" and its emotional demands, and that participated in the world without attempting to impose its own meaning onto it. Cage saw his music as "an affirmation of life – not an attempt to bring order out of chaos nor to suggest improvements in creation, but simply to wake up to the very life we're living."[11] To avoid the tyranny of personal expression or personal taste, Cage had been using chance methods, such as the I Ching, to determine his compositions since 1950. Though Cage was primarily involved in music, he also made his ideas manifest in writings, drawings, and as of the late 1960s, prints.

Cage's edition with Calvin Sumsion *Not Wanting to Say Anything About Marcel* (1968) has obvious similarities with Rauschenberg's *Shades* (1964), the artist's inventive response to Tatyana Grosman's suggestion that he make a book. *Shades* was printed on six transparent plexiglass sheets, which were propped vertically in a wooden base, and could be arranged and rearranged as desired by the owner. The Cage edition similarly consisted of a set of screenprinted plexiglass sheets that were accompanied by two lithographs, repeating elements from the "plexigrams." Cage used the I Ching to select images and fragments of words, and to structure them on the page. The sheer multiplicity of solutions eradicates any hint of imposed meaning, suggesting an open field in which the mind of the viewer is allowed to play. If the Abstract Expressionist ambition had been, as Rothko and Gottlieb put it, "to make the spectator see the world our way – not his way,"[12] that of Cage and Rauschenberg was to free the spectator to perceive the world as he chose, no longer a passive receptor of artistic genius, but an active collaborator in the creation of meaning.[13]

The vision of a flexible, multifarious art

object implicit in these editions owed much to Marcel Duchamp. *Shades* and *Not Wanting to Say Anything About Marcel* knowingly invoke Duchamp in both Cage's title, and in their use of transparency, reminiscent of Duchamp's magnum opus, *La Mariée mise à nu par ses célibataires, même* (1915–23), commonly known as *The Large Glass*. Already, in the first decades of the century, Duchamp had dismissed such supposedly fundamental elements of art as hand labor, rarity, even visual appeal. He wanted "to wipe out the idea of the original,"[14] and for most of his life Duchamp busied himself, as Richard Hamilton put it, "in the propagation of his achievements through the media of printed reproductions and certified copies," until the distinction between original and substitute was almost moot.[15] The famous "readymades" – objects purchased in stores and exhibited, usually unaltered, as art – were often replicated, most audaciously in a 1964 set of limited-edition facsimiles, which were signed and numbered, and quite expensive. *The Large Glass* spawned a virtual cottage industry of replicas and addenda. A masterpiece of hermetic symbology and mechanized sexuality, it was largely incomprehensible without a gloss, which Duchamp willingly and repeatedly provided: *The Green Box*,[16] a facsimile collection of ninety-four working notes and drawings (which Duchamp considered an essential part of *The Large Glass* itself) was published in 1934; a celluloid miniature *Large Glass* was included in Duchamp's museum-in-a-suitcase, *de ou par Marcel Duchamp ou Rrose Sélavy (Boîte en Valise)*; a second collection of facsimile notes, *The White Box*, appeared in 1966; eighteen etchings of the piece were made in the late 1960s and a table-top replica of one passage from *The Large Glass*, *The Occulist Witness*, was made by Richard Hamilton. All this prolific revision and reiteration suggested that art objects are not self-sufficient universes, but reference points in a larger ongoing conception. Duchamp also revealed the eloquence of qualities frequently perceived as shortcomings of the print: insubstantiality and contingency.

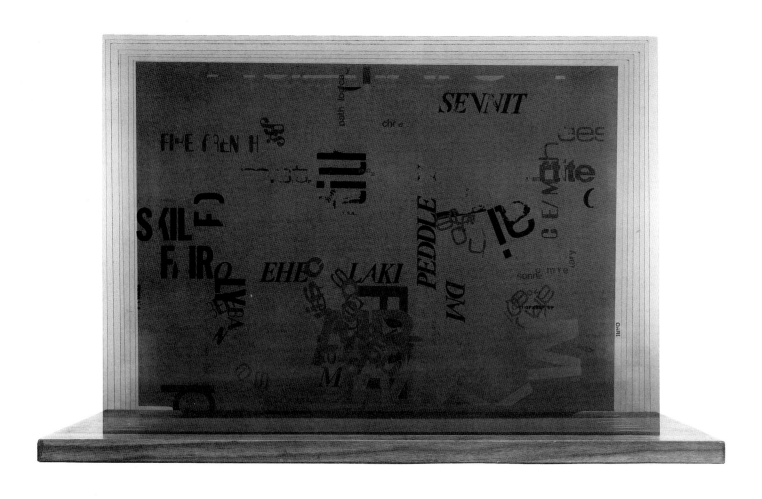

24 John Cage and Calvin Sumsion
Not Wanting to Say Anything About Marcel 1969
Plexigram
35.5 × 50.8 cm (14 × 20 in.)

Opposite:
25 John Cage and Calvin Sumsion
Not Wanting to Say Anything About Marcel 1969
Lithograph
69.8 × 101.6 cm (27¹/₂ × 40 in.)

Rauschenberg and Johns, like Duchamp, understood that the best work in print is not necessarily the masterful, singular statement we expect of painting, but an orchestration of linkages. For Johns, Duchamp's work presented "in literal terms the difficulty of knowing what anything means."[17] This is a difficulty that is exacerbated in print – the seemingly simple question of where one object leaves off and another one begins becomes perplexing when the image exists in multiple copies; when it is reversed; when what you hold in your hand is not the thing the artist drew, but something that has simply rubbed against it. For Johns the fact of multiple impressions raised intriguing questions: "should they all be identical or should each be different? What kind of differences do you tolerate and what kinds do you encourage?"[18]

When he first began working at ULAE in 1960, Johns knew little about lithography, but he had picked up the idea that a single stone could generate a succession of revised images, and he conceived a sequence of the figures zero through nine, printed from the same stone in consecutive states. On his first stone, Johns drew a large zero above a set of smaller, sequential numerals. After printing, the zero was partially erased to create a large numeral one, which was then partially erased to draw the two, and so on. At each transition, traces of the old number were retained,[19] leaving a visible history of the development of the image. This idea was always important to Johns – he chose the arduous paint medium of encaustic because it preserved earlier brushstrokes even as they were superseded by later ones – and the kind of explicit

sequentiality of *0–9* (1960–63) was a natural convergence of Johns's interests and the procedures of printing.[20] In a similar manner, Johns found in printing a parallel for the plaster casts of body parts that featured in his paintings, using his body as a printing element. *Hand*, *Skin with O'Hara Poem*, and *Pinion* (all 1963) were not pictures of the body, but direct impressions of it, uncomfortably personal yet dispassionately mechanistic.

Most of Johns's early prints, however, were based on drawings, often quite closely. But to dismiss these works as "reproductive," which many print connoisseurs did at first, is to ignore the fact that Johns habitually re-uses his images: drawings become prints, sculptures become drawings, prints occasionally become paintings. Instead of fading into the shades of once interesting ideas, Johns's images seem to

grow in weight and resonance with each repetition. By changing the physical form, but repeating the image, Johns can elucidate "what it is that connects them and what separates them."[21] In *1st Etchings* (1967) and *1st Etchings 2nd State* (1967–69), Johns presents hand-drawn and photo-engraved etchings of his early sculptures and reliefs. Each sheet of the first portfolio bears a line etching and photo-engraving of a sculptural work, as if for didactic comparison of representational modes – linear versus tonal; subjective versus objective. In the second portfolio, both the photographic and hand-drawn plates are scratched up and scribbled over, made richer and more equivocal. Johns describes the advantage of etching as "the ability of the copper plate to store multiple layers of information. One can work in one way on a

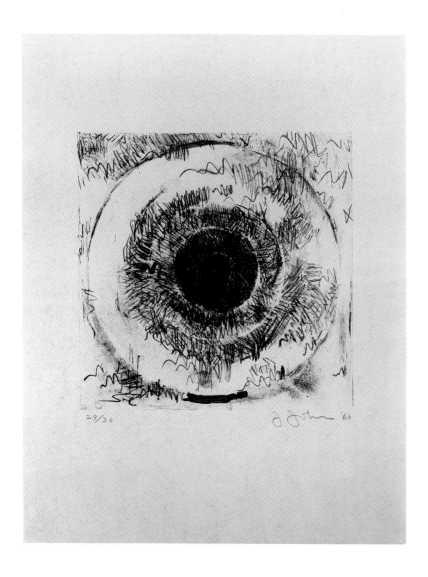

26 Jasper Johns
Target 1960
Lithograph
57.5 × 44.7 cm (22⅛ × 17⅛ in.)

of one another. The offset lithograph *Decoy* (1971) is one of Johns's most masterly arrays of semiotic relationships and cognitive quandaries. The print is made up almost entirely of re-used and recombined materials. Its compositional underpinning is an old plate from an earlier print, *Passage I* (1965–66), itself a photolithographic reproduction of the painting *Passage II* (1966). The painting, in turn, was an agglomeration of objects and ways of meaning: colors existing as paint, colors described by words, words made out of wood, words made out of neon lights, legs made out of plaster casts. Much of this remains visible behind the diverse additions to *Decoy*, which includes a frieze of etching plates from *1st Etchings 2nd State* and a photograph of a Ballantine Ale can, the model for Johns's seminal sculpture and all its descendants. In all, *Decoy* (pl. 38) was printed from one stone and eighteen separate lithographic plates. This technical complexity, unusual for Johns, was made practical by ULAE's acquisition of an offset proofing press.

In offset lithography the image is printed from a metal plate onto a rubber blanket and thence onto paper, thereby eliminating the problem of right/left reversals. Less labor intensive on a plate-for-plate (or plate-for-stone) basis, it can be used to attain extremely subtle effects through multiple passages of very thin inks. It is the method by which all commercial high-speed lithography is accomplished, and was for many years scorned by fine-art printers who preferred Bavarian limestones and hand-pulled presses. Tamarind's June Wayne once described the speed and efficiency of the modern offset proofing press as "indecent." ULAE's press was small, and had to be fed by hand, but it constituted a minor concession to industrial "progress," and to the desire of artists to push at the boundaries of accepted practice.

plate, later work in another way and the print can show all these different times in one moment," adding that "this is not the nature of lithography."[22]

Nonetheless, it was in lithography that he most often chose to work, perhaps because when these multiple layers are spread out, they became more open to inspection and comparison than they do when stacked on top

For Johns and Rauschenberg, among others, this desire led to collaboration with other, less traditional artisans and printers, most notably

Gemini GEL. Founded in Los Angeles in 1966, and led by master printer Ken Tyler, Gemini rejected ULAE's and Tamarind's reverential approach to lithography. (Tyler once dismissed the adherents of Tamarind, where he had been technical director, as "hopeless craft romantics."[23]) Its reputation for high-tech ingenuity and its willingness to approach art production on an industrial scale appealed especially to Rauschenberg, who had become increasingly involved with live performance and technological art.

Rauschenberg's Gemini projects, such as *Booster and Seven Studies* (1967), were physically and technologically more ambitious than anything attempted at ULAE. *Booster* (pl. 39), whose central image is an X-ray of Rauschenberg's body printed to scale, was larger than any available litho stone, and had to be printed in two sections onto a single sheet. And yet in its suggestion of an allegorical self-portrait, it is less radical than many of Rauschenberg's earlier, less decipherable, prints. Increasingly, Rauschenberg's selection and use of photographic material carried topical content and iconographic meanings. The *Stoned Moon Series* (1969), which combined lithography and screenprinting in the same image, was Rauschenberg's response to having witnessed the launch of the Apollo 11 rocket that sent men to the moon. Far from being a casual sampling of pictorial flotsam, the prints were assembled from official photographs provided by NASA, along with pictures from the history of aviation and specimens of Florida fauna. Its scale was exhaustive: a cycle of thirty-three prints, whose central work *Sky Rocket* was, at 2.25 meters high, the largest fine-art lithograph ever made.[24] Critic Lawrence Alloway called it a printerly form of history painting, "a technological equivalent of Rubens' *Medici* cycle."[25]

Johns also took advantage of the technical possibilities presented by Gemini, expanding his scale dramatically in the *Color Numerals* (1969) and *Black and White Numerals* (1968) and

abandoning traditional print methods for embossings of lead sheets in *Lead Reliefs* (1968). The repetition of images, which was such a fundamental part of Johns's ULAE prints, continued, though in a cooler key. While the *1st Etchings* portfolios treated Johns's early sculptures with equal parts cerebral inquiry and physical grit, his 1972 Gemini lithographs render his early paintings in sleek, schematic

27 Jasper Johns
0–9, Edition A/C, page 5 1960–63
Lithograph
52.1 × 39.4 cm (20½ × 15½ in.)

translation: the original colors are reduced to a shimmer of gray and gold;[26] topographic surfaces of encaustic paint are recast as lithographic stain; and the brooms, cups, and other objects affixed to the original canvases appear as tracings, silhouettes, or words.

Four Panels from Untitled 1972 (pl. 35) is a restatement of a crucial painting in Johns's development, a work that ushered in the crosshatch pattern that was to occupy him for most of the 1970s, and that articulated with greater precision than ever before his concern with wholeness and fragmentation. The print repeats the painting's quadripartite design: a panel of crosshatch (freely redrawn); two of a slightly overlapping "flagstone" pattern (drawn in fairly close imitation of the painting); and a fourth of fragmented body parts on a haphazard wooden armature (reproduced photographically). The juxtaposition of this "psychologically loaded" panel with coolly repetitive abstractions was an attempt to treat widely divergent subjects with equivalent emotional distance.[27]

In the crosshatch prints that followed, the question of "what connects and what separates" two versions of the same image was relentlessly pursued in a language of abstract marks and material differences in manufacture. Mechanical and logical permutation became dominant devices: hatch patterns roll over and recombine, step through paces of reversal, inversion, mirroring and stammering, or repeat themselves in different materials. *Scent* (1975–76) was composed of stuttering panels of offset lithography, linocut, and woodblock. In his many screenprints of the 1970s, the flat and stolid surface that usually characterizes the medium was transformed into a study of subtlety and variety. The shimmering *Usuyuki* screenprints (pl. 36) were built up from a multitude of overlapping, hand-painted screens, to create delicate, even painterly, images that balance change and repetition.[28] ("Of course," Johns acknowledged, "this may constitute an abuse of the medium, of its true nature."[29]) In the screenprint *Flags 1* (1973, pl. 37), which

relies not on crosshatching but on an earlier flag painting, two flags are given subtly different textures through the use of varnish.

These deliberate statements of permutation can be seen in the context of conceptual art, as explications of process, but they are also open to metaphorical interpretation about the splitting, reflecting, and fracturing of identity. Finally, they are maneuvers which are natural – often unavoidable – in printing, while being attainable in painting, as Johns says, "only out of perversity."[30] In Johns's work, as in Rauschenberg's, aspects of the print that had merely been problems – irritating moments of cognitive dissonance that most artists preferred to ignore rather than resolve – were revealed as sources of content, and not only for prints. Johns observed that "the process of printmaking allows you to do things that make your mind work in a different way than, say, painting with a brush does… things which are necessary to printmaking become interesting in themselves and can be used in painting where they're not necessary but become like ideas."[31]

Canto *VII* 1/18   Barnett Newman 12/63

28 Barnett Newman
Canto VII from *18 Cantos* 1963
Lithograph
41.5 × 40.2 cm (16⅜ × 15⅞ in.)

29 Sam Francis
The White Line 1960
Color lithograph
90.5 × 63.3 cm (35½ × 25 in.)

30 Antoni Tàpies
Ditades damunt diari 1974
Etching and aquatint
65.5 × 50.2 cm (25¼ × 19¼ in.)

31 Pierre Soulages
Eau-forte XVI 1961
Etching
76 × 56 cm (30 × 22 in.)

32 Pierre Alechinsky
Prisma 1988
Color etching and aquatint
191 × 90.5 cm (75¼ × 35½ in.)

33 Pierre Alechinsky
Panoplie 1967
Color lithograph
54 × 53 cm (21¼ × 20¾ in.)

34 Corneille
Enchantement de l'été 1962
Color lithograph
56.2 × 76 cm (22⅛ × 30 in.)

35 Jasper Johns
Four Panels from Untitled 1972 1973–74
Four-color lithograph with embossing
101.6 × 72.4 cm (40 × 28½ in.) each sheet

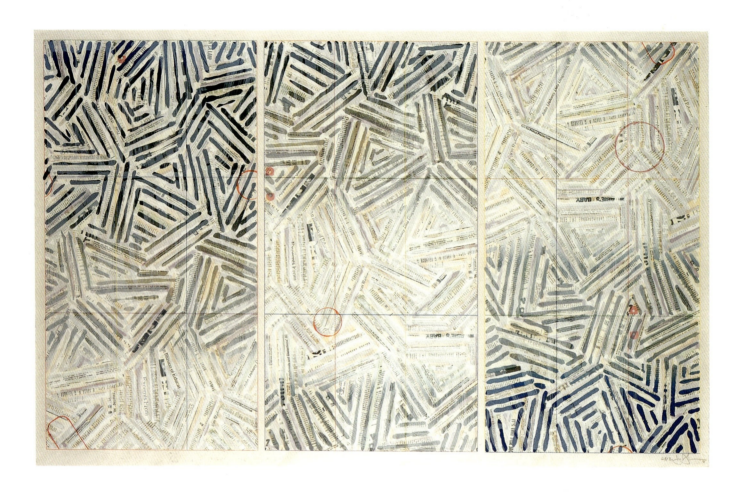

36 Jasper Johns
Usuyuki 1979–81
74.9 × 120.6 cm (29¹/₂ × 47¹/₄ in.)

Opposite:
37 Jasper Johns
Flags I 1973
Color screenprint
69.9 × 88.9 cm (27¹/₂ × 35 in.)

38 Jasper Johns
Decoy 1971
Color lithograph
104.1 × 73.6 cm (41 × 29 in.)

39 Robert Rauschenberg
Booster 1967
Color lithograph and screenprint
182.8 × 90.2 cm (72 × 35¹/₂ in.)

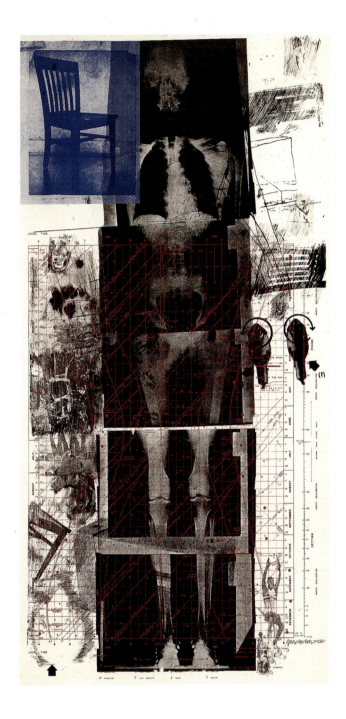

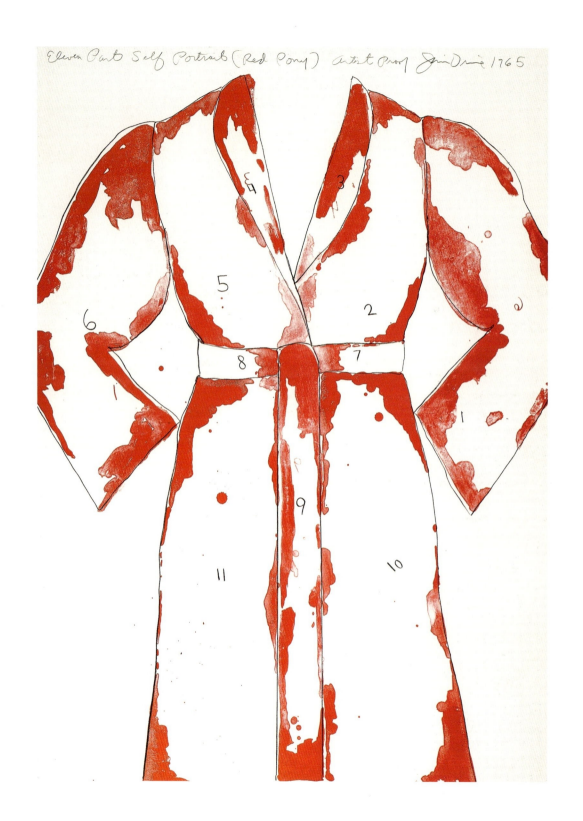

3

POP AND PRINT

op art is largely defined through its relationship to reproduction – its fascination with advertising, comic books, photographic celebrity, the visual appearance and social mechanisms of commerce – and its impact on the print was profound. In America and Britain, which gave birth to the two most influential strains of Pop, prints were granted a new pride of place by artists who exploited many of the very characteristics that had repulsed previous generations: reproductive infidelity, wanton association with commerce, impersonality, and distance from the artist's hand.

Significantly, one of the first important assemblies of works by the artists who would later be grouped under the rubric of American Pop occurred in print – the black-and-white etchings that made up the *International Anthology of Contemporary Engraving: The International Avant-Garde: America Discovered* (1962–64).[1] Jim Dine, Red Grooms, Robert Indiana, Allan Kaprow, Roy Lichtenstein, Claes Oldenburg, James Rosenquist, Wayne Thiebaud, and Andy Warhol all participated. Dine had been an enthusiastic printmaker since art school and Lichtenstein had won a prize in 1951 for a whimsical woodcut at the Brooklyn Museum's National Print Annual, but most of these artists had shown no previous interest in printmaking. They were, however, interested in art that was not unique, precious, or distinct from all the life that goes on around it; art

that, in Claes Oldenburg's famous phrase, "does something other than sit on its ass in a museum."[2] Many had been actively involved in "Happenings" – mixed-media, theatrical events meant to shatter the confines of painting and the distinctions between observers and participants. Dine's and Oldenburg's first professional prints stemmed from Happenings. Dine's *Car Crash I–V* and *End of the Crash* (1960) derived from a frantic performance piece about an automobile accident in which a friend had died, and the prints echo this emotional pitch – tangles of distraught lines, spinning wheels, crosses, and the scribbled word "CRASH." Oldenburg's contribution to *The International Avant-Garde* portfolio, *Orpheum Sign* (1961), was a tiny etching in the shape of a mangled movie marquee, a "jewelry version"[3] of the rough-and-tumble reliefs that stocked his environments like *The Street* (1960), which Oldenburg described as celebrating "irrationality, disconnection, violence and stunted expression – the damaged life forces of the city street."[4] *Orpheum* and the *Crash* prints reflect the tenor of Happenings, but they mark a critical point in the artists' transition from time-based performances to objects, and from Happenings to Pop.

There is some irony in the fact that Happenings, which Allan Kaprow, the form's chief theoretician, intended to be part of an "anti-capitalist effort to prevent the stockpiling

40 Jim Dine
Eleven Part Self-Portrait (Red Pony)
1964–65
Lithograph
104.8 × 75.2 cm (41¼ × 29⅛ in.)

49

The Crash #2 $\frac{7}{33}$ Jim Dine

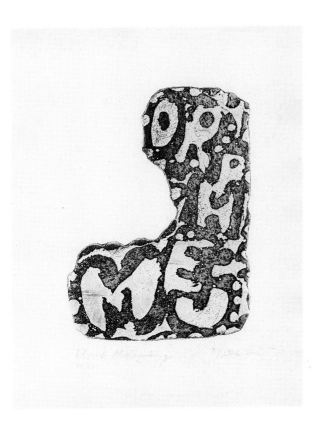

42 Claes Oldenburg
Orpheum Sign 1961
Etching and aquatint
29.8 × 23.8 cm (11¾ × 9⅜ in.)

43 Jim Dine
Toothbrushes #1 1962
Lithograph
64.2 × 51.7 cm (25³/₁₆ × 20½ in.)

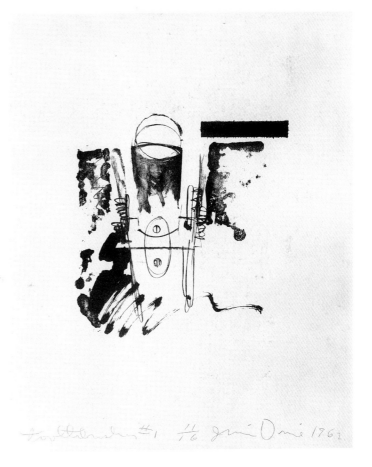

Opposite:
41 Jim Dine
The Crash #2 1960
Lithograph from the set of five
81.3 × 50.8 cm (32 × 20 in.)

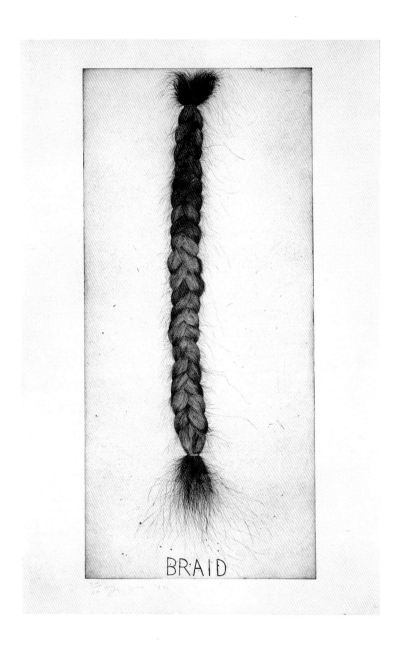

BRAID

44 Jim Dine
Braid State II 1972
Etching
97 × 63 cm (38 × 25 in.)

abandoned the raw emotion of the *Crash* in favor of neutral household items as carriers of meaning. In 1961 Dine made several drypoint etchings of fanciful colored ties, and of *Ten Useful Objects Which No One Should Be Without When Traveling*. The following year Johns brought him to ULAE, where he began to make lithographs of the tools and bathroom paraphernalia that occupied his paintings. In the paintings, Dine placed real objects against lushly painted canvas backdrops; in the prints, all his attentive brushwork is brought to bear on describing the subject rather than decorating its background. These are not simply tools and toothbrushes but "surrogates for human activity"[8] – especially that of the artist. After the tools and toothbrushes came palettes and sexually suggestive paintbrushes, and then the overtly self-referential bathrobe of *Eleven Part Self-Portrait (Red Pony)*, 1964–65.

In the mid-1960s Dine moved to England, and for three years devoted himself to writing and to print portfolios that proclaim his physical delight with etching and lithography. (By contrast, Oldenburg tended "to think of printmaking as an excruciatingly unpleasant activity, like going to the hospital for an operation."[9]) Although the subject of *Braid* (1972) – a disembodied hank of hair – ought to seem repulsive, in Dine's hands it is transformed into something approachable, even sentimental. Fascinated by the human will to recognize the personal within the generic, Dine recognized in prints a provocative meeting of intimacy and mechanical detachment. His art was considered Pop because he depicted the flotsam of everyday life – even his "autobiographical" bathrobe was lifted from an advertisement – but the allegorical use he made of these things, and his romantic pleasure in the artist's touch, was distinctly un-Pop.

Wayne Thiebaud was also, briefly, considered a Pop artist because of his vernacular subjects (almost anything you find in an early Thiebaud could be purchased at a well stocked Woolworth). But Thiebaud's

of art of the rich,"[5] gave birth to Pop art, which resulted in such an unprecedented stockpiling of art by the upper-middle class (largely in the form of editions). But there are points of continuity. Oldenburg saw his editioned sculptures as exhibiting the "balance of individuality, objectivity, and chance" that had characterized Happenings.[6]

Dine, on the other hand, later discounted his involvement with Happenings as "immature" and "theatrical,"[7] and he

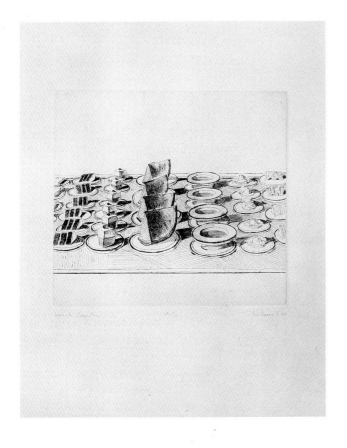

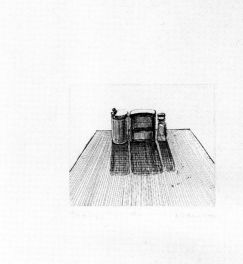

pictures are suffused with a quiet lyricism and concentration on the particular that had little to do with the brash culture of advertising. The distinction is poignantly clear in his use of print. His 1964 portfolio, *Delights*, was executed in etching – a medium dropped by Lichtenstein, Warhol, and most other Pop artists as soon as the plates for *The International Avant-Garde* were finished, but one that suits the deliberation with which Thiebaud composes his subjects, and the slow perusal that he seems to request from the viewer. Modest in scale (the sheets are just 15 by 11 inches, and the images much smaller), Thiebaud's *Delights* are intimate invitations to shared pleasures: a set of

restaurant tabletop dispensers, a plate of olives, a display of stately cake wedges. Later prints, like *Big Suckers* (1971), employ etching and aquatint with a classical purity and discretion, endowing lollipops with an unlikely air of dignity and consequence.

Thiebaud and Dine were not interested in what Oldenburg called "the false and cynical treatment of real emotion, as in today's publications,"[10] nor in the "blatantly trashy subjects and confrontation with the issue of merchandizing"[11] which artists such as Lichtenstein found fascinating. By 1961, Lichtenstein, Warhol, Rosenquist, and Ruscha

45 Wayne Thiebaud
Lunch Counter from the portfolio
Delights 1964
Etching
38.1 × 27.9 cm (15 × 11 in.)

46 Wayne Thiebaud
Dispensers from the portfolio
Delights 1964
Etching
38.1 × 27.9 cm (15 × 11 in.)

47 Wayne Thiebaud
Big Suckers 1971
Color aquatint
55.9 × 74.9 cm (22 × 29½ in.)

were all imitating in paint the infelicities of cheap print: overblown dot screens, crudely misregistered colors, ragged inkings. In painting them large, by hand, and on canvas, they elevated these characteristics to formal elements that could then be transferred to prints. But their fascination with commercial print did not immediately translate into a fondness for etching plates or lithography stones. Despite Lichtenstein's award-winning woodcut, *To Battle* (1950), his early Pop prints were almost all reproductive screenprints or offset lithographs. This hands-off approach, however, did not diminish the power of the prints – if anything it enhanced the mix of distance and intimacy, melodrama and catatonia that characterized Lichtenstein's art. Lichtenstein used the ham-fisted visual syntax of comic books – the thick black outlines, flat color shapes, and Ben-Day dots – to parody the ways in which emotion is emblematized and the way content can be altered, simplified, misregistered, and dispersed by reproduction.

The screenprints *Sweet Dreams, Baby!* (1965, pl. 76) and *The Melody Haunts My Reverie* (1965) each present melodramatic emotional states, intentionally disconnected from personal experience. *Brushstroke* (1965) gives the same treatment to the Abstract Expressionist emblem of deep emotion, the gestural swathe of paint. *Brushstroke* pulls the rug out from under the mystical pretenses of Expressionism, but the issues raised are broader than mere intergenerational sniping. Visually these prints succeed because their appearance is so geared to print media; conceptually they succeed because their subject is, in essence, mediation.

The most famous of Ruscha's early prints, *Standard Station* (1966, pl. 72), also manipulates clichés of commercial art: a gleaming gas station rising with absurd and awesome majesty against a dyspeptic tri-tone sky (the latter was achieved by Ruscha's appropriation of the commercial "split-fountain" inking technique, and soon became a screenprint cliché). Above it stands the solid word

"STANDARD," with its triple connotations of "mediocre or commonplace," "the model against which all others should be measured," and "buy gas here." Ruscha, like Thiebaud and Warhol, had worked as a commercial artist, and from his first proto-Pop paintings in 1959, his territory has been the objectified word, or more particularly, the curious epistemological gaps that open between words, representations, and objects.

Standard Station is based (with the substitution of day for night) on his painting *Standard Station, Amarillo, Texas* (1963), which in turn is derived from a photograph that appeared in the first of Ruscha's quixotic books, *Twentysix Gasoline Stations* (1963). The book reproduced snapshots of twenty-six gasoline stations encountered on the road between Los Angeles and Ruscha's home town of Oklahoma City. The photographs and the architecture reproduced are unremarkable, and the book does not qualify as a social or geographical document since it does not reproduce all the gas stations en route, nor does it present them in order. Like many of Ruscha's subsequent books, *Twentysix Gasoline Stations* seems always to be approaching some definitive statement only to fall critically, enigmatically, and purposefully short. In fact, Ruscha had designed the cover before the contents: "I like the word 'gasoline' and I like the specific quality of 'twenty-six'. If you look at the book you will see how well the typography works – I worked on all that before I took the photographs."[12] Ruscha's books represented two important departures from the traditional artist's book: they were cheaply printed and distributed by the artist in an unnumbered, unsigned, and unlimited edition; and the structure of the book was identical with its content. Instead of a collection of individual artworks bound to a literary text, Ruscha presented a cinematic narrative in which the individual frames were interesting mainly as parts of a whole.

Ruscha perpetually confuses the tasks of viewing, reading, interpreting, and knowing.

With the "liquid words" (pl. 73) that he began in 1967, representational sleight of hand, iconography, and the meaning of the word represented all vie for attention. In 1970, Ruscha took these conundrums further when he began to print with organic substances rather than merely portraying them.[13] In London, Ruscha produced a portfolio of rhyming English theme words – "Mews, Brews, Stews" – printed with substances such as blackcurrant pie filling, red salmon roe, axle grease, and chocolate syrup. One version of his famous *Hollywood* (1971) was a three-color organic screenprint made from grape jam, apricot jam, and Dutch Chocolate Metrecal (a 1960s diet food), another version offered a Pepto-Bismol sky and hills of squeegeed caviar.

Ruscha, along with his childhood friend Joe Goode, was part of a Southern Californian manifestation of Pop which arose parallel to, but largely independent of, New York Pop. Goode, like Ruscha, preferred to exploit the smooth and unreal suavity of print media, rather than the choppy foibles that intrigued Lichtenstein (pl. 75, 76). Both were

48 Roy Lichtenstein
Brushstroke 1965
Color screenprint
58.4 × 73.6 cm (23 × 29 in.)

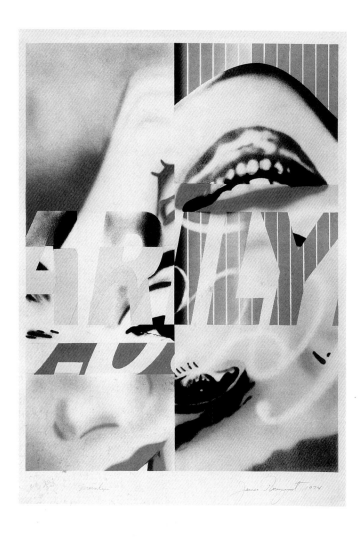

49 James Rosenquist
Marilyn 1975
Color lithograph
106 × 75 cm (41¾ × 29½ in.)

dissociated from objects of desire – even the car trim was "too old to excite acquisitiveness, too new for nostalgia"[14] – just as Rosenquist's choice of colors was dissociated from the task of representation, a printer's overlay of chromatic excitement quite divorced from its subject. There is an alluring dissonance between the fine, subtle, handmade quality of manufacture and the brashness of the images. Later prints, such as *Marilyn* (1972), exhibit a cleaner, more mechanized sheen: sharper edges, flatter colors, just as his painting assumed a more industrial appearance and scale. In the prints *Horseblinders* (1974) and *F-111* (1974), Rosenquist applied the environmental scale of his painting to multi-part prints that literally wrap around the room.

Mistrust of the machine gave way to a self-conscious embrace of it. Warhol said, famously, that "the reason I'm painting this way is that I want to be a machine."[15] Lichtenstein wanted his art "to look as if it had been programmed. I want to hide the record of my hand."[16] These ambitions flew in the face of recent print tradition, which had struggled to preserve and expose the artist's hand, and to minimize the presence of the machine. The visibility of the artist's hand was, in fact, considered a prerequisite of the original print. High-minded shops like Tamarind insisted that all artists must draw their stones by hand, and the Print Council of America's booklet *What is an Original Print?* specifically enjoined the use of photomechanical means. But offset lithography and screenprint continued to gain favor with artists fascinated with the artifacts of commerce. Both techniques could photo-mechanically reproduce an image simply, quickly, and – if the image was composed of solid blocks of color rather than subtle gradations of tone – fairly accurately.

Prints allowed artists to address not just isolated individuals, but a community of art consumers. Postwar affluence and education had resulted in an art public that was younger, hipper, and larger than at any time in the past.

appropriations of advertising syntax that lent themselves naturally to print, but for Rosenquist, whose paintings simulated the fracturing of imagery that occurs when an image is too large to be seen at once (as when billboards are viewed from too close), the small scale of print required the invention of alternative strategies. *Dusting Off Roses* (1964, pl. 78) offers a typical scramble of images – chrome car trim, tea roses in full bloom, a woman's hand fluttering a handkerchief. The juxtapositions carry personal significance for the artist, but aren't meant to be read as a rebus. Rather, they form a fluid structure of suggestion, allowing different viewers to construct different meanings. Though lifted from advertising, these fragments were

At the same moment that artists found broad distribution of their work to be desirable conceptually, it became practical financially. Prints sold – especially if intriguingly packaged. Clever production concepts flourished among new independent print publishers such as Multiples, Inc., Rosa Esman, and Tanglewood Press – publishers who did not run printshops and who often worked primarily with commercial printers and fabricators.

Most of the early Pop prints were made at the behest of publishers putting together group portfolios. *The International Avant-Garde* was the first of these, though its reliance on small, black-and-white etchings gave it a bookish quality that was to prove utterly atypical. Ruscha's publications notwithstanding, the book was not a Pop form. The decade's most important *livre d'artiste*, *1¢ Life*, is famous for including some of the great images of Pop, but still held close to the European fine book heritage. Equal parts expressionist tradition and Pop irreverence, *1¢ Life* brought together artists as diverse as Pierre Alechinsky, Karel Appel, Sam Francis, Roy Lichtenstein, and Andy Warhol, but it remained the only cross-over of its kind (pl. 74, 75).

The new American print portfolios were rarely tied to a text. Put together by galleries, museums, and independent publishers, these portfolios were assembled like small, portable exhibitions, promoting connections and ideas. The prints were often reproductive and the editions were often large (the portfolio *Ten Works × Ten Painters* was run in an edition of five hundred). The three volumes of *Eleven Pop Artists* (1965) circulated widely in America and in Europe and helped to define the look of Pop.[17] Multiples, Inc. made a specialty of concept portfolios like *Mirrors of the Mind*, a psychedelia-by-way-of-surrealism collection of reflections on reflection. The Multiples portfolio *Four on Plexi* (1966) included perhaps the only plastic multiple by a first-generation Abstract Expressionist (Barnett Newman), as well as one of the great art objects of the decade: Oldenburg's *Tea Bag* (1965).

Tea Bag was part print, part multiple (the term coined to refer to all manner of editioned objects that didn't qualify as prints): clear plexiglass molded in relief to depict a soggy, collapsed tea bag lying in a screenprinted puddle. Like *Baked Potato*, created for the portfolio *Seven Objects in a Box* (1966), it was a "hard" version of one of Oldenburg's "soft" sculptures.[18] In *Tea Bag*, the "hard" sculpture appears only as a ghost, in transparent sculptural relief. Inside sits a felt cut-out depicting the "bag," which Oldenburg describes as "a kind of 'before' to the dropped bag's 'after,' or an ideal state in relation to the

50 Claes Oldenburg
Tea Bag 1966
Screenprint on felt, plexiglass, and plastic
99.8 × 71.4 × 7.6 cm
(39¹¹⁄₁₆ × 28¹⁄₁₆ × 3 in.)

Indiana prints, *LOVE* began life as a painting, it was designed for reproduction, and has been reproduced so many times, and in so many forms, that reproduction has become central to its effect: a Christmas card, a desktop multiple, an eighteen-karat gold ring, a stainless steel sculpture, and thousands of unauthorized mass-market posters for which the artist received nothing. Indiana himself has produced no fewer than 21 different screenprint editions of *LOVE*. On Valentine's Day 1973, the US Bureau of Engraving and Printing released the *LOVE* postage stamp in an edition of 330 million, with the line "a special stamp for someone special." The ludicrous idea that there were 330 million special someones out there, all of whom could be specially favored by the identical item, demonstrated the essential conundrum of *LOVE*.

51 Robert Indiana
Love 1967
Color screenprint
91.4 × 91.4 cm (36 × 36 in.)

52 Andy Warhol
Self-Portrait 1967
Screenprint on silver coated paper
58.4 × 58.4 cm (23 × 23 in.)

dropped bag's circumstantial character. The formulation also creates a separation of the senses: what the hands touch is not what the eyes see."[19]

The print was no longer despised for its association with the market-place – in fact, the democratizing principle of the market was welcomed. "I think it would be great if you had an art that could appeal to everybody," Oldenburg said.[20] "Printmaking," Ruscha said, "is glorified as a great art at the expense of people knowing it's a fantastic marketable item."[21] The two most famous art images of the 1960s – Robert Indiana's *LOVE* and Andy Warhol's *Soup Cans* – exploited the clean-edged vibrancy of commercial design, and were, in turn, reincorporated into mainstream, commercial culture. The first *LOVE* was designed as a Christmas card for the Museum of Modern Art in 1964. While much of Indiana's art is assertively American, often regionalist, in its iconography, *LOVE* was universal – an impersonal, even corporate logo for what we like to think of as the most personal of emotions. Though, like most

It was Warhol, however, who took the notion of mechanization and the false intimacy it enabled to the decade's most memorable extremes. As a commercial artist in the 1950s, Warhol had become fluent in commercial print processes and, like Rauschenberg, Warhol had begun to use screenprint in his paintings in 1962. For Rauschenberg, the photomechanical image was one more painterly effect, a way to inject the real world into art without the burden of narrative. But for Warhol it was the iconographic content of the photograph, the distance and the desire that the photograph interposed, that were at issue. When Rauschenberg first began to make prints, he paralleled the look of his screenprinted paintings in lithography; Warhol simply substituted paper for canvas. For Warhol, the distinction was of little consequence: "I suppose you could call the paintings prints, but the material used for the paintings was canvas."[22] Warhol liked the "assembly-line" effect of screenprint,[23] and he used it to generate paintings, sculptures, and prints.[24]

Warhol's "original" works were so close to being mass-produced (at its peak the Factory was producing eighty paintings a day)[25] that producing proper print editions may have seemed both tedious and beside the point. In any case commercial screenprinters were engaged to run the editions of *Birmingham Race Riot* for *Ten Works × Ten Artists*, and *Jackie I, II,* and *III* for the three *Eleven Pop Artists* portfolios. Jackie Kennedy, glamorous and tragic, embodied Warhol's twin preoccupations with celebrity (paintings of Elizabeth Taylor, Elvis Presley) and disaster (fatal car accidents, race riots, anonymous suicides). In the three Jackie prints, her face is presented in stammering repetition – once, twice, four times – constructing an image that is sad, distant, and vaguely prurient, a reprise of the public fascination with looking as a substitute for comprehending.

After Warhol's famous "retirement" from painting in 1965, he concentrated on movies and other prototypes for reproduction; his show the following year at Castelli featured helium-inflated silver pillows and the infamous *Cow* wallpaper (pl. 81) – bovine, bucolic, and relentlessly repetitious. He also set up his own in-house print-publishing vehicle, Factory Additions, whose first publication was the screenprint portfolio, *Marilyn* (1967, pl. 80).

Marilyn Monroe was a subject of Warhol's earliest screenprinted paintings: there was the iconic Marilyn, isolated against a gold field, and there was the incessant Marilyn, repeated from

canvas edge to canvas edge. In print, the portfolio format allowed for isolation and repetition to co-exist. Taken together, the ten garish color variations of the same impassive face suggest not a portrait or a personality, but a tabula rasa for the dreams of others.

Marilyn may well be Warhol's greatest graphic work, but Warhol placed an assistant in charge of the project, and was apparently not even present when the prints were proofed.[26] Warhol typically entrusted his assistants with both responsibility and latitude, and enjoyed the "minor misunderstandings" which affected the work. Critic John Coplans observed that "what obviously interests Warhol is the decisions, not the acts of making."[27] Although the *Marilyns* were clearly based on an appropriated, photographic image, the viewing public could be comforted by the evidence that someone had bothered to add a bit of color. The shocking thing about the Campbell's soup cans was their utter fidelity to their commonplace source. They suggested (which very little of Pop actually did) direct appropriation and unhindered mass production. It was often forgotten that the first soup cans

53 Andy Warhol
Jackie II 1966
Color screenprint from the *Eleven Pop Artists II* portfolio
61 × 76.2 cm (24 × 30 in.)

had been hand-painted on canvas. Instead, it was the portfolio, *Campbell's Soup I* (1968, pl. 79) – crisp, machine-made, banal and impersonal – that became an enduring symbol of Pop.[28]

By 1970, printmaking had established itself as a vital forum for avant-garde art. Dine, Rauschenberg, Ruscha, and Warhol all gave up painting for some years, but continued to concentrate on graphic works. Prestigious European art events such as Documenta in Kassel, Germany, and the Biennale des Jeunes in Paris, began to incorporate graphic sections, and the 35th Venice Biennale was to have featured a survey of American printmaking, and included a printshop where artists would make prints in situ. A boycott by artists protesting the American involvement in Vietnam quashed the plan, but the fact remains that prints had achieved a presence at the forefront of art production that they never enjoyed before, or since.

In Britain, printed matter was also, conspicuously, the subject and the substance of contemporary art. Though American Pop had its intellectual component (most obviously in the person of Claes Oldenburg), it was largely a visceral response to the artists' actual environment. In postwar Britain, where responding to the environment had resulted in a decade of what Joe Tilson described as "tiny, brown, sad paintings,"[29] Pop art, as exemplified in the prints of Richard Hamilton, Eduardo Paolozzi, R. B. Kitaj, and Tilson, was ideological and analytical.

Hamilton and Paolozzi were key figures in the Independent Group of artists, architects, and writers, who met at London's Institute of Contemporary Arts in the 1950s, and who began to formulate a new art that would respond to the gleamingly mechanical aspects of modern life. In England at the time, however, the gleamingly mechanical remained largely fictive, a concoction of images exported from America, while the objects they represented stayed behind. The artists' fascination was not with the objects

themselves, but with the mechanisms whereby knowledge of these objects was communicated: television, film, electronic communications, photography, and print.

Hamilton was by training a painter and etcher. He was deeply influenced by Duchamp[30] and, like him, was more intrigued by the cerebral aspects of visual experience than by retinal stylistics. He wanted to make art in which no "signature style" could be discerned – a perplexing task with brush or pencil, but an obvious one for photomechanical print processes. In 1963, Hamilton began working with Christopher Prater, a screenprinter who had the skills, insight, imagination, and patience necessary in a great artists' printer. For more than a decade, Prater's Kelpra Studio was to dominate print production in Britain the way ULAE, Tamarind, and Gemini did in the United States. And just as the 1960s was the decade of lithography in the United States, it was the decade of screenprinting in Britain. The difference is instructive: lithography is adept at reproducing painterly nuance; screenprinting, on the other hand, is an art in which painterly touch is irrelevant. For artists who worked with collage, the screenprint offered a new seamlessness, as it allowed images to be peeled away from their sources and built into something else altogether.

Hamilton's early prints with Prater were all adaptations of found images. The idea of making prints by reworking photographic material was not new – as far back as the 1940s Picasso had made photogravures of his drawings and reworked them, layering autographic mark, photographic translation, and autographic mark again. Hamilton, however, tried to steer clear of the autographic altogether. In *My Marilyn* (1965, pl. 82), Hamilton's intention was to produce "a painterly result without actually making marks."[31] Through an elaborate series of positive/negative reversals and color changes, Hamilton mechanically reworked George Barris's contact sheets of Marilyn Monroe. All the marks that appear on the photos – the crosses of rejection and arrows of preference – are Monroe's, a fact that turns the work into a compelling portrait of a self-portrait, and in the light of Monroe's suicide, a poignant memento mori.

With the print, Hamilton was able to develop an art-making process that had less to do with the traditional habits of drawing, or even composing collages, than with subtle editorial interferences in the act of reproduction: selection, placement, revision, deletion. "I was less interested in subject matter," Hamilton explained, "than in the print structure, the way the image is transmitted."[32]

Hamilton's masterpiece *I'm Dreaming of a Black Christmas* (1971, pl. 83) is the culmination of a series of works derived from a film still of Bing Crosby. The final collotype (with screenprint additions) was made from a color negative, which was made from a color transparency of Hamilton's painting *I'm Dreaming of a White Christmas* (1967), which itself was a handmade color-negative version of a 35mm frame from the movie. In theory the double reverse ought simply to cause the image to revert to its original state, but since every step of the process was subjected to interference, the net result is a strange displacement – as if Bing, walking in an unfamiliar street, had carefully retraced his footsteps only to find himself on a foreign continent.

Paolozzi engaged in a far more aggravated restructuring of visual material. *As Is When* (1965), his screenprint suite based on the life and writings of Ludwig Wittgenstein, splices together fragments of typed language, photographs, manufactured patterns, and even cannibalizes itself in parts: proofs of the print *Tortured Life* were cut up and re-used in two other prints of the series. "For me," said Paolozzi, "the day of the artist struggling with his bare hands is finished. Nobody would expect an aerodynamicist to build his own wind tunnel."[33] Paolozzi's fascination with the mechanical world had been apparent in his

Brutalist "mechanomorph" sculptures of the 1950s. *As Is When* announced a transformation in Paolozzi's style, mirroring the global transformation, just becoming evident, from the brutal, comprehensible mechanics of industry to the more sparkling and surreptitious power of electronic communications. Considered the first great masterpiece of screenprint, the portfolio was a showpiece of Prater's tremendous skills as a stencil cutter and printer. The screens were all made by Prater, working from collages prepared by Paolozzi, and the colors were changed with every printing (thus there was no question of "replicating" the collage, and no question of a standard, uniform edition). The impression of instability, of a visual world in which everything might change at any moment, is literally true. As a printmaker, Paolozzi interlocks two preoccupations of 1960s culture: a visual fascination with the dazzlingly decorative, and an intellectual fascination with the "information overload."

In 1963 the Institute of Contemporary Arts in London commissioned a portfolio of prints by twenty-four artists selected by Richard Hamilton, who presciently managed to include almost every major British artist of the coming decade.[34] All were screenprinted at Kelpra, but the images ranged from Peter Blake's photo-typographic collage *Beach Boys* (pl. 85) to the pure optical abstractions of Bridget Riley. But they shared a brazenness and chromatic brilliance that was deeply startling to a nation that had, as Bryan Robertson wrote, "tended to equate tonality with moral rectitude and pure color with irresponsibility."[35]

When six prints from the ICA portfolio were chosen to represent Britain at the Paris Biennale, French officials refused to hang them alongside "original" prints, because of the nature of their manufacture. Patrick Caulfield's *Ruins* (pl. 88) – which might seem a banner image for the portfolio, with its dull grey bricks sitting on top of, and nonetheless giving way to, brilliant blades of grass – won the

54 Allen Jones
Life Class 1968
Book in the form of seven two-part,
recombinable lithographs
upper: 34.3 × 56.5 cm (13½ × 22¼ in.)
lower: 46.3 × 56.5 cm (18¼ × 22¼ in.)

Press were chastised for their involvement with suspect techniques, but with little effect.

Given the abuses that had occurred in Paris and elsewhere, there was some legitimate concern about what constitutes an "original" print and what constitutes a reproduction or a copy, but what many people seemed to miss was the critical distinction between how an image was made and how it was presented. The real concern was deception. Prints such as Paolozzi's did not even pretend to be hand-drawn. The award-winning *Ruins* was, in fact, a reproduction of a gouache, but a gouache from which all idiosyncratic, autographic marks had been rigorously eliminated by the artist. In an open challenge to what Walter Benjamin called our "fetishistic fundamentally anti-technological notion of art,"[36] artists were dramatically blunt about the nature and extent of their contributions: Caulfield said "I couldn't do a silkscreen of my own if I was given the chance. I don't see why it's necessary really…"[37]

Unlike most of the artists classified as Pop, Caulfield didn't borrow photographically from mass media, but drew pictures of things and places that were as graphically gripping, as flawlessly designed, as deceptively seductive, as the made-up world of advertising. His bold black lines and bright blocks of color look as if they were printed even when applied by hand. Caulfield once said he would have been happy to screenprint his paintings if screens could only be made large enough. But he has shrewdly used the smaller scale of prints to evoke intimate interiors and quiet still-lifes, most remarkably in a set of illustrations to accompany the poems of Jules Laforgue (pl. 87).

But it was the photomechanical manipulation of found imagery that drew most artists to screenprint. Allen Jones intercut pop-culture borrowings with hand-drawn elements, moving between artifice and nature, style and sexuality. Joe Tilson, Peter Blake, and R. B. Kitaj worked with sliced and re-combined newspaper and magazine clippings that set up complicated internal relationships and ambiguous meanings. Tilson likened the task

unofficial Prix des Jeunes Artistes, nonetheless. This episode, along with other, concurrent clashes between artists, publishers, curators, and print pedants, dramatically exposed the growing gap between the definition and the practice of "originality." As in America, the prospering of prints that relied on photomechanical and commercial techniques was greeted by the print establishment with something less than enthusiasm. The screenprint was regarded with special suspicion. Unlike lithography, it had little in the way of fine-art pedigree, and it allowed the artist to work at a considerable manual distance. The most innovative British publishers of the 1960s, Marlborough Graphics, Editions Alecto, and Petersburg of explicating the precise content of his work to making "an ordnance survey map of a cloud of steam."[38] In the 1960s Tilson's eclecticism, technical adventurousness, and complete disregard for the two-dimensional propriety of the print redefined the limits of printmaking for many younger artists. Tilson said, "I made a list of the things you weren't meant to do, such as make it bulge, tear it up, cut it, make it out of materials that fell to pieces, make it out of plastic, and so on…"[39] *Rainbow Grill* (1965) was screenprinted on card and vacuum-formed polystyrene; *Transparency Vallegrande Bolivia, October 10th* (1969), a portrait of Che Guevara that was one of several political tributes Tilson

made at the time, was a screenprint on rigid PVC, lumiline, and paper (pl. 89). There was a fluid exchange of ideas and images between Tilson's printed work and his unique, constructed work. The *Sky* prints (1967, pl. 90) link the night sky, a large human finger, and a packet of vacuum-formed and metalized toys (*Sky One*), torn paper pictures of helicopters, trees, and birds (*Sky Two*), or the plastic letters S, K, Y (*Sky Three*). As in his reliefs (which often include printed elements), these are combined not for novelty, but as an assembly of metaphors.

R. B. Kitaj's pictures of the 1960s were composed of so many densely interlocked

55 R. B. Kitaj
The Flood of Laymen from *Mahler Becomes Politics, Beisbol* 1965
Color screenprint
76.2 × 50.8 cm (30 × 20 in.)

56 R. B. Kitaj
Partisan Review from *In Our Time* 1970
Screenprint
78.7 × 57.2 cm (31 × 22½ in.)

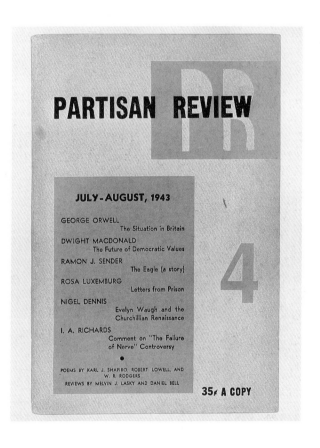

references that they have been described as "painterly lectures."[40] Like Tilson and Paolozzi, Kitaj concentrated on the accumulation and arrangement of images, and allowed his printers considerable independence with regard to execution. In 1967 Chris Prater described "a Kitaj print we are about to start working on, [which] arrived from California by mail as a page of instructions, a small pencil sketch, and about twenty photographs from newspapers and magazines."[41] Kitaj's three-year-long series of screenprints collectively titled *Mahler Becomes Politics, Beisbol* (1964–67), had its origins in a group of poems written by Jonathan Williams in response to Mahler symphonies. The prints, with their nested visual quotations and references, reiterate the sense, implicit in the title, of successive layers of interpretation and reinterpretation, progressing outward until the original event has disappeared from view. Kitaj's other major print series, titled *In our Time – covers for a small library after the life for the most part*, replicated the covers of books Kitaj owned. Reproduction was no longer anathema, it was the vehicle for portraying both intellectual concerns and historical context.

In 1975, Kitaj abandoned photographic and reproductive modes of art and announced that he was interested only in "representing the face and human form."[42] He was not alone in changing direction. A few years earlier, Tilson had moved from London to the Wiltshire countryside, where he traded hyper-modern screenprint for rusticated etching, and turned from headline topicality to the more enduring cycles of nature and myth. His *Mantra* etchings, produced in Italy, build repetitions of a single word – "Earth," "Seed," "Moon," "Sea" – into a large grid, a kind of apothecary chest for thought (pl. 91). Blake also abandoned contemporary technology, turning in the mid-1970s to wood engraving – the technique that had supplied the vast bulk of newspaper and magazine illustrations through the nineteenth century.[43] With the arrival of photomechanical means of making relief blocks, wood engraving had been permanently displaced in commercial practice. It enjoyed a brief blaze of popularity among British artists in the first decades of this century before finally petering out, a victim of its extraordinary demands upon time and labor. Blake's superb, painstaking depictions of Victorian circus freaks in *Side Show* (1974–78) took five years to produce – a fact reflected in their poignant, fly-in-amber look of incarceration.

This withdrawal from the slickness of commerce, popular culture, and high technology could be ascribed to the late 1960s disillusionment with progress, but it should be remembered that these artists had long been concerned with political, cultural, and humanist issues. Tilson's statement that he thinks "of art as a tool of understanding, an instrument of transformation to put yourself in harmony with the world and life,"[44] is virtually unimaginable on the lips of an American Pop artist.

"I take," David Hockney has said, "a rather old-fashioned view of a print: you should actually draw it."[45] Though he contributed a not entirely successful screenprint (his only one) to the ICA portfolio, virtually all his important early prints occurred in the unfashionable medium of etching, a medium that gives full power to his perspicacious, descriptive line. (Marco Livingstone described Hockney as "taking a line not just for a walk, as Paul Klee had done, but also for a talk."[46]) Hockney was initially judged to be part of Pop – a result of the bleached hair and lamé jacket, as much as of his fondness for picturing quotidian life – but his art was, from the start, more concerned with the intimate world of friends visited, places seen, and stories told, than with the machinations of media. While other artists were condensing an eclectic array of images into individual prints, Hockney recognized the expanded narrative potential of prints in series. *A Rake's Progress* (pl. 92), Hockney's brilliant print cycle of 1961–63, takes its title from Hogarth's eighteenth-century morality tale, and with a mix of autobiographical accuracy and imaginary

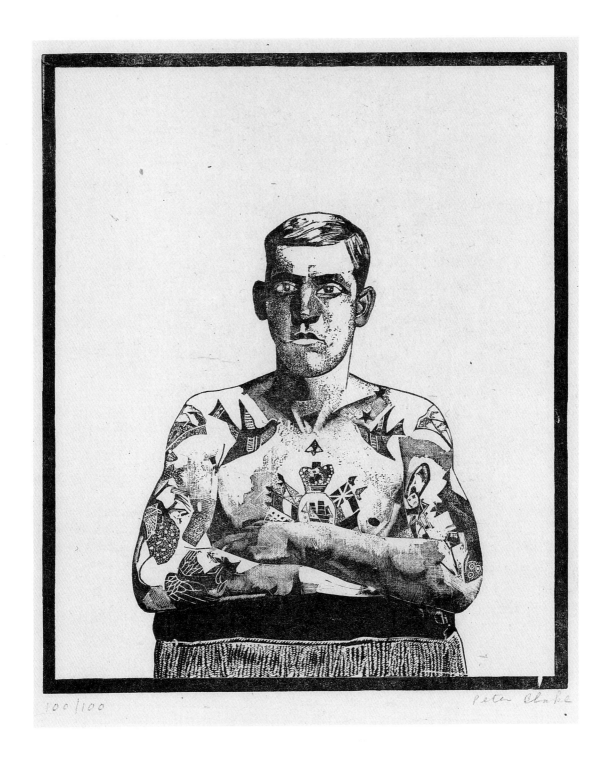

100/100   Peter Blake

57 Peter Blake
Tattooed Man from *Side-Show* 1974–78
Wood engraving from the set of five
26.7 × 21 cm (10½ × 8¼ in.)

58 David Hockney
Paris, 27 rue de Seine 1971
Etching and aquatint
89.5 × 71.1 cm (35¼ × 28 in.)

parable, chronicles the artist's first trip to the Eldorado of America. Hogarth wrote "I treat my subject as a dramatic writer; my picture is my stage, and men and women my players,"[47] and Hockney tells his tales with a quirky vocabulary of flat figurines and scattered props within a shallow theatrical space.[48] The crucial moment of Hockney's transformation from brunette to blond (and by implication, from struggling artist to glamorous wastrel) is captured in *The Start of the Spending Spree and the Door Opening for a Blond*, where a thin wooden door separates the artist's somber profile from a paradisiacal sunset while a bottle of Lady Clairol perches on his head like a crown. The insouciance of *A Rake's Progress* appeared not just in its content, but also in its technique. A series of straightforward line etchings with occasional flourishes of aquatint, it revealed a simplicity and directness in etching that had almost been forgotten in the search for expanded intaglio effects. Bruce Nauman remembers it being roundly attacked by the American academic printmaking establishment: "They thought the work had nothing to do with printmaking."[49]

Lithography would later become one of Hockney's most eloquent instruments, but his concentration in the 1960s was on etched books and portfolios: *A Rake's Progress* was followed by *Illustrations for Thirteen Poems from C. P. Cavafy* (1966), and *Illustrations for Six Fairy Tales from the Brothers Grimm* (1969), both of which moved closer to naturalistic representation and demonstrated the artist's remarkable gift for capturing a mood. Unlike most contemporary *livres d'artistes*, such as Motherwell's *A la pintura*, where images are meant to invoke "essences" parallel to those of the text, Hockney's etchings illustrate precise events without ever looking "illustrative." They work both in and out of their binding: the Brothers Grimm series was released as a large-scale limited edition *livre d'artiste*, as a portfolio of individual prints, and in a pocket-sized facsimile edition that was small and inexpensive enough to be given and read to children.

The possibility of producing and distributing art in massive quantity, which fine-art print media seemed to promise but never deliver, was avidly pursued by artists, publishers, businessmen, and musicians (many English rock bands came out of art schools). Blake and Hamilton both designed album covers for the Beatles. Blake's *Sgt Pepper's Lonely Hearts Club Band* (1967) is a masterpiece of dysfunctional nostalgia; Hamilton's design for the "White Album" (1968), with its individually numbered, pristine, blind-stamped jacket, was meant to place it "in the context of the most esoteric art publications."[50] These albums are undoubtedly the most widely distributed works either artist has made, though few of those who can recite the lyrics might remember who designed the covers.

While most art editions remained limited to dozens, or, at most, hundreds, a Munich publisher named Dorothea Leonhart was producing editions in sufficient quantity to make artists' prints once again a popular and populist form of art. Leonhart published Friedrich Hundertwasser's *Good Morning City* in an aggregate edition of 10,000; a Paolozzi edition of 3,000, and Hamilton's *Kent State* (1970), in an edition of 5,000. *Kent State* proved to be a technical nightmare, given the near-impossibility of applying to an edition of 5,000 the standards kept for an edition of 30, but it is also one of Hamilton's most important prints. Searching for an appropriately mass-market image, Hamilton set his camera up in front of his television set for one week in May 1970; it was the week that National Guardsmen opened fire on students protesters at Kent State University in Ohio, killing four. After reviewing the ethics of using a photograph of a wounded student lying bleeding on the ground,[51] Hamilton concluded that "the wide distribution of a large edition print might be the strongest indictment I could make."[52] The prone figure lies congealed in layer upon layer of screenprinted ink (Hamilton decided to overlay color rather than break them up by dot screen). The text that Hamilton wrote on the piece speaks only of the transmittal of information from event to camera to satellite to television to camera to print, finishing: "Fifteen… screens are used to print pale transparent tints on paper. Fifteen layers of pigment; a tragic chorus monotonously chanting an oft-repeated story. In one eye and out the other."[53]

4

MULTIPLICITY

For better or for worse, art objects that exist in multiple are commonly seen as less authoritative than unique works, less ringed about with the nebulous, charismatic quality that Walter Benjamin called "aura." For June Wayne, "the multiple potential of lithography was a secondary, even irrelevant, characteristic,"[1] but to many artists of the 1960s, the condition of multiplicity promised a radical and much desired redefinition of art. It was multiplicity, rather than printerly techniques or effects, that drew many younger artists to print.

In 1959, the Swiss artist Daniel Spoerri established the organization MAT (Multiplication d'Art Transformable) to produce editioned artworks that would challenge the economic and social isolation that plagued art. Spoerri laid down three criteria: the works should not depend on the "personal handwriting" of the artist (since replication would then be mere imitation of an absent original); they should not be fabricated by the usual reproductive art methods – no printing, casting, or tapestry – and they should include some variable or kinetic element, such that the existence of multiple examples would not lead simply to increased repetition of a static idea, but would allow a profusion of works to arise from a single design. Among the works included in the first MAT collection were a reissue of Duchamp's *Rotoreliefs* of 1935; a screenprinted plexiglass construction by Jesus

Rafael Soto which changed appearance as the viewer moved; and motorized objects by Pol Bury and Jean Tinguely.

Though the initial MAT venture was a financial failure, the essential concept of art that was broadly available, that avoided the pretensions and manipulations of the art market, and that responded to its viewer, proved enormously popular, especially in Europe. It appealed to two continuing strains of artistic theory: one, following in the tradition of Dada, that aimed to dismantle the rickety apparatus of aesthetic value and institutional standards; and the second, following in the tradition of the Bauhaus, that wanted to develop a truly democratic and universal practice of art manufacture.

As early as the 1920s, Bauhaus artists had rejected the elitism of the handmade – what Laszlo Moholy-Nagy described as "the collector's naive desire for the unique, [which] hampers the cultural potential of mass consumption."[2] They proposed a rationally determined, universally accessible, and potentially mass-produced abstraction that would reconcile industrial production with the spiritual life of man.[3] Their forms were predicated on the idea that, rather than force a machine to imitate, ineptly, luxury ornament developed for the human hand, the artist should collaborate with the machine, answering human need from mechanical strengths. These

59 Fluxus (George Brecht, Joe Jones, Ay-O, Takehisa Kosugi, Ben Vautier, George Maciunas, etc.)
Fluxkit 1964 (this example 1966)
Vinyl case with mixed media
30.5 × 43.2 × 12.7 cm
(12 × 17½ × 5 in.) overall

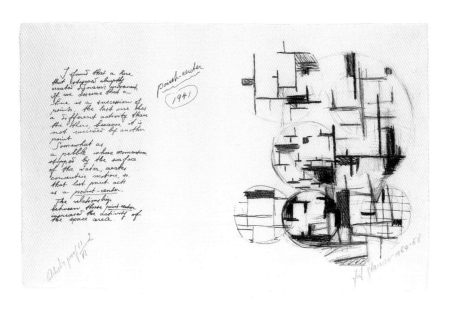

60 Fritz Glarner
Point Center 1941, page 2 of
Recollection 1964–68
Lithograph
36.5 × 57.2 cm (14¼ × 22½ in.)

was already designing works like *Diagon 31* (1956–62, pl. 93), in which the image is composed of screenprinted strips of PVC and wood that can be manipulated by the viewer into a wide variety of patterns.

Albers became the strongest representative of the Bauhaus in America. In his positions at Black Mountain College and Yale University Albers taught that artists – like designers, engineers, or doctors – must have absolute comprehension of their working materials, and he immersed himself in studies of the interaction of color. The nesting squares of carefully calibrated color that occupied Albers throughout the 1960s and 1970s were perfectly geared to mechanical reproduction, and, with the flourishing of lithography and silkscreen shops in America, he became an intensely prolific printmaker, completing nearly three hundred prints between 1961 and his death in 1976. The *White Line Squares* (1966, pl. 95) were the first major publications of Gemini GEL, and initiated its reputation for cool technological mastery: the project required an unprecedented precision of edge, color, and registration, and in the spirit of the Bauhaus, it was executed by telephone and post (to guarantee fidelity of color, Albers cut his studies in half, sending one part to Gemini to work from and retaining the other for proofing).[5] "I never touch the stone, never the rule, never the ink, it's all done by my friend Ken [Tyler], but I watch him like Hell!" Albers said.[6]

The Bauhaus pursuit of mass-produced visual art influenced a number of younger artists, including Victor Vasarély and Richard Mortensen, who renounced traditional painting to concentrate on prototypes for multiplication. "The value of the prototype," Vasarély said, "does not consist in the rarity of the object, but the rarity of the quality it represents."[7] In manifestos issued throughout the 1950s, Vasarély had argued for a mechanically produced art of standardized shapes and colors. Following his own advice, he produced a vast array of screenprints, lithographs, rugs, puzzles, and sculptural objects, eventually

ideas were carried into the 1960s by a diaspora of older European artists including Joseph Albers, Max Bill, Richard Paul Lohse, and Fritz Glarner. As a painter, Glarner banished all signs of casual or personal touch, but in his lithographs, especially the suite *Recollection* (1964–68), which details the development of his aesthetic, the hard edges and polished surfaces of his paintings have been replaced by sketchiness and informality.

Bill and Albers were veterans of the Bauhaus, concerned with principles of industrial and graphic design as well as with art, and Lohse was trained as a graphic designer, and for them collaboration with the machine necessitated little alteration of style, and enabled a permutational investigation of shape, line, color, and compositional structures. All these artists had produced prints since the 1940s, but in the 1960s the public for geometric abstraction expanded dramatically. The influence of Bill and Lohse (pl. 94) was primarily felt in Europe. The Swiss artist Karl Gerstner, who shared with his older compatriots both a fascination with mathematically determined images and a history as a professional designer, was an important advocate of the multiple, which he saw as a way "to produce the greatest possible originality and the lowest price."[4] In the 1950s, Gerstner adopting the principle of mass manufacture to such a degree that he came to seem less an artist than a small industry. Vasarély saw these works as efforts at social reform: "the thought and methods of art can only develop parallel with the most advanced thought and technique of their time. In this way the dream of the concomitance of culture and civilization will be realized."[8]

These ideas were taken up by many "kinetic" and "optical" artists who wanted to rationalize the experience of art, employing carefully calibrated optical effects, or actual

herself feared that they would be seen as "gimmicks") and many of the more technologically bizarre works have not fared well in recent opinion.

Though Spoerri had proscribed the use of traditional graphic methods, most artists and publishers saw printing as one more option on the menu of reproductive technologies. And, as the Belgian kinetic sculptor Pol Bury observed, the physical awkwardness of distributing three-dimensional works inclined sculptors to "rêveries postales."[9] Bury animated his two-dimensional prints with various

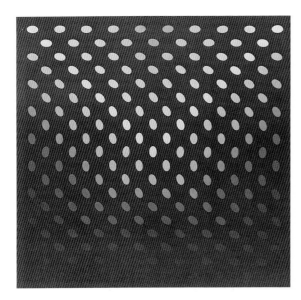 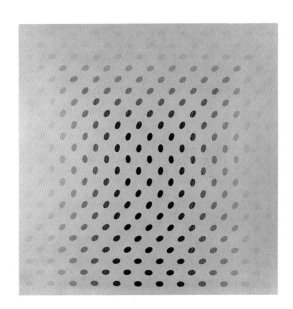

moving parts, to imbue works of art with the quality of motion. The Parisian gallery run by Denise René (which Vasarély had helped to found) and Cologne's Galerie Der Spiegel (which in 1964 revived MAT in association with the artists Daniel Spoerri and Karl Gerstner) were among the most prominent publishers of multiples and prints that either moved physically, or appeared to move. From the mid-1960s to the mid-1970s such multiples were extremely popular and enjoyed the respect of collectors, dealers, and museums. But novelty was a notable factor (Denise René

devices: his "Ramolissements" used flexible mirrors to distort famous places and faces into rubbery fantasies; while his "Cinétisations" were images sliced and reassembled to produce "linear hiccups."[10]

The optical art of the British artist Bridget Riley, on the other hand, was far closer to Albers' exploration of vision and perception than to the multiplicity and trompe-l'oeil topography that fascinated Vasarély. Riley's subdued tonal range (she worked in black and white for the better part of decade) and her careful orchestration of visual frequency and

61 Bridget Riley
19 Greys A 1968
Screenprint
76.2 × 76.2 cm (30 × 30 in.)

62 Bridget Riley
19 Greys C 1968
Screenprint
76.2 × 76.2 cm (30 × 30 in.)

63 Robert Watts
Fingerprint c. 1965
Plastic box, offset on paper, plaster, ink
10.2 × 12 × 2.5 cm (4 × 4¾ × 1 in.)

optical bounce accords her work a characteristic sobriety. Her masterly screenprint set *19 Greys* (1968) exploits the suave tonal gradations, crisp edges, and unconditional flatness of screenprint to create images of unexpected emotional poignancy. "No matter what I do," Riley said, "it will be subjective."

Drawing on the other, Dadaist strain of thought about multiplicity, Fluxus attempted to separate the experience of art from a fixation on objects, and its publications were largely ignored by art institutions and markets of the time. A loose gathering of American, European, and Asian composers, poets, and artists, Fluxus was held together mainly by the figure of George Maciunas, who acted as its administrator, archivist, publisher, and ideological policeman. The artists who participated in Fluxus were many and varied: George Brecht, Nam June Paik, Robert Watts (who burlesqued the official side of print with artworks that impersonated money, stamps, and fingerprints), Robert Filliou, Ben Vautier, Wolf Vostell, LaMonte Young – even Joseph Beuys was briefly considered (by Maciunas if

not by himself) a Fluxus artist. They had in common what Maciunas called a "preoccupation with insignificances,"[11] derived from a mixture of Cage, Duchamp, and Zen, and they had a strong distaste for tradable commodities. Early Fluxus activities consisted of small, informal performances, but by the mid-1960s Fluxus was operating mainly as a publishing house, distributing its wares through mail-order and an international sprinkling of Fluxshops run by Fluxus artists. The *Fluxboxes* and *Fluxkits* of the mid-1960s contained a loose array of printed matter, found objects, games, and performance scores by a changing selection of artists. The boxes were assembled as orders came in, always with a slightly different set of ingredients.

Maciunas, whose aspirations were as much social as aesthetic, envisioned Fluxus as a collective, defeating the notion of the artist as an exceptional creative hero, just as the irregularities and cheap production values of Fluxus publications defeated the consideration of art as a luxury consumable.

Fluxus publications can be seen, as Simon Anderson has written, as "a series of utopian fantasies interspersed with sporadic, uneven productions and held together by the overweening ambitions of a fanatically flawed genius."[12] But of the two models for multiplicity – Kinetic/Op art and Fluxus – it was Fluxus that proved the more influential. Its anarchic attempt to restructure publishing, distribution, creation, and consumption was a precursor to much Conceptual art, and to a wealth of alternative print activities: artists' books, xerox art, and mail art. Certainly the thread of multiplicity that weaves through serious art of 1970s and 1980s owed a great deal more to the mischievous, and occasionally mystical, nature of Fluxus absurdities than to Op art's utopian certainties.

In America, multiples were often associated with Pop art, as in Oldenburg's editioned sculptures, mimicking the look and feel of consumer merchandize, in much the way Pop prints did. They were also, sometimes, manifestations of more cerebral inquiries, as in Richard Artschwager's *Locations* (1969). The ovoid "blps" contained in Artschwager's formica-clad display case were intended as non-referential marks for punctuating space much as periods and commas punctuate writing. Each "blp" in the box is of a different material: redwood, mirror, formica, rubberized horsehair. And in keeping with the participatory nature of multiples, their disposition was left entirely in the hands of their owners.

In Europe, multiples and prints often aimed for both greater social conscience and greater spiritual transcendence. Multiplicity's appeal for Beuys, who made limited editions a critical part of his practice, was understandable: editions could be disseminated widely, and they were less likely to inspire materialistic idolatry. The most influential postwar artist in Germany, Beuys saw his role not as a manufacturer of luxury goods, but as a kind of shaman – a conductor of spiritual energy made visible in actions, teachings, and indirectly, in objects. Objects were, Beuys felt, the waste products of real art, which lay in the interaction of living beings. The distinction between unique and multiple, or between original and reproduction, was immaterial. His lithographs, etchings, films, wooden postcards, offset lithograph posters, and other productions were essentially relics of communication. The *Minneapolis Fragments* (1977, pl. 100) lithographs were released in both a black-on-white version that took on the private look of scribbled notes, and a white-on-black version that suggested the public venue of a blackboard. *Zeige deine Wunde* (Show Your Wound) of 1977 documented a performance, not in the casual offset lithography of so much documentary art, but in a massive, iron-clad glass sandwich. *Erdtelephon* (Earth Telephone, pl. 99) of 1973 is printed on the heavy grey felt Beuys so often used to allude to the event when his life was saved, during the Second World War, by Tatars who wrapped his frozen body in fat and felt. The

screenprinted telephone is not a Pop citation of consumer culture, but a cogent metaphor for physical and metaphysical contact.

In works such as these, the distinction between "print" and "multiple" becomes a

murky one. Dieter Roth, who crossed the boundary often, settled on a definition of graphics as "all objects that have appeared in a series and are not thicker than two centimeters."[15] As unconventional editions gained in popularity, artist-instigated enterprises like Fluxus and MAT were joined by art dealers and galleries throughout the US and Europe: Edizioni Danese, Arte Multiplicata, Sergio

64 Richard Artschwager
Locations 1969
Box (formica on wood) and five objects of wood, glass, formica, plexiglass, and rubberized horsehair
38.1 × 27.3 × 12.7 cm (15 × 10¾ × 5 in.)

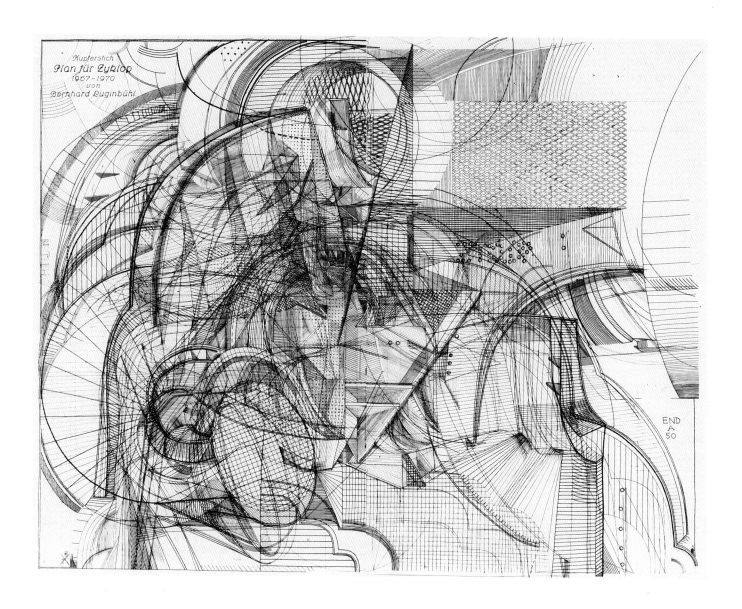

Kupferstich
Plan für Zyklop
1967–1970
von
Bernhard Luginbühl

65 Bernhard Luginbühl
Grosser Zyklop II 1967–70
Copper engraving
85.7 × 105.7 cm (33¾ × 41½ in.)

Tosi, and Arturo Schwarz all published multiples in Milan; René Block in Berlin published Joseph Beuys's famous felt suit and Dieter Roth's *Literature Sausage* (a mulch of printed pages, water, gelatin, lard, and spices in a plastic sausage casing); Multiples, Inc., in New York, produced gigantic banners, artist-designed tableware, and an edition of robots by Robert Breer. GEM Montebello manufactured jewelry editions with Joe Tilson, Pol Bury, and Lucio Fontana; EAT ART Gallery[14] in Düsseldorf specialized in edible editions: a bread telephone by Daniel Spoerri,

a Lichtenstein brushstroke made from gingerbread dough, a chocolate sculpture (with copperplate engraving) by Bernhard Luginbühl.

For the most part, the ethos of the multiple operated independently of – and in ideological opposition to – the world of the limited-edition, fine-art print. There was in continental Europe no parallel to the print revival that overtook the States – no large flurry of new printmaking establishments courting avant-garde artists and perfecting old techniques. Most of the important prints by younger European artists of the 1960s and 1970s occurred in the materially unpretentious and economically viable forms of screenprint and photo-offset lithography. Gerhard Richter sounded a typical note when he said he chose print media that were "the cheapest... anything that could be produced in vast quantity."[15]

There was, nonetheless, a handful of artists and printers who were able to take the inspiration of multiplicity – the excitement of defining a new type of art object – and give it life in traditional techniques. In Switzerland, Bernhard Luginbühl produced elaborate engravings that paralleled the mad mechanical invention of his sculptures. Lucio Fontana created remarkable intaglio prints which succeeded by violating the very fundaments of printerly craft, much as he had violated the sanctity of canvas in his paintings. As part of his visionary attempt to integrate art into the world, Fontana had sliced and punctured the pictorial plane of his canvases and allowed the notional space of painting and the actual space of real life to interpenetrate. In the intaglio works, Fontana's plates were etched very deeply, and printed under such enormous

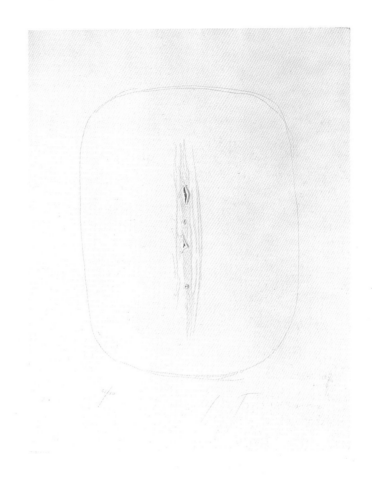

66 Lucio Fontana
Plate 5 from *Sei Acquaforti Originali* 1964
Etching, printed in yellow-white
44.1 × 33.2 cm (17⅜ × 13¹⁄₁₆ in.)

67 Diter Rot (Dieter Roth)
Bok 3b and *Bok 3d: Reconstruction*
1961–74
Reconstruction of two books, originally published in 1961 by Forlag editions (Reykjavik), made from perforated comics and coloring books
23 × 17 cm (9 × 6½ in.)

pressure that the paper would burst, leaving a pattern of violent ruptures through the mossy field of aquatint. The effect is deliberate and visceral, revealing not a bent for perfunctory destruction, but an intensity of formal purpose.

No artist brought greater inventiveness and intellectual acuity to print than Dieter Roth (also known as Diter Rot). In his books, multiples, and prints, Roth attempted nothing less than a complete reappraisal of visual culture and visual meaning. Roth's "Bok" books of the late 1950s and early 1960s were not only concerned with the creative manipulation of text or image, but went on to reinterpret the very structure of the book. Roth transformed it from a familiar vehicle for narrative structures into what Richard Hamilton has described as "a multiplicity of surfaces which project a set of precisely conditioned variations."[16] His contribution to the first MAT collection was a book of black-and-white patterned sheets that the viewer could rearrange to produce endless variations of rectilinear moiré. Roth had trained as a designer in Switzerland, the lodestar of intellectually rigorous design, and his best works join astute analysis of forms and functions to a subversive imagination. Roth worked interchangeably with unconventional multiples, concrete poetry, records, video, and traditional, elegant, printmaking techniques.

In the 1960s Roth began to employ pre-fabricated imagery, most often postcards, and to incorporate a wide variety of odd and unstable substances. *Braunschweiger Landshaft mit Käsebäumen* (Braunschweig Landscape with Cheese Trees, 1973, pl. 96) is a photo-offset picture-postcard street scene smeared with soft cheese and encased in plastic that may curtain the olfactory evidence of decay but not the visual clues. Roth exploited and exposed the layering and mutability inherent in print processes, and his works investigate visible change and permutation: the variable moiré, the instability of form, the putrefying cheese.

Though Pop is often considered an American and British phenomenon, there is an undeniably Pop quality to Roth's recycling of cheap popular printed material, his concern for social and graphic mechanisms, and his irreverence. Across Europe, in fact, artists were looking to the "real" and the commonplace much as their colleagues in the States and Britain had done, though with less concentration on prints and more on politics. In France in the early 1960s, artists associated with Nouveau Réalisme attempted to capture "sociological reality"[17] by incorporating in their work objects from everyday life: Arman collected them; Christo wrapped them; Klein coated them in his signature pigments. The literalism of this project found a natural form in multiples, but not initially in print. Arman's early prints are hand-drawn attempts to recreate the profusion and imprisonment of his sculptures, with irregular success. Martial Raysse and Alain Jacquet, like the German artists Wolf Vostell and Sigmar Polke, took to screenprinting their canvases. In Jacquet's 1964 restatement of Manet's *Déjeuner sur l'Herbe* overly assertive printing colors and the dot screens overwhelm the original painting.

The Italian artist Enrico Baj developed a singular marriage of Expressionism and Pop that, like Theater of the Absurd, was funny and grim in equal measure. Baj produced both traditional prints, such as his grotesquely contorted, pleasingly decorated, *Generals* of the 1960s (pl. 98), and innovative multiples, such as *Do It Baj Yourself* (1968), described as "the biggest art-book in the world with 137.952.460.800 colour plates and 479.001.600 pages for musical accompaniment"[18] (in fact, a book-shaped box containing wooden blocks with rearrangeable Baj images on them). Operating in Franco's Spain, the group Equipo Crónica (Rafael Solbes, Manuel Valdés, and briefly, J. A. Toledo) made screenprints that took a Pop sensibility and turned it toward direct political commentary.

In Germany, a number of artists had begun commandeering the imagery of newspapers, magazines, and television: the 1967 portfolio *Grafik des Kapitalistischen Realismus* (Graphics of

68 Wolf Vostell
Starfighter 1967
Screenprint with glitter from the
Graphik des kapitalistischen Realismus
portfolio
53 × 81.5 cm (20¾ × 32 in.)

Capitalist Realism) included, among other
works, a flower-draped dream house
disintegrating into a dot screen (Sigmar Polke),
an enigmatic snapshot of two men in a hotel
room (Gerhard Richter), a cigar-smoking
advertising moll sitting on seed packets (K. P.
Brehmer), and glitter-bedecked war-planes
(Wolf Vostell). The name Capitalist Realism,
with its slightly camp, sinister allusion to the
Social Realism of Nazi Germany and East
Germany, was originally coined to title a
Happening-type event staged by Konrad Lueg[19]
and Gerhard Richter in a Düsseldorf
department store; but it came to describe a
German art that rejected the expressive
premise of Informel painting in favor of the
images and mechanisms of contemporary life.

Brehmer made great use of the
photographically produced relief blocks used
for newspaper illustrations, manipulating them
in much the way that Joe Tilson manipulated
screenprint. His purpose, like Tilson's, was
often ideological: the oversized postage
stamp prints that he began making in 1966
commented on contemporary social issues, on
the political legacy of Germany, and generally
on the power of print to institutionalize
imagery, establish market values, and legitimize
a particular world view.

Vostell has been primarily concerned with
actions, rather than objects, and many of his
prints document ephemeral events. A number
of his early screenprints, however, fuse political
principles and Pop aesthetics, linking the
niceties of consumer culture to appalling
images of war and death. When he showed a
screenprinted B-52 bomber dropping bombs
of real lipstick, or gave German fighter planes
a dazzle of glitter, it was not a glorification, he
said, but a "danse funebre."[20]

The prints of Polke and Richter are
considerably more enigmatic. Polke's range
from the bikini-clad, Pop-ish *Freundinnen*
(Girlfriends, 1967) and to the nonsensically
methodical portfolio *Höhere Wesen befehlen*
(Higher Beings Command, 1968), a group of
fourteen offset photographs, most of palm
trees that Polke had modeled out of everything
from buttons to gloves to his own body. Any
attempt to read these images for content is
thwarted so consistently and wilfully, and
Polke's decisions appear so stubbornly

69 Sigmar Polke
Freundinnen 1967
Offset lithograph on cardboard
48 × 61 cm (19 × 24 in.)

irrational, that the work begins to assume an almost mystical character. In his 1971 *Self-portrait*, a cryptic offset photograph of the shadow of a Janus-head, the patches of light and shadow look less like inept printing than a Spiritualist emanation, complete with dripping photographic ectoplasm. Printed in pointedly shabby offset lithography, on cheap paper, these images take on a degraded material presence that only enhances their otherworldliness.

Richter's elusive subject lay in the seemingly reflexive process of transferring an image from photograph to paint, and from paint to print. From 1965 to 1974 Richter produced offset

lithographs, screenprints, and photogravures – most of them fuzzy and not-quite-credible manipulations of photography: the offset lithographs in the portfolio *9 Objekte* (1969) presented retouched photographs of mind-bending, physically impossible geometric structures; his lithographs and gravures (Richter's one foray into printerly elegance) of seascapes and clouds were made from cleverly constructed photomontages of subtle and insidious artificiality; the toy boat in *Schiff* (Ship, 1972, pl. 102) is blurred to such an extent that it no longer appears as a real toy and yet retains the photographic aura of a real thing in the real world. Richter had begun painting from photographs in an attempt to elude personal touch. In blurring the photographs, he avoided the narrative implications of a specific incident. In printing the images in editions, he freed them from identification with both the artist as singular creator, and the canvas as singular object.

Richter's last series of prints were altogether different visually. Eliminating the last vestiges of style, composition, and judgment, *Farbfelder: 6 Anordnungen von 1260 Farben* (Colorfields: 6 Arrangements of 1260 Colors, 1974, pl. 103) mocked both personal preference and impersonal systems. Richter constructed a grid of methodical color variations produced by applying a simple formula,[21] but the posture of supreme rationality is undone by the fact that the formula yields the same 999 colors in each print, and that an extra 261 colors were added and interspersed among the 999 systematic ones, so that the system loses all legibility and meaning. "How I feel and what I think is rather uninteresting," Richter said. "Therefore I am always tempted to generalize."[22]

The rise of multiplicity in the 1960s inspired dramatic predictions of the impending transformation of art and society. Events like the 1967 Swedish exhibition "Multikonst," which opened at a hundred locations simultaneously, were seen as the wave of the future. In 1967 Pierre Restany wrote: "Abandoning the old concept of the unique object, the luxury product for individual use, the artist is in the process of inventing a new language of communication between men."[23] A 1968 Documenta catalogue stated hopefully: "Now that the work of art has lost its quality as a prestige object, its spiritual value may be uninfluenced by its market value."[24] It was expected that, faced with such a clear alternative to its artificially constructed values, the traditional gallery and museum systems would collapse, and the line between creator and consumer would blur into indistinction. Art would now be sold in supermarkets and

department stores next to pulp paperbacks and fashion magazines.

"It is time," wrote the artist Öyvind Fahlström, "to incorporate advances in technology and to create mass produced works of art, obtainable by rich or not rich. Works where the artist puts as much quality into the conception and the manufacturer as much quality into production as is found in the best handmade works of art."[25] Fahlström exemplified both the political idealism and the creative generosity of the era with his "variable" pictures, in which the visual elements are not fixed, but rearrangeable at whim. Some used magnets to adhere picture parts to a metal background (pl. 97), some were boats that floated around in small pools. There was a print called *Eddie (Sylvie's Brother) in the Desert* (1966), which came like a paper-doll set, with printed landmarks and characters meant to be cut up and arranged. Fahlström's visual sources were comic books, maps,

70 Gerhard Richter
9 Objekte 1969
Offset lithograph from the set of nine
45 × 45 cm (17¾ × 17¾ in.)

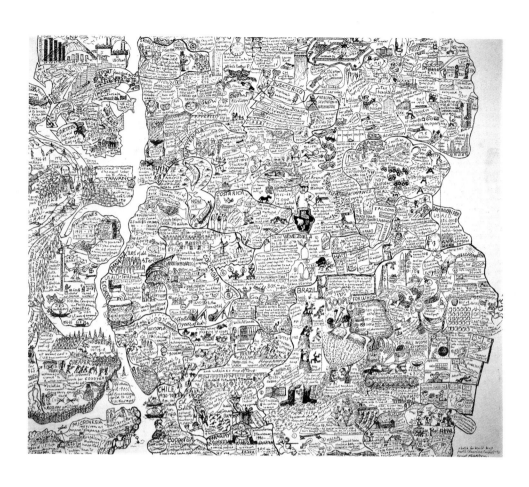

71 Öyvind Fahlström
*Sketch for "World Map" Part I
(Americas, Pacific)* 1972
Offset lithograph
86.5 × 101.5 cm (34 × 40 in.)

puzzles, and board games – printed material that provided a Pop visual style, a set of structures for conveying complex information in simple ways, and an aura of mass production. In 1964 he wrote, "the role of the spectator as a performer of the picture-game will become meaningful as soon as these works can be multiplied into a larger number of replicas, so that anyone interested can have a picture machine in his home and 'manipulate the world' according to either his or my choices."[26] These picture-games were to parody the games of world power broking, but they also allowed the viewer – or more precisely, the owner – something approaching a collaborative role.[27]

Fahlström's vision of mass production never came to pass. With a couple of exceptions,[28] his editions were produced and consumed within the confines of the art world,

in modest editions of a hundred or so. For Fahlström and for other artists, the problems of quality control, of financial viability, and of effective distribution proved insurmountable. In the 1990s the major surviving purveyor of inexpensive artists' multiples is the museum gift shop – a conflation of the very two institutions the multiple was supposed to make obsolete. But the working principles that underlay the ideal of multiplicity – the compound linkage of art, economy, social reform, and spiritual content – remain vital presences in the art of our time.

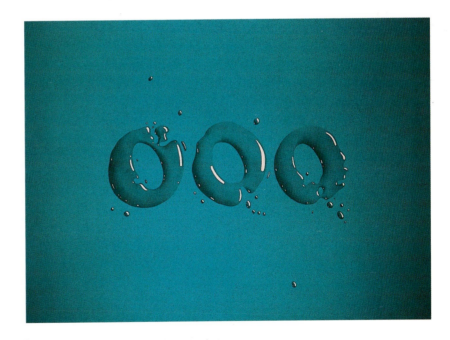

72 Ed Ruscha
Standard Station 1966
Color screenprint
65.4 × 101.9 cm (25¾ × 40⅛ in.)

73 Ed Ruscha
OOO 1970
Color lithograph
50.8 × 71.1 cm (20 × 28 in.)

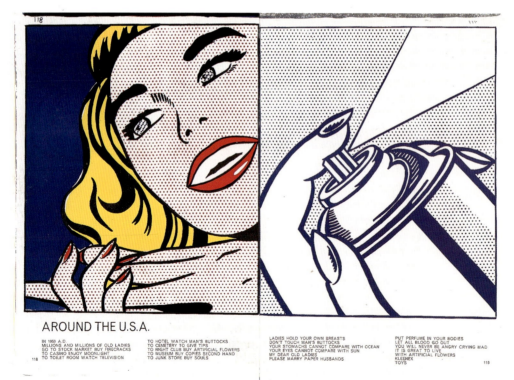

74 Sam Francis
with text by Walasse Ting
from *1¢ Life* 1964
Color lithograph with type
40.2 × 57.8 cm (16 × 22¾ in.)

75 Roy Lichtenstein
with text by Walasse Ting
Girl and *Spray Can*
from *1¢ Life* 1964
Color lithograph with type
40.2 × 57.8 cm (16 × 22¾ in.)

Opposite:
76 Roy Lichtenstein
Sweet Dreams, Baby! 1965
Color screenprint from the
11 Pop Artists III portfolio
95.6 × 70.2 cm (37½ × 27½ in.)

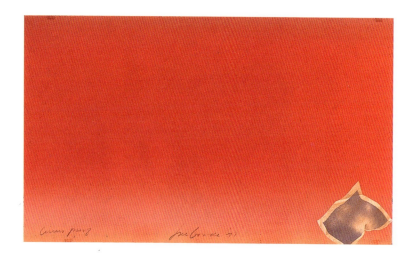

77 Joe Goode
Untitled 1971
Lithograph and screenprint
35.6 × 58.4 cm (14 × 23 in.)

78 James Rosenquist
Dusting Off Roses 1965
Color lithograph
78.1 × 55.1 cm (30¾ × 21¹¹/₁₆ in.)

79 Andy Warhol
Tomato from *Campbell's Soup I* 1968
Screenprint from the set of ten
88.9 × 58.4 cm (35 × 23 in.)

80 Andy Warhol
Marilyn 1967
Color screenprint from the set of ten
91.5 × 91.5 cm (36 × 36 in.)

81 Andy Warhol
Cow 1966
Screenprinted wallpaper
115.5 × 75.5 cm (45½ × 29¾ in.)

82 Richard Hamilton
My Marilyn (a) 1965
Color screenprint
69 × 102 cm (27¼ × 40¼ in.)

83 Richard Hamilton
I'm Dreaming of a Black Christmas 1971
Screenprint on collotype with collage
74.7 × 100 cm (29½ × 39⅜ in.)

84 Richard Hamilton
Kent State 1970
Color screenprint
73 × 102 cm (28 × 40 in.)

85 Peter Blake
Beach Boys 1964
Color screenprint from the Institute
of Contemporary Arts portfolio
75.6 × 51 cm (30⅛ × 20⅛ in.)

86 Eduardo Paolozzi
As Is When: Tortured Life 1965
Color screenprint
96.5 × 66 cm (38 × 26 in.)

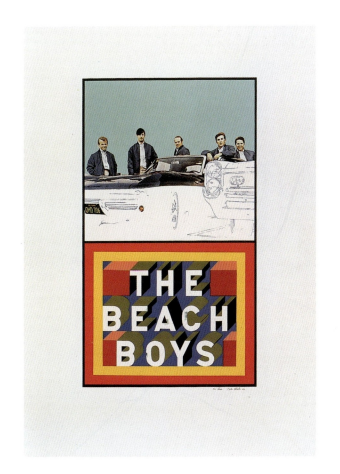

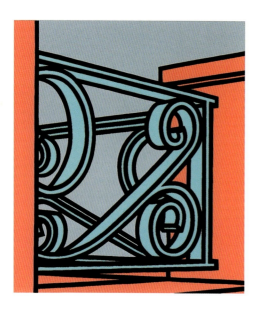

87 Patrick Caulfield
Ah! storm clouds rushed from
the Channel coasts from *The Poems*
of Jules Laforgue 1973
Book of 22 screenprint illustrations
for 12 poems, accompanied by
a slipcase of loose prints
40.5 × 35.5 cm (16 × 14 in.)

88 Patrick Caulfield
Ruins 1964
Color screenprint
50.8 × 76.2 cm (20 × 30 in.)

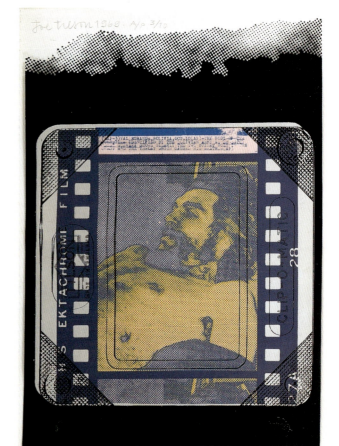

89 Joe Tilson
Transparency Vallegrande Bolivia,
October 10th 1969
Screenprint on rigid PVC,
lumiline and paper, collaged
71 × 51 cm (28 × 20 in.)

90 Joe Tilson
Sky One 1967
Three dimensional screenprint
with vacuum-formed and vacuum-
metallized objects
124 × 69 cm (48¾ × 27⅛ in.)

91 Joe Tilson
Earth Mantra 1977
Soft-ground etching and aquatint
106 × 76 cm (41¾ × 30 in.)

Inside the image:

LADY
CLA

A RAKE'S PROGRESS
LONDON | NEW YORK | 1961-62

PLATE No. 3 THE START OF THE
SPENDING SPREE AND THE DOOR OPENING FOR A BLONDE

Artist's proof   *David Hockney*

92 David Hockney
The Start of the Spending Spree and
the Door Opening for a Blonde from
A Rake's Progress 1961–63
Etching from the set of 16
50.8 × 61.6 cm (20 × 24¼ in.)

93 Karl Gerstner
Diagon 31² 1956–67
Alterable object made of screenprint on
plastic bars, shown in two possible
arrangements
62 × 62 cm (24½ × 24½ in.)

94 Richard Paul Lohse
Zentrum aus vier Quadraten 1976
Silkscreen
58 × 58 cm (22¾ × 22¾ in.)

95 Joseph Albers
White Line Square VIII 1966
Lithograph
53.3 × 53.3 cm (21 × 21 in.)

96 Dieter Roth
*In Oelper scheperts (Braunschweiger
Landschaft mit Käsebäumen)* 1973
Soft cheese on hand-printed offset
lithograph in plastic
32×49 cm (12½ × 19 in.)

97 Öyvind Fahlström
Elements from "Masses" 1976
Baked enamel on metal with magnets
70×70 cm (27½ × 27½ in.)

98 Enrico Baj
Generale Urlante (Shouting
General) 1966
Color lithograph
100×70 (39½ × 27½ in.)

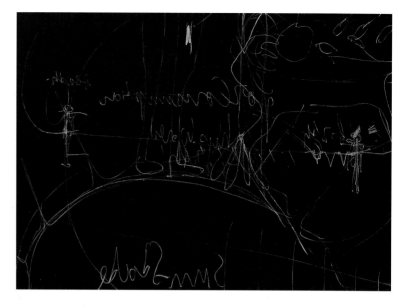

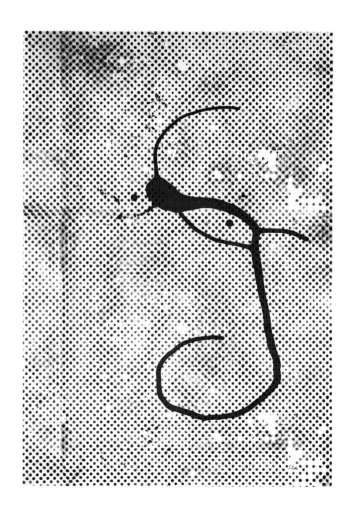

99 Joseph Beuys
Erdtelephon 1973
Screenprint on felt board
99 × 60 cm (39 × 23½ in.)

100 Joseph Beuys
Minneapolis Fragments 1977
Six lithographs printed in white on
black printed surface, with pencil line
(alternate version of edition printed in
black on white)
64 × 89 cm (25½ × 35 in.)

101 Sigmar Polke
Untitled 1988
Screenprint and offset lithograph
98.5 × 69 cm (38½ × 27 in.)

102 Gerhard Richter
Schiff 1972
Color offset lithograph
50×65 cm (19½ × 25½ in.)

103 Gerhard Richter
Farbfelder: 6 Anordnungen von
1260 Farben 1974
Offset lithograph from
a portfolio of six
64.4×79.2 cm (25¼ × 31 in.)

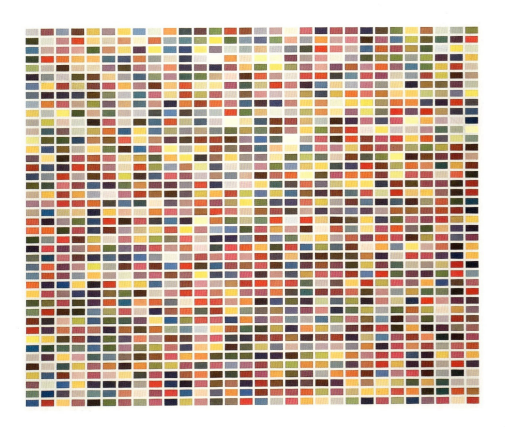

5

MATERIAL FORMS AND SOCIAL FUNCTIONS: 1960s INTO 1970s

The 1970s saw a radical rethinking of the print by artists who were neither specialist printmakers nor painters, and for whom the critical question about prints was not "what does it look like?" but "how does it work?" Around 1970, as Richard S. Field observed, "the perception of gravity, tension, strength, texture, and color as integral aspects of materials rather than as abstract qualities became the central focus of anti-illusionism."[1] At the same time, the physical and cognitive processes of art-making came to be seen as subjects in their own right, and artists worked to make them visible. Finally, the contextual circumstances surrounding art – from the effects of optics to the effects of economics – were explored in increasing detail as determinants of meaning. In printmaking, these strategies brought about a renewed investigation of the complex materiality of paper and print media, especially etching; of serial progressions; and of the accepted roles of printed matter in the conveyance of knowledge and the transference of wealth.

Formally reductive, geometric abstraction was employed throughout the 1960s and 1970s by a range of artists who worked with similar vocabularies, but to radically different ends. The painter Ellsworth Kelly had, while working in Paris in the 1950s, developed abstract syntheses of shape and color that were distillations of visual moments – a shadow on

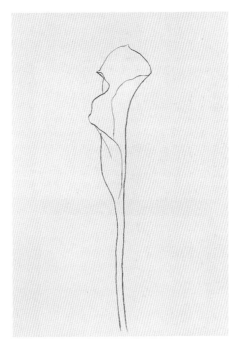

a wall, the shape of a leaf – capturing the essence of an experience, but removing it from its circumstantial trappings. His first print project was a mini-retrospective of his own early work, and fell foul of Tatyana Grosman's definition of originality (as Richard Axsome put it, "Grosman's 'listening to the stone' was not his cup of tea"[2]). But for Kelly, printing was a further, vital stage in the distancing of the image from its origins. Even in his paintings Kelly had avoided visible

105 Ellsworth Kelly
Calla Lilly 3 1983
Lithograph
91.4 × 63.5 cm (36 × 25 in.)

Opposite:
104 Jannis Kounellis
Untitled 1975
Offset lithograph with embossing and preserved butterfly, in galvanized iron case
57 × 42 cm (22½ × 16½ in.)

of an enormous wall of paintings, Kelly's manipulation of size, surface texture, color, and the interaction of designated form and surrounding space is both visually subtle and physically extreme.

The ambitions of American Minimalists of the early 1960s were quite different, and far more difficult to encapsulate in print. In creating forms of such obviousness and simplicity the mind could know them at a glance, these artists proposed a new, phenomenological approach to art objects – examining their irreducible materiality and the conditions that governed their perception by the viewer. The sculptor Donald Judd and the painter Frank Stella, among others, sought to reach beyond expressionist clichés or the clever compositions of European abstraction. Expanding on the logic that required Abstract Expressionist painters to part with all things not inherent to paint and canvas, they produced art that claimed neither to depict, nor to express, but simply to be. "What you see is what you see" was Stella's famous dictum.[4] Prints in this situation were problematically pictorial, given their reductive scale, margins, and the inescapable reminder of an absent mirror image, the template from which they were made. Judd's sculpture emphasized an unambiguous unity of material and composition. In Stella's painting, the painted image and the canvas object were not physically identical, but his simple stripe

brushstrokes because such souvenirs of facture bind the image to a specific individual and emphasize the historical act of making rather that the experience of the final image.[3] Kelly's prints have continued to reflect the forms of his paintings, but they are also carefully calibrated for their specific material situation. In works such as *Large Grey Curve* (1974), or *18 Colors Cincinnati* (1981, pl. 170), which repeats the composition not of a single painting, but patterns reduced the gap between painted illusion and physical fact.

Judd's first prints were literal by-products of his sculptures, made by inking and printing thirteen plywood wall sculptures from 1961.[5] Later, he employed engraving and more conventional forms of woodcut to offer two-dimensional equivalents of the sculptures' periodic masses (pl. 172). The implication of systematic variation, uncompromised by personal preference, is clearly visible in his untitled woodcuts of 1988, with their serial

viewer's mind hopped between the image and the paper, the paper and the painting, the reproduction and the original. The first part of Stella's solution was to draw the images by hand on the litho plate so that, while the design of the drawing replicates the design of the painting, its surface properties and visual character are strictly lithographic. Secondly, the eccentric placement of the image in the lower left corner causes the paper itself to appear as part of the composition rather than as background and margins. Finally, Stella

Opposite:
106 Ellsworth Kelly
Large Grey Curve 1974
Screenprint with embossing
62.3 × 213.7 cm (24⅛ × 84⅛ in.)

107 Ellsworth Kelly
Wall 1979
Etching and aquatint
80 × 71.1 cm (31½ × 28 in.)

permutations of solid and void, which Judd used as a antidote to compositional cleverness.

Stella's first print series, done in 1967, was based on his Black Paintings of the late 1950s, such as *Marriage of Reason and Squalor*. To make prints from these paintings presented several difficulties, foremost among them the task of providing the prints with the same phenomenological stance as the paintings – to prevent the splintering of attention as the

compensated for the inevitable loss of scale and confrontational power by bringing the images together as a series. The prints were meant to be placed in acetate sleeves in loose-leaf albums so that one could collect the entire series – an arrangement that emphasized relationships and context rather than a singular presence. Stella's subsequent prints followed the increasing complexity of his paintings. In works like *Double Gray Scramble* (1972–73, pl.

108 Frank Stella
Marriage of Reason and Squalor 1967
Lithograph
38.1 × 55.9 cm (15 × 22 in.)

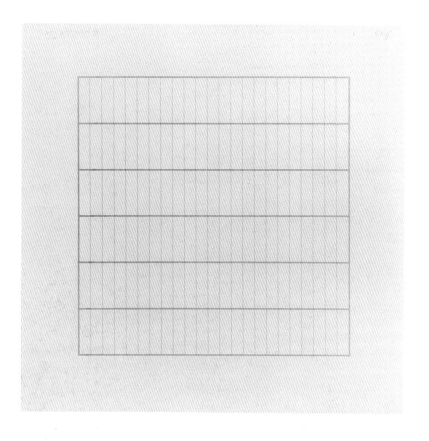

artists the demeanor of materials and surfaces was as important as the structuring of shape and color – Marden worked for many years with monochrome surfaces of paint rich in beeswax; Ryman made white-on-white paintings in which the composition was revealed by changes in surface texture, rather than changes in color. In contrast to the smoothness of lithography, etching is dimensional, and can be used to provoke an intense awareness of physical structure. Lithography, said Marden, "is like ice-skating. I'd rather walk through the mud."[6]

The idea of multiplicity was relatively unimportant for these artists. Ryman said he was "not really interested in the reproductive aspect of printmaking," but rather in the "results that can only be achieved through the medium itself, the actual process of printing, the ink, the paper, and how to make the medium become the images."[7] In Ryman's *Seven Aquatints* (1972, pl. 179), the image is conducted without recourse to color or contrast, by barely visible distinctions of surface texture and reflectivity. The shape of the aquatint, the signature, edition number, and printer's chop all operate as elements of the composition. However transcendently beautiful Ryman's aquatints are, attention is always recalled to physical reality.

Rockburne's *Locus* aquatints (1975) are defiantly physical: each of the sheets was etched with thin grey lines along which the paper was folded, then printed with a white aquatint, and folded again. Sold in this state, the print had to be unfolded to be seen, providing the viewer with both a tactile and a cerebral understanding of the processes and materials that structure it. In the *Radiance* lithographs (1983, pl. 181) Rockburne printed intense color on both sides of translucent paper before folding it, transferring "the inside poignancy of feeling to an outside visual form."[8] Both Rockburne's analytic formulae and their material treatment – folding and unfolding, adding and subtracting, displaying and retreating – can be understood literally,

109 Agnes Martin
On a Clear Day 1973
Screenprint from the set of thirty
30.8 × 30.5 cm (12⅛ × 12 in.) each

Opposite:
110 Brice Marden
Adriatics 1973
Etching from the set of seven
82.8 × 92.4 cm (32⁹/₁₆ × 36⅜ in.)

111 Brice Marden
Adriatics 1973
Etching and aquatint
from the set of seven
82.8 × 56.5 cm (32⁹/₁₆ × 22¼ in.)

173) the sense of progression and variation became incorporated into individual images, and by the 1980s, Stella was producing prints of unprecedented visual and technical complexity.

At the same time, the simple geometries and emphatic materiality that Stella and Judd employed to escape the implications of personal choice were being used by other artists as a means to evoke emotional states. Largely at the behest of a new publishing concern, Parasol Press, a number of painters, including Brice Marden, Robert Mangold, Robert Ryman, and Dorothea Rockburne became actively involved in printmaking, especially etching, in the early 1970s. The appearance in the late 1960s of Picasso's "347" prints and of Johns's *1st Etchings* had demonstrated the formal discretion of which etching was capable, and Parasol established an early and close working relationship with the etching shop Crown Point Press. For these as physical processes, or metaphorically, as signifiers of emotion. Similarly, Agnes Martin's evanescent grids are not mathematical games, but evocations of the experience of nature through pure abstraction. In her print project, *On A Clear Day* (1973), thirty screenprints work as a group to establish the visual and emotional power occasioned by subtle disruptions of expectation.

Marden, who became one of the most eloquent etchers of his generation, has acknowledged his admiration of Abstract Expressionist painters, especially Newman.

stains of a smooth plate. *Adriatics* (1973) conjures the experience of a long boat journey to the Greek island of Hydra – the mesmerizing rhythms of water, the contrasting densities of sea and sky. As in all Marden's etchings, the compositional severity is enlivened by myriad irregularities – visibly imperfect lines, white spaces permeated by subtle tone, and the random scratches and scars of "foul biting." In works such as these Marden was able to synthesize the calm tonal fields of his paintings with the nervous linear articulation of his drawings. Toward the end of

 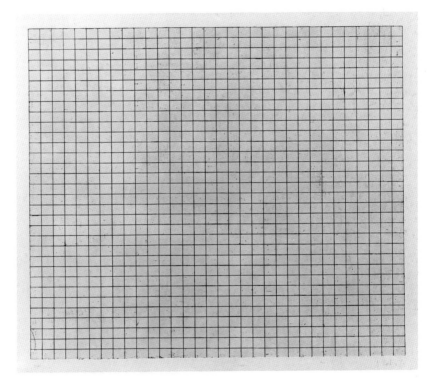

After a few attempts to capture the chromatic concentration of his paintings in screenprint, Marden entered into a serious engagement with etching in the *Ten Days* portfolio, executed at Crown Point Press in 1971. Using a vocabulary of bisected or trisected rectangles and grids, Marden examined the physicality of tone – the soft black of aquatint, the hand-made marks of cross-hatching, the vestigial

the decade, architectonic linear structures and irregular gestural marks merged in etchings such as *Tiles* (1979), which was drawn with a long stick that, like a telephoto lens, exaggerates every jiggle and twitch of muscle.

All these artists were closely involved with the physical presence of the art object (Judd said bluntly, "art is something you look at"[9]).

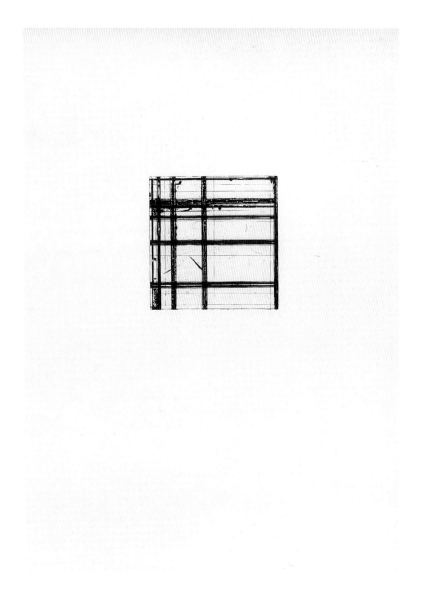

Other artists, however, were more concerned with explicating the process by which the image was achieved. For Mel Bochner and Sol LeWitt, printmaking represented a way to reveal a process governed by what Bochner called "the application of rigorous governing logics" rather than personal preferences.[10] Bochner's aquatint *Rules of Inference* (1974–77) displays what initially appears to be an arbitrary, if appealing, arrangement of white dots and dot patterns against a rich black aquatint field. It becomes apparent, however, that the dots articulate a spiral of increase: the single dot in the center, a pair of dots to the lower right, a triangle of dots above, and so on to the grid of nine at the lower left. The print is neither a spontaneous creation nor a rote execution of program – Bochner said the origins of his images were "emotional and intuitive"[11] – and his choice of scale and medium confer a commanding material presence on what is an essentially immaterial image of structure and change. In Bochner's later, and far more painterly, prints of 1988 and 1990 (pl. 180), the intertwining of conceptual structure and material presence is still more complex. Splashily painted cubes tumble around four sheets that are arranged so that together they frame a central, square void – a material absence to match the cubes' illusionistic presence.

LeWitt's early print sequences were based, like his wall drawings, on the principle of a system defined and executed without editorial intervention. *Squares with a Different Line Direction in Each Half Square* (1971) is typical: each of nine prints presents one possible solution to the condition described in the title, while a tenth brings together nine further options in miniature. But while the wall drawings are usually temporary, the prints are immutable and portable; and while LeWitt's involvement in the wall drawings consists of composing instructions that could be executed by anyone with a meticulous hand, the etchings were drawn by the artist himself. The crisp industrial look favored by Albers would

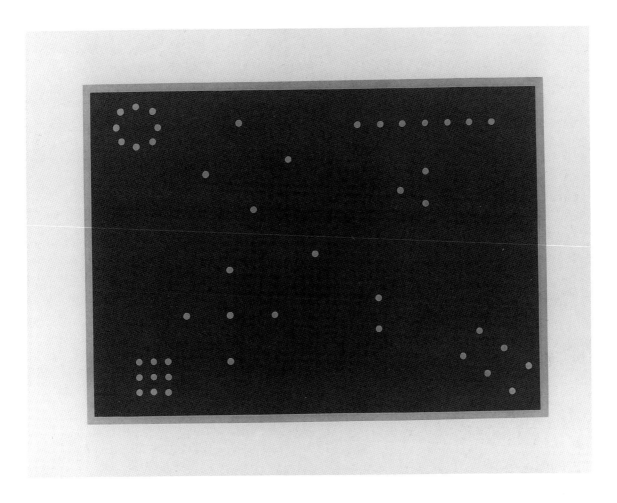

have been too strong a statement about the importance of facture for an artist who wrote that "execution is a perfunctory affair,"[12] and the slight waver of the artist's line as it strives for regularity is actually a stronger statement of the demands of the system. At the same time, LeWitt took full advantage of the print's aptitude for mechanical mutation, taking a single plate and printing it in multiple directions and combinations to realize all possible solutions.[13] Recognizing the consonance of print and permutation, LeWitt became a prolific printmaker, producing limited-edition etchings, screenprints, and woodcuts, as well as more affordable offset lithographs and artist's books.

Performance art, land art, and site-specific installation art were some of the most visible developments of the 1970s, and prints served

to formalize, to document, and to popularize (within a limited sphere) all these forms. They provided, as Vito Acconci said, "convenient and cheap distribution for conceptual art."[14] Artists exploited the print's beguilingly flimsy presence, its reassuring history of low economic prestige, and the aura, acquired through centuries of use for botanical diagrams and encyclopedia illustrations, of a visual form with a practical purpose. Some documentation art relied on a standard formula – a map or sketch, a photograph or two and a written explanation, laid out on a page and easily reproduced as inexpensive offset lithographs, such as those of Dennis Oppenheim. But rarely was it a straightforward recording of fact, and often documentation provided the occasion to explore the complex quandaries of representation.

113 Mel Bochner
Rules of Inference 1974–77
Etching and aquatint
75.6 × 99 cm (29¾ × 39 in.)

Opposite:
112 Brice Marden
Tiles 1979
Etching and sugarlift aquatint from
the set of four
75.5 × 57.2 (29¾ × 22¾ in.)

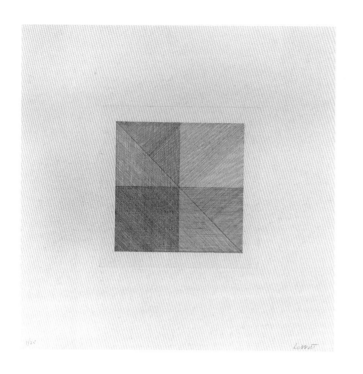

115 Sol LeWitt
A Square Divided Horizontally and
Vertically into Four Equal Parts, Each with
a Different Direction of Alternating Parallel
Bands of Lines 1982
Woodcut
76.2 × 76.2 cm (30 × 30 in.)

116 Sol LeWitt
Lines In Color On Color From Corners
Sides and Centers to Specific Points on a
Grid 1978
Color screenprint from the set of seven
76.2 × 76.2 cm (30 × 30 in.)

Opposite:
114 Sol LeWitt
Squares with a Different Line Direction
in Each Half Square 1971
Four from the set of ten etchings
36.8 × 36.8 cm (14½ × 14½ in.) each

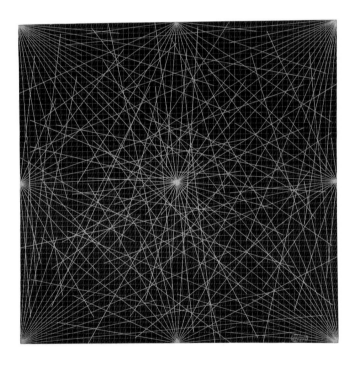

117 Richard Long
From *Nile: Papers of River Muds* 1990
Book of paper handmade from the
muds of 14 rivers and screenprinted
with the name of each river
22 leaves, each leaf 38 × 31 cm
(15 × 12¼ in.)

Opposite:
118 Claes Oldenburg
Print IV from *Notes* 1968
Color lithograph with embossing
57.6 × 40 cm (22¹¹/₁₆ × 15¾ in.)

Many land and environmental artists
developed inventive ways to bridge the
distance between the work of art and its
public: Richard Long, whose primary work
takes the form of thoroughly documented
walks in the countryside and arrangements
of the stones and other things he finds there,
has made prints in both a diaristic fashion –
matching photographs of his stone circles or
lines of twigs with strings of words that recall
his experiences of the site – and in a more
metonymic way. In *Papers of River Muds* (1990),
mud from specific sites was made into papers,
which were then screenprinted with the name
of the location. Sandy Gellis allowed nature to
inscribe herself: the plates for *Spring 1987: In the
Northern Hemisphere* (1987–88, pl. 182) were

sent to locations scattered over the Northern
Hemisphere and left outside for three months,
then returned to the artist, etched, and printed
to reveal of record of physical experience.

Transitory interior works, such as site-
specific installations, were also regularly
recorded in print. The German artist Blinky
Palermo, who was a student of Beuys, often
made prints related to, but not exactly
documenting, his wall-paintings: *Fenster*
(Window, 1970) repeats the design of a wall-
painting based on the design of the front
window mullions of the space in which it
occurred, but in print it appears simply as
a mysteriously irregular abstraction, the logic
of its development allowed to drop into
invisibility. The screenprint *Flipper* (1970, pl.
183) was intended to replicate a painting of
the same name – a red-and-white checkerboard
held in place by a grid of blue lines – but the
print evolved into a diptych of first and second
states, one like the painting, and one of just
red squares floating on a white field. It is a
mechanical variation, but also a poetic one –
a demonstration of faith in an organizing
principle that has been reduced to a suggestion,
whispered from the right-hand page.

The British artist Tom Phillips, whose
fascination with commonplace documentary
images had led him to work for many years
from touristic postcards, discovered and
documented evocative incident within the
utterly quotidian in works such as *64 Stopcock
Box Lids* (1976, pl. 190). The screenprint was
part of an extended project of documenting
the unremarkable walk between his home and
studio in South London. Like *The Birth of Art*
(1972–73, pl. 184–89), it is typical of Phillips's
use of print to play external, arbitrary struc
tures off against quixotic, private concerns. *The
Birth of Art* could be seen as a didactic work of
process art – a set of zinc stencils were placed
in acid and printed in ten progressive states of
deterioration – but its didacticism is betrayed
into allegory by his use of the letters A R T,
punning between subject and object, and by
his decision to print the stencils in reverse

order, rewriting history to replace degeneration with progress.

Revitalizing one of the most popular historical functions of the print, artists such as Christo and Oldenburg used it to record actual constructions, and also to disseminate visions of imaginary or projected ones.[15] Christo's editions on paper range from lucid photographic records of his spectacular, temporary environmental works such as the *Valley Curtain* (1970–72), to hand lithographs, collotypes, and screenprints that picture the artist's wrappings of sundry historical monuments through a mix of expressive drawing, photo-montage, and collaged fabric, polyethylene, or twine.[16] For an artist whose major works depend on gigantic scale and transitoriness, the printed sheet offers tactile and ongoing contact with works most people can never see. More pragmatically, the editions have raised money to support the artists' grander projects, which are executed independent of government or private patronage.[17]

"In printmaking," Oldenburg said, "I'm concerned with thinking in terms of circulating ideas – with book and illustration, with explanations and ways of stimulating thinking."[18] His lithographic portfolio *Notes* (1968) is purposefully didactic. Done at a time when his improbable monuments were not yet being built, *Notes* appears to represent a group of facsimile workbook pages, like the reverently reproduced workbooks of some famous architect, containing a collection of observ-ations, photographic clippings, and sketches that reflect on the landscape and culture of Los Angeles. The fourth print presents a sober discussion of the ice cream cone:

> For a thorough use of ice cream cones, buy two: eat one and drop the other. The city has a program of beautifying oil derricks and the dropped cone is proposed as a design. The proposal is influenced by the megaphone-like structure on the Venice beach and its echoes in the sails of boats beyond. The shapes of "draw-downs" made to test color in the lithography shop suggest the cone-

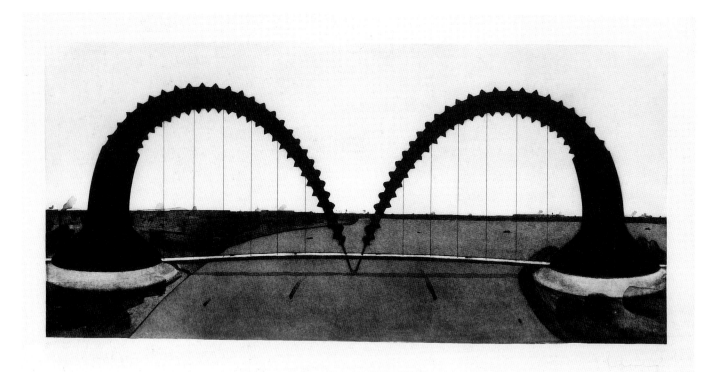

119 Claes Oldenburg
Screwarch Bridge (State II) 1980
Etching (hard ground, spitbite, and
aquatint)
80 × 147.3 cm (31½ × 58 in.)

Opposite:
120 Gilbert and George
The Sadness in Our Art 1970
Offset lithograph on charred paper
37.4 × 25.4 cm (14¾ × 10 in.)

form and also, by their translucence suggest
the sea and sky. A derrick is placed where
there is a well. It may be in your back yard.
The flat roofs around it are like the fragments
of tape. The Punching Bag again – ice cream,
the bag. The circular outlines of the disks,
top and bottom, are separated by miles of
vanishing perspective.

In later prints, Oldenburg abandoned
verbal exegeses in favor of visual ones that try
to convince, like an architect's drawing, on the
basis of sheer visual charm. In *Screwarch
Bridge*,[19] Oldenburg's proposal for spanning the
Nieuwe Maas River in Rotterdam, the actual
cityscape has been replaced with an epic
landscape in the style of the Dutch
seventeenth-century etcher Hercules Seghers.
Sobriety of presentation is firmly wedded to
the preposterous.

Performance artists such as Eleanor Antin
and Gilbert and George similarly used printed
materials to "document" fictive personalities.
Gilbert and George solved the problem of the

rift between idea and object, and between life
and art, by declaring themselves "living
sculptures," thereby placing all of their prolific
output of posters, postcards, books,
photographs, and videotapes in a position
somewhere between conceptual art document
and theatrical prop. "The early conceptualists
were primitives," Antin declared. "Contrary to
their beliefs, documentation is not a neutral list
of facts. It is a conceptual creation of events
after they are over. All description is a form of
creation."[20] Antin used postcards as both a
form of casual documentary object, and as a
self-sufficient form of alternative distribution.
The fifty-one postcards of *100 Boots* (1971–73)
were mailed over the course of two and a half
years to some 1000 people – installments
in a serialized "conceptual picaresque novel,"[21]
starring rubber boots in a variety of
photographically verified adventures.

Throughout the decade, photography and the
printed word were recruited for two

Gilbert George

THE SCULPTORS

4th July 1970   London

George and Gilbert would like you to accept this written picture explanation.

The Sadness in Our Art

The Ritz we never sigh for, the Carlton they can keep
There's only one place that we know and that is where we sleep
Underneath the arches we dream our dreams away
Underneath the arches on cobblestones we lay
Every night you'll find us tired out and worn
Happy when the day-light comes creeping, heralding the dawn
Sleeping when its raining and sleeping when its fine
We hear trains rattling by above
Pavement is our pillow no matter where we stray
Underneath the arches we dream our dreams away

'ART FOR ALL,' 12 FOURNIER STREET, LONDON, E.1, ENGLAND   Tel. 01 247 0161

121 Eleanor Antin
*100 Boots on the Way to Church,
Solana Beach, California, Feb. 9,
1971 11:30 AM* 1971
Postcard mailed April 15, 1971
One of a series of 51 postcards sent
from 1971 to 1973
11.4 × 17.8 cm (4½ × 7 in.)

contradictory functions: to provide credible, easily understood documents of absent art works, and to question fundamental assumptions about the credibility of knowledge and communication. The claims of photography to be an impartial record of objective reality were actively challenged by many artists.

The Italian sculptor Anselmo made editions that expose the gap between photographic illusion and physical experience: in *Verticale* (1966–73), a photographically reproduced spirit-level, with its bubble neatly centered, appears to verify the gravitational orientation of the picture, but the print could be hung any which way and the bubble would remain in place. The Dutch artist Jan Dibbets, like the Swiss artist Markus Raetz, took the mannerist technique of anamorphic art[22] into the twentieth century, exposing the traps awaiting the eye as it tries to perceive space in a two-dimensional image. In Dibbets's untitled print from a portfolio on the theme of landscape (pl. 192),[23] photographic strips of sea and sky are altered by the simple addition of a white bar, robbing them of spatial illusion, and reducing them to flat, numbered stripes. As photography became a more frequent element

of contemporary art, it became a more frequent element of contemporary editions. Some used photomechanical techniques, like the Dibbets collotype, others were actual photographs. Workshops may have drawn the distinction between printerly means that use a physical template pressed against paper, and photographic means that work by light, but print publishers rarely did.

Markus Raetz went beyond the specifics of photography. A prolific printmaker, he has contrived myriad metaphors for the duplicity of vision: pictures of hands reaching into eyesockets, a spill of marbles on the ground that can also be read as a portrait, Cozens-like blots that coalesce into landscapes. In his installation works, apparently arbitrary arrangements of objects are transformed into legible pictures when viewed from the right angle. The six photogram-gravures of *Schatten* (1991) were made by dangling a piece of shaped wire above a photosensitized plate, such that the shadow cast by the wire was etched photographically. The looping black line that occupied the first five gravures resolves, in the last, into the unmistakable outline of Magritte's famous pipe (itself a recognized emblem of the

122 Giovanni Anselmo
Verticale 1966–73
Color photograph
83 × 56.5 cm (32½ × 22¼ in.)

123 Marcus Raetz
Schatten, 1991
photogram-gravure and aquatint
176.5 × 67.3 cm (69½ × 26½ in.)

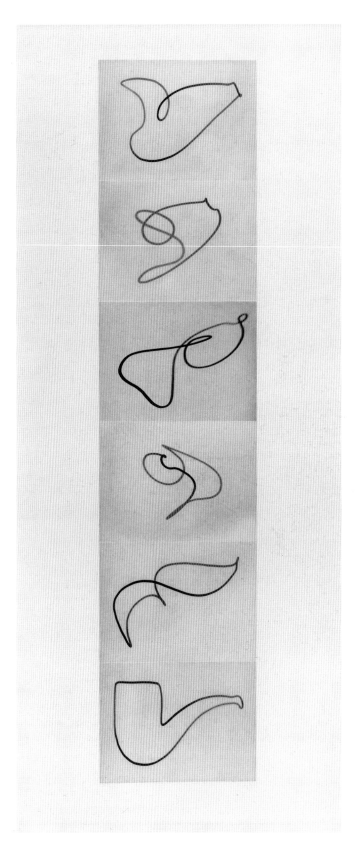

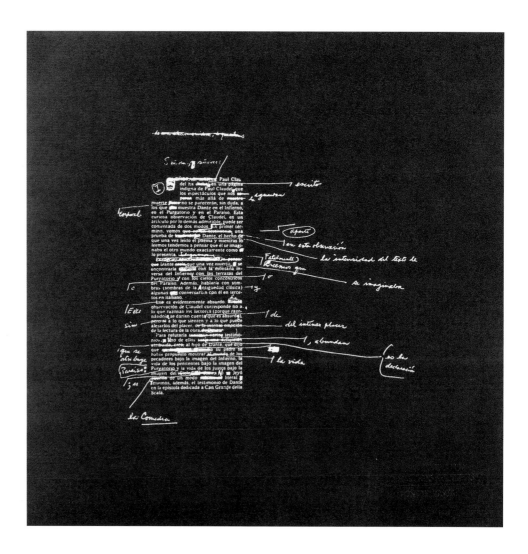

124 Joseph Kosuth
From *Ten Unnumbered Corrections* 1991
Relief-printed photoengraving
25.4 × 25.4 cm (10 × 10 in.)

complexity of representation). The shadow pipe only exists from a single viewpoint, for a brief moment, in a dance of shifting shapes.

The questioning of appearances that motivates the work of Raetz, or the disarming and insidious etchings of Pieter Holstein, who uses the artificial clarity of children's book illustration to present complex issues of epistemology (pl. 193), is at its heart a philosophic inquiry into reality and its distance from perception.

Language was equally suspect, and equally at home in print media. When Joseph Kosuth defined the kind of art in which he was involved as an "inquiry into the foundations of the concept 'art,' as it has come to mean,"[24] he suggested a cognitive rather than a visual inquiry, one best articulated in language rather than color, shape, or pictorial reference. Such work, by Kosuth and others, was derided at the time as a triumph of the classroom over the studio,[25] and, by extension, of printed matter over painted matter. Kosuth has often worked with quite plebeian forms of printing, such as photostats, but has also indulged in more rarified, "fine-art" forms, as in his *Ten Unnumbered Corrections* (1991). These relief-printed etchings reproduce hand-corrected galley proofs of the blind Argentinian writer Borges in an elegant and tactile manner, but also make clear the mutability of meaning. The

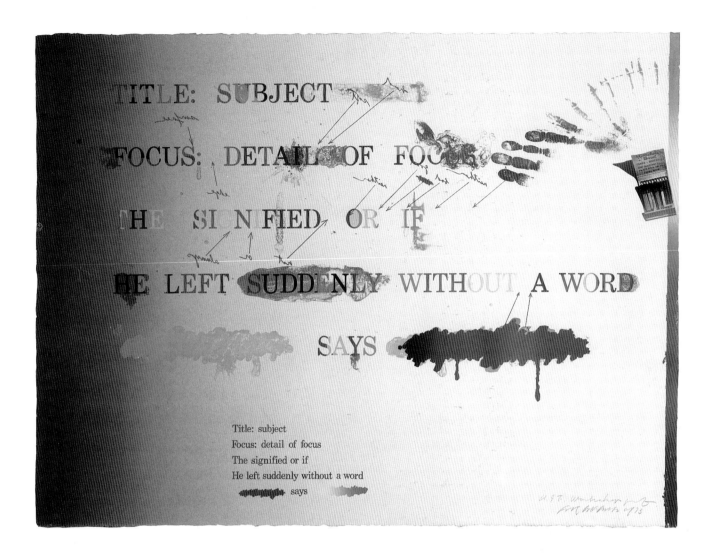

Title: subject
Focus: detail of focus
The signified or if
He left suddenly without a word
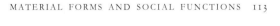 says

artist Arakawa makes paintings and films, but it is in print that his "visual *koans*"[26] connect most closely to the kind of affable texts that they vexingly deconstruct. His first print series, *"No!" Says the Signified* (1973–74), is filled with reasonable-looking language that means nothing, and with instructions that self-destruct upon reading. Though language is predominant, it is embedded in an elaborate pictorial structure – color, depth, surface detail, collaged objects, split-fountain ink rolls, palm and finger prints are enlisted as contradictory elements that negate each move toward understanding as it occurs.

Bruce Nauman, the sculptor and installation artist, maintained that "the point where language starts to break down as a useful tool for communication is the same edge where poetry or art occurs."[27] Nauman's enigmatic, vaguely malevolent word games explore the interplay of language and power in specifically printerly terms.[28] The fuzzy warmth of drypoint in *Violins/Violence* (1982–83), or the melding of loose lithography and sharply mechanical screenprint in *Oiled Dead* (1975),[29] are deployed just as the words themselves are: drawing the viewer forward one moment, pushing him back the next. Nauman has also exploited the visual reversals endemic to printing: "I like the way front/back interplay confuses the information. Not knowing what you're supposed to look at keeps you at a

125 Shusaku Arakawa
Untitled 5 from *No! Says the Signified*
1973–74
Color lithograph with screenprint
57.2 × 76.4 cm (22½ × 30⅛ in.)

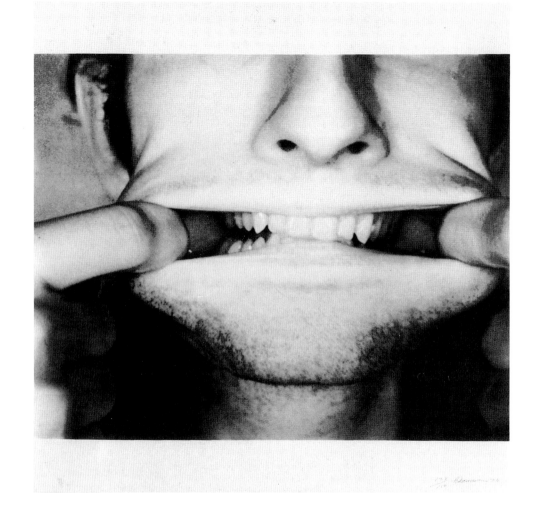

126 Bruce Nauman
Studies for Holograms 1970
Screenprint from the portfolio of five
66 × 66 cm (26 × 26 in.)

Opposite:
127 Bruce Nauman
TV Clown 1987–88
Lithograph
76.2 × 111.8 cm (30 × 44 in.)

128 Bruce Nauman
Violins/Violence 1982–85
Drypoint
71.1 × 99.4 cm (28 × 39⅛ in.)

distance from the art, while the art keeps you at a distance from me."[30]

While his word pieces are naturally embedded in print, Nauman has used print to touch upon all aspects of his work: drypoints and lithographs of his sculptures and video installations reiterate his ongoing fascination with the confusion between inside and outside, intrusion and observation. The lithographs *Studies for Holograms* (1970) record an early performance piece "about the body as something you manipulate."[31] Dramatically distorting his facial features, first in documentary photography, then in illusionistic holograms, and finally in accessible offset lithographs, Nauman transgressed the

accustomed boundaries between intimacy and exposure, between artist and audience.

Prints, as Nauman recognized, are uniquely situated to negotiate the space between public and private experience. Simultaneously populist and elitist, the print is as enmeshed with the idea of private ownership as it is with the idea of a broad audience. This facet of the print as, in Acconci's words, "a kind of instrument in the world,"[32] was recognized and manipulated by artists concerned with the sociological, economic, institutional, and architectural structures that govern how art is received and how its meaning is construed. The French artist Daniel Buren, the Belgian Marcel Broodthaers,

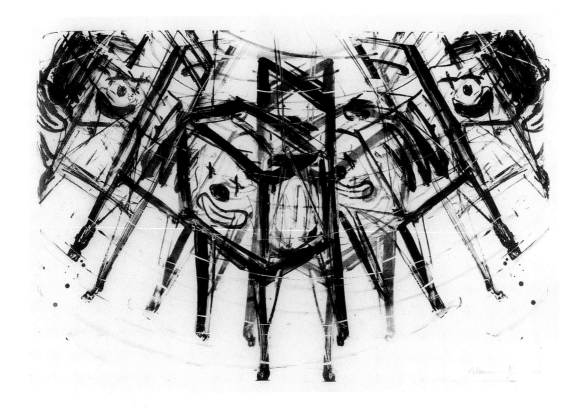

the German Hans Haacke, and the Americans Vito Acconci and Chris Burden were among those who used printmaking to explore the interaction of art objects and social forces.

For Acconci, as for Nauman, prints offered a way of transferring private activities into a defiantly public forum. Acconci's first prints, done at the Lithography Workshop at the Nova Scotia College of Art and Design, were literally "performances on stone:"[33] in *Kiss Off* (1971) lipstick stains (grease-based, like lithographic tusche) are transferred from mouth to hand to stone, and in *Trademarks* (1971) Acconci bit himself in as many places as he could reach, and then printed from the bite marks. In Acconci's later prints the viewer is promoted from a voyeur to a subject of direct provocation. The portable, printed installation *Stones for a Wall* (1977–79) imprisons the viewer within a hostile lithographic barrier of guns, explosions, and psychopathic graffiti. *3 Flags for 1 Space and 6 Regions* (1979–81, pl. 195) construct a "wall" that, like both architectural and political structures, simultaneously defines and divides.[34]

Acconci and Nauman were able to make limited-edition prints work to their own ends, but for other artists the edition presented problems. Buren deploys his trademark stripes in unlikely locations in order to call attention to sites and situations. "No one of my works is independent of a wall where it is to begin with," Buren has said.[35] But the belief that it is contextual circumstance that determines meaning in art presented a challenge to the static concept of the edition. If context is everything, how is the artist to deal with a form that is expected to exist in many places at once and mean, more or less, the same thing in each? With *Framed/Exploded/Defaced* (1979) Buren devised an edition that defies expectations of portability, uniformity, and tidy scale. A large square aquatint of colored bands was printed in forty-six unique color impressions, then cut up into twenty-five squares that were individually framed. Instructions accompanying the piece advise

that the fragments must be hung in an even grid stretching to all four corners of the wall. If there are obstructions on the wall – windows, doors, fireplaces – where a fragment would be placed, the Buren fragment must be removed and put aside. These instructions are the only element of the piece that is signed by the artist, and if "the work is not installed as described... the artist considers the work neither completed nor authentic."
Framed/Exploded/Defaced is essentially an edition of installations that are identical in concept and instruction, but unique in color, adaptation to their surroundings, and the collaborative efforts of their owners.

As artists moved from simple condemnation of art as an economic commodity toward an active investigation of the phenomenon, the contradictions of the limited-edition print

became more intriguing. Chris Burden's *Diecimila* (1977, pl. 198), a two-sided photo-etching of an Italian 10,000 lira note, directly confronts the pleasures and problems of the limited-edition print in a capitalist art culture. *Diecimila* is clearly not a counterfeit bill – the image is surrounded by margins and the paper is all wrong – but it is also problematic as a work of art: printed on both sides of the paper, it cannot be framed or hung on the wall without hiding half the image. *Diecimila* is nonetheless extremely appealing – the bill Burden selected is more beautiful than dull American greenbacks and more extravagant in its denomination (ten thousand lira sounds so much grander than the ten dollars it was worth). The owner ends up with an object that can be neither spent nor fully displayed, but that suggests the power, beauty and endless promise

130 Daniel Buren
Framed/Exploded/Defaced 1979
Color aquatint in 25 individually framed fragments
20.3 × 20.3 cm (8 × 8 in.) each fragment

Opposite:
129 Vito Acconci
Stones for a Wall #7 1977–79
Lithograph from the set of ten
76.2 × 59 cm (30 × 23¼ in.)

ARE THE RICH A MENACE?

Some people think they are, so let's look at the record.

Suppose you inherit, win or otherwise acquire a million dollars net after taxes. That would make you rich, wouldn't it? Now, what's the first thing you'd do? Invest it, wouldn't you?—in stocks, bonds or in a savings bank.

So, what does that mean? It means that you have furnished the capital required to put about 30 people to work.

How is that? National statistics show that for every person graduating from school or college, at least thirty thousand dollars of capital must be found for bricks, fixtures, machinery, inventory, etc. to put each one to work.

Now, on your million dollar investments you will receive an income of sixty thousand, eighty thousand, or more dollars a year. This you will spend for food, clothing, shelter, taxes, education, entertainment and other expenses. And this will help support people like policemen, firemen, store clerks, factory workers, doctors, teachers, and others. Even congressmen.

So, in other words, Mr. Rich Man, you would be supporting (wholly or partially) perhaps more than 100 people.

Now, how about that? Are you a menace? No, you are not.

TIFFANY & CO.

FIFTH AVENUE & 57TH STREET
NEW YORK

Advertisement in The New York Times, June 6, 1977

The 9,240,000 Unemployed in The United States of America Demand The Immediate Creation of More Millionaires

131 Hans Haacke
Tiffany Cares 1978
Photo-etching
73.6 × 104.1 cm (29 × 41 in.)

of unspent cash.[36] Haacke, who has made a specialty of exposing unholy alliances between capitalism and art, manipulates both the social connotations of the intaglio medium and the snobbery of the limited edition in *Tiffany Cares* (1978) to "bite the hand that feeds" them.[37] On one side of the photo-etched diptych Haacke reprints an opinion piece run by Tiffany & Co. in the *New York Times*, claiming that the rich are good for society because they spend money, which creates jobs. Opposite it, in the elegant script of engraved invitations, runs the line, "The 9,240,000 Unemployed in The United States of America Demand The Immediate Creation of More Millionaires."

"I do not believe," Broodthaers said, "it is legitimate to seriously define art other than in light of one constant factor – namely the transformation of art into merchandise."[38] Broodthaers recognized early the failure of multiples to alter the treatment of art as commodities or to democratize the consumption of art, and in works such as *Museum-Museum* (1972), he used printed editions as a means not to escape, but to comment on the social, economic, and especially, institutional dependency of art. In black and gold screenprint Broodthaers equates the names of famous artists – Bellini, Ingres, Duchamp – with gold bars and more mundane commodities such as butter, chocolate, and tobacco. He also toyed with the nature of the edition: in *La Signature Série I Tirage Illimité* (The Signature Series I Unlimited Edition) of 1969, the artist's signature, which is supposed simply to validate the image to which it is attached, supplants the image altogether; and while the title, printed at bottom, announces that the edition is unlimited, in fact only sixty prints were made, each one initialed by the artist, though not numbered.

Again and again, prints in the 1970s were used in ways that emphasized their didactic and practical history. But just as the geometries of Minimalism could be employed to negate or to stress emotional content, so the modest materiality and commonplace social uses of printed matter could be invoked in search of a more transcendent experience of art. For sculptors such as the Art Povera artists Jannis Kounellis and Mario Merz, prints offered a pictorial option free of the cultural weight of painting. Kounellis and Merz both recognized the print's poignant physical frailty, its engagement with history, and its role as a time-honored housing for images of nature. Merz's *Da un Erbario Raccolto nel 1979 Woga-Woga* (1989, pl. 199) and Kounellis's untitled photo-etching of 1979 (pl. 200) evoke old-fashioned botanical scrapbooks of pressed leaves and flowers, and contrast the ephemerality of plants with solidly abstract forms of man's invention: the black aquatint square of Kounellis's print, or Merz's use of the Fibonacci number sequence (in which each number is the sum of the preceding two), which can be interpreted as a metaphor for the way in which the small and manageable can be overtaken by unmanageable proliferation, both biologically and socially. In 1974 Kounellis made an edition of asbestos, glassine, and phosphorus that was meant to be ignited. The charred remains form the finished artwork, a poetic marriage of death and rebirth, history and nature, artificiality and inevitability – subjects also implicit in an untitled print from 1975 which pairs a real butterfly with a grisaille reproduction of *The Death of Marat*.

Even the serial "application of rigorous governing logics" could be used poetically, as in the printed sequences of the German artist Hanne Darboven, which compose cerebral elegies to the passage of time. *Wende "80"* (Turning Point "80") of 1980 is a boxed set of 416 offset lithographs that include reproductions of page after page of Darboven's hand-scrawled "Tagesrechnungen" (calendrical calculations), drawings she made as a child, a magazine interview with candidates for the chancellorship of West Germany, and a short biography of Giorgio de Chirico. There are also nine records of music derived from the "Tagesrechnungen." Each of these elements represent a way of coming to terms with the inevitable transformation of "present" into "past," and the futile attempt of memory to reverse the process. While Darboven's unique works are usually presented as massive installations on the wall, the boxed set is manageable and intimate, more like going through the letter boxes of an aged aunt than like visiting a war memorial.

One way to view the trajectory of the print through the 1960s and 1970s is as a progression from interior to exterior – an expansion of attention from the image itself, to the full sheet of paper, to the wall on which the paper hangs, and finally, to the surrounding cultural and economic structures that govern its reception. As artists actively searched for the print's essential attributes – the singular mix of material qualities and social functions that set it apart – they made visible both the intricate relationship of physical form and cognitive systems, and the persistent eruption of the personal within apparently impersonal structures.

132   Hanne Darboven
Wende "80"   1980
Portfolio of 416 offset lithographs and
six records (detail)
58.4 × 43.2 cm (23 × 17 in.) each sheet

genesis I   R. Artschwager

6

HIGH TECH AND THE HUMAN TOUCH

In 1971, when the Museum of Modern Art devoted an exhibition to the achievements of Gemini GEL, it was an official validation of the technological sophistication epitomized by Gemini, but it marked the apex of a manner already on the wane. In both high culture and low, the promise of technology had given way to distrust, and the optimistic rush to industry that typified art production in the 1960s was supplanted by the desire for a more atavistic experience of the world. There was, however, no retreat from print production. Instead artists and printers turned toward the craft traditions – both Western and non-Western – from which print technologies had sprung. It was a period that art critics found singularly difficult to summarize. In place of such useful, if simplistic, verbal handles as "Abstract Expressionism" or "Pop," the 1970s in America were identified by "Pluralism," a term meant to encompass rather than delimit. It failed, however, to suggest that among its myriad parts – Realism, Pattern Painting, New Figuration, and so on – lay a common will to re-invest art with a human presence, without abandoning the anti-expressionist bias or clear conceptual structures of the previous decade. Pat Steir verbalized this "Pluralist" consensus when she stated that "separation between thinking and emotion is a stupid person's way of defining the way things are."[1]

Photorealism, one of the most visible new developments of the time, has been described as both a conceptualization of Pop and as a realist response to Minimalism. For artists such as Chuck Close, Vija Celmins, and Franz Gertsch, copying photographs represented a way to dispense with self-consciously expressive pictorial elements, and to isolate, as Celmins said, "something that could still be art after removing obvious composition and obvious invention."[2] What remained clearly visible were the tantalizing negotiations between human will, the human hand, and the tractable material upon which they work. In their prints especially, these artists sought to give to their meticulous marks a substantial presence as both independent beings and conspirators in illusion: Close has built faces from fingerprints, from patches of wood, and from sturdy clots of colored paper pulp. When first invited to make a print, Close chose, eccentrically, to work in mezzotint, a medium with which neither he nor his printer, Kathan Brown, had any experience, and which had never been used on the huge scale that Close proposed.[3] He was drawn to it because its fuzzy slide from light to dark resembled airbrush, which he used in painting to imitate the grain of photography. But a side effect of this visual softness is that mezzotint plates wear down quickly, and the areas Close began working on first had visibly eroded by the time

133 Vija Celmins
Concentric Bearings B 1983
Aquatint, drypoint, and mezzotint
43.2 × 38.1 cm (17 × 15 in.)

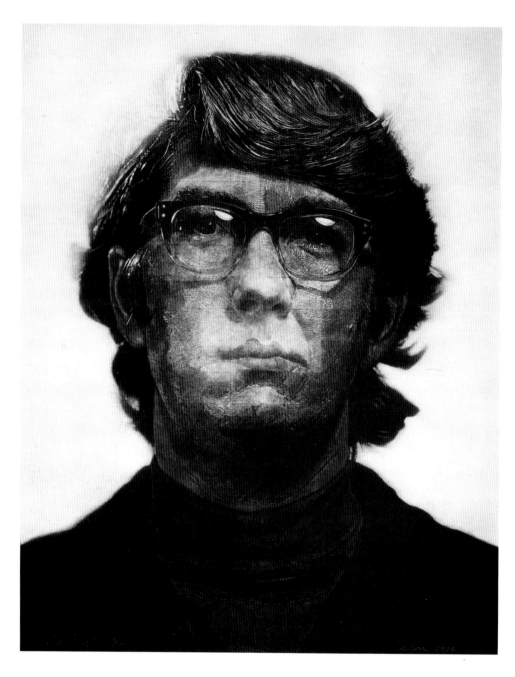

134 Chuck Close
Keith 1972
Mezzotint
132.1 × 106.7 cm (52 × 42 in.)

135 Chuck Close
Phil Manipulated 1982
Handmade paper
177.8 × 137.2 cm (70 × 53½ in.)

136 Vija Celmins
Ocean 1992
Woodcut
49.5 × 39.4 cm (19½ × 15½ in.)

Opposite:
137 Robert Cottingham
Hot 1973
Color lithograph
58.4 × 58.4 cm (23 × 23 in.)

138 Richard Estes
Ten Doors from the *Urban Landscape*
Portfolio 1972
Color screenprint
50 × 70 cm (19¹³/₁₆ × 27⅛ in.)

the rest of the image was complete. The result is a patchy likeness in which Close's working grid, concealed in his earlier paintings, stands as a visible structure (a presence that Close later extended to the rest of his work).

Like Close's faces, Celmins's galaxies, oceans, and deserts are not so much subjects as armatures for mark-making,[4] but instead of the human face grown to architectural proportions, Celmins gives us unencompassable vastness, reduced to intimacy. Her images thrive in situations where the act of drawing encounters the greatest physical resistance: in mezzotinted night skies or in the scratches of drypoint and gouges in wood that cause her

oceans to stiffen and condense. The same is true of Gertsch, whose enormous portrait and landscape woodcuts (pl. 201) are created by picking away tiny spots of light – approximating by hand the speckle of photographic grain, but not the casualness of chemical dispersion. The visible labor in works like these is often astonishing – Celmins spent a year cutting the woodcut *Ocean* (1992) – but drudgery is not the point. The point is the visceral presence of what Close calls a "record of decisions having been made."[5]

Another group of photorealists, including Robert Cottingham, Robert Bechtle, and Richard Estes, used deadpan American cityscapes to explore the "syntax" of photography. (Ivins, who had written so effectively about the historical implications of the syntax of engraving, was blind to the limitations of photography, and thought it free of syntactic distortion.) In Estes's intricate screenprints, space is compressed, the play of reflective surfaces prolonged, and visual events evenly dispersed over the surface. Like Cottingham's fragmented signage, his *Urban Landscapes* describe spaces without people, garbage, or irrational incident; they are vistas in which the real world has adjusted itself to the tidy simplifications of graphic design – smoothly edged, sharply lit, manipulated and false.

139 Sylvia Plimack Mangold
Flexible and Stainless 1975
Color lithograph
53.3 × 74.3 cm (21 × 29¼ in.)

Realist printmaking of the 1970s was not concerned with representing the "reality" of life, but with using images from the real world to explore issues of perception and cognition, much as some Conceptual art had done, but extending its investigation outward from the cerebellum to the hand. The hand, with its involuntary ellipses and sometimes cumbersome muscularity, is a restrained but critical presence in the prints of Sylvia Plimack Mangold and Philip Pearlstein. Plimack Mangold's *Flexible and Stainless* (1975), for example, can be seen as a conceptual still life – deceptively realistic floorboards and rulers that imply receding space while keeping the image glued fast to the flat paper – but the visible fact of it as a hand-drawn lithograph changes its meaning, calls attention to the process of its facture, while imbuing it with the lyricism of the handmade.

Pearlstein said that "complete verisimilitude …is not my goal. It is a process, my experience during the attempt to achieve the likeness, that is my purpose."[6] This concern with making process visible connects Pearlstein's work to

that of Close and Celmins, but Pearlstein works entirely from life. His subject, the usually eroticized female nude, is rendered with disconcerting dispassion – the result, Pearlstein says, "of suppression."[7] Flesh becomes flat pattern and sinuous line intertwined with decorative fabrics and furnishings, the whole of it charged with a formalized sensuality, similar to that of Japanese Ukiyo-e woodblock prints (pl. 204). The clean but sketchy human-hand-at-work quality of his early lithographs was abandoned in his later aquatints in favor of a clean-edged chromatic intensity. This quality of formal precision and emotional distance inflected the prints of many contemporary realists, including Jack Beal, Richard Haas, Neil Welliver, and Alex Katz.

Katz is a naturally "graphic" artist, with a gift for transforming the dimensional complexities of life into a play of abstract form and social type. Though he began making screenprints out of a wish to produce financially accessible art, Katz quickly found affinities between the flatness, precision, and balance of form that is essential to his art and the plates, blocks, and screens of print techniques. He has worked in virtually every print medium, but his strongest prints tend to be those woodcuts and intaglio works in which his dapper stylishness is given a tough physical housing.

"Style" – that intricate alliance of manual quirks, habitual exaggerations, and inexplicable visual preferences – once again became a subject of fascination. No longer seen as either the Expressionist manifestation of an inner state, nor as an arbitrary ornament that impeded meaning, style was viewed by artists such as Pat Steir and Jennifer Bartlett as yet another form of visual syntax, to be appropriated, analysed, and manipulated. Bartlett, in her early prints, systematically examined the material, manual, and compositional permutations of picture making. The intaglio series *Day and Night* (1978)[8] employed a compare-and-contrast format of paired houses that transformed the exploration of technique (Bartlett had never worked in etching before) from a necessity into a virtue, and from a virtue into a subject. Straight lines oppose curved ones, light opposes dark, the warm burr of drypoint opposes trim line etching.

Steir's first major etching project, *Drawing Lesson* (1978), was conceived as a "dictionary of marks,"[9] each signaling a turn of technique and of historical voice, roaming from Rembrandt to LeWitt. In later prints such as *The Wave/From the Sea/After Leonardo, Hokusai, and Courbet* (1985), Steir has hand-copied whole passages from the pages of art history contrasting the styles of the originals, but also revealing the filtering process that brings them together in a twentieth-century mind.

This fascination with style is a natural extension of the kinds of critique that drove Pop art, and many Pop artists who had established their reputations with anonymous mass-market imagery were increasingly looking to art history for inspiration. In his *Haystacks* and *Cathedrals* lithographs of 1969 Lichtenstein had paraphrased Monet, substituting Ben-Day

dots for Impressionist dabs and mechanical ink variations for nuances of light. Hockney's prints had long played host to art-historical spirits from Hogarth in *A Rake's Progress* to Matisse in *Rue de Seine* (1971). It was Picasso, however, who inspired the most repeated appropriation by artists in the 1970s. Picasso's ceaseless invention of pictorial styles and his codification of autobiographical experience

140 Alex Katz
The Swimmer 1974
Aquatint
71.4 × 91.1 cm (28⅛ × 35⅞ in.)

appeared suddenly timely. *The Blue Guitar* (1976–77), the last of Hockney's great etching series, was subtitled "Etchings by David Hockney who was inspired by Wallace Stevens who was inspired by Pablo Picasso," and the cycle's subject was the meshing of influence, inspiration, and invention: quotations from Picasso's paintings are arrayed like props in stage sets of Hockney's devising, leaping, like Hockney's own art, between naturalism and stylization. Richard Hamilton's *Picasso's Meninas* (1973) is a tour-de-force of visual wit and technique that paraphrases Velazquez's masterpiece, *Las Meninas*, with a chronological catalogue of Picasso periods: the lounging mastiff is replaced by a Guernica-esque bull, the dog-kicking dwarf by a Rose Period

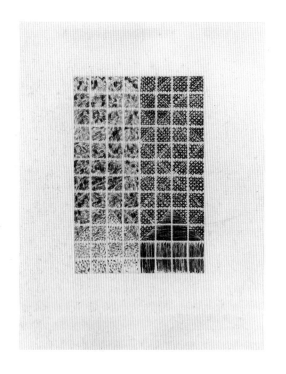

141–143 Jennifer Bartlett
Day and Night 1978
One etching and two drypoints
38.1 × 27.9 cm (15 × 11 in.) each

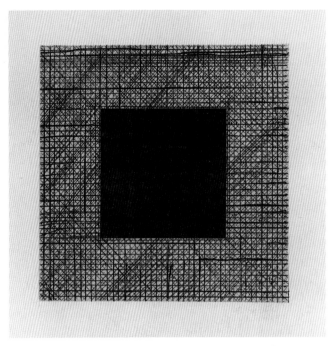

144–146 Pat Steir
Drawing Lesson, Part I, Line 1978
Three etchings from the set of seven
30.5 × 30.5 cm (12 × 12 in.)

147 Richard Hamilton
Picasso's Meninas 1973
Etching (hard- and soft-ground, stipple,
open-bite and lift-ground aquatint,
engraving, drypoint, burnishing) from
the portfolio *Hommage à Picasso*
75 × 50.5 cm (29½ × 20 in.)

harlequin, the Infanta by a patch of analytic
Cubist prismatic jottings. This confrontation
of styles articulates both time (Picasso's
succession of styles) and space (Velazquez's
ricochet of glance and reflection). Printed by
Aldo Crommelynck, the etcher who had
worked so closely with Picasso, the print is
also a compendium of etching techniques.[10]
In *Bull Profile Series* (1973), Lichtenstein took
on Picasso's great lithographic series from
1945–46 in which a bull gradually
transmogrifies from naturalism to abstraction

in eleven successive reworkings of the same
stone.[11] Lichtenstein's bulls progress from
illustrative clarity to rectilinear abstraction,
but the prints are not successive states, but
are made from completely separate printing
elements. They are connected visually, but
not materially, and parody both "process"
and "style."[12]

As style came to be seen as an independent
entity, some artists chose to divorce decorative
mannerisms from any claims about content:
"I don't think there is any reason to transcend

pure decoration," Robert Kushner proclaimed. "Pure decorations are the highest goals... of mankind."[13] Kushner was one of the few "Pattern and Decoration" painters to become seriously involved with print. Kushner took on the full decorative potential of intaglio and lithography, driving them to heights of witty and acerbic garishness. *Music* (1981) shows a lyre-playing, cross-looking cartoon cherub, tarted up with sequins, peacock feathers, and a synthetic floral wreath.

This reappraisal of style and decoration owed much to feminist cultural critiques, which had exposed a wealth of visual practices previously dismissed in Western art history as secondary forms of visual invention. This was not simply a question of elevating "women's work," but of encouraging artists to consider a wide variety of non-European traditions, including those of Islamic, Asian, and Native American cultures.[14] The pattern prints of Joyce Kozloff, which were meant to be applied directly to the wall, free of any isolating and legitimizing frame, derive from a political and anthropological consideration of pattern and its meanings. Nancy Spero printed and collaged

totemistic images onto long expanses on paper, merging contemporary feminist politics with ancient myth. Michelle Stuart's *Tsikomo* lithographs, made in 1974 at Tamarind's new location in Albuquerque, take their names from sites sacred to local Native Americans, and were designed more as talismanic objects than as images on a page: the paper for *Tsikupuming* is printed the color of earth, pocked with "rock marks" (actually embossings from a sculpmetal plate), then torn and mounted on cheesecloth.

In works such as these, the printed image and the paper support come close to being one and the same thing,[15] and the desire to integrate image and object was one of the distinguishing features of printmaking in the 1970s, inspiring both technical innovations, especially in handmade papers, and the revitalization of older techniques, such as woodcut. In the mid-1970s, Helen Frankenthaler created woodblock prints that, for the first time, merged substance and image to the degree that distinguished her painting. Working with a bandsaw rather than gouges or chisels, Frankenthaler developed a non-linear

148 Robert Kushner
Music 1981
Color lithograph with sequins, feathers, and bronze painted crowns
58.4 × 76.8 cm (22⅛ × 30¼ in.)

149 Michelle Stuart
Tsikupuming 1974–75
Embossed lithograph on paper mounted on cheesecloth
34.9 × 28 cm (13¾ × 11 in.)

150 David Hockney
Celia in an Armchair 1981
Lithograph
101.5 × 121.9 cm (40 × 48 in.)

Opposite:
151 Robert Motherwell
The Stoneness of the Stone 1974
Lithograph
104.1 × 76.2 cm (41 × 30 in.)

mode of working with wood, registering its weight, resistance, and grain, and giving equal consideration to the paper to which it was wedded: for *Essence Mulberry* (1977, pl. 208) the artist employed four different woods and allowed unmarked mulberry paper to compose almost half the image. *East and Beyond* (1972–73) "marked a departure so profound," according to Field, "that virtually all subsequent woodcuts incorporated the thinking it embodied."[16] For most of the preceding hundred years, woodcuts had been closely associated with figurative Expressionism.[17] From the late 1970s onward, however, woodcut, linocut, and other forms of relief printing came into broader use. The British sculptor Barry Flanagan played with both the grainless pliancy of linoleum and its cultural associations, in linocuts that stressed both homeliness and elegance: the buttery curl of line in *Killary Harbour* (pl. 209) blazons the

presence of linoleum (as does the torn edge at the bottom and the peculiarly kitchen-floor color). Roy Lichtenstein used woodcut as a way to combat technical slickness, and to give his mechanistic images a rougher and more substantial feel (pl. 207).[18] Though Lichtenstein used technicians to carve his blocks, and though workshops such as Tyler Graphics and Graphicstudio invented photographic and laser-based systems for cutting wood, the fascination with relief printing nonetheless represented a return to the most basic of printing techniques.

The other basic element, the paper on which the print is printed, also received serious attention. Robert Rauschenberg's work in 1973 with the venerable French paper mill Richard de Bas resulted in the first handmade paper editions by a major contemporary artist:[19] *Fuses*, which were brightly colored, shaped sheets with screenprinted chine collées, and *Pages*, which were white-on-white shaped papers that bore no printing at all. In these works, and in subsequent editions such as *Bones & Unions* (1975), with their Indian silks and "paper mud," or the diaphanous fabric *Hoarfrost Editions* (1974, pl. 210), with their medleys of California references, Rauschenberg merged subtle poetics of substances with a potent sense of place.

Sedulous print publishers such as Tanya Grosman had long made paper the subject of careful consideration, but it now appeared as a medium in its own right. Ken Tyler, who left Gemini abruptly in 1973, quickly established papermaking facilities at his new workshop, Tyler Graphics in New York State. In California, Garner Tullis's International Institute for Experimental Printmaking was largely dedicated to paper production and manipulation. Kenneth Noland, Ellsworth Kelly, and Chuck Close were among many artists who worked directly with paper pulp, creating repeatable images by applying pulp through molds or stencils, or with direct hand manipulation. By far the most ambitious of these works were David Hockney's ninety-five *Paper Pools* of 1978 (pl. 211). (Despite their Californian glow the pools were drawn from Tyler's pool in Westchester County, New York.) Ranging from single-panel studies to grand twelve-panel vistas, the *Pools* were made by pouring colored pulp into metal "cookie-cutter" molds made after the artist's drawings, then working freehand over the surface, with pulp, dyes, turkey-basters, brushes, and dog combs.[20]

Whether or not such paper works qualify as "prints" depends on which work is judged and which definition is used. Frank Stella and his cataloguer, Richard Axsome, agree that his paper reliefs are not prints. By other definitions many "made-paper" projects would qualify as prints; applying pulp through molds is not dissimilar to the application of pigments through stencils in pochoir printing. The question, in any case, may be more museological (which department gets to buy

which works) than useful.[21] Certainly, the development of paper as an active medium rather than a passive support dramatically affected all forms of print production, promoting the fusion of material and immaterial image. One of Robert Motherwell's most masterly prints, *The Stoneness of the Stone* (1974), arose from the marriage of two Zen-like lithographic strokes with a two-tone handmade

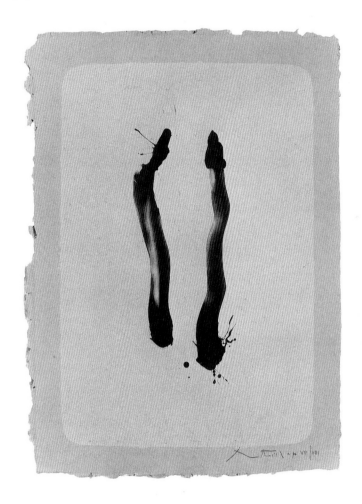

paper the color, size, and texture of the lithographic stone. William Weege and Alan Shields created flamboyant constructions from eccentric papers by cutting, sewing, weaving, and layering, for an appearance at once novel and archaic (pl. 212).

Handmade paper was also essential in transforming Frank Stella's printmaking from an elegant mode for cataloguing earlier paintings to an inspired departure from precedent.[22] In the late 1970s, as his paintings exploded out from the picture plane in baroque profusions of color and form, Stella's prints also began to display a new geometric and gestural exuberance. The pseudo-graph paper on which the *Exotic Bird Series* was printed was a rectilinear backdrop for an eruption of scribbly lines, glitter inks, and the winsome irregularity of French curves (pl. 213). With the *Circuits* series (1982–84) and the *Swan Engravings*

(1982–85) Stella broke free of the habit of "painting with printmaking techniques. Now," Stella said, "I'm using the process to make prints about printing." The *Swan Engravings* were printed from enormous metal collages, which included cut-outs and other refuse left over from the reliefs (as well as industrial plates for making plastic "lace" tablecloths). The initial inspiration for the *Circuit* prints came from another by-product of the reliefs: the wooden tabletop upon which the reliefs had been cut by laser, and which bore laser-etched

152 Eduardo Chillida
Eldu 1971
Etching
12.9 × 9.8 cm (5 × 3¾ in.)

153 Eduardo Chillida
Euzkadi IV 1976
Etching
159.5 × 115 cm (62¾ × 45¼ in.)

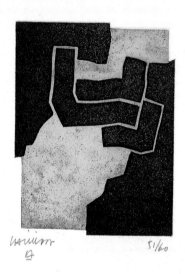

scars in overlapping patterns. *Pergusa Three, State 1* (1983, pl. 214) was printed in relief from hand-carved woodblocks inlaid with hand- and photo-etched magnesium plates, onto handmade paper, with a total of ten dye colors in the paper pulp and thirty colors of ink printed on top. It is in no respect a restatement on paper of visual discoveries made in paint; it stands aside from traditional categories, fitting neither the demeanor of prints nor that of painting.

The technical complexity of prints like these makes clear that the retreat from industrial

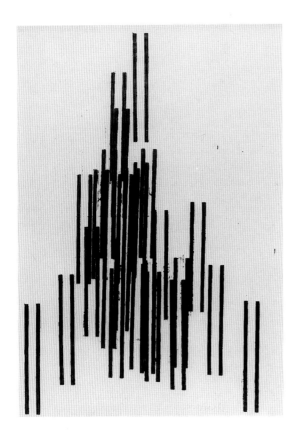

imagery and surfaces was far from a Luddite procedure. In fact, technically and economically, the major American printshops enjoyed tremendous expansion through the first part of the 1970s. More artists were making more prints, in more styles, and with more varied techniques than at any point in history.

One of the remarkable achievements of the print in the 1970s was its extension to artists who did not normally work in two-dimensional forms: landworks and performances were documented or expressed through analogues in print, as were the ideas of an increasing number of sculptors. Sculptor's prints had been a more common feature in Europe than in America. Alberto Giacometti and Henry Moore were among many European modernists who made prints that closely resembled their drawings. The etchings and woodcuts of the Spanish sculptor Eduardo Chillida, however, demonstrated the way in which printmaking

could be used to combine the virtues of drawing and sculpture. Works such as the tiny etching *Eldu* (1971) meld the linear naturalism of Chillida's drawings of hands with the architectonic, interlocking masses that propel his sculptures. And in the far larger *Euzkadi* (1976), a shaped and textured plate is allowed to run off the edge of the page, elevating the blank paper to an equal compositional role with the printed form, and allowing the two to interpenetrate. The Dutch sculptor Carel Visser had, in the late 1950s and 1960s, made remarkable prints by repeatedly printing a single, simple woodblock, compiling geometric structures in which abstraction appears unexpectedly to be subjected to gravity and other real world forces.

In America, Lee Bontecou's compelling lithographs of 1963–64 were among the few important sculptor's prints of the 1960s, followed in the early 1970s by Richard Serra's lithographs, such as *Circuit* (1972). Serra's

154 Carel Visser
Composition 1961
Woodcut
61 × 85 cm (24 × 33½ in.)

155 Mel Kendrick
Untitled (B) 1990
Woodcut from the set of eight
152 × 119.3 cm (60 × 47 in.)

156 Martin Puryear
Dark Loop 1982
Woodcut
57.8 × 76.2 cm (22¼ × 30 in.)

157 Richard Serra
Videy Afangar #5 1991
Etching
24.5 × 30.5 cm (10 × 12 in.)

prints were influential, though most of the sculptors who followed preferred more tactile techniques, such as woodcut. It offered stubborn physicality and the grain of nature, and unlike lithography and etching, which were developed to allow artists to draw as they would on paper, with woodcut it is possible to use a sculptural process to arrive at a two-dimensional result. Mel Kendrick was able to make prints only when he learned how to "draw" with a jigsaw. Martin Puryear's *Dark Loop* (1982), in which an arching, tent-like form emerges from woody solidity, clearly reveals the sculptor's fascination with the marriage of natural forms and human uses. Judy Pfaff, who says she "never wanted to make objects,"[23] and whose circumambient installations are meant to be viewed in overlapping bits and pieces as the viewer walks through them, transferred her catholic imagination to print by transferring her working method from the wall to the press bed. The series *Six of One...* (1987, pl. 217) was printed from a multitude of discrete parts – found objects, hand-carved gewgaws, lattices, and type blocks. Images duck away, spill out, and reappear in different locations and forms throughout the series, providing not the scale of her sculptures, but their sense of surprise and sequential revelation.

Joel Shapiro has made prints by laying out small pieces of lumber on the press bed, much as he arranged his wooden beam figures in space, and also with incised wood blocks, in which he isolated simple geometric shapes, and printed them in combinations that imply motion: trapezoidal cups seem to tip, balls appear to collide, even while the surrounding gouge marks keep them clearly tethered in place. But Shapiro, who has made prints throughout his career, has also worked in the distinctly unsculptural techniques of lithography and pochoir. In his aquatints with Aldo Crommelynck, blocks of color appear as a kind of weightless sculptural matter, airy and suave (pl. 215).

None of these artists use the print to portray sculptures. "I do not draw to depict, illustrate, or diagram existing works," Serra wrote of his prints. "The shapes originate in a glimpse of volume, a detail, an edge, a weight." Serra sees the color black as "synonymous with a graphic or print procedure" from Gutenberg on,[24] and his prints explore its essence just as his sculptures elucidate the essential weight, stress, and volume of their materials and surroundings. Serra's 1992 *Afangar* aquatints refer to an island off the coast of Iceland, around which Serra placed pairs of basalt slabs that articulate the topography and an elegiac sense of passage.[25] The aquatints were made in sizes ranging from that of the height of a short adult (these support about one pound of ink) to that of

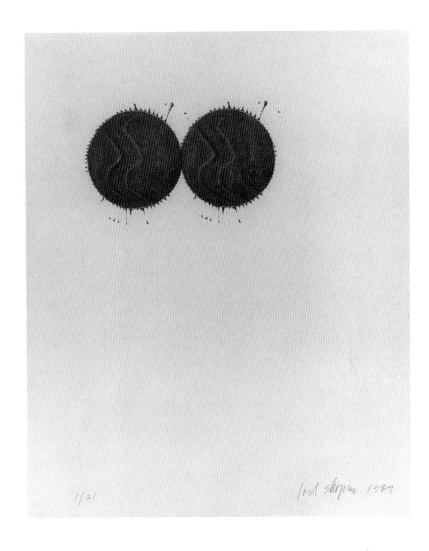

158 Joel Shapiro
Untitled 1989
Woodcut
53.3 × 43.8 cm (21 × 17¼ in.)

a paperback novel, and were printed with overstated relief onto paper of concrete-like roughness, strongly reflecting the constitution of stone.

This duality between literalism and illusion, the picture and the thing, is one of the singular riches that the print can offer sculptors. In his four-print set *Muzot* (1987) Richard Deacon mixed shapes drawn on plates and shapes physically cut from plates, and printed them on both plain paper and old "woodgrain" oilcloth, a material whose feel is at odds with its appearance, setting off a chain of comparisons between exterior and interior, literalism and illusion.[26] The Swiss sculptor Not Vital, who often weds constructed elements to found objects, has used intaglio techniques to transmute base and ephemeral nature into rarified art. The totemic *Tongue* (1990) was made by dipping an ox tongue in lift ground and pressing it to the plate.

In his early screenprints, Richard Artschwager used gridded photographs much as he used wood-grained formica in his sculptures, as a way of splitting surface from substance, and substance from subject. Both *Sailors* and *Interiors* (both 1972) reproduce on a defiantly flat surface paintings he had made on celotex, an industrial paper product with a surface so emphatically textured that it shatters the images. In later prints, Artschwager created assertive intaglio surfaces that persistently impose themselves between the attempt at pictorial effect and its reception.

The pursuit of palpable imagery and a tangible personal presence led some artists and printers away from standard editions altogether. The 1960s rediscovery of the print as a kind of mass-production manqué gave way to the 1970s rediscovery of the unique print. The painter and printmaker Nathan Oliveira wrote that his "ideas grew out of the lithographic drawing materials – as the ideas of Abstract Expressionists grew out of their paint. I was satisfied with a singular visual event, and as a result, my editions were limited or even

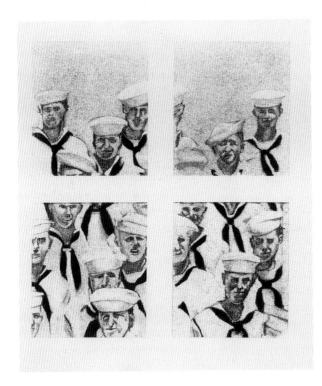

161 Richard Artschwager
Interior 1972
Screenprint
83.2 × 116.8 cm (32¾ × 46 in.)

162 Richard Artschwager
Sailors 1972
Screenprint
62.9 × 45.1 cm (24¾ × 17¾ in.)

Opposite:
159 Richard Deacon
Muzot 1987
Etching on oilcloth from
a portfolio of four prints
64 × 64 cm (25³/₁₆ × 25³/₁₆ in.)

160 Not Vital
Tongue 1990
Lift-ground aquatint made
from a cow tongue
107.9 × 107.9 cm (42½ × 42½ in.)

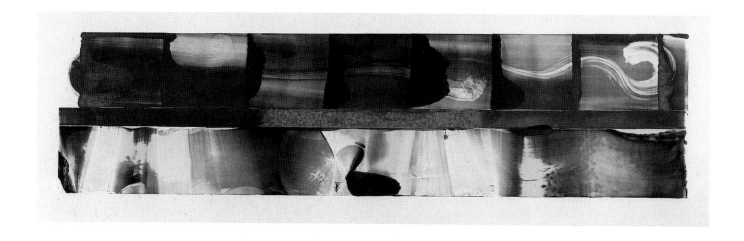

163 David Reed
For Fransesco de Cairo 1987
Monotype
71.1 × 233.7 cm (28 × 92 in.)

164 David Storey
Untitled (series X, impression II) 1988
Monotype
94 × 59.7 cm (37 × 26 in.)

Opposite:
165–167 Oleg Kudryashov
Composition (triptych) no. 284 1982
Set of three: drypoint uninked
with monotype watercolor;
drypoint with additional lines
incised after inking; and drypoint
with monotype watercolor and
additional lines incised after inking
72.4 × 121.3 cm
(28½ × 47¼ in.) each sheet

nonexistent."[27] In 1972 Oliveira began working in monotype (pl. 216), a form of unique print made by painting or drawing with ink on a smooth glass or metal plate; there is no fixed matrix and the image is unrepeatable. (The monoprint, on the other hand, combines fixed matrices, such as woodblocks, with direct hand-work, and is often simply a unique variant of an otherwise editionable work.) Invented in the seventeenth century and revived in the

nineteenth, monotype is a liquid and spontaneous medium – more so than painting or drawing, since the thin inks can be wiped so easily from the plate. An exhibition of Degas monotypes at the Fogg Art Museum in 1968 and a later survey of monotype at the Metropolitan Museum of Art stimulated the interest of numerous painters. Abstract Expressionists, such as Sam Francis and the Italian Emilio Vedova, were able to make full use of its buoyant spontaneity. Younger painters such as the American David Reed and the British Thérèse Oulton (pl. 219) exploited its luminosity and its peculiar mix of surface compression and illusory depth. (Reed's monotypes in particular maximize its cinematic, backlit look.) Michael Mazur, an ardent proponent of the medium, describes both its genius for improvisation and its "sequential advantage:"[28] after printing, pale traces of the image remain on the plate and can be used for faint printing or for further elaboration and alteration. These "ghosts" (or "cognates") can form the basis of ongoing deliberations, as in Mazur's monumental series, *Wakeby Day/Wakeby Night* (1982–83, pl. 218). The preservation and manipulation of ghosts has become a specialty of certain printers: Maurice Sanchez of Derrière l'Etoile is able to produce something like an edition from a single monotype drawing.[29] David Storey's monotypes, done with Sanchez, have the intense blacks and dusty spatterings of his drawings, but convey a more relaxed imagination – the result, perhaps, of knowing the image is infinitely adjustable and can deliver up multiple solutions.

Even within conventional print media, hand-applied marks and unrepeatable variations became increasingly common through the decade: hand-colored prints were made by Mel Bochner, Claes Oldenburg, Pat Stier, Wayne Thiebaud, and Andy Warhol, whose hand-colored *Flowers* (1974) can be seen as a definitive marker of the swing from mechanical image generation to the hand. Nancy Graves, whose sculptures merged scientific observation and shamanistic invocation of the unknown, made lambent hand-colored intaglio prints as well as densely worked monoprints (pl. 220). Oleg Kudryashov made large-scale drypoints of loosely piled geometric forms that are hand-colored, irregularly inked, and sometimes cut, folded, and pasted into three-dimensional reliefs. John Cage's fascination with chance procedures extended to the use of fire and smoke to "print" paper. He made monotypes by placing dampened paper over burning newspaper and running it through the press, where it picked up both scorches and newsprint ink, then branding the sheet with rings (made by the bottoms of Japanese iron teapots) whose placement was determined by the I Ching. He also made editions, such as *Missing Stone* (1989, pl. 221), in which the etched outlines of randomly positioned stones was printed on smoked sheets of paper, each one unrepeatable.

Richard Tuttle's response to a publisher's request for a hand-colored print was *In Praise of Economic Determinism* (1973) – a paper sheet with a pencil-drawn arc, two punched holes, and printed instructions on the back. All the required qualities are present, but perversely: the printing cannot be seen, the hand-coloring is hardly colorful, and the customary, respectful presentation of paper in a flattering frame is mooted by the two nail holes. In a related group, *In Praise of Historical Determinism I, II, and III* (1974), two framed lithographs are

168 Richard Tuttle
In Praise of Historical Determinism I, II, and III 1974
Two lithographs and one screenprint
76.2 × 55.9 cm (30 × 22 in.) each

accompanied by a bright yellow screenprint, stiffened with wooden runners at the back and leaning at a 45-degree angle between wall and floor. These works cannot be approached with the usual frame of reference with which we regard prints – there is no way to isolate the image from the paper, or the paper from the installation.

But the interleaving of printed and hand-applied marks as a working method is at its most refined in the prints of Howard Hodgkin (pl. 222–224). The hand-coloring in these works is not simply a chromatic overlay on printed structures, but an integral element of the composition, and is repeated, with as much consistency as possible, to produce a regular edition. Hodgkin often uses the same plates to create both color and grisaille images: in *Monsoon* and *Black Monsoon* (1987) the red frame, so prominent in the former, recedes in the latter into invisibility, while gray splatter erupts over the surface, conveying a profoundly different emotional content. These prints, like Hodgkin's paintings, take as their subject emotional moments embedded in memory. His paintings, which are small, heavily layered, and painted on board, are often reworked over a period of years, the slow accretion of insight and reconstruction imitating the adjustments that subsequent events impose on recollection. The prints, however, are large and luminous, their layers attenuated and exposed. Significantly, the hand-coloring is not done by the artist, but by an assistant following his instructions. The character of the gestures, like that of memory, is both intimate and detached; and it is emotionally moving because (rather than in spite) of its distance and intangibility.

The fascination with material warmth, tactile incident, and accessible imagery that affected printmaking in the 1970s did not, after all, signal a rush to primitive expression, but a cagey distrust of both direct emotion and cerebral purity – a way to acknowledge the personal experience of the artist and complex mediating presence of the work of art.

169 Ellsworth Kelly
Colors on a Grid, Screenprint 1976
screenprint and lithograph
122.6 × 122.6 cm (48¼ × 48¼ in.)

170 Ellsworth Kelly
18 Colors (Cincinnati) 1981
Color lithograph
40.6 × 229.9 cm (16 × 90½ in.)

171 Donald Judd
Untitled 1988
Set of ten woodcuts
60×80 cm (23⅛ × 31½ in.) each

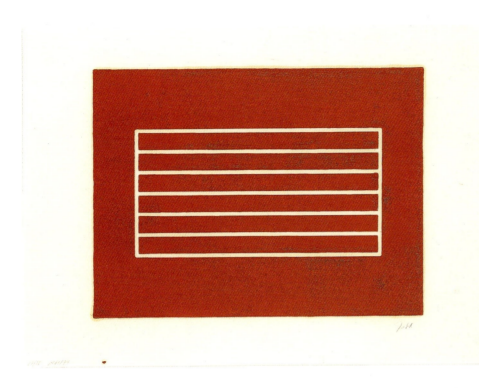

172 Donald Judd
Untitled 1961–79
Woodcut printed in oilpaint
on Japanese paper, from set
of two
53.3 × 73.7 cm (21 × 29 in.)

173 Frank Stella
Double Grey Scramble 1972–73
50-color screenprint
73.6 × 128.9 cm (29 × 50¾ in.)

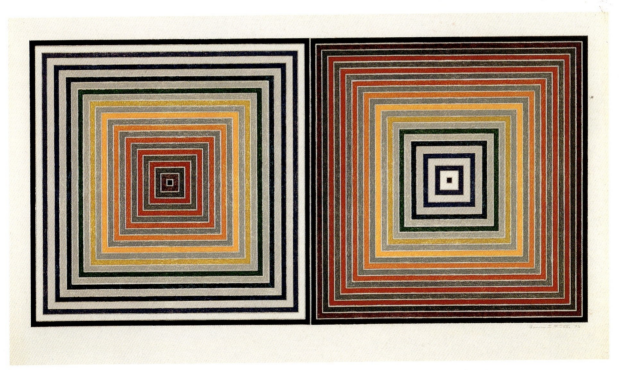

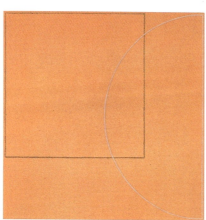

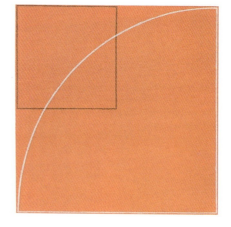

174–178 Robert Mangold
Five Aquatints 1975
Portfolio of five color aquatints and
soft-ground etchings
22.9 × 22.9 cm (9 × 9 in.) each

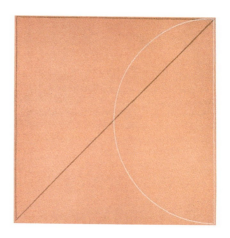

179 Robert Ryman
Seven Aquatints 1972
Aquatint from the set of seven
61 × 61 cm (24 × 24 in.)

180 Mel Bochner
Second Color Quartet 1990
Color lithograph on four sheets
88.9 × 114.3 cm (35 × 45 in.) overall

181 Dorothea Rockburne
Radiance 1983
Color lithograph printed on
both sides, cut and folded
101.6 × 81.3 cm (40 × 32 in.)

182 Sandy Gellis
Spring 1987: In the Northern Hemisphere
1987–88
Twelve color photo-etchings
30.5 × 30.5 cm (12 × 12 in.) each

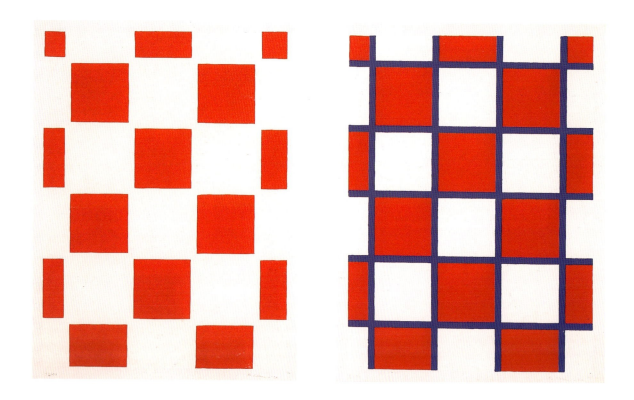

183 Blinky Palermo
Flipper 1970
Screenprint on two sheets
85.5 × 66 cm (33½ × 26 in.) each sheet

184–189 Tom Phillips
The Birth of Art 1973
Zinc stencil progressively eroded and
relief printed, six from set of ten
26.4 × 58.4 cm (10⅜ × 23 in.)

Opposite:
190 Tom Phillips
Sixty-four Stopcock Box Lids 1976
Screenprint
101.3 × 71.1 cm (39⅞ × 28 in.)

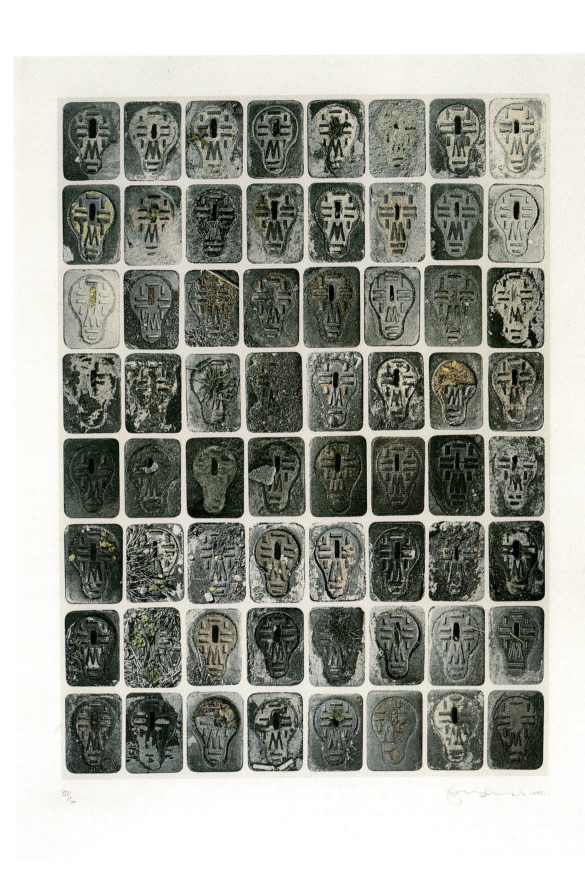

37/56

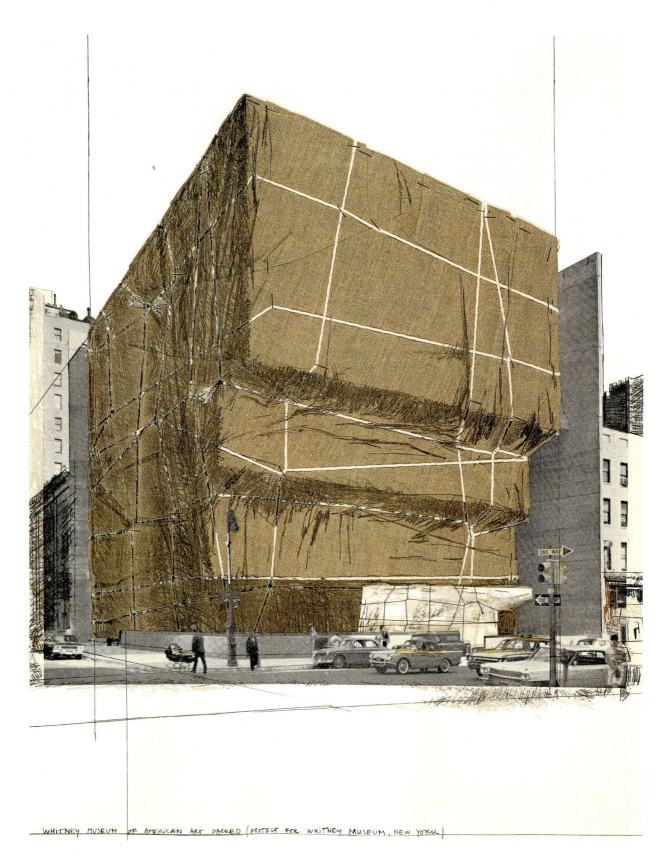

WHITNEY MUSEUM OF AMERICAN ART PACKED (PROJECT FOR WHITNEY MUSEUM, NEW YORK)

diblect 79 VII/VIII

192 Jan Dibbets
Untitled 1974
Collotype and screenprint from
the portfolio *Landscape*
33×40 cm (13×15¾ in.)

193 Pieter Holstein
Dog Watching Omnipresence 1975
Hand colored etching
50×65 cm (19¾ × 25½ in.)

Opposite:
191 Christo
(Some) Not Realized Projects: Whitney
Museum of American Art, Packed, Project
for New York 1971
Color lithograph with collage
71.1×55.9 cm (28×22 in.)

194 Bruce Nauman
Oiled Dead 1975
Lithograph and screenprint
115.6 × 125.7 cm (45½ × 49½ in.)

195 Vito Acconci
3 Flags for 1 Space and 6 Regions 1979–81
Color photo-etching in six parts
182.9 × 162.5 cm (72 × 64 in.) overall

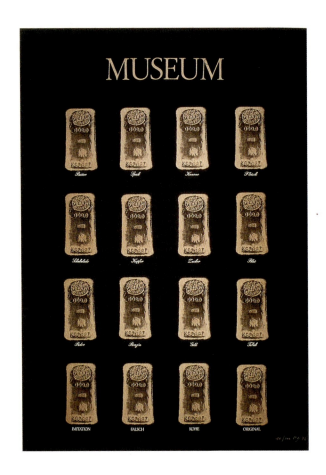

196 Marcel Broodthaers
La Signature Série 1
Tirage illimité 1969
Screenprint on tracing paper
54.5 × 73.8 cm (21½ × 29 in.)

197 Marcel Broodthaers
Museum-Museum 1972
Color screenprint, two parts
83.9 × 59.1 cm
(33 × 23¼ in.) each sheet

Opposite:
198 Chris Burden
Diecimila 1977
Color photo-etching printed on
both sides of the paper (shown
front and back)
25.4 × 35.5 cm (10 × 14 in.)

4/35 Diecimila   Chris Rinden 1977

199 Mario Merz
*Da un Erbario Raccolto nel 1979
Woga-Woga, Australië* 1989
Color lithograph from the set of
fourteen
46 × 34 cm (18¹⁄₈ × 13¹⁄₂ in.)

200 Jannis Kounellis
Untitled 1979
Aquatint and photo-etching
114.3 × 91.4 cm (45 × 36 in.)

Opposite:
201 Franz Gertsch
Schwarzwasser 1990–91
Woodcut
274 × 217 cm (108¹⁄₄ × 85¹⁄₂ in.)

202 Alex Katz
Black Shoes 1987
Color etching and aquatint
57.2 × 73.7 cm (22⅛ × 29 in.)

203 David Hockney
What Is This Picasso?
from *the Blue Guitar* 1976–77
Color etching and aquatint
from the set of twenty
45.7 × 52 cm (18 × 20½ in.)

204 Philip Pearlstein
Models with Mirror 1983–85
Color etching and aquatint
90.5 × 137.2 cm (35⅛ × 53¼ in.)

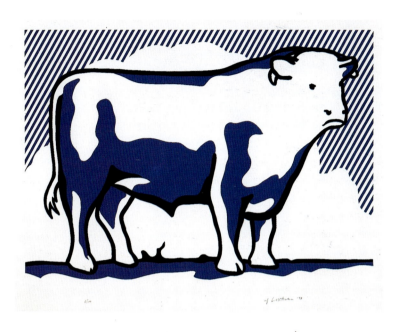

205 Roy Lichtenstein
Bull Profile Series: Bull II 1973
Lithograph and linecut from the
series of six
68.6 × 88.9 cm (27 × 35 in.)

206 Roy Lichtenstein
Bull Profile Series: Bull IV 1973
Lithograph, screenprint and linecut
from the series of six
68.6 × 88.9 cm (27 × 35 in.)

207 Roy Lichtenstein
Goldfish Bowl 1981
Woodcut
63.5 × 46.3 cm (25 × 18¼ in.)

208 Helen Frankenthaler
Essence Mulberry, State I 1977
Color woodcut
100.3 × 47 cm (39½ × 18½ in.)

Opposite:
209 Barry Flanagan
Killary Harbour 1979 1980
Linocut
38.5 × 57 cm (15¼ × 22½ in.)

210 Robert Rauschenberg
Hoarfrost Editions: Plus Fours 1974
Transfer and collage on silk
170.2 × 241.3 cm (67 × 95 in.)

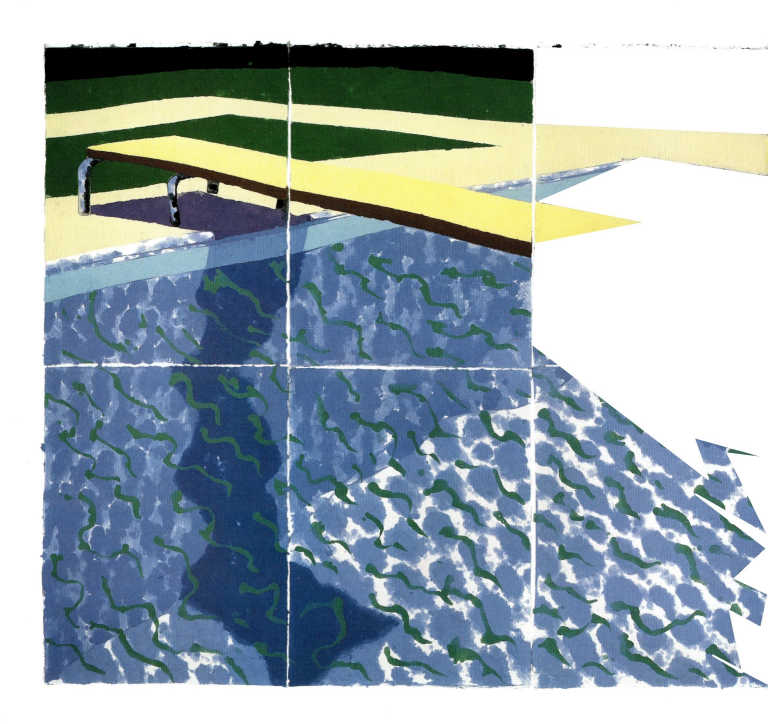

211 David Hockney
Le Plongeur, Paper Pool 18 1978
Colored, pressed paper
pulp in twelve sheets
182.9 × 217.2 cm (72 × 171 in.) together

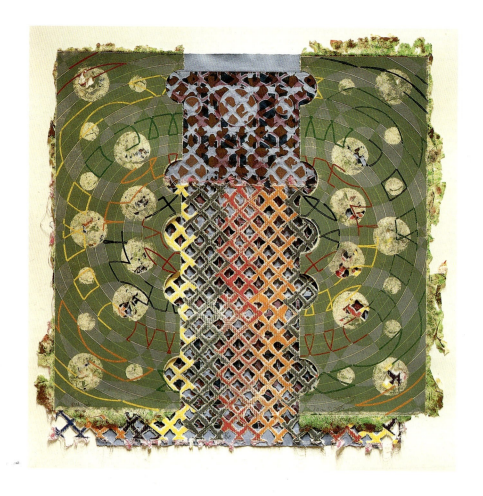

212 Alan Shields
Odd-Job 1984
Woodcut, etching, stitching, and collage
on handmade papers
106.7 × 106.7 cm (42 × 42 in.)

213 Frank Stella
Noguchi's Okinawa Woodpecker from the
Exotic Bird Series 1977
Color lithograph and screenprint
86 × 116.5 cm (33⅞ × 45⅞ in.)

Opposite:
214 Frank Stella
Pergusa Three, State I 1983
Relief print in 40 colors from
magnesium plates and woodblocks on
handmade dyed paper
167.6 × 132 cm (66 × 52 in.)

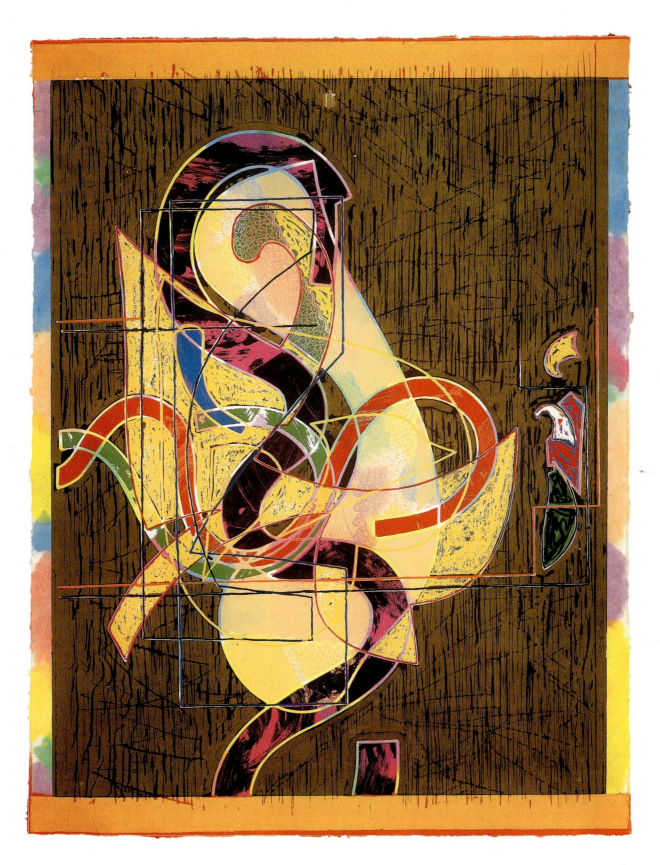

215 Joel Shapiro
Untitled 1990
Color aquatint from a portfolio of four
94.9 × 69.2 cm (37⅜ × 27¼ in.)

216 Nathan Oliveira
London Site 8–11 1984
Monotype with hand painting
66 × 55.9 cm (26 × 22 in.)

Opposite:
217 Judy Pfaff
Manzanas Y Naranjas
from *Six of One...* 1987
Color woodcut
149.9 × 177.8 cm (59 × 70 in.)

218 Michael Mazur
Wakeby Day II 1983
Pastel and monotype
182.9 × 365.8 cm (72 × 144 in.)

219 Therese Oulton
Untitled 1989
Monotype
97.1 × 66 cm (38¼ × 26 in.)

220 Nancy Graves
Ngetal 1977
Hand-colored etching with
aquatint, engraving, and drypoint
80 × 90.2 cm (31½ × 35½ in.)

221 John Cage
The Missing Stone 1989
Color spitbite and aquatint
etching on smoked paper
137.2 × 104.1 cm (54 × 41 in.)

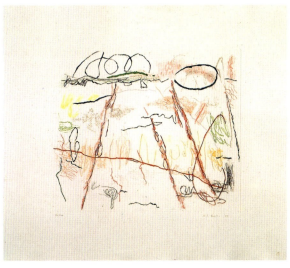

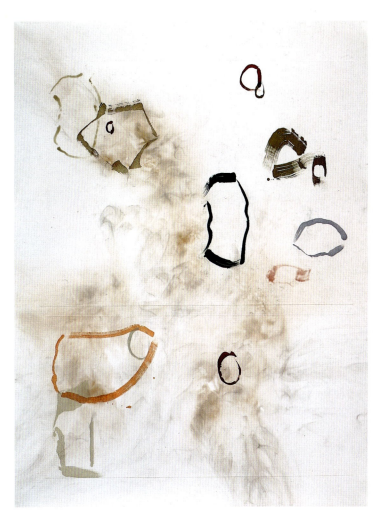

222 Howard Hodgkin
Monsoon 1987
Lithograph, watercolor, and gouache
107.5 × 135 cm (42³/₈ × 53¹/₈ in.)

223 Howard Hodgkin
Black Monsoon 1987
Lithograph and gouache
107.5 × 135 cm (42³/₈ × 53¹/₈ in.)

Opposite:
224 Howard Hodgkin
In an Empty Room 1990
Etching with carborundum and gouache
120 × 150 cm (47¹/₄ × 59 in.)

7

USES OF HISTORY

In the early 1980s, for the first time since the Second World War, New York relinquished its hegemony as the global capital of contemporary art. The decade saw the creation of masterful prints by American artists, but it also saw European prints once again become an international force. Europe, it should be remembered, has never developed the large printer/publisher organizations that so dominated American printmaking after 1960, and contemporary European prints have, with a handful of exceptions, never enjoyed the economic clout or high visibility of recent American prints. Most are produced at small, specialized shops that lie scattered over the continent or, quite often, by the artists themselves, using simple techniques and self-conscious muscularity. It is a mode well suited to much of the art that emerged in the early 1980s in Europe and America – art that was marked by an apparent resurgence of tradition: a return to familiar images, especially the human figure; to familiar systems of content, such as narrative and allegory; and to familiar physical forms, such as woodcuts and etchings. Painting, which had been pronounced dead more than once in the preceding two decades, sprang back to life. Rough-and-ready, hands-on printmaking flourished, the sign of a desire for technical simplicity and for a keener cohesion of emotional experience and printed image.

These prints were not just the work of younger artists – many of the most influential were produced by artists such as the Austrian Arnulf Rainer and the German Georg Baselitz, who had come of age in the 1950s and who, while dedicated to the direct expression of personal emotion, had sought alternatives to the international abstract style then sweeping the continent. In Austria, printmaking was an important extension of "Aktionismus" – a movement of expressionist performance works that were brutal, ritualistic, and often (literally) visceral. Hermann Nitsch, famous for covering volunteers with animal blood and entrails, also made large, jittery screenprints on blood-splattered paper. Günter Brus began his extraordinary *Bild-Dichtungen* (Picture-Poems) in the isolation of exile (in the late 1960s he had been sentenced to prison for committing obscene acts while singing the national anthem), and used a fidgety etched line to elaborate fantasies that leap between grotesque sadomasochism and cloying sweetness. But the most enigmatic and powerful prints to come out of Austria were those of Rainer, who since the mid-1950s has pursued concealment as a form of expression – making or taking an image only to obliterate it in a tangle of swift gestures. Rainer explained that when he looked at his early pictures, he saw only mistakes, "places that called out to be painted over in black... Only in total blackness did I see no

225 Georg Baselitz
LR 1966
Chiaroscuro woodcut from three blocks
approximately 45 × 35 cm
(17¾ × 13¾ in.)

177

more mistakes, no more weak spots."[1] In his drypoints (some of which are done over photogravures of the artist's face) this eradication is literally a scratching-out, evidence of the simultaneous will toward destruction and creation. A collaboration between Rainer and Brus, *Depth Obscured* (1985–86), used old copper plates from botanical illustrations, which were drawn on by Brus and then overworked by Rainer in a layering of objective observation, fervid embellishment, and extirpatory "correction."

In Germany, Baselitz had begun his rough, expressive, figurative etchings and woodcuts in the early 1960s, when most forward-looking European artists were pursuing abstraction or abandoning canvas and paper altogether.[2] A collector of both African art and Mannerist prints, Baselitz employed figurative motifs as a way to merge potent symbolism with glorious contrivance. In 1969 he began composing his images upside down, a conceit that created dynamic tension between his imagery and his increasingly abstract barrage of marks: viewing his large woodcuts and linocuts of the late 1970s, the eye flips between passive acceptance of the flying strokes and an active struggle to recognize the simple subjects: men eating oranges, women leaning in windows, eagles at rest and on the wing.

Not the least disturbing thing about Baselitz's work was its explicit Germanness: his pin-headed "heroes" could be seen as dark twins to the figurative fictions of Social Realism; his eagles could be uncomfortable reminders of the imperial past. Even the woodcut medium itself might be considered a particularly German choice: its greatest early master was Dürer, and its most significant revival in this century was in the hands of German Expressionists. Baselitz's relationship to the history he cited was the subject of much debate – observers could not decide if he was being nostalgic, critical, or merely sensationalist.

This bewilderment also greeted the younger German artists, including Jörg Immendorff, Anselm Kiefer, and A. R. Penck, who used

226 Arnulf Rainer and Gunter Brus
Depth Obscured 1985–86
Etching, photoetching, and drypoint
45.2 × 31.2 cm (17¹³/₁₆ × 12⁷/₁₆ in.)

woodcut and linocut to enact historical or
primitivist motifs, and who, like Baselitz,
exploited its implicit violence of form. (Markus
Lüpertz, who is often jumbled in with these
artists under the fuzzy rubric "Neo-
Expressionism,"³ employed Picasso quotations,
First World War headgear, and other historical
flotsam as elements in a self-consciously
sophisticated game of allusion, rather than
emotion – a distinction substantiated in
Lüpertz's preference for lithography over
woodcut.) Kiefer and Immendorff were former
students of Beuys who began in the 1970s to
survey the forbidden territory of German
myths, politics and history. Kiefer used home-
made photographs and woodcuts as the
underpinnings of grandly operatic paintings,
books and works on paper. *Wege der
Weltweisheit – die Hermanns-Schlacht* (Paths of
Worldly Wisdom – Hermann's Battle, 1980)
offers a gallery of German historical figures
from Kant to Bismarck to the legendary

227 Georg Baselitz
Adler (Eagle) 1981
Woodcut from the portfolio *Erste
Konzentration II*
65 × 50 cm (25½ × 19¾ in.)

228 Markus Lüpertz
Flasche II (Bottle II) 1980
Lithograph
95.5 × 65.5 cm (37½ × 25¾ in.)

Wege der Weltweisheit + die Hermanns-Schlacht

Hermann,[4] each represented by a separate
woodcut portrait head and joined together in
a web of painted lines, suggesting a variable
collection rather than an organic whole.

Immendorff focused on more recent
history, devising pictorial morality plays of East
and West, Left and Right, the macro-politics of
nation states and the micro-politics of the art
world. In his *Café Deutschland* (1982, pl. 275)
linocuts he makes the most of the medium's
lean, spiky contours, its propagandistic
distortions and oversimplifications.

The prints of Baselitz, Kiefer, and
Immendorff were cut, inked, and printed with
conscious imprecision by the artists to achieve
an image of recklessness, integrity, and physical
substantiality.[5] They have nothing to do with
modern ideals of multiplicity, and little to do
with the contemporary collaborative print

practice of professional shops. Kiefer ignored
the edition potential of woodcut altogether.[6]
The medium worked for these artists because
of its simple graphic power, its suggestion of
something hoary and time-worn, and its
capacity to appear simultaneously primitive
and elaborate.

Penck sees the woodcut as a medium of
crisis and transition, both in his own life and
historically. He made the woodcuts of *Acht
Erfahrungen* (Eight Experiences, 1982) shortly
after emigrating from East Germany to the
West, and though they were printed by a
master printer (François Lafranca), the prints
are purposefully coarse: the blocks were cut
with power tools, accentuating urgency and
minimizing control, and the paper is stone-like,
reinforcing the prehistoric tone of the images.
In Penck's earlier silkscreen set *Ur End Standart*

(1972, pl. 276–279), by contrast, these pictograms have much more the look of hastily painted graffiti.[7] Penck's abstracted, visual Esperanto of symbols and archetypes was developed to embody "direct signals" – a form of human communication that did not enjoin or instruct the way language so often does, and that harbored no hidden agenda: "I want my pictures to be open, so that one can see the development, the categories 'ur' and 'end,' so that one can tell… that nothing has been hidden, destroyed, or altered."[8]

The meshing of political and aesthetic issues in the prints of German artists was not just a prophylactic legacy of Nazism, but also a creative legacy of Beuys, for whom the distinction between spiritual and political life was immaterial. Elsewhere in Europe, the tendency toward greater emotional content took less politicized form: the Danish artist Per Kirkeby, whose art reflects an almost mystical involvement with geology, scratched turbulent compositions into stiffly resistant wood and metal (pl. 280); the Swiss artist Martin Disler made fierce yet elegant etchings of wildly distorted, orgiastic scenes.

In Italy, where younger artists began drawing on their own local myths and cultural histories, the tone was more lyrical. While Immendorff said "ideological and political determination run like a red thread through my art and my life,"[9] Mimmo Paladino envisioned the artist's role as "a magician, shaman, juggler of this great mystery, art."[10] Paladino, along with Sandro Chia, Francesco Clemente, and Enzo Cucchi, were identified as the "Transavantgarde," a term coined to indicate that the relentless forward motion of the avant-garde had been abandoned in favor of an equable skittering over the surface of history, borrowing styles and motifs at will. Chia once characterized art as a "theater of fictions,"[11] and he made the most of printmaking's literary and illustrative qualities: his puffy superheroes bounce through mysterious narratives while making coy

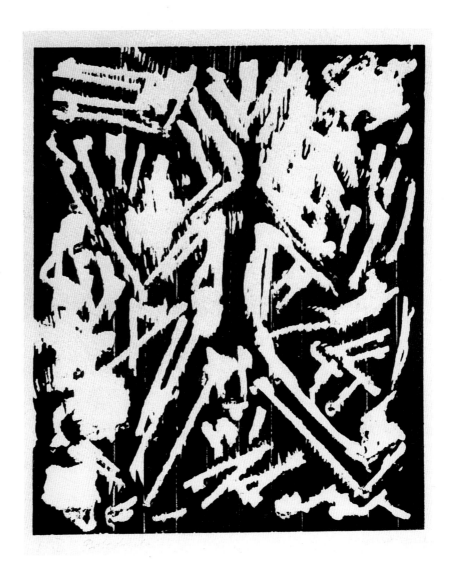

the enigmatic subject of his enormous etching *Un'Immagine Oscura* (An Obscure Image) of 1982 as "a kind of irradiation of life lived, also making itself felt to me as a sort of smell, a spicy odor."[12] Paladino's touch is lighter, and the solemnity of his figures is regularly deflected by unexpected, often ludicrous, juxtapositions of materials. In the etching *Muto* (Mute) of 1985 (pl. 283) enormous fake fur ears keep the silent figure suspended between the imaginary and the physical world. Paladino's art depends more on draftsmanship than on painterly regulation of tone, but his drawing is adept at conforming to the material it inhabits – in the lift-ground etching of *Muto* it is broad and expressive; in line etching it is mellifluous and serpentine; in linocut, obdurate and forceful. "I am not interested in reproducibility," Paladino said. "I am fascinated with working on a hostile surface."[13] The expansive triptych *Sirene*, *Vespero* and *Poeta Occidentale* (1986) was etched, not on the usual copper or zinc, but on iron, a material with an archaic, shambolic feel. The figures are not meant as actors in a cogent Christian or Pagan tale (despite the golden cross), but as open allegories through which individual experience can be made universally accessible.

Likewise, the polymorphous sexuality and scatology that feature in Clemente's work were not meant as either erotica or expressions of personal anguish. "Keep to the surface," Clemente said. "Don't look for meanings... In every mystical tradition, whatever paradoxical or poetic notion you come across, there is the idea that you don't have to add meaning to it."[14] A connoisseur of surfaces, Clemente avoids chunky impasto in favor of a pointedly thin membrane between man and image. His most famous print, an untitled self-portrait of 1984, is a woodcut made in the traditional Japanese Ukiyo-e manner, and looks very much like one of his light, improvisatory watercolors. On closer examination, however, the washes of color are revealed as the impressions of dozens of wood blocks, cleverly carved and superimposed in forty-nine

231 Enzo Cucchi
La Mano di Pietra 1982
Etching and aquatint
85 × 60 cm (33 × 23½ in.)

Opposite:
232 Enzo Cucchi
Un'Immagine Oscura... 1982
Color etching
120 × 176 cm (47¼ × 69¼ in.)

233 Francesco Clemente
Self Portrait No. 2 1981
Etching
40.6 × 52 cm (16 × 20½ in.)

allusions to art history and their own fictive natures. The *Figure Looking Out* (1982) gazes over, and is embedded within, a ground of decorative looping lines, like a farmer in a field of sentimentalized Pollock (pl. 282).

Prints not only offered appealing visual qualities, but more allusively, a history of borrowed form and even of pocket mysticism (in the fifteenth century woodcuts were made as religious souvenirs). The dreamscapes of Cucchi or Paladino are ambiguously suggestive of psychic or spiritual states: Cucchi described

meticulous passages of printing. Unlike the watercolors, which can almost seem to dissipate off the page, the print, with its painstaking recreation of seemingly inadvertent detail, is a vision of motion made solid, a frozen waterfall. The bleeding edges and liquid pools of watercolor are far from the natural aptitudes of Japanese technique, but the Ukiyo-e tradition, is in other respects an apt one for Clemente: it was dedicated to portraying the ephemeral pleasures of the world – snow, fireworks, feminine beauty, sexual diversion – and it is a mode in which surface is everything: compositions without depth, moments without time.[15]

At the same time that Clemente and others were using the print in a romantic engagement with historical figurative forms, artists such as Günther Förg, Stephen Ellis, Helmut Federle,

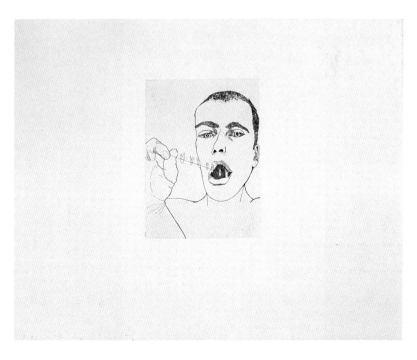

Marden's balance of austerity and sensuality, as well as Palermo's interplay of transcendence and irreverence. Ellis's intaglio series pit insistent geometric patterns against irregular spreading stains of aquatint, balancing precise intent against controlled accident. The Dutch artist René Daniëls (pl. 285) established a vocabulary of forms that flip between pictorial description (the receding corner of a room) and emblematic concision (a bow tie). For Förg in particular, print techniques offered an opportunity to explore the tension between ideal form and sensual improvisation. In his etchings and lithographs animated brush- and fingerstrokes push at the edges of classical stasis, just as in his photographs of faces and neoclassical architecture ideal structures are undermined by the myriad irregularities, the nicks and pores, that constitute people and buildings in the real world. Förg's prints almost always appear in series, allowing him to articulate similarity and difference over an unexpected range of objects, as in the *Krefeld Suite* (1987, pl. 286), in which four smudgily elegant, defiantly flat lithographs are accompanied by one bronze relief – tactility and immediacy are set against the displaced action that is the essence of the print.

Other younger European artists worked still more eclectically, drawing on both abstract and figurative traditions in works whose emotional tenor hovered between the cheeriness of Pop and the probity of both geometric and expressive abstraction. The Danish artist Troels Wörsel, whose paintings merge seemingly Expressionist impasto with snippets of mass-market texts and images, found in etching a medium that could marry diverse elements with grace and translucency.

In America also, historicizing impulses were being felt, and ancient techniques were being revived, but to somewhat different ends. The venerable Japanese tradition of woodblock printing was rediscovered by American artists such as Sol LeWitt and Jennifer Bartlett, who remarked that placing the virtuosity of

234 Stephen Ellis
Plate VI from *Escorial* 1991
Drypoint and aquatint from the set of eight
32 × 24 cm (12½ × 9¼ in.)

Opposite:
235 Troels Wörsel
The Spanish Set 1990
Etching and aquatint from the set of 25 etchings and one screenprint on plexiglass
76.2 × 55.9 cm (30 × 22 in.)

and Imi Knoebel were using it in a critical engagement with the radical geometries of earlier twentieth-century art. Ellis described the contemporary artist inhabiting "a studio overpopulated by the enormous ghosts of modernism."[16] For while the geometrical forms employed by Joseph Albers or Donald Judd were still available (as they had been since Euclid), the rational or logical certainties that inspired them as art no longer were tenable. Instead of projecting the purity and consistency of mechanistic production, the prints of these younger artists acknowledged both the machine and the hand, recalling

5/15   T. Wentzel

236 Philip Guston
Pile Up 1979
Lithograph
50.8 × 76.2 cm (20 × 30 in.)

Japanese printers at her disposal "was like giving a Ferrari to a six-month-old baby."[17] The Japanese method is capable of great graphic drama, like Western woodcut, but emphasizes flatness, subtlety, and control. The combination was appealing to both artists and printers, who increasingly incorporated elements of Japanese technique. Crown Point Press established a program with Japanese printers in Kyoto,[18] which lead to a number of remarkable images including Chuck Close's shimmering mosaic portrait *Leslie* (1986), and Wayne Thiebaud's darkly luminous *Candy Apples* (1987, pl. 288). The fact that the block is, traditionally, cut and printed by artisans in imitation of the artist's drawings, briefly rekindled the "original print" debate, but for Western artists it was not a way to reproduce,

but to recast, their work. Diebenkorn observed that even with the technical mastery of the Japanese block-cutters, "distortions do present themselves…you begin to work with the distortions and finally find yourself quite a distance away from the original thrust…it isn't far from what can happen in one's studio when one is alone."[19]

Field, writing in 1982 about the unexpected resurgence of woodcut, observed: "the magic of the new woodcut is that it is two things at once; while increasing the felt presence of the artist, it maintains the basically anti-expressionist bias of the 1960s."[20] Richard Bosman's woodcut *Man Overboard* (1981, pl. 289), which became a mascot of the "Neo-Expressionist" woodcut revival in America, is typical in its mix of emotional urgency and parodic distance:[21] despite all the vigorous slashing and the exaggerated and distended limbs, the falling figure is as perfectly composed and motionless as an Ukiyo-e courtesan. The emotional stimulus for Bosman's print was the artist's childhood memory of a shipboard suicide; but its visual inspiration came from the cover of a cheap detective novel. In America, the artifacts of cycloptic heads, tangled legs, and severed fingers.[22] In Chicago, the artists in and around the "Hairy Who"[23] had been scrambling the influences of popular culture, Surrealism, and Expressionism since the 1960s: Jim Nutt and Gladys Nilsson made giddy, maniacal etchings and offset lithographs that were clearly enamored of the graphic efficiency of the comic strip; Roger Brown's aquatints and

237 H. C. Westermann
The Human Fly 1971
Woodcut
62.5 × 46 cm (24⅛ × 18¹/₁₆ in.)

238 Roger Brown
Standing While All Around Are Sinking
1977
Aquatint
61 × 50.8 cm (24 × 20 in.)

popular culture, such as the pulp paperback or comic-book, often served the function that native history and myth played in Europe – providing a graphic language to embody the emotional issues that had been suspended in recent contemporary art. The late, cartoonish figuration of Philip Guston was extremely influential, with its thick black lines, and its expressive, dyspeptic vocabulary of shoes, lithographs were more formal but no less phantasmal; and the lithographs and woodcuts of H. C. Westermann were important precursors of the ingenuous, ideographic imagery that erupted in the 1980s.

The mixture of high culture and kitsch, and the use of juvenile imagery as a foil for serious issues, became something of a global trend in the early 1980s. It arose in the virulent,

collage-based work of David Wojnarowicz who, like Fählstrom, mixed Pop aesthetics with political fervor (pl. 290). And it appeared in the more sanguine work of artists such as George Condo, Donald Baechler, Keith Haring, Jonathan Borofsky, and Robin Winters. Baechler's befuddled but dignified figures are as much pictograms as portraits, and in his portfolio *Increments* (1987), he used the layering of intaglio processes to mark the progression from happy inspiration to formal icon: brisk sugar-lift drawing, geometric bolsters of solid aquatint, hazy splashes of spit-bite. Condo, working with Aldo Crommelynck, indulged the atmospheric aquatint wash that is Crommelynck's trademark, suffusing a goofy clown head with an aura at once idiotic and urbane, an American innocent awash in Parisian sophistication. Haring's first lithographs were made at the time of his renegade drawings in the New York City subways, and reflect the inspired speed of both his hand and his imagination. The phenomenal popularity of his work, from the huge tarpaulin paintings to the Radiant Baby and Barking Dog buttons he gave away in their thousands,

240 George Condo
Clown 1989
Color aquatint
62.9 × 54 cm (24³⁄₄ × 21¹⁄₄ in.)

241 Keith Haring
Untitled #1 1982
Lithograph from the group of six
61 × 91.4 cm (24 × 36 in.)

Opposite:
239 Donald Baechler
Increments 1987
Etching and aquatint from
the set of five
90.1 × 69.8 cm (35¹⁄₂ × 27¹⁄₂ in.)

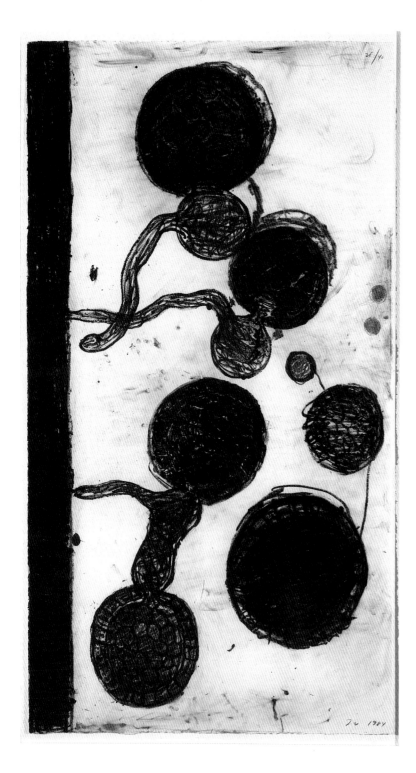

242 Terry Winters
Double Standard 1984
Lithograph
198.1 × 108 cm (78 × 42½ in.)

arose from the qualities that initially drew him to graffiti: "its energy and publicness – the way it gets into the culture and the people."[24]

These quick-witted cartoons are far from the aromatic trance-states of Cucchi or Paladino, but they rely on the same premise: that the most subjective experiences are also archetypal and universal. This premise is inherent in the print, with its dual role as intimate treasure and public spectacle, and it was knowingly exploited by Winters and Borofsky, who used prints to create a ricochet between private and public experience; between massed images and isolated ones; between, essentially, social relationships and individual identities. Winters's *Fiddleback Fleamarket* (1987, pl. 291) is a mounted collection of woodcuts printed on wood veneer, a grid of disconnected scenarios that make no pretence at rational narrative, but whose medium (an image made of wood printed onto wood) suggests an allegorical mother-and-child reunion. Borofsky mixed public and private with punning clarity in the lithograph *Berlin Dream Stamp* (1986), where a dream image is mechanically repeated as if on a sheet of stamps, a single page engineered for separation and dispersal. His portfolio *2740475* (1982) is composed of both tiny intimate etchings ("subconscious doodles"[25] mixed with his ongoing project of counting to infinity)[26] and screenprints of Borofsky's clean-cut, generic man-with-briefcase – both private "brain chatter," as Borofsky calls it, and public life.

A great deal of attention was paid to the resurgence of painting in the early 1980s, though much of the work appearing on canvas was distinctly unpainterly. In place of chromatic nuance and the fluid manipulation of pictorial depth, the painting of Penck, Paladino, or Baechler relied on essentially graphic qualities – bold linearity, high contrast, space that recedes like the stacked planes of a 3-D postcard – exactly the qualities endemic to the print. At the same time, however, another group of artists were deeply engaged in the specific

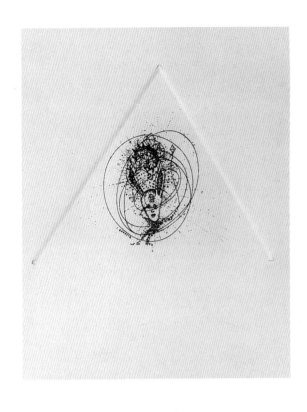

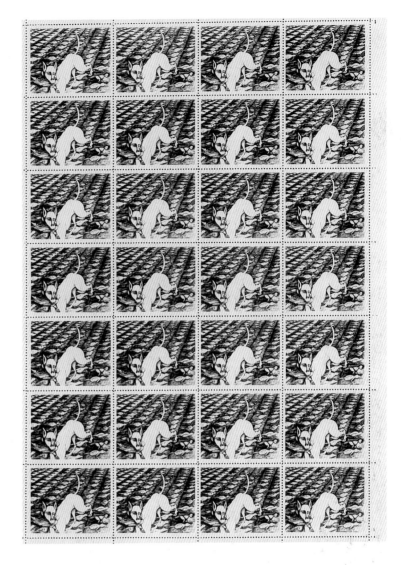

243 Jonathan Borofsky
2740475 1982
Etching from the portfolio of six
etchings and seven screenprints
76 × 56 cm (30 × 22 in.)

244 Jonathan Borofsky
2740475 1982
Screenprint from the portfolio of six
etchings and seven screenprints
76 × 56 cm (30 × 22 in.)

245 Jonathan Borofsky
Berlin Dream Stamp 1986
Black and white photo print with
perforations
33 × 49.5 cm (13 × 19½ in.)

246 Susan Rothenberg
Pinks 1980
Hand-inked woodcut in two colors
48.3 × 68.6 cm (19 × 27 in.)

Opposite:
247 Elizabeth Murray
Untitled State I 1980
Lithograph from a set of five
57.8 × 45.7 cm (22¼ × 18 in.)

248 Elizabeth Murray
Untitled State IV 1980
Lithograph from a set of five
57.8 × 45.7 cm (22¼ × 18 in.)

materiality, history, and struggles of painting. For Susan Rothenberg, Elizabeth Murray, or Terry Winters, the leap to printmaking was not a simple recognition of formal affinities, but a search for particular forms of emphasis, quite different from those of painting.

In Rothenberg's early woodcuts, she used the physical resistance of the block to magnify the sense of an image that has been pulled from within rather than simply planted upon the surface. The nested head-and-hand in *Pinks* (1980) and the horse figure in *Head and Bones* (1980) are both defined and disrupted by flurries of strokes (which Rothenberg calls "weather"). At the same time their constructive/destructive action reflects the essential psychological dichotomies presented in the images: mind versus body, nature versus culture, bridled versus unbridled emotion. *Between the Eyes* (1983–84, pl. 294) is a more sophisticated study in oppositions: male and female, woodcut and lithograph, sharp linear sketches and a diffuse scattering of marks that accumulate into forms like iron filings adjusting to a distant and invisible magnet.[27]

Elizabeth Murray's first professional prints, *Untitled I–V* (1980), were inspired by Picasso's sequential lithographic variations, and constitute five stages in the development of a single stone. As Johns had done in *0–9*, Murray allowed traces of each previous image to remain in its successor, revealing a narrative of decisions, but the development is full of divagations, and no state seems more "final" than any other.

Murray and Rothenberg captured with particular vividness the essential drama of drawing – the visible decision of an artist to take up and emphasize one line while allowing another to fall into insignificance. (Murray said she wanted to expose all the "layers that in a painting get covered up.") In the work of Terry Winters, the similarity between drawings and prints is intentionally played up. Early lithographs such as *Double Standard* explored the medium's textural properties – the powdery, greasy, or liquid qualities of marks –

just as his drawings did (and on more than one occasion Winters made lithographs with a backdrop of thin horizontal lines, as though they were sketched on note-book paper).[27] Later woodcuts elucidated his fascination with organic structure and tactile response, and ceased to resemble casual drawing.

Carroll Dunham intended his prints to be "specifically about printmaking – about marks specific to working on stone."[28] Dunham's early paintings consisted of spectacular priapic abstractions in day-glo colors on panels of wood or wood veneer, but his early lithographs are graphically black and white, and the solidity of the wood panels is replaced with a printerly game of illusion, and false margins into which the composition spills. Jane Kent, who unlike these other artists is primarily a printmaker, "draws" in the discrete accretions of mezzotint, where one can see formal elements – polka-dot patterns, loopy grin, surface texture – laid out as incremental stages of image-making and associative exegesis. Like Winters's burgeoning zygotes or Dunham's flying penises, her images alternate between high-minded biomorphic abstraction and cartoonish figuration; both form and style appear to be in a constant state of mutability.

Such mutability was not just a feature of abstract art, but reflected a broader fascination with ambiguity and narrative, which also erupted in the work of figurative artists such as David Salle and Eric Fischl. Salle's trick of layering contradictory images was easily transferred to print, where such impositions of unrelated plates had existed as printerly accidents for centuries. Fischl took a more complex approach. The six prints of *Year of the Drowned Dog* (1983, pl. 287) can be viewed separately, sequentially, or arranged by the viewer to form a single scene. Each print portrays its own action: an empty beach, a group of sailors looking into the distance, a man in the process of changing his clothes, a boy bent over the body of a dog. It is a formally clever and visually elegant example of Fischl's specialty of rendering the deepest fears

of bourgeois plenitude, depicting a world which craves security in a way that implies profound instability. "Dreadful things often occur in beautiful light," Fischl observes, "which makes the event more intolerable."[29] As in Rothenberg's prints, options are presented but not resolved – the beach is beautiful, the figures are beautiful, the color is beautiful, but the whole is charged with the irrational contingency of life.

Such even-handed examination of opposing options is partly a legacy of Johns, who remained a profoundly influential artist. Johns, however, did not take up the emotional implications of his approach until the 1980s, when he turned from the abstract investigations of cross-hatching to more conspicuously autobiographical content. In *The Seasons*, the title of both a group of four paintings and of eleven separate editions,[30] Johns charts the passage of time with a silhouetted figure (traced from the artist's shadow and that of a young boy) and a complex iconography of art-historical and personal references: earlier works about illusion and double-readings, the Mona Lisa, George Orr pots, the Isenheim altarpiece, the familiar Johnsian device of

250 Jane Kent
Untitled 1990
Aquatint and mezzotint
66 × 55.9 cm (26 × 22 in.)

Opposite:
249 Carroll Dunham
Untitled 1984–85
Two-color lithograph
71 × 48.5 cm (28 × 19 in.)

a hand and arm marking out a semicircle from apex to nadir. The first *Seasons* prints, a set of color etchings from 1987, were jewel-like reductions of the paintings, but in subsequent black-and-white variations Johns reworked both the imagery and the order, confounding the seemingly inexorable progression from cradle to grave. In the horizontal *Seasons* of 1989 the sequence begins (assuming one reads left to right) in Summer and ends in Spring, where the plate has been altered to eradicate the adult silhouette and emphasize the child. At the same time, by printing the plates edge to edge, Johns establishes the stammering repetition of his earlier prints.[51] "My experience of life is that it's very fragmented," Johns has said. "In one place, certain kinds of things occur, and in another place, a different kind of thing occurs. I would like my work to have some vivid indication of those differences."[52]

For better or worse, Johns's work has repeatedly been read as a barometer of the state of contemporary printmaking. In the early 1960s, his persistent repetition of images developed in drawing or painting helped to

ignite the debate over originality; in the 1970s, his cooler abstract prints were seen as indicative of a broad-based retreat into the cerebral. In the 1980s, Johns's prints were most often discussed as a measure of the market. Like all markets, the print market cycles through stages of boom and bust: the boom which accelerated through the 1960s wound down in the early 1970s, only to pick up and collapse again at the end of the decade, a victim of overproduction and a limp economy. There was, however, no precedent for the print boom of the mid-1980s. The popularity of painting and painters' prints, the new internationalism of the market, and trickle-down from the freshly deregulated financial markets conspired to bring a flood of money and interest into contemporary art. Existing printshops expanded, and new printers and publishers flourished on both sides of the Atlantic. Bi-continental publishers, such as Peter Blum, brought European artists to American printers and American artists to European printers, fostering cultural friction to spark new ideas. Print prices skyrocketed (Johns prints traded at the price of a large house), and prints were discussed in terms of "asset appreciation" and "liquidity." One publisher described himself happily as "a market-maker in Johns and Hockney." (As in the previous booms, however, the marketability and visibility of specialist printmakers was barely affected.) All this tended to overshadow the actual achievements of artists and printers. Without doubt, the boom brought with it indiscriminate and unnecessary production, but it also provided the opportunity for younger artists such as Rothenberg and Winters to

in the 1980s, created etchings and drypoints that captured complicated psycho-sexual dramas in simple forms, and she was able to publish for the first time plates made at Atelier 17 in the 1940s.[33] David Hockney, Jim Dine, Sam Francis, and other artists whose work had always found an appreciative audience continued as productive and eloquent printmakers.

Brice Marden discovered a new intensity of purpose with the pivotal series, *Etchings to Rexroth* (1986). Abandoning the rectilinear

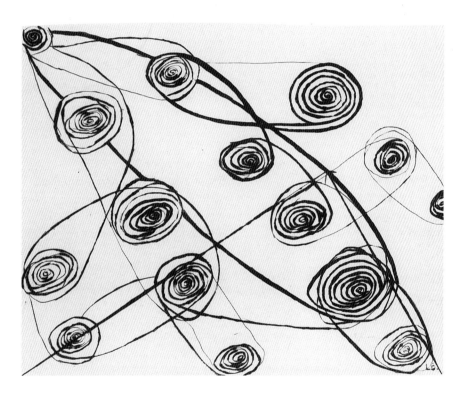

develop into dedicated and accomplished printmakers. And it brought the prints of certain older artists to public attention for the first time.

The Abstract painter Joan Mitchell produced brilliant lithographs of light-filled spaces and expansive gesture in the last decade of her life (pl. 292). The sculptor Louise Bourgeois, whose blend of Surrealism and abstraction finally found a significant audience

structures that had sustained his work for two decades, Marden developed a vocabulary of calligraphic glyphs – marks that, as in certain traditions of Asian calligraphy, were meant as channels for spiritual thought and the energy of nature.[34] The *Rexroth* etchings emphasize manual gesture, but as in his earlier work, carefully map the border where control breaks down and artistic intent gives way to external incident.

254 Richard Diebenkorn
#5 from *Five Aquatints with Drypoint*
1978
Aquatint and drypoint
48.3 × 33.6 cm (19 × 13¼ in.)

255 Richard Diebenkorn
Passage 1 1990
Etching and aquatint
74.9 × 50.8 cm (29½ × 20¼ in.)

Richard Diebenkorn, who had returned to printmaking in 1977 after a twelve-year hiatus, produced some of the most beautiful prints of the decade. The *Five Aquatints with Drypoint* (1978) are indicative of his rich elaborations of intaglio technique. Drawn with water-soluble solutions (soap ground or sugar lift) which could be applied, smudged, and removed with evocative delicacy, the plates were then reworked in the more muscular and resistant drypoint and burnishing – sculptural manipulations of the metal that are felt in the printed image as tough skeletons beneath the seductive fur of aquatint. In the radiant color aquatints that Diebenkorn began in 1980 (pl. 295), this toughness is overlaid with translucent blocks of color. Manipulating that particular quality of etching that Johns described as "the ability of the copper plate to store multiple layers of information,"[35] Diebenkorn was able to reveal a history of decisions, adjustments, and changes of heart, structuring not just an illusion of surfaces retreating, but a record of time passing. These are not technically simple prints, but they are expressive ones, and they serve as a reminder that for many artists – Clemente and Rothenberg as well as Diebenkorn – searching to imbue materials and images with transcendent emotion, printmaking is a vital tool, not in spite of its indirectness, but because of it.

256 Brice Marden
Etchings to Rexroth #9 1986
Etching from the set of 25
50×41 cm (19½ × 16 in.)

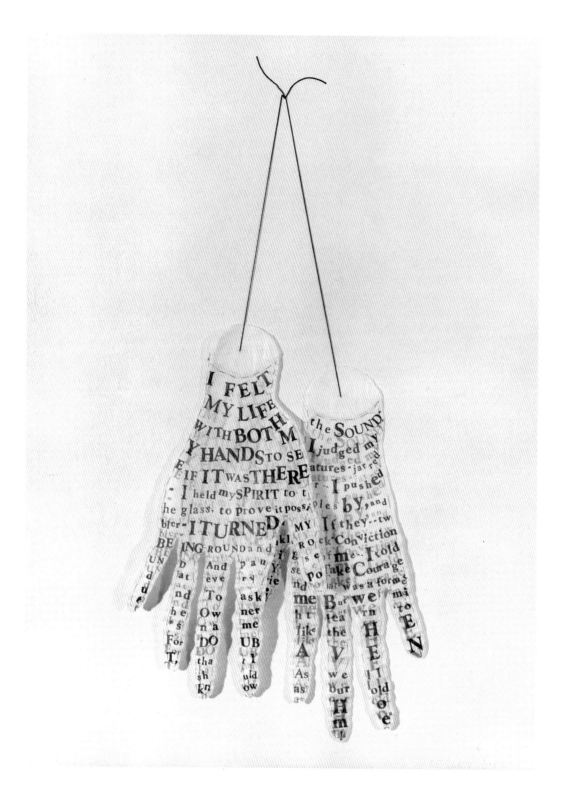

8

THE ETHOS OF THE EDITION

The "original print" is, as its oxymoronic designation suggests, an often uncomfortable compromise between the conventional aesthetic values of hand-facture and the progressive social values of commercial mass production. Revealingly, neither of the two significant theoretical texts on the print address themselves to the original print at all: Ivins dealt with the impact on European history of "exactly repeatable pictorial statements" – an impact that was largely scientific and technological. He had no patience with the muddy, nostalgic use of antiquated media, and saw photography as the ultimate development of reproductive technologies. Benjamin was interested in the ramifications of *mass* reproduction and its dramatic *removal* from "originality." In the 1980s the questions addressed by Ivins and Benjamin about the social and psychological consequences of reproduction became once again a critical influence on art. The omnipresent fictions of advertising, television, movies, and art that had fascinated Pop artists were no longer seen as banal or mindless, but as purposeful tools of power, social control, and individual self-determination. In editions and in unique works, artists employed the materials and devices of commercial image production: utilitarian offset printing, photostats, and photography.

Art photography had for most of the century been isolated from the mainstream of art much the way printmaking was – practiced by dedicated specialists and collected by connoisseurs who valued craftsmanship, rarity, and aesthetic refinement. The invasion of photography into the art of the 1980s paralleled, in some ways, that of printing in the 1960s: artists again purposely stressed the commercial associations that had been played down by specialists, and many who used photography did so while steering clear of the darkroom, relying on technicians to develop and print the work to their specifications.

The use of photography by Rauschenberg, Warhol and Hamilton in the 1960s had been seen as an attack on the hallowed, painterly virtues of "originality, authenticity and presence,"[1] even though the photographic image had remained firmly embedded in the traditional forms of painting and lithography. Subsequent decades saw the steady preferment of the photographic image, and increasingly subtle forms of manipulation: while Hamilton's early screenprints employed radical re-colorations and collage-based displacements of the original photographic material, his 1988 print *The Apprentice Boy* (pl. 296) is itself a photograph – a dye-transfer print of a photographic image that has been restructured using computer software. Digital technology provided Hamilton with a way to manipulate the image while preserving its photographic

257 Lesley Dill
The Poetic Body: Poem Gloves 1992
Letterpress and collage
45.7 × 33.02 cm (18 × 13 in.)

aura of reality found rather than constructed.

Rauschenberg moved from the obfuscatory splashes and scribbles of *Accident* (1963), to the clean and eloquent *Bellini* series of the 1980s (pl. 297), in which luminous photogravures of contemporary urban life and of fifteenth-century painting abut and overlap. Photogravure, a photomechanical intaglio technique in which the soft translucency of aquatint is used in place of a dot screen, allowed Rauschenberg to preserve the broad tonal range of photography, which had been a necessary sacrifice in screenprint, while replacing its often offputting surface with something lush and sensually appealing. An obscure printing specialty in the 1970s, photogravure was offered by virtually every major intaglio printshop by the end of the 1980s, a reflection of photography's new cultural clout.

As photography came to occupy the space of painting both physically and economically, more photographers were invited, as painters had been, to work with print publishers: Joel-Peter Witkin, Lee Friedlander, Thomas Ruff, and Cindy Sherman were among those who released editions through print publishers. Robert Mapplethorpe, for whom the sensuality of surfaces was a crucial photographic subject, used gravure, screenprint, and lithography to explore textures unobtainable in photography. In his gravure series, the pictured surfaces of flower petals, ceramics, and black skin are played off against the actual, tactile surfaces of the images, which were enhanced with screenprint, hand-coloring, and even flocking (pl. 298). While photographs tend to repel the urge to touch, these works actively solicit it within a framework of cultural oppositions: the carnal and the ascetic, the majestic and the debased, the Bacchanal lurking beneath Apollonian formality.

Photography had sneaked into "serious" art in the late 1960s and early 1970s as a means of documenting land works, performance works, and conceptual paradigms. But in addition to those, such as Richard Long or Joseph Beuys,

for whom the photograph was a tangible record of an intangible art, there were others, including John Baldessari and Ger van Elk, who used photography in much the same way that Ruscha used language: toying with its narrative credibility and its apparent literalism in an art poised midway between Pop and Conceptualism. Searching for a form that partook of photography's casual authority, but which was not a photograph *per se*, these artists composed photographic collages, printed photographs on canvases, and shaped photographs into semi-sculptural constructions. Baldessari had made occasional prints in the 1970s, but it was not until the etching portfolio *Black Dice* (1982, pl. 300–308) that he found a way to use print techniques to slip between the photograph and its restructuring. Taking up a method he used in the early 1960s, Baldessari divided an old movie still into nine sections and developed each one as a self-sufficient composition that can be viewed as a print in its own right, or as an "alienated fragment" of the whole.[2] "One of the worst things to happen to photography," Baldessari once said, "is providing cameras with a view-finder"[3] – the implication being that, by allowing the photographer to select a perfectly composed shot, the viewfinder encouraged the fiction that the fragment seen was in fact complete and self-sufficient. In *Black Dice* Baldessari reasserts the fragmentary nature of experience and imposes it, with no small amount of irony, on a scene concocted exclusively for the viewfinder. In his subsequent prints and printed constructions, such as *Fallen Easel* (1988), his operations are both more minimal and more stylized: photographic images[4] are cropped, colored, and masked, marking out networks of glances and implicit action.

Van Elk's reworked photographs, which cite specific art-historical moments (*About the Reality of G. Morandi,* 1972) or compositional conceits (*The Symmetry of Diplomacy,* 1972), investigate the interval between real things and the alterations imposed on them by art. In his screenprinted photographs and photolithographs (pl. 310), the rich irregularity of nature is set against the artificiality of human manipulation with no attempt at a Hamiltonian mingling of photograph and painterly amendments; the silkscreen strokes remain firmly disengaged from the photographic surface, emphasizing difference even when neither is handmade.

Many younger artists had a more politicized suspicion of narrative structures and saw photography as a means to occupy popular or commercial forms and subvert them from within. While fine-art print techniques such as lithography and gravure had none of that mass-media edge, they provided something of an equivalent – a way to occupy the cliché of fine art. Laurie Simmons's *Ventriloquism* (1986, pl. 311) portfolio reproduces, in sober black-and-white photogravure and almost glamorous color photolithography, a world populated by dummies who, like the models in advertisements, cannot speak but are spoken through. Sarah Charlesworth's *Tartan Sets* (1986) presents a lithographed equivalent of the artist's photographic strategy of isolating cultural icons and presenting them as emblems. In most of Charlesworth's work these icons are recognizable photographic clippings isolated in a color field, but the three tartans are both image and field, and the real-world specificity of the photograph has been replaced with an unnatural clarity: the original photos of fabric, replete with errant hairs and lint, were scanned into a computer and digitally reconstructed into a flawless simulation of the tartans' former self.

Print projects not only provided photographers with an opportunity to work with different materials, they were also, ironically, an occasion to explore the proliferation of editions. Though photography is itself a print medium, inherently reproducible, its reproducibility was intentionally played down by artists who wanted their work to be given the same attention as paintings, and who understood that the number of copies of a work is an element of meaning like any other.

The colossal portrait photographs of Clegg & Guttmann, for example, were pointedly unique, purposefully intertwining the masquerades of corporate power and aristocratic patronage. When Clegg & Guttmann did make an edition, it was directed at the populist fantasy of the viewer as a subject manqué, and included not just a large photograph, but chairs that allowed viewers to place themselves "in the picture." Many photographers chose similar approaches to working with print publishers: not abandoning the photograph but encasing it in some more elaborate structure. Thomas Ruff's edition for the art periodical Parkett (pl. 313) placed C-print photographs (negative prints of the night sky) in translucent papers screenprinted with astronomical data – a seemingly instructive object that works best not on the wall, but held in the hand.

The most radical and direct use of photographic reproduction came in the work of Richard Prince and Sherrie Levine, both of whom made art by re-photographing existing images – Marlboro magazine advertisements or masterpieces of modern art – and displaying it as their own work. By isolating and reproducing work that everyone knew had originated elsewhere, they questioned the value and definition of originality in a way that took it out of the confines of the print world and into the broader arena of cultural criticism. To preserve their deviancy, these works were presented as unique rather than in the realm of editions, where such acts of reproduction would have held no novelty. While Prince made books using his re-photographed magazine pictures – bound volumes of unrelenting imagery without context or verbal framing – he only began making prints when he took up handwritten and typeset jokes, which appeared on both canvas and paper. His lithographic portfolio "*(no title)*" of 1991 carries layers of loosely scribbled gag-lines and pseudo-suave cartoons reiterated so incessantly that the humor fades away, leaving just the residue of fear, anger, and anxiety that prompted them.

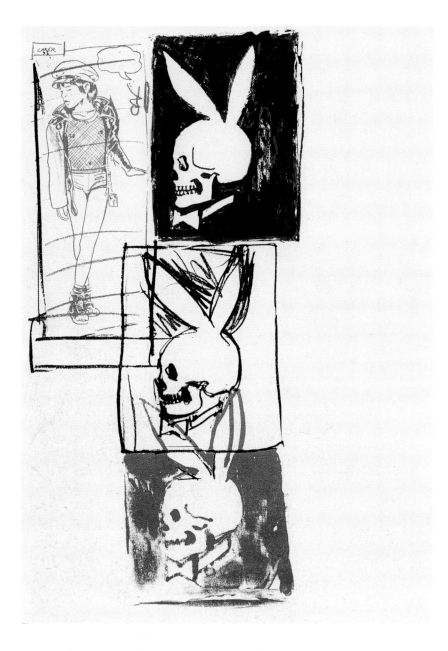

258 Richard Prince
"(no title)" 1991
Lithograph from the set of twelve
38.1 × 27.94 cm (15 × 11 in.)

Opposite:
259 Ed Ruscha
Rooster 1988
Etching
111.8 × 77.5 cm (44 × 30½ in.)

Levine, however, has made several print editions based on her "copies" of other art, all of them carefully structured to emphasize her mediation. The four woodblock prints of *Meltdown* (1989, pl. 314) are based on Levine's 1983 photographs of reproductions of paintings by Monet, Kirchner, Mondrian, and Duchamp (appropriately, his own revision of Leonardo, *LHOOQ*). The photographs were scanned into a computer which divided each image into twelve quadrants and analysed the predominant color value for each; Japanese woodblock prints were made from the computer analysis, resulting in four geometric abstractions that look very much like each other, while looking nothing like the pictures that spawned them – pictures whose aims and intentions are as different as the aims and intentions of Impressionism, Expressionism, Dada, and de Stijl. A madly exaggerated example of the restructuring syntax that all forms of reproduction impose on their subjects, *Meltdown* is not a work of appropriation but of interpretation, albeit interpretation through automation. A large amount of contemporary printmaking, from Hamilton to Johns to Levine, can be seen as a study of the involuntary revelation of content that occurs when a supposedly transparent mechanism of repetition – printing, photography, memory – becomes occluded. The critical question, proposed as much by Levine's prints as by Baldessari's, was one of how to draw connections between things in the world and invest them with personal meaning, when almost all of them have been created by someone else for some other purpose.

Throughout the decade both the "high" culture of art history and classic literature, and the "low" culture of advertising, television, and movies were claimed and recycled by artists who cited the original source and filled it with unexpected or contradictory content. In prints this appeared as both a flirtation with commerce on the one hand, and an exaggerated embrace of small-scale historicism and intimacy on the other. Joan Nelson's lithographs (pl. 315)

picture fragments that appear to derive from
old landscape paintings, preserving the romance
and otherworldliness that have accumulated
around the images over time, but dispensing
with the original compositional content. Matt
Mullican has courted both the industrial and
the nostalgic affiliations of the print in works
that invoke systems of knowledge and
representation. In 1990 Mullican had
magnesium relief plates made from the
illustrated pages of a nineteenth-century
encyclopedia, and then made oilstick rubbings
of the plates, "duplicating," he said, "an
artificial world in much the way a school
does,"[5] and transforming the original optimistic
precision of the illustrations into thickly
pigmented, fuzzy approximations (pl. 316).

One of the older artists whose use of print
media seemed suddenly influential was Ed
Ruscha, who continued to produce etchings
and lithographs in which deadpan literalism is
given a poignant emotional twist. His *World
Series* lithographs presented sketchily drawn,
panoramic cusps of earth that are labeled, like
maps or file drawers, with the locations of
invisible objects and events (pl. 321). In the
silhouettes that followed, tee-pees, picket
fences, lawn jockeys, roosters, and other filmic
emblems of Americana are invested with both
corny nostalgia with quixotic majesty.

Reflecting the perception that reality and
representation were becoming increasingly
confused, words and literature appeared in
printed art not simply as an inspiration
accompanied by imagery, as in the traditional
livre d'artiste, but as the physical stuff of which
images were made: in Lesley Dill's print cycle
The Poetic Body (1992) excerpts from the poems
of Emily Dickinson were printed by letterpress
and used to build physical attributes of a
human figure: ears, eyes, gloves, a dress. In
Goethe Quote (1992, pl. 317) Mike Kelley, an
astute observer of the ways in which people
project themselves onto the inanimate world,
placed a photograph of a fetishistic head in
a matt apparently calligraphed (actually
screenprinted) with Goethe's description of

260 Tim Rollins + K.O.S.
*The Temptation of St Antony XXV –
the Solitaires* 1990
Aquatint with photogravure
and chine collé
41.3 × 29.8 cm (16¼ × 11¹¹⁄₁₆ in.)

261 Tim Rollins + K.O.S.
*The Temptation of St Antony XVI –
the Solitaires* 1990
Aquatint with photogravure
and chine collé
41.3 × 29.8 cm (16¼ × 11¹¹⁄₁₆ in.)

Opposite:
262 Jenny Holzer
Truisms 1978
Poster installation (photostats)

imagination as "a savage who takes delight in grimacing idols." Tim Rollins and K.O.S.'s *Temptation of St Antony* etchings (1990) were printed onto pages from Flaubert's hallucinogenic prose poem. The text is partially obliterated by a host of indistinct forms that, like those of Dubuffet's *Phenomena* lithographs, arose from chemical experimentation as much as from artistic intent, and suggest laboratory stains, viruses, the cloudy masses of X-rays – invisible and terrifying monsters of the modern world. Rollins has said that the pages are not meant to be read, but whether they are read or not, their presence confirms the collaborative genesis of the imagery – not just the joint effort of several artists and printers, but also a response to the external stimulus of the text. And since K.O.S. ("Kids of Survival") is an association of teenagers and young adults from a largely Hispanic area of the South Bronx,[6] their use of the European literary canon also raises issues of the interaction of individual identity with the dominant culture.

Barbara Kruger and Jenny Holzer employed the more dynamic, economic language of mass media to address similar issues of language, representation, and power. Holzer's famous *Truisms* first appeared as offset lithograph posters plastered around New York City in the late 1970s. Printed pages of deadpan epigrams, which she calls her "*Reader's Digest* version of Western and Eastern thought,"[7] the *Truisms*

TWOJE CIAŁO

BROŃ PRAW KOBIET

WALCZ O PRAWO DO ABORCJI

RZĄDAJ EDUKACJI SEKSUALNEJ

TO POLE WALKI

WOMEN IN AMERICA EARN ONLY 2/3 OF WHAT MEN DO.
WOMEN ARTISTS EARN ONLY 1/3 OF WHAT MEN ARTISTS DO.

A PUBLIC SERVICE MESSAGE FROM **GUERILLA GIRLS** CONSCIENCE OF THE ART WORLD

offer a panorama of sentiments that slide from benign to terrifying. Their design and execution was pragmatic, a tool for entering the world that lay beyond gallery walls: "because my work is primarily information," Holzer said, "it [makes] sense to have it in something that could be considered print form, a kind of unlimited multiple. I'm even happy when people steal it because then they do part of the work of distribution for me."[8] Kruger's work takes the guise of snazzy magazine layouts – startling, cropped photographs overlaid by banners of text – but in place of the numbing reiteration of advertising, Kruger attempts to open a rift between image and content.[9] In wall works, T-shirts, matchbooks, print editions (pl. 318), and billboards, she has used this format to prompt a general awareness of the ways in which images are manipulated to further particular economic and social agendas, and also as exhortations to direct political action, as in the *Your Body is a Battleground* abortion rights campaign.

The print's historical function as a tool of political agitation has been often revived since 1960: the late 1960s brought an eruption of anti-war and anti-Nixon editions by artists (of which Warhol's bilious Nixon in *Vote McGovern*, 1972, is one of the most memorable); the 1970s brought a spate of prints and artists' books that inveighed against racism and sexism. One of the most substantive political uses of lithographs and etchings in recent years has been as campaign fund-raisers. At the same time, more utilitarian printing was employed at street level with surprising success, especially when the projected audience was neatly defined by both geographic limitation and cultural homogeneity. The Guerilla Girls, the self-styled "conscience of the art world,"[10] made effective use of the poster throughout the 1980s, plastering the art districts of Manhattan with "public service messages" that detailed sexism and racism within the art world.[11] Other artists took advantage of the increasingly permeable border between art-market and mass-market audiences to propagate works

265 Art Spiegelman
Mickey, Mouse & Maus 1992
Three-color lithograph
from the set *4 Mice*
20.3 × 15.2 cm (8 × 6 in.)

Opposite:
263 Barbara Kruger
Your Body Is a Battleground 1989
Offset lithograph poster
Polish edition

264 Guerilla Girls
Women In America... 1988
Offset lithograph poster

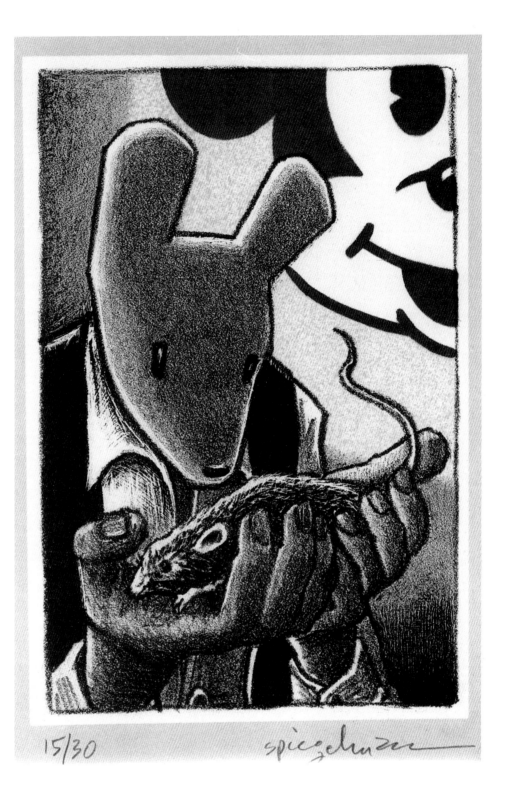

15/30   spiegelman

masses, for the millions of people that read newspapers and magazines," though she has also produced etchings of Piranesian depth and drama.

The prints of Coe and Spiegelman are firmly autographic, giving visible priority to the artist's hand and eye, and recalling the great social realist prints of the 1930s. Despite the high visibility of photographic means in much socially critical art of the 1980s, there was concurrently a strong practice of purposely handmade images that worked with similar techniques of fragmentation, reproduction, and replication. Some printmakers, such as Randy Bolton (pl. 319) and Matthew Lawrence, shattered and restructured print imagery rather than photographic imagery, exploiting and undermining the nostalgia endemic to handmade pictures. Christopher Wool found a way to merge painterly touch and automation, using the venerable wallpaper technique of cut rollers to print unique "all-over" abstractions on canvas and on paper, and using letter stencils to paint dense, confrontative word pieces. Kiki Smith, whose work concentrates on the functions and experiences of the human body, has used printing to evoke mechanical, organic forms of reproduction. In *All Souls* (1988), a unique work built out of multiple sheets of translucent tissue paper, the splotchy gangs of newborns picture both repetition and individuality. Smith undermines what she described as the "deadness" of screenprint – its gift for precise and endless reproduction – at the same time she exploits its capacity to make images that are less personal than drawings. Like Jenny Holzer and Robin Winters, Smith was a member of the loose artists' collective Co-Lab in the early 1980s,[12] where she gained her first exposure to screenprint making T-shirts. In the print editions she has made with ULAE, Smith has used repetition in a vertical rather than horizontal fashion, layering images into dense recombinant forms. While there is always a temptation to read insistent repetition as a deliberate invocation of automation, Smith's

266 Sue Coe
The Selection 1991
Lithograph
76.2 × 55.9 cm (30 × 22 in.)

with a strong social content: Art Spiegelman brought the comic strip into the realm of serious art and literature with *Maus*, his book addressing the Holocaust through a cast of cats and mice who subsequently featured in his concisely dramatic lithographs. Sue Coe has diligently documented the moral turpitude of Capitalism in books, modest and inexpensive photo-etchings, and editorial illustrations for mainstream publications such as the New York Times. Coe says that she is "a print artist," doing all her work "for reproduction, for the

prints hark back to an older, more mystical tradition in which each act of repetition is a new statement of respect and creation.

Smith's emphatically organic images are meant to present an alternative to the anonymity of commercial facture, but elsewhere in the art world commercial

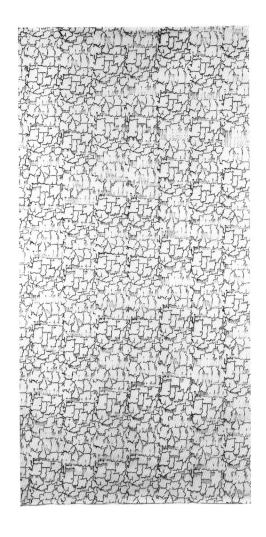

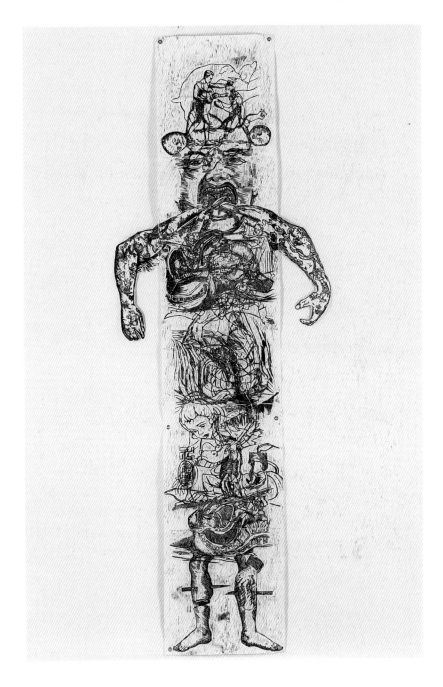

manufacture was exploited as never before. Artists designed works disguised as everyday artifacts, and the consuming public appeared to delight in anything with an artistic pedigree, from paintings to tea kettles. Unlike in the heyday of the multiple, however, the aim was not a radically new type of art object that would define a new era of social and aesthetic

interaction, but the occupation of utilitarian forms, well known and well used in the real world. Sol LeWitt, Roy Lichtenstein, and Richard Tuttle were among dozens who produced editions of functional furniture; Cindy Sherman designed jigsaw puzzles and Limoges porcelain; Jenny Holzer designed stockings; Donald Sultan designed playing

267 Christopher Wool
Untitled 1989
Monotype
187 × 94 cm (73⅛ × 37 in.)

268 Matthew Lawrence
The Cleansing 1992
Woodcut
304.8 × 121.9 cm (120 × 48 in.)

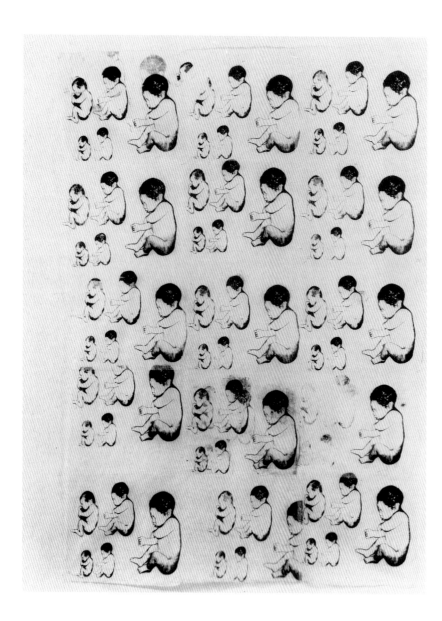

cards; Gerhard Richter, David Hockney, and Barbara Kruger all designed carpeting. For several artists in both Europe and America who came out of conceptual art or performance art backgrounds, and for whom the subtle alteration of familiar life was a preferred modus operandi, "cross-over" editions were especially effective: Sophie Calle's *Tie* (1993, pl. 322) is a wearable tie and, at the same time, illustration, prop, and script for a story in which the narrator takes an interest in an attractive man in an ugly tie, and decides to dress him from head to foot with anonymous Christmas presents.[13]

The musician and visual artist Christian Marclay has based almost all his work on a single household item – the phonograph record – corrupting its use while distilling its iconic presence: in his monotypes, made by inking records on the press bed, the record appears transparent and ethereal – the promise, but not the presence, of sound. General Idea (the collaborative persona of A. A. Bronson, Felix Partz, and Jorge Zontal) described themselves as "parasitically" inhabiting popular forms. Their most widely visible work was *AIDS* (pl. 324), a mutation of Robert Indiana's *LOVE* that, like its model, has appeared in myriad incarnations: posters, paintings, stamps, screenprints, public sculptures, desktop multiples. But while the word LOVE was resonant with possibilities – noun or verb, benevolent gift or Christian injunction – AIDS is inscrutable. Neither advertisement nor protest, but simply bitter allusion, it captured the essentially ambiguous function of the printed logotype, inspiring universal recognition while making no specific claims.

The position of the print, perched on the border between the rarified and the commonplace, made it particularly useful to artists such as Barbara Bloom, Christian Boltanski, and Felix Gonzalez-Torres, whose works invoke the elusive promises and betrayals of possession. Bloom's editions figure both as elements within, and souvenirs of, her installations: as part of *Esprit de l'Escalier* (1988), a multi-room piece about visibility

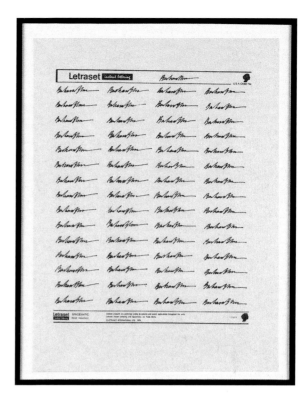

and invisibility, presence and absence, faith and doubt, she exhibited sheets of handmade paper in which photographs of UFOs were reproduced as watermarks. Since watermarks are only visible when lit from behind, the sheet in repose appears completely blank, and the viewer must suspect the presence of the image in order to find it.[14] The *Reign of Narcissism* (1989) appeared to present a neoclassical room, but each and every detail, from books to plaster busts to chair upholstery, was a portrait of the artist. Among the editions it spawned were tea cups with the artist's face impressed into the bottom, chocolates that bore her profile, and letraset sheets of the artist's signature (a witty update of Broodthaers's *La Signature Série 1 Tirage illimité*).

Boltanski, like Bloom, has often invoked the model of the museum – both the way it structures diverse objects to promote particular readings, and the semi-automatic reverence it inspires – and has used the edition rather like the museum gift shop: as a way to bridge the divide between public monuments and private collections. His vast gatherings of anonymous photographs convey the elusiveness of memory, and the ultimate failure of images and objects to retrieve that which has been lost. In the *Gymnasium Chases* (1991) portfolio, Boltanski recast found photographs in photogravure: twenty-four fuzzy black-and-white faces are identified in the frontispiece as members of the graduating class of a Jewish high school in Vienna in 1937. The portfolio constitutes a yearbook of sorts, but the faces have no names, and Boltanski has so blurred the features that the line between the specific and the general has been eradicated. In using gravure Boltanski abandoned the commonness of found photographs, but gained a tactile intensity that provides in a small and subtle way what all the dramatic lighting, enlargement, framing, and structuring lend in his installations – a reverence for the otherwise ordinary.

Gonzalez-Torres has even more directly used the essential properties of the printed

270 Christian Marclay
Untitled 1990
Surface monotype from phonograph records
114.3 × 114.3 cm (45 × 45 in.)

271 Barbara Bloom
Signature Lettraset from *The Reign of Narcissism* 1989
Letraset sheet
33 × 25.4 cm (13 × 10 in.)

Opposite:
269 Kiki Smith
All Souls 1988
Screenprint on fifteen attached sheets
228.6 × 156.2 cm (90 × 60½ in.)

edition to interpret between public and private experience: his "stack" sculptures are reminiscent of Minimalist blocks, but instead of impregnable units, they are temporary consolidations of printed paper sheets that viewers are invited to take away with them. The stacks are in a constant state of flux (the exhibitor is obliged to reprint and restack the sheets to maintain the work's designated dimensions), with each stack occupying both the concise space of sculpture and the dilute space of the edition. The images they carry are usually abstract or photographic – a black bordered white sheet; a photograph of the ocean surface – open subjects on which viewers can impose their own meanings. Virtually all the stack pieces are "unique works," which is to say the stack exists in only one place even while the pieces out of which it is made may exist in an unlimited number of locations. One was produced as an edition with the proviso that the entire edition, all 190 signed and numbered impressions and ten artist's proofs, had to be kept together.[15]

Gonzalez-Torres's work articulates the profound difference between the singular domineering art object, and the multiple, adaptable, social character of the edition, and he reminds us that repetition is possessed of two very different kinds of power – the mass of something in one place, and the more elusive power of an equal mass dispersed to the limits of visibility.

At the cusp of the millennium, printmaking is more thoroughly integrated into artistic practice that would have been imaginable in 1960. The crudest and most venerable methods of printing have been revitalized; new levels of technological subtlety and sophistication have been broached in lithography, intaglio, relief printing, and paper-making; and, most recently, the digital technologies that have transformed commercial printing have become accessible to artists. David Hockney has demonstrated the opportunities for visual invention and easy distribution provided by common office equipment, such as copiers and faxes, and computer hardware and software become daily more sophisticated and less expensive.

For artists, the computer offers new means for manipulating images; new printing technologies for getting those images onto "hard copy;" and new opportunities for distribution. To date it has been the first of these that has been the most significant: the images of Victor Burgin's portfolio *Fiction Film* (1991), an imaginary recreation of a lost film of André Breton's Surrealist novel *Nadja*, were composed and edited on computer, then "outputted" as duotone screenprints. Hamilton's *Apprentice Boy*, Charlesworth's *Tartan Sets*, and Levine's *Meltdown* are all examples of images produced by scanning a photograph into a computer and editing or altering it with software. All these artists, however, reverted to older technologies for printing: photography, lithography, and woodcut. Computer printers offer unparalleled speed and fidelity. But, computer printers have until very recently been limited in both the size and surface quality of their images. The two most common technologies[16] are laser printers, which work essentially like copiers and use powdered toner; and ink-jet printers, which are becoming increasingly sophisticated and varied in the forms of inks they can use, and hence in the surfaces they can produce. (As with photography, of course, ink-jet or laser-printed images are not properly "prints:" there is no fixed matrix, no physical press of paper against a template. But until museums and libraries invent departments for dealing with paper-based works produced by electronic media, such works will probably continue to be categorized as prints or as photographs, depending on the image and the artist.)

The most dramatic potential of the digital domain lies in its capacity for image distribution – traditionally the purview of printing, whether rarified or commercial. On electronic bulletin boards artists can send out images to be viewed on monitors, or printed on paper, by vast numbers of

272 Christian Boltanski
Gymnasium Chases 1991
Portfolio of 24 photogravures and
colophon
52.3 × 41.9 cm (23¼ × 16½ in.)

273 Victor Burgin
Fiction Film 1991
Duotone screenprint with varnish from
the set of nine
76.2 × 95.3 cm (30 × 37½ in.)

people, and the distinction between the image and its physical housing, which has troubled so many people throughout the history of the print, finally achieves a complete separation.

Whether or not such technical opportunities revolutionize art production and consumption in the future (past experience suggests that the market and human habit will succeed in minimizing any impending revolutions), it seems likely that print production will remain a critical part of contemporary art, exploited for its seductive formal properties and epistemological quandaries; for its historical associations with literature, science and art; for its fun-house mirroring of the commercial world; and finally, for its singular ability to suggest both the commonality of a shared culture and the singularity of individual experience. "Everybody knows a different world, and only part of it," Baldessari observed. "We communicate only by chance, as nobody knows the whole, only where overlapping takes place."[17]

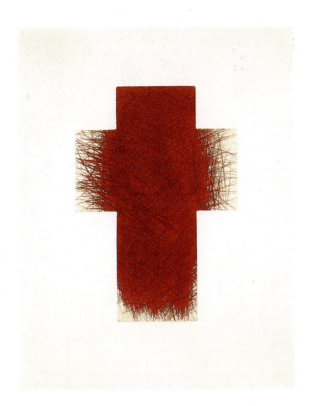

274 Arnulf Rainer
Dornenkreuz 1990–91
Drypoint on shaped plate
65 × 50 cm (25½ × 19¾ in.)

275 Jörg Immendorff
Erbe from the *Cafe Deutschland
Gut* series 1982
Linocut
180 × 230 cm (70¾ × 90½ in.)

276–279 A. R. Penck
Ur End Standart 1972
Four screenprints from the
portfolio of 15
70×70 cm (27½ × 27½ in.) each

280 Per Kirkeby
Untitled 1987
Woodcut
69.5 × 64.5 cm (27⅜ × 25⅜ in.)

281 Francesco Clemente
Untitled 1984
Woodblock print
42.7 × 57.2 cm (16¹³/₁₆ × 22½ in.)

282 Sandro Chia
Figure Looking Out 1983
Etching
75.5 × 56 cm (29¾ × 22 in.)

4/25   J Cla 82

283 Mimmo Paladino
Muto 1985
Etching and aquatint
with fur collage
156.5 × 88 cm (61½ × 34½ in.)

284 Mimmo Paladino
Sirene, Vespero, Poeta Occidentale 1986
Three-part etching, aquatint, and
drypoint with gold leaf
199.5 × 98.5 cm
(78½ × 38¾ in.) each sheet

285 René Daniëls
Lland Stival 1985
Screenprint
115.5 × 85.5 cm (45½ × 33½ in.)

286 Günther Förg
Krefeld Suite 1987
One bronze relief and
four two-color lithographs
Bronze: 77 × 49 × 5 cm (30½ × 19½ in.)
Lithographs: 69 × 53 cm (27½ × 21 in.)

Opposite:
287 Eric Fischl
Year of the Drowned Dog 1983
Set of six color etchings
58.5 × 175.3 cm (23 × 69 in.) overall

288 Wayne Thiebaud
Candy Apples 1987
Woodblock print
59.7 × 61.6 cm (23½ × 24¼ in.)

Opposite:
291 Robin Winters
Fiddleback Fleamarket 1987
Sixteen woodcuts on wood veneer,
mounted and framed
118.1 × 85 cm (46½ × 33½ in.) overall

289 Richard Bosman
Man Overboard 1981
Color woodcut from one block
72.4 × 48.3 cm (28½ × 19 in.)

290 David Wojnarowicz
*Four Elements: Earth, Wind, Fire and
Water* 1990
Color lithograph in two parts
62.9 × 76.2 cm (24¾ × 30 in.) each sheet

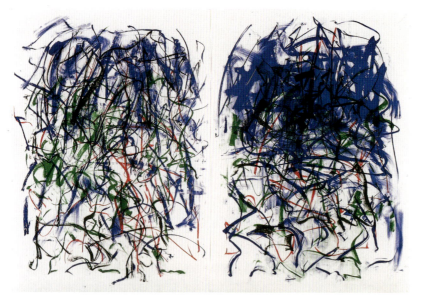

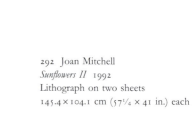

292 Joan Mitchell
Sunflowers II 1992
Lithograph on two sheets
145.4 × 104.1 cm (57¼ × 41 in.) each

293 Sam Francis
Green Buddha 1982
Color lithograph
149.8 × 127 cm (59 × 50 in.)

Opposite:
294 Susan Rothenberg
Between the Eyes 1983–84
Handpainted lithograph and woodcut
with collage
146 × 86.4 cm (57½ × 34 in.)

295 Richard Diebenkorn
Large Bright Blue 1980
Etching and aquatint
101.6 × 66 cm (40 × 26 in.)

296 Richard Hamilton
The Apprentice Boy 1988
Dye-transfer of an electronically
collaged image
64 × 63 cm (25⅛ × 24¾ in.)

297 Robert Rauschenberg
Bellini #4 1988
Color intaglio
152.4 × 97.8 cm (60 × 38½ in.)

298 Robert Mapplethorpe
Ken Moody (Untitled #1) 1985
Color gravure and screenprint
76.9 × 63.2 cm (30¼ × 24⅞ in.)

Opposite:
299 John Baldessari
Fallen Easel 1988
Nine-part color lithograph and
screenprint on paper and photo-
sensitized aluminum
188 × 241.3 cm (74 × 95 in.) overall

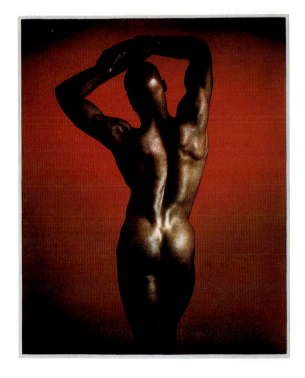

309 John Baldessari
Two Sets (One With Bench) 1989–90
Photogravure with color aquatint
120.6 × 75.6 cm (47½ × 29¾ in.)

310 Ger van Elk
Roquebrun II 1980
Screenprint and photolithograph
56 × 103 cm (22 × 40½ in.)

Opposite:
300–308 John Baldessari
Black Dice 1982
Nine color etchings (aquatint, photo
etching, soft ground and sugar lift) with
accompanying photograph
42 × 50 cm (16½ × 19¾ in.) each

311 Laurie Simmons
Ventriloquism 1986
Color lithograph from the
portfolio of two photogravures
and one photolithograph
85 × 67.6 cm (33½ × 26⅛ in.)

312 Sarah Charlesworth
Tartan Sets 1986
Photolithograph from
the set of three
81.3 × 61 cm (32 × 24 in.)

313 Thomas Ruff
C-Prints 1991
C-prints in translucent
wrappers, screenprinted
both sides with astronomic data
49.5 × 49.5 cm (19½ × 19½ in.)

314 Sherrie Levine
Untitled from *Meltdown* (after
Kirschner) 1989
Woodblock print
92.7 × 65.4 cm (36½ × 25¾ in.)

315 Joan Nelson
Untitled 1990
Lithograph and screenprint
40.6 × 40.6 cm (16 × 16 in.)

316 Matt Mullican
Untitled 1990–91
Wooden cabinet containing 449 oilstick
rubbings from magnesium relief plates,
the plates produced photographically
from a nineteenth-century encyclopedia
Cabinet: 144 × 77.5 cm (56¼ × 30½ in.)
Paper: 66 × 48.3 (26 × 19 in.)
and 66 × 96.5 cm (26 × 38 in.)

Opposite:
317 Mike Kelley
Goethe Quote 1992
Photograph with screenprinted mat
63.5 × 44.5 cm (25 × 17½ in.)

318 Barbara Kruger
Read Between the Lines 1989
Offset lithograph and engraving
63 × 58 cm (25 × 23 in.)

Imagination lies in wait as the most powerful enemy. Naturally raw, and enamored of absurdity it breaks out against all civilizing restraints like a savage who takes delight in grimacing idols.
(Goethe)

story, *n.* **1.** *Archaic.* **a.** A connected narration of past events. **b.** A history. **2. a.** An account of some incident. **b.** A report; statement. **c.** An anecdote, esp. an amusing one. **3.** In literature: **a.** A narrative in 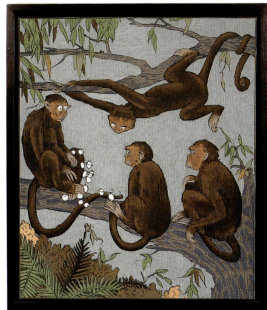 r verse; a tale; esp. narrative less elabo vel. **b.** The plot of a narrative. **4.** *colloq.* A fib; a lie. **5.** *U.S. Journalism.* Any news article. —*v.t.;* **1.** *archaic.* To narrate or describe in story. **2.** To adorn with a story, or scene from history, etc.

319 Randy Bolton
Seeing and Believing 1990
Three-panel screenprint
151.1 × 81.3 cm (59½ × 32 in.)

320 Ed Ruscha
Tails from *Cameo Cuts* 1992
Suite of six two-color lithographs
with title page and colophon
designed by the artist
30.5 × 30.5 cm (12 × 12 in.)

321 Ed Ruscha
World Series: Girls 1982
Color lithograph
63.5 × 86.36 cm (25 × 34 in.)

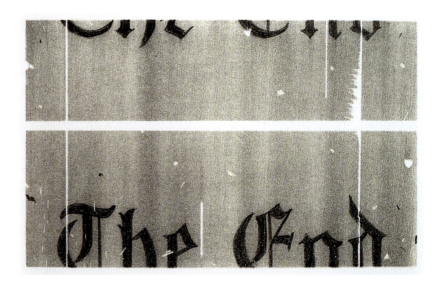

322 Sophie Calle
The Tie 1993
Screenprint on silk tie

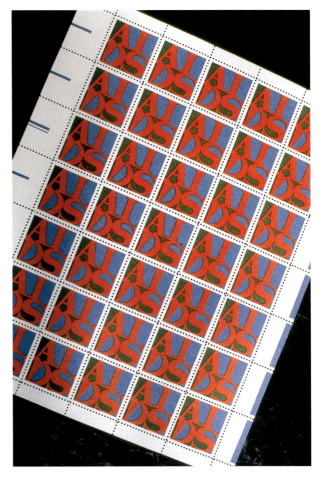

323   Felix Gonzalez-Torres
Untitled (The End) 1990
Stack of offset lithographs
55.9 × 71.1 × 59.7 cm (22 × 28 × 23½ in.)

324   General Idea
AIDS Stamps 1988
Offset lithograph on perforated paper
25.4 × 20.3 cm (10 × 8 in.)

INFORMATION

NOTES

INTRODUCTION

1 William M. Ivins, Jr., *Prints and Visual Communication*, Cambridge, Mass.: Harvard University Press, 1953, reprinted by Cambridge Mass., and London: the M.I.T. Press, 1969. Walter Benjamin, "The Work of Art in the Age of Mechanical Reproduction," in *Illuminations*, edited by Hannah Arendt, translated by Harry Zohn, New York: Schocken Books, 1969.

2 In one telling example of how our lives are structured by print media and their distortions, Chuck Close, who spent many years rendering human faces in fantastically enlarged detail, but in black and white, recalled that growing up in Seattle his only exposure to the great painting of the 1950s was through art magazines which were, at that time, printed in black and white: "I went over these magazines with magnifying glasses. As far as I was concerned, all these de Koonings and stuff were black and white. I had never seen any of the originals."

3 Benjamin, "The Work of Art in the Age of Mechanical Reproduction," in *Illuminations*, p. 224.

4 Pat Gilmour, "Kenneth Tyler: A Collaborator in Context," in *Tyler Graphics Catalogue Raisonné 1974–1985*, Minneapolis: Walker Art Center and New York: Abbeville Press, 1987, p. 10.

5 Lithography, which is based on the resistance of grease and water, was invented in 1798 by the Bavarian Aloys Senefelder (1771–1834).

6 Such definitions have an important function in the legal world, where they can be used to protect the uneducated art consumer from buying Dalí reproductions at exorbitant prices, but they are seldom useful in directing or even following the flow of art.

7 Kenneth Tyler in Stephanie Terenzio and Dorothy C. Belknap, *The Prints of Robert Motherwell*, New York: Hudson Hills Press, 1980 (reprinted 1984, 1991), p. 84.

8 Vincent Katz, "Interview with Peter Blum," *The Print Collector's Newsletter*, Vol. XXI, No. 4, September–October 1990.

1 PAINTERS AND PRINTERS

1 Richard Hamilton, "Glorious Technicolor, Breathtaking Cinemascope and Stereophonic Sound," a lecture presented in 1960 and reprinted in Hamilton, *Collected Words 1953–1982*, London: Thames and Hudson, 1983.

2 This was the blessing and curse of encouragement given to print, especially lithography, by the Works Progress Administration programs in the 1930s. The medium came to be identified with the regionalist and social realist styles that predominated at the time, and therefore held little appeal for artists with other aims.

3 Larry Rivers, "Life Among the Stones," *Location I* (Spring 1963), p. 93, quoted in Elizabeth Armstrong, *First Impressions*, Minneapolis: Walker Art Center, 1989, p. 11.

4 Pollock pulled trial proofs of the prints, but it was not until 1967 that his estate hired Emiliano Sorini to print editions from them.

5 Lanier Graham, *The Spontaneous Gesture: Prints and Books of the Abstract Expressionist Era*, Canberra: the Australian National Gallery, 1987, and Seattle: University of Washington Press, 1989, p. 9.

6 Quoted in P. M. S. Hacker, "The Color Prints of Stanley William Hayter," *Tamarind Papers*, Vol. 14, 1991–92, p. 33.

7 Una Johnson, *Ten Years of American Prints 1947–1956*, Brooklyn: The Brooklyn Museum, 1956. Quoted in Barry Walker, "The Brooklyn Museum's National Print Exhibitions," *The Tamarind Papers* No. 13, 1990, p. 43.

8 Though few important artists were to follow closely in the steps of Lasansky and Peterdi, dedicating themselves exclusively to intricate intaglio techniques, the establishment of printmaking as a serious discipline within art schools and universities had its effect: many artists whose fame would rest in other media, but who would make important contributions to the art of the print, received their first exposure to printmaking in school. Among the many who passed through Peterdi's classroom were Brice Marden and Chuck Close, both of whom would later help to restore the vitality and reputation of intaglio media in the 1970s.

9 Robert Motherwell in John J. McKendry, Diane Kelder, and Robert Motherwell, *Robert Motherwell's A la pintura: The Genesis of a Book*, New York: The Metropolitan Museum of Art, 1972. Quoted in Stephanie Terenzio and Dorothy C. Belknap, *The Prints of Robert Motherwell,* New York: Hudson Hills Press and The American Federation of Arts, 1991, p. 53.

10 Once stone lithography was overtaken in commercial shops by aluminum plates, it became common practice to use lithographic stones as paving stones, edging stones, or porch buttresses.

11 In 1970 the Ford Foundation grant that had supported Tamarind expired and Tamarind Lithography Workshop was transformed into the Tamarind Institute, a division of the College of Fine Arts at the University of New Mexico in Albuquerque. It continues most of the same programs, and has added a contract publishing section.

12 In addition to the commercial shops founded by Tamarind master printers (Gemini GEL, Tyler Graphics, Hollander's, Solo Press, Derrière l'Etoile, Cirrus, Landfall, and others), the not-for-profit structure of Tamarind has become a model for community and academic printshops in which artists are invited for residencies that act as training grounds for aspiring printers. At the same time they produce saleable editions which are divided between printshop and artist. (The standard arrangement with professional publishers is that the profits are split with the artist, but the product remains in the hands of the publisher).

13 June Wayne, "To Restore the Art of the Lithograph in the United States," 1959, Tamarind Archive File No. 16-717. Quoted in Lucinda H. Gedeon, *Tamarind: From Los Angeles to Albuquerque*, Los Angeles: Grunewald Center for the Graphic Arts, 1985.

14 Robert Motherwell, in Terenzio and Belknap, *The Prints of Robert Motherwell*, p. 35.

15 The friends were George Miyasaki and Nathan Oliveira, both artist-lithographers.

16 There is a distinction between the way the terms *livre d'artiste* and 'artist's book' are used: the former usually signifies a fairly luxurious volume combining an artist's images and a writer's text (Motherwell's *A la pintura* with poems by Raphael Alberti, or Jasper Johns' and Samuel Beckett's *Foirades/Fizzles*). The latter has come to refer to less precious books, often produced by offset lithography, xerox, rubberstamp, or other cheap means, whose entire structure is directed by the artist's concept. (Sol LeWitt, Dieter Roth, etc.).

17 The first plates for *21 Etchings and Poems* were printed as early as 1955, but the book was not released until 1960 because there was no market interest. See Lanier Graham, "The Rise of the *Livre d'Artiste* in America: Reflections on *21 Etchings and Poems* and the Early 1960s," *The Tamarind Papers*, Vol. 13, 1990.

18 The artist/writer pairings were: Pierre Alechinsky and Dotremont; Fred Becker and T. Weiss; Ben-Zion and David Ignatow;

Letterio Calapai and William Carlos Williams; Willem de Kooning and Harold Rosenberg; Peter Grippe and Dylan Thomas; Salvador Grippi and Richard Wilbur; Stanley William Hayter and Jaques-Henry Lévesque; Franz Kline and Frank O'Hara; Jacques Lipchitz and Hans Sahl; Enzio Martinelli and Horace Gregory; Ben Nicholson and Herbert Read; I. Rice Pereira and George Reavey; Helen Phillips and André Verdet; André Racz and Thomas Merton; Kurt Roesch and Alastair Reid; Attilio Salemme and Morris Weisenthal; Louis Schanker and Harold Norse; Karl Schrag and David Lougee; Esteban Vicente and Peter Viereck; Adja Yunkers and Theodore Roetchke. See Lanier Graham, "The Rise of the Livre d'Artiste in America…".

19 Graham, *The Spontaneous Gesture*, p. 21.

20 Tatyana Grosman in Terenzio and Belknap, *The Prints of Robert Motherwell*, p. 52.

21 In addition to two uneditioned prints done at Atelier 17 in 1943–44, there were three editions produced at ULAE between 1961 and 1963, as well as a silkscreen reproduction of a collage, included in the *Ten Works × Ten Painters* portfolio in 1964. But these were sporadic events, and seemingly, not entirely satisfactory to Motherwell.

22 Motherwell, in *Robert Motherwell's À la pintura: The Genesis of a Book*. Quoted in Terenzio and Belknap, *The Prints of Robert Motherwell*, p. 65.

23 Barnett Newman, preface to *18 Cantos*, West Islip: Universal Limited Art Editions, 1964.

24 Richard Diebenkorn began working with Kathan Brown in the midst of a lull in his painting activity that followed his 1963 retrospective at the M. H. DeYoung Museum, and the death in 1960 of his close friend David Park. Robert Motherwell began working with Irwin Hollander during a depression following his 1965 retrospective at the Museum of Modern Art: "in the silence of my studio after it was over, my work went badly. I was overcome by an almost metaphysical loneliness. By chance, I came across a master printer… I had always instinctively loved working on paper, but it was the camaraderie of the artist-printer relationship that tilted the scale definitively, a phenomenon that I think often happens when artists grow older and more isolated." (Motherwell in "A Special Genius: Works on Paper," *Bulletin of Rhode Island School of Design*, Winter 1977, pp. 20–34.)

25 Hugh M. Davies, *The Prints of Barnett Newman*, New York: The Barnett Newman Foundation, 1983, p. 13.

26 The original function of margins was to give the printer something to hold onto. In the nineteenth century it became a popular location for decorative embellishment, and in the twentieth it became home to the artist's signature and the edition number. Until recently, it was common practice for collectors or dealers to crop print margins to fit a print into a handy drawer or frame, and only in the 1960s did it become popular to float prints in a frame, with the margins – and signature – as prominent as the printed image.

27 When Robert Motherwell, who had worked in French shops, drew his first stone at ULAE he requested that a printer come and clean up the margins for him. Grosman told him "It's your stone, your margins," out of a conviction that the margin is an integral part of the image, and only definable by the artist. See Esther Sparks, *Universal Limited Art Editions: A History and Catalogue: The First Twenty-five Years*, Chicago: The Art Institute of Chicago, and New York: Harry N. Abrams, Inc., 1989, p. 166.

28 Newman, preface to *18 Cantos*.

29 *Ibid.*

30 Robert Hughes, *Frank Stella: the Swan Engravings*, Fort Worth: the Fort Worth Art Museum, 1984, p. 6.

31 Quoted in Graham, *The Spontaneous Gesture*, p. 24.

32 Francis in Sam Francis and George Page, *Sam Francis: The Litho Shop, 1970–1979*, New York: Brooke Alexander Gallery, 1979.

33 E. C. Goosen, *Helen Frankenthaler*, New York: the Whitney Museum of American Art, 1969. Quoted in Sparks, *Universal Limited Art Editions: A History and Catalogue*, p. 84.

34 The Hayter tradition emphasized color, line, and heavily textured surfaces; etchers like Kathan Brown preferred the rich tonalities of black and white, employing aquatint, which was not used by Hayter, and relying on careful hand-wiping of the plate.

35 Brown in Nancy Tousley, *Prints: Bochner, LeWitt, Mangold, Marden, Martin, Renouf, Rockburne, Ryman*, Toronto: Art Gallery of Ontario, 1975, p. 58.

36 *Ibid.*

37 Riva Castleman, *Prints of the Twentieth Century*, New York: the Museum of Modern Art and Oxford University Press, 1976, p. 134.

38 How the role of these technicians was treated has changed with history: in earlier centuries it was often explicit, with each worker signing his own work. In our own century, the preoccupation with originality and the artist's hand has meant that the role of such technicians is often covert.

39 These terms, like "Abstract Expressionism" or "Pop," do not signify a formal movement but a rather loose set of stylistic and aesthetic affinities.

40 Graham, *The Spontaneous Gesture*, p. 7.

41 Antoni Tàpies, "A Statement on Art," in Achille Bonita Oliva, *Antoni Tàpies: Ossevatore/partecipante, depinti e sculture* Rome: Cleto Polcina Edizioni, no page numbers, 1988. Quoted in Deborah Wye, *Antoni Tàpies in Print*, New York: the Museum of Modern Art, 1991, p. 51.

42 *Karel Appel: Works on Paper*, New York: Abbeville Press, 1980.

43 Graham, *The Spontaneous Gesture*, p. 15.

44 Jean Dubuffet, "Notes on Lithographs by Transfers of Assemblages, and on the 'Phenomena' Series," in Kneeland McNulty, *The Lithographs of Jean Dubuffet*, Philadelphia: The Philadelphia Museum of Art, 1965. No page numbers. All subsequent Dubuffet quotes taken from this source.

2 JOHNS AND RAUSCHENBERG

1 Harold Rosenberg, "The American Action Painters," *Art News* 51, December 1952, p. 23. Quoted in Barbara Haskell, *Blam! The Explosion of Pop, Minimalism, and Performance, 1958–1964*, New York: The Whitney Museum of American Art in association with W. W. Norton & Co., 1984, p. 13.

2 "He did a beautiful job," Rauschenberg said, "but I consider it my print." Quoted in Dorothy Gees Seckler, "The Artist Speaks: Robert Rauschenberg," *Art in America* 54, May–June 1966, p. 81.

3 Rauschenberg in Edward A. Foster, *Robert Rauschenberg: Prints 1948/70*, Minneapolis: Minneapolis Institute of Arts, 1970, no page numbers.

4 *Merger* (1962) was intended to be collaboration between Rauschenberg, Jim Dine, and the Swiss sculptor Jean Tinguely, in conjunction with the "Dynamische Labyrinte" exhibition at the Stedelijk Museum in Amsterdam. The proposed merger of artistic talent never materialized (either at ULAE or in Amsterdam), and the print is somewhat airier than Rauschenberg's usual compositions.

5 Quoted in Calvin Tompkins, *The Bride and the Bachelors*, New York: The Viking Press, 1962, pp. 193–94.

6 Robert Rauschenberg in Esther Sparks, *Universal Limited Art Editions: A History and Catalogue: The First Twenty-Five Years*, Chicago: the Art Institute of Chicago, and New York: Harry N. Abrams, Inc., 1989, p. 222.

7 *Accident* won the Grand Prize at the 1963 International Print Exhibition in Ljubljana. In the 1990s, when the international print market is a substantial institutional body in its own right, it is difficult to understand the importance of such juried exhibitions, but at a time when prints were virtually invisible as a medium, they provided the only global

network for exhibition. And such shows do not always favor the arcane or the reactionary – Rauschenberg won in Ljubljana the year *before* he took the prize at the Venice Biennale.

8   This was not an unprecedented occurrence: the stone for *License* (1962) also broke, and pieces were re-used in *Stuntman I, II,* and *III* (all 1962).

9   Quoted in Andrew Forge, *Rauschenberg*, New York: Harry N. Abrams, 1972, p. 227.

10 Quoted in Calvin Tompkins, "The Sistine on Broadway," in Roni Feinstein, *Rauschenberg: the Silkscreen Paintings 1962–64*, New York: The Whitney Museum of American Art and Boston, Toronto, London: Bulfinch Press, Little, Brown and Company, 1990, p. 14.

11 John Cage, *Silence: Lectures and Writings*, Middletown, Connecticut: Wesleyan University Press, 1961. Quoted in Calvin Tompkins, *Off the Wall: Robert Rauschenberg and the Art World of Our Time*, New York: Penguin Books, 1980, p.69.

12 Mark Rothko and Adolph Gottlieb, letter to the *New York Times*, 1943, quoted in Alice Goldfarb Marquis, *The Art Biz*, Chicago: Contemporary Books, 1991, p. 50.

13 The art historian E. H. Gombrich, in *Art and Illusion*, drew attention to the inevitable role of the spectator in determining the meaning of a work of art, and Richard Field has pointed out the degree to which Gombrich acted as a bellwether of upcoming changes in the attitudes of artists.

14 Marcel Duchamp, quoted in Otto Hahn, "Passport No. G255300," *Art and Artists I*, No. 4, July 1966, p. 10. Cited in John L. Tancock, *Multiples: the First Decade*, Philadelphia: The Philadelphia Museum of Art, 1971, no page numbers.

15 Richard Hamilton, "The Pasadena Retrospective," *Collected Words*, London: Thames and Hudson, 1982, p. 199.

16 The proper title is *La Mariée mise à nu par ses célibataires, même (Boîte verte)*.

17 Johns in Grace Glueck, "The 20th-Century Artists Most Admired by Other Artists," *Art News* 76, November 1977, pp. 87–89. Quoted in Riva Castleman, *Jasper Johns: A Print Retrospective*, New York: the Museum of Modern Art, 1986, p. 14.

18 Johns in Christian Geelhaar, *Jasper Johns Working Proofs*, New York and London: Petersburg Press, 1980, p. 48.

19 The obvious precedent for this process was Picasso's famous *Bull* series of 1945–46, though according to Sparks, Johns was unaware of the Picasso work.

20 Johns further elaborated the sequential variation by printing three different editions of each stage of the stone. One was printed in black on cream paper, one in gray on gray paper, and one in a different color for each

number, on white paper. Finally, in each numbered member of the edition of ten, the numeral in the bottom set that corresponded to the number of the edition was overprinted. (Thus in the impression 3/10, the numeral three was overprinted).

21 Johns in the film *Hanafuda/Jasper Johns*, directed and produced by Katrina Martin, 1980.

22 Johns in Geelhaar, *Jasper Johns Working Proofs*, p. 38.

23 Kenneth Tyler in Michael Knigen and Murray Zimiles, *The Contemporary Lithographic Workshop Around the World*, New York: Van Nostrand Reinhold, 1974, p. 75.

24 *Autobiography*, done the previous year, was larger, but was considered a billboard rather than a lithograph.

25 Lawrence Alloway, *The Graphic Art of Robert Rauschenberg*, Philadelphia: the Institute of Contemporary Art, University of Pennsylvania, 1970.

26 There was a second state in shades of charcoal black.

27 The interdependence of the panels is accentuated in the print by the fact that each sheet is embossed with the image of the sheet to the left. The first panels bears the stamp of the last one, suggesting a cyclical return. In the grisaille version of the print, the margins of each sheet are printed with a strip of the adjacent pattern.

28 Johns had begun to work seriously in screenprint in 1972 and, disregarding the uses to which other contemporary artists had put the medium – mainly photographic manipulation and bold, clean-edged design – Johns chose to paint directly on the screens. The practice of painting directly on the screen had been the first validated, "fine art" method of screenprinting, adopted in the 1930s. Because of the directness of the artist's involvement, it was held to be artistic and original, and was dubbed "serigraphy" in an attempt to distinguish between "the free creative work of artists and commercial products for signs and advertisements." (Letter from print curator Carl Zigrosser to the editor of the *Springfield Union and Republican*, 21 April 1940, quoted in Pat Gilmour, *Kelpra Studio: An Exhibition to Commemorate the Rose and Chris Prater Gift*, London: Tate Gallery, 1980, p. 15.)

29 Johns in Geelhaar, *Jasper Johns Working Proofs*, p. 37.

30 Johns in *Hanafuda/Jasper Johns*.

31 Johns in *Hanafuda/Jasper Johns*.

3   POP AND PRINT

1   Published by the Italian art dealer and Duchamp expert Arturo Schwartz, working with Billy Klüver, a Bell Laboratories engineer and curator familiar with the New York scene.

2   Claes Oldenburg in *Environments, Situations, Spaces*, New York: Martha Jackson Gallery, 1961. Quoted in Elizabeth Armstrong, *First Impressions: Early Prints by Forty-six Contemporary Artists*, New York: Hudson Hills Press and Minneapolis: Walker Art Center, 1989, p. 34.

3   Claes Oldenburg, interview with Judith Goldman, "Sort of a Commercial for Objects," *The Print Collector's Newsletter*, Vol. II, No. 6, January–February 1972, p. 118.

4   Oldenburg in Gene Baro, *Claes Oldenburg: Drawings and Prints*, London and New York: Chelsea House, 1969, p. 15.

5   Allan Kaprow, "Happenings in the New York Scene," *Art News* 60, May 1961, quoted in Barbara Haskell, *Blam! The Explosion of Pop, Minimalism, and Performance 1958–1964*, Whitney Museum of American Art in association with W. W. Norton & Co., 1984, p. 46.

6   Claes Oldenburg, *Multiples in Retrospect 1964–1990*, New York: Rizzoli, 1991, p. 34.

7   Dine in Thomas Krens (ed.), *Jim Dine Prints: 1970–1977*. New York: Harper and Row in association with Williams College, 1977.

8   "I don't consider my involvement with the avant-garde invalid – only immature." Dine in Krens, *Jim Dine Prints*, p. 16.

9   Oldenburg, interview with Goldman, *The Print Collector's Newsletter*, p. 118.

10 Oldenburg in Barbara Rose, *Claes Oldenburg*, New York: The Museum of Modern Art, and Greenwich: New York Graphic Society, 1970. Quoted in Barbara Haskell, *Blam!*, p. 83.

11 Lichtenstein in Haskell, *Blam!*, p. 77.

12 Ed Ruscha in John Coplans, "Concerning 'Various Small Fires,' Edward Ruscha Discusses His Perplexing Publications," *Artforum 3*, February 1965, p. 26.

13 The organic screenprints are an outgrowth of the *Stains* portfolio of 1969 in which various substances were smeared on paper, but not incorporated as elements of larger images.

14 Esther Sparks, *Universal Limited Art Editions: A History and Catalogue: the First Twenty-Five Years*, Chicago: The Art Institute of Chicago and New York: Harry N. Abrams, Inc., 1989, p. 257.

15 Warhol, quoted in Gene Swenson, "What Is Pop Art?, Part I: Jim Dine, Robert Indiana, Roy Lichtenstein, Andy Warhol." *Art News*, 62, November 1963, p. 26.

16 Lichtenstein in John Coplans, "Talking with Roy Lichtenstein," *Artforum 5*, May 1967, p. 34, reprinted in Haskell, *Blam!*, p. 81.

17 The three volumes were all published in 1965 by Original Editions (New York). Each included a work by Allan d'Arcangelo, Allen Jones, Gerald Laing, Roy Lichtenstein, Peter

Phillips, Mel Ramos, James Rosenquist, Andy Warhol, John Wesley, and Tom Wesselmann.

18 The master was made by filling the stitched canvas of a soft sculpture with plaster and allowing it to set before peeling the canvas away.

19 Claes Oldenburg, *Multiples in Retrospect, 1964–1990*, New York: Rizzoli, 1991, p. 36.

20 Oldenburg in Bruce Glaser, "Oldenburg, Lichtenstein, Warhol: A Discussion," *Artforum 4*, February 1966, pp. 20–24.

21 Ed Ruscha in Howardena Pindell, "Words with Ruscha," *The Print Collector's Newsletter*, January–February 1973, p. 125.

22 Warhol in Gerard Malanga, "A Conversation with Andy Warhol", *The Print Collector's Newsletter* 1, January–February 1971. Apparently the distinction was unclear to others as well. Warhol's first appearance in an art publication was in the "New Talent USA" issue of *Art In America* 50, 1962, where one of his paintings (ironically *not* one that was screenprinted) appeared in the printmaking section. There were screenprints on paper produced at the Factory, though never run in regular editions.

23 Warhol, quoted in Andy Warhol and Pat Hackett, *POPism: The Warhol 60s*, New York: Harcourt Brace Jovanovich, 1980, p. 22.

24 The single exception was *Cooking Pot* (1962), a photo-engraved reproduction of a newspaper advertisement, made for *The International Avant-Garde*.

25 Calvin Tompkins, *Off the Wall: Robert Rauschenberg and the Art World of Our Time* New York: Penguin Books, 1981, p. 260.

26 Marco Livingstone, "Do It Yourself: Notes on Warhol's Techniques," in *Andy Warhol: A Retrospective*. New York: the Museum of Modern Art, p. 74.

27 John Coplans, *Andy Warhol*, Greenwich Conn.: New York Graphics Society, 1970, p. 51.

28 Warhol's attitude, radical for its time, echoed much earlier opinions about what mattered in a work of art. As Robert Rosenblum noted, Jacques-Louis David would exhibit two copies of the same painting together, and freely employed assistants in copying, since "the image, being his invention, mattered more than the execution." In a more printerly example, in the eighteenth century, the responsibilities for drawing, engraving, border design of a single image would often be distributed among different artisans in order to bring about a more polished image, in which any single artist's hand is effectively hidden.

29 Joe Tilson, in conversation with the author, February 1993.

30 Hamilton has written extensively on Duchamp, has produced a typographic rendering of "the Green Box", has replicated *The Large Glass* from Duchamp's working Notes, and collaborated on a multiple reproducing a section of the Large Glass, *The Occulist Witness*.

31 Richard Hamilton, *Collected Words*, London: Thames and Hudson, 1982, p. 90.

32 Hamilton, *Collected Words*, p. 88.

33 Eduardo Paolozzi in Christopher Finch, "Spotlight on Moonstrips Empire News – Eduardo Paolozzi's dialogue with the mass media," *Vogue* 1967, quoted in Pat Gilmour, Silvie Turner, *Kelpra Studio, An Exhibition to Commemorate the Rose and Chris Prater Gift*, London: Tate Gallery, 1980, p. 28.

34 *The ICA Print Portfolio* consisted of works by: Gillian Ayres, Peter Blake, Derek Boshier, Patrick Caulfield, Bernard Cohen, Harold Cohen, Robyn Denny, Richard Hamilton, Adrian Heath, David Hockney, Howard Hodgkin, Gordon House, Patrick Hughes, Gunther Irwin, Allen Jones, R. B. Kitaj, Henry Mundy, Eduardo Paolozzi, Victor Pasmore, Peter Phillips, Bridget Riley, Richard Smith, Joe Tilson, and William Turnbull.

35 Bryan Robertson, introduction to *Patrick Caulfield Prints 1964–81*, London: Waddington Galleries, 1981, no page numbers.

36 Walter Benjamin, "A Short History of Photography," *Screen*, Spring 1980.

37 Quoted in Gilmour and Turner, *Kelpra Studios*, p. 37.

38 Tilson, in conversation with Pat Gilmour (Tate Gallery Archive 4, November 1975), quote in Gilmour and Turner, *Kelpra Studios*, p. 34.

39 Pat Gilmour, *Joe Tilson: Graphics* (exhibition catalogue), Vancouver: The Vancouver Art Gallery, 1979, no page numbers.

40 Werner Haftman, *R. B. Kitaj: Complete Graphics 1963–69*, Berlin: Galerie Mikro, 1969, no page numbers.

41 Christopher Prater, "Experiment in Screenprinting," *Studio International*, December 1967, p. 293.

42 R. B. Kitaj and George MacBeth in dialogue, *Art Monthly*, April 1977, quoted in Gilmour and Turner, *Kelpra Studios*, p. 34.

43 Wood engraving was used instead of lithography because the wood relief block could be printed along side lead type, on the same press at the same time. Lithography was far quicker for the artist, but required separate presses.

44 Tilson, in Gilmour, *Joe Tilson/Graphics*, no page numbers.

45 David Hockney in Ruth E. Fine. *Gemini GEL: Art and Collaboration*. Washington: National Gallery of Art, and New York: Abbeville Press, 1984, p. 146.

46 Marco Livingstone, *David Hockney Etchings and Lithographs*, London: Waddington Graphics and Thames and Hudson, 1988, no page numbers.

47 Quoted in A. Hyatt Mayor, *Prints and People*, Princeton: Princeton University Press, 1971, p. 550.

48 Stage design is one of Hockney's great loves. See Martin Friedman, *Hockney Paints the Stage*, London: Thames and Hudson, 1983, reprinted 1985.

49 Bruce Nauman, interview with Chris Cordes, in *Bruce Nauman Prints 1970–89*, New York: Castelli Graphics and Lorence Monk Gallery and Chicago: Donald Young Gallery, 1989, p. 25.

50 Hamilton in Richard Field, *The Prints of Richard Hamilton*, Middletown, Conn.: Wesleyan University, Davison Art Center, 1973, p. 42.

51 The wounded student captured in Hamilton's photograph, Dean Kahler, was not killed but paralyzed.

52 Hamilton, *Collected Words*, p. 94.

53 Hamilton, *Collected Words*, p. 96.

4 MULTIPLICITY

1 June Wayne, "Broken Stones and Whooping Cranes: Thoughts of a Wilful Artist," *The Tamarind Papers*, Vol. 13, 1990, p. 22.

2 Laszlo Moholy-Nagy, "The Naive Desire for the Unique," *Art and Artists IV*, no. 3, June 1969, p. 30. Quoted in John L. Tancock, *Multiples: the First Decade*, Philadelphia: Philadelphia Museum of Art, 1971, no page numbers.

3 In 1922 Moholy-Nagy made five "paintings" by telephone order from a sign factory, using the factory's color chart and a piece of graph-paper as reference.

4 Karl Gerstner in *1→∞: New Multiple Art*, London: Whitechapel Art Gallery and the Arts Council of Great Britain, 1970, p. 5.

5 Tyler and Albers did meet before beginning the project.

6 Quoted in Pat Gilmour, review of Riva Castleman: American Impressions, *The Tamarind Papers*, Vol. 9, No. 1, Spring 1986.

7 Victor Vasarély, "Homage to Alexandre Dauvillier," *DATA Directions in Art, Theory and Aesthetics*, Anthony Hill (ed.), London, 1968, p.104. Cited in John L. Tancock, *Multiples: the First Decade*, Philadelphia Museum of Art, 1971.

8 Victor Vasarély, "Homage to Alexandre Dauvillier, cited in Tancock *Multiples*.

9 Pol Bury, *du Point à la Ligne/van Punt tot Lijn*, Brussels: Musées Royeaux des Beaux-Arts de Belgique/Koninklijke Musea voor Schone Kunsten van Belgie, 1976, no page numbers.

10 Pol Bury, *du Point à la Ligne/van Punt tot Lijn*.

11 George Maciunas, "Diagram of Historical Development of Fluxus and Other 4 Dimensional, Aural, Optic, Olfactory, Epithelial and Tactile Art Forms," 1973, cited in

Elizabeth Armstrong, "Fluxus and the Museum," *In the Spirit of Fluxus*, Minneapolis: Walker Art Center, 1993, p. 16.

12 Simon Anderson, "Fluxus Publicus," *In the Spirit of Fluxus*, p. 56,

13 *Dieter Roth Collected Works, Vol 40: Books and Graphics (Part 2), from 1971 to 1979*, Stuttgart and London: Hansjörg Mayer and Dieter Roth, 1979.

14 EAT ART Gallery was established by Daniel Spoerri as part of his Düsseldorf restaurant.

15 Gerhard Richter in interview with Dorothea Dietrich, *The Print Collector's Newsletter,* Vol. XVI, No. 4, September–October, 1985, p. 131.

16 Richard Hamilton, "The Books of Diter Rot," *Typographica 3*, June 1961, p. 29.

17 Pierre Restany, quoted in Edward Lucie-Smith, *Movements in Art Since 1945*, London: Thames and Hudson, 1984, p. 128.

18 Tancock, *Multiples*, no page numbers.

19 Konrad Lueg later became well known as the Düsseldorf art dealer Konrad Fischer.

20 Wolf Vostell in René Block, *Grafik des Kapitalistischen Realismus*, Berlin: Edition René Block, 1971, p. 173.

21 Each print is titled with the words 'red', 'yellow,' and 'blue' in a different order; the position of each color in the title corresponds to its place in a three-digit number from 001 to 999; color mixes were determined by the number in that position. In the print *Yellow-Red-Blue*, 001 would be made up of no yellow, no red, and one part blue, while 999 would be made up of nine parts each of all three colors.

22 Richter in *The Print Collector's Newsletter*, Vol. XVI, No. 4, p. 130.

23 Pierre Restany, *Superlund* (exhibition catalogue), Lund, Sweden, 1967, quoted in Lucie-Smith, *Movements in Art*, p. 24.

24 Günther Gerken, "Graphik und Objeckte: Vervielfältige Kunst," *Documenta 4*, Kassel: Museum Fridericianum, 1968, p. xiv. Cited in Todd Aldgren, "Marcel Broodthaers: On the Tautology of Art and Merchandise," *The Print Collector's Newsletter*, Vol. XXIII, No. 1, March–April 1992, p. 7.

25 Öyvind Fahlström, "Ta vara på världen: ett manifest" (Take Care of the World: a Manifesto), *Bonniers Litterära Magasin*, 7, 1966. Reprinted in Swedish in *Öyvind Fahlström*, Stockholm: Moderna Museet, 1979, and in English in *Öyvind Fahlström*, New York: The Solomon R. Guggenheim Foundation, 1982.

26 Öyvind Fahlström, *Manipulating the World, Art and Literature* 3, 1964. Reprinted as above.

27 A better known, and much cagier version of this idea occurs in Jasper Johns's *Target* (1970). A lithographic line drawing of a target with a paintbrush and three watercolor paint pads affixed to the sheet, it also bore a rubberstamp that read "Target 1970 for ———— and

————" with Johns's signature occupying the first slot. It was based on a ten-year-old drawing that also had paint pads attached to it, but the unique drawing doesn't proffer the same open-hearted invitation or indifference to defacement as either the hand-signed edition of 50 or the offset lithograph edition of 22,500 (included as part of a boxed catalogue for an exhibition at the Museum of Modern Art). But by 1970, Johns was far too bankable an artist for a collector to want to improve upon. And in Johns's work, unlike in Fahlström's work, the suggested collaboration can only occur once. It is an open question whether painting in the target would "complete" the piece, or alternatively, negate a piece whose whole point is promise and provocation.

28 *Sketch for "World Map" Part I (Americas, Pacific)* (1972) was published as the centerfold of the *Liberated Guardian* in an edition of 7,000 or more, and at a price of 25 cents; *Column No. 1 (Wonderbread)* and *My White Skeleton* (1964) also appeared in the thousands.

5 MATERIAL FORMS AND SOCIAL FUNCTIONS

1 Richard S. Field and Ruth E. Fine, *A Graphic Muse, Prints by Contemporary American Women*, South Hadley, Mass.: Mount Holyoke College Art Museum, 1987, p. 19.

2 Richard H. Axsome, *The Prints of Ellsworth Kelly: a catalogue raisonné, 1949–1985*, New York: Hudson Hills Press in association with the American Federation of the Arts, 1987, p. 18.

3 In later prints of the 1980s, Kelly has used a very obviously "brushed" surface texture but, significantly, the strokes are done by technicians, not by the artist.

4 Stella in "Questions to Stella and Judd," interview with Bruce Glazer, edited by Lucy R. Lippard, *Art News*, September 1966, reprinted in Gregory Battcock (ed.), *Minimal Art: A Critical Anthology*, New York: E. P. Dutton & Co. Inc., p. 158.

5 The prints were apparently pulled by the artist's father, Roy Clarence Judd.

6 Brice Marden in Jeremy Lewison, *Brice Marden: Prints 1961–1991*, London: Tate Gallery, 1992, p. 31.

7 Robert Ryman in Nancy Tousley, *Prints: Bochner LeWitt Mangold Marden Martin Renouf Rockburne Ryman*, Toronto: Art Gallery of Ontario, 1976, p. 49.

8 Dorothea Rockburne in Ruth E. Fine, *Gemini GEL: Art and Collaboration*, Washington: National Gallery of Art and New York: Abbeville Press, 1984, p. 228.

9 Donald Judd in "Questions to Stella and Judd," p. 164.

10 Mel Bochner, "Serial Art, Systems, Solipsism," *Arts Magazine*, Summer 1967, revised version printed in Battcock (ed.), *Minimal Art*, p. 100.

11 Bochner in Tousley, *Prints*, p. 13.

12 LeWitt, "Paragraphs on Conceptual Art," *Artforum*, Vol. 5, No. 10, Summer 1967, p. 80.

13 Sol LeWitt quoted in Ronny H. Cohen, "Minimal Prints," *The Print Collector's Newsletter*, Vol. XXI, No. 2, May–June 1990, p. 44. Frank Stella's first print at Gemini, *Star of Persia I* (1967), was accomplished in a similar way: a single V shape was drawn, then photographically turned and reprinted to form a six-pointed star.

14 Vito Acconci, quoted in Elizabeth Armstrong, *First Impressions: Early Prints by Forty-six Contemporary Artists*, New York: Hudson Hills Press and Minneapolis: Walker Art Center, 1989, p. 72.

15 Both artists have also produced multiples in which their ideas for colossal projects assume a more domestic scale, or which act as portable models of visionary proposals.

16 There are no hand-drawn lithographs of the major projects with the exception of *Surrounded Islands, Project for Biscayne Bay, Greater Miami, Florida*, 1987.

17 For the last several years, the environmental works have been credited as the joint creations of Christo and Jeanne-Claude.

18 Oldenburg, interview with Judith Goldman, "Sort of a Commercial for Objects," *The Print Collector's Newsletter*, Vol. II, No. 6, January–February 1972, p. 117.

19 There were three published states of the *Screwarch Bridge* print: the first, a straight line etching; the second, filled out in aquatint; the third was a color monoprint, accomplished by hand-coloring the plate before printing. In addition there was a large sculpture of the piece, and drawings.

20 Eleanor Antin, "On Self-Transformation," *Flash Art*, Vol. 44–45, March–April 1974, p. 69.

21 Antin, *Flash Art*, p. 69.

22 Anamorphic paintings, when viewed head-on, appear illegibly distorted, but when viewed from an extreme angle, or reflected by cylinders or other devices, become naturalistic representations of people and things.

23 *Landscape* (1975), published by Edition Schellmann, Munich. The other artists were Christo, Richard Hamilton, and Dennis Oppenheim.

24 Joseph Kosuth, "Art After Philosophy, I & II," *Studio International*, October and November 1969, reprinted in Gregory Battcock (ed.), *Idea Art*, New York: E. P. Dutton, 1973, p. 93.

25 Harold Rosenberg, "The Art World: American Drawing and the Academy of the Erased de Kooning," *New Yorker*, March 22, 1976, p. 109.

26 Jean-François Lyotard, "Longitude 180° W or E," *Arakawa*, Milan, 1984, quoted in Fine, *Graphicstudio*, p. 104.
A *koan* is a Zen Buddhist riddle that has no solution, and is used to teach the limits of reason, and to foster enlightenment.

27 Bruce Nauman, interview with Christopher Cordes, *Bruce Nauman: Prints 1970–89*, New York: Castelli Graphics and Lorence Monk Gallery and Chicago: Donald Young Gallery, 1989, p.25.

28 Nauman has also made word pieces in neon, but felt it was "encumbering the information …with this technology that didn't seem very important." Nauman, in Cordes, *Nauman: Prints 1970–89*, p. 23.

29 The stones for "Dead" were also used to print *Help Me Hurt Me*; *Help Me Hurt Me (State)*; *Dead*; and a second state of *Oiled Dead* (all 1975).

30 Nauman, in Cordes, *Nauman: Prints 1970–89*, p.24.

31 Nauman in Cordes, *Nauman: Prints 1970–89*, p.25.

32 Vito Acconci, interview with Robin White, *View*, Vol. II, No. 5/6 October–November 1979, Oakland: Point Publications, p. 18.

33 "I wanted to give myself a way to be involved with the printmaking process – and I wasn't about to use my hand, let my hand show – so I could find a way in: I could perform on the stone, act on the stone." Vito Acconci quoted in Armstrong, *First Impressions*, p. 72.

34 *3 Flags for 1 Space and 6 Regions* was part of a group of prints in which Acconci tried to encompass the effects of architecture: the squarish wall of superpower flags was accompanied by the eight-part photo-etching *20 Foot Ladder for Any Size Wall*, 1979–80 (the print climbs up the wall as far as possible and then onto the ceiling), and the twelve-part photo-etching *2 Wings for Wall and Person* (1979–81) which incorporated human presence as an element of the work.

35 Daniel Buren, interview with Robin White, *View*, Vol. 1, No. 9, February 1979, Oakland: Point Publications, p. 12.

36 Etchings and paper money are united by roughly the same method of manufacture and the social and economic value of both is constructed through a strictly controlled artificial imposition of rarity. Both require of the holder faith in the object's authenticity (a record of genius or a portion of gross national product). Burden is not the only artist to have noted these connections: Robert Watts's contribution to the *International Avant-Garde* portfolio was a hand-etched dollar bill, and J. S. G. Boggs has made an art of imitating both the appearance of bills and their mode of exchange, to the distress of treasury officials around the world.

37 Hans Haacke, interview with Robin White, *View*, Vol. 1, No. 6, November 1978, Oakland: Point Publications, p. 3.

38 Marcel Broodthaers, "To Be a Straight Thinker or Not to Be/To Be Blind," *No Photographs Allowed*, artist's book accompanying the 1974 exhibition *The Privilege of Art*, the Museum of Modern Art, Oxford, quoted in Todd Aldren, "Marcel Broodthaers: On the Tautology of Art and Merchandize," *The Print Collector's Newsletter*, Vol. XXIII, No. 1, March–April 1992, p. 5.

6 HIGH TECH AND THE HUMAN TOUCH

1 Pat Steir in "Expressionism Today: An Artists' Symposium," *Art in America* Vol. 70, No. 11, December 1982, p. 75.

2 Vija Celmins, interview with Chuck Close, in William S. Bartman (ed.), *Vija Celmins*, A.R.T. Press, 1992, p. 17.

3 Brown noted at the time that "only a few people have done [mezzotints] in the past hundred years, and even… when they were popular their size range was about 9 × 12 [inches]." Kathan Brown, in Elizabeth Armstrong and Sheila McGuire, *First Impressions: Early Prints by Forty-six Contemporary Artists*, New York: Hudson Hills Press and Minneapolis: Walker Art Center, 1989, p. 82.

4 "I feel the image is just a sort of armature on which I hang my marks and make my art." Vija Celmins in interview with Chuck Close, *Vija Celmins*, p. 14.

5 Close in *Vija Celmins*, p. 11.

6 Philip Pearlstein, "Process Is My Goal," *New York Times*, 31 October 1976, p. D29.

7 Pearlstein in Sanford S. Shaman, "An Interview with Philip Pearlstein," *Art in America* 69, September 1981, reprinted in Ruth E. Fine and Mary Lee Corlett, *Graphicstudio: Contemporary Art from the Collaborative Workshop at the University of South Florida*, Washington D.C.: National Gallery of Art, p. 62.

8 The *Day and Night* etchings take their composition from the painting *27 Howard Street/Day and Night* (1977).

9 Pat Steir, interview with Robin White, *View*, Vol. 1, No. 3, June 1978.

10 *Picasso's Meninas* was produced as part of a portfolio, *Hommage à Picasso*, in honor of Picasso's ninetieth birthday. Work on the portfolio introduced Crommelynck to a number of artists, including Hamilton, Dine, and Hockney, with whom he would form long working relationships.

11 Picasso's *Bull* series can also be seen as a precursor to Johns *0–9* (1960–63), in its successive revisions of a single stone, but apparently Johns was working with no awareness of this precedent. (See Esther Sparks, *Universal Limited Art Editions*, Chicago: The Art Institute of Chicago and New York: Harry N. Abrams, Inc., 1989).

12 Johns's citations of Picasso are of a somewhat different character: the illusionary print *Cups 4 Picasso* (1972) in which Picasso's doubled profile defines the shape of a vase, cites Picasso's persona, though not his work. In the 1980s elements from Picasso's 1936 painting *Minotaur Moving His House* appeared in Johns's *The Seasons*, not as an exploration of stylistic vocabulary, but as a study of the ways in which profound personal meaning can be encoded in cryptic form.

13 Kushner, interview with Robin White, *View*, Vol. 2, February–March 1980, p. 9.

14 It must be noted, however, that this broadened view did not bring about any benign embrace of contemporary artists of color. Though there was a dramatic surge in community-access printshops in America that encouraged the articulation of minority experiences, and though few older black American painter/printmakers such as Jacob Lawrence and Romare Bearden finally achieved some wider recognition, print publishers and professional shops continued to reflect the demographics of the galleries and museums: predominantly white, and only slightly less predominantly male.

15 The term "works on paper" came to replace "drawings" or "prints," which seemed somehow inadequate with their emphasis on what was done *to* the paper rather than emphasizing the paper itself.

16 Richard S. Field, "On Recent Woodcuts," *The Print Collector's Newsletter*, Vol. XIII, No. 1, March–April 1982, p. 2.

17 Having ceased to be a commercial force in Europe in the early seventeenth century, the woodcut was revived by artists in the late nineteenth, for exactly the reasons it had earlier been abandoned. Gauguin and Munch were among the artists who exploited its boldness, roughness, and impatience with detail, and they brought to the European woodcut some of the flatness and decorative reduction they had learned from the Japanese woodblock prints that flooded Europe in the mid-nineteenth century. Later, German Expressionists such as Kirchner and Schmidt-Rotluff took up woodcut, and still later, American figurative expressionists like Leonard Baskin led its revival in the 1950s.

18 "I want a kind of mechanical image in my prints. But after a while, I was able to achieve that technical quality too easily. Woodcuts resist that. I like the way you have to fight against the block to get the image you want."

Lichtenstein in Deborah C. Phillips, "Looking for Relief? Woodcuts Are Back," *ARTnews*, April 1982, p. 93.

19 Rauschenberg's *Cardbirds* (1969) were editioned cardboard constructions that were precursors of his later paperworks, in which printing is incidental.

20 These molds were set down on newly made white pulp base sheets, so that the colored pulp and the white pulp would consolidate as a single mass.

21 Tyler Graphics addresses the problem by describing works like Hockney's *Steps with Shadow N, Paper Pool 2*, as existing in an edition of "16 variants;" while the "unique" *Le Plongeur* has an almost identical counterpart, clearly made from the same molds, but titled in English, *A Diver* (all works 1978).

22 "Stella admits that three giant technical advances won him the aesthetic freedom that helped to make prints as important to him as paintings. These advances were the surface and sculptural possibilities of handmade paper, the scale and fidelity of etched magnesium, and the ability to superimpose repeated veils of ink from the offset press…" Pat Gilmour, "Kenneth Tyler: A Collaborator in Context," *Tyler Graphics: Catalogue Raisonné, 1974–1985*, Minneapolis: Walker Art Center, 1987, p. 21.

23 Judy Pfaff in interview with Constance Lewallen, *View*, Vol. V, Summer 1988, p.11.

24 Richard Serra in *Richard Serra at Gemini 1983–1987*, Los Angeles: Gemini GEL, 1987, no page numbers.

25 Nancy Princenthal describes the sculpture as follows: "Thin slabs of indigenous basalt were installed in pairs in nine locations, one slab in each pair at a nine-meter elevation from the sea and the other at ten. The difference is compensated by their respective heights, the lower slabs each being four meters high and the upper three, so their tops are level. Since the steepness of the grade changes from place to place, sometimes the paired slabs are as close as seven feet, sometimes as far as 25." "The 'Afangar Icelandic Series': Richard Serra's Recent Etchings", *The Print Collector's Newsletter*, Vol. XXII, No. 5, November–December 1991, p. 158.

26 Of the set of four prints, two were to be printed on oilcloth, but the material proved too difficult and the last ten impressions of each were printed on paper.

27 Nathan Oliveira, "The Monotype: Printing as Process," *The Tamarind Papers*, Vol. 13, 1990, p. 58.

28 Mazur in Jane M. Farmer, *New American Monotypes*, Washington: the Smithsonian Institution Traveling Exhibition Service, 1978, p. 28.

29 Sanchez apparently uses a variation on "dry lithography" to create his "multiple monotypes."

7 USES OF HISTORY

1 Rainer in Barbara Catoir, "Interview mit Arnulf Rainer," *Das Kunstwerk*, January 1985, p. 35; translation by Peter Champe in *Kunst als Kultur/Art as Culture: Recent Art from Germany*, Middletown: Ezra and Cecile Zilkha Gallery, Wesleyan University, 1986, p. 53.

2 Andreas Huyssen described the situation of postwar German artists as follows: "Auschwitz cast a prohibition over any form of visual or literary representation, and artists were fundamentally insecure as to which traditions were still usable, which aesthetic strategies not contaminated by Nazi abuse. In painting, abstraction – no matter how secondary and imitative – provided a possible way out." Andreas Huyssen, "Back to the Future: Fluxus in Context," in Elizabeth Armstrong and Joan Rothfuss, *In the Spirit of Fluxus*, Minneapolis: Walker Art Center, 1993, p. 148.

3 The term "Neo-Expressionism" was broadly used in the early 1980s, and was applied to almost all painting that was not clean and hard-edged, from Julian Schnabel, to Anselm Kiefer, to Susan Rothenberg. In retrospect the distinctions between these artists appear far stronger than the simple similarities of active paint handling and recognizable forms. The term's best application is perhaps illustrated in Richard Bosman's description of the *New York Post* as a "Neo-Expressionist newspaper" – an articulation of the mechanisms of melodrama so blatant that they cease to function.

4 Arminius, the German national hero who defeated the Roman legions in 9 AD.

5 These tasks were often performed with the help of studio assistants, or family members, but not with professional printers in shops.

6 Kiefer's woodcut book *Der Rhein* was released in an edition but there is an enormous amount of variation within the edition, and each book is essentially unique.

7 *Ur End Standart* was published by Heiner Friedrich Gallery in Munich while Penck was still living in East Germany. The prints that Penck actually produced in the East with East German printers are quite different in feel: quick expressive sketches of specific people and experiences that have more the character of notes passed between friends.

8 Penck in Dorothea Dietrich, "A Talk with A. R. Penck." *The Print Collector's Newsletter*, Vol. XIV, No. 3, July–August 1983, p. 92.

9 Immendorff in Elizabeth Armstrong, *Images and Impressions: Painters Who Print*, Minneapolis: Walker Art Center, 1984, p. 34.

10 Paladino in Danny Berger, "Mimmo Paladino: An Interview," *The Print Collector's Newsletter*, Vol. XIV, No. 2, May–June 1983, p. 50.

11 Chia in conversation with Heiner Bastian in the exhibition catalogue of the Kunsthalle Bielefeld, 1983, p. 40. Quoted in Bice Curiger, *Looks et Tenebrae: Nine Monographs on the Portfolios Published by Peter Blum Edition*, New York and Zurich: Peter Blum Edition, p. 127.

12 Cucchi, text accompanying print.

13 Paladino in Elizabeth Armstrong, Introduction to *Images and Impressions: Painters Who Print*, p. 8.

14 Clemente, interview with Robin White, *View*, Vol. III, No. 6, 1981.

15 While the Western woodcut is made by cutting away the surface of a block to isolate a raised design, then rolling it with opaque, oily ink and passing it through a press, the Japanese cut blocks into solid shapes, paint them with water-based inks, fit the different blocks together, and rub them by hand. Because the inks are transparent a single color may be printed again and again to produce sensitive gradations of hue.

16 Ellis quoted in Patrick McGrath, "Abstract Monsters," *Parkett*, No. 34, 1992, p. 120.

17 Bartlett in Deborah C. Phillips, "Looking for Relief? Woodcuts Are Back," *ARTnews*, Vol. 91, No. 4, April 1992, p. 96.

18 Crown Point has subsequently also started a program with printers in Shanghai, working in the somewhat different Chinese tradition of woodblock printing.

19 Richard Diebenkorn in Gerald Nordland, *Richard Diebenkorn: Graphics 1981–1988*, Billings, Montana: Yellowstone Art Center, 1989.

20 Richard S. Field, "On Recent Woodcuts," *The Print Collector's Newsletter*, Vol. XIII, No. 1, March–April 1982, p. 6.

21 Bosman, whose work was seen as typically American, was actually born in Madras, India, and had a peripatetic upbringing.

22 In the last year of his life Guston produced an important group of lithographs with Gemini GEL. Seven of these editions remained unsigned at the time of his death (he had signed the RTP to authorize the edition), and are embossed with an estate stamp in place of the artist's signature. Interestingly, in overall compositional tone, the Gemini prints are not dissimilar to the abstract, lyrical lithographs Guston made at Tamarind in the 1960s.

23 "Hairy Who" was the title given to several group exhibitions in the 1960s of artists James Falconer, Art Green, Gladys Nilsson, Jim Nutt, Suellen Rocca, and Karl Wirsum. It has since come to be more generally applied, often embracing Roger Brown and Ed Paschke. The

other term commonly used is the somewhat more banal "Imagism."

24 Haring in Gerrit Henry, "Keith Haring: Subways are for Drawing," *The Print Collector's Newsletter*, Vol. XIII, No. 2, May–June, 1982, p. 48.

25 Borofsky quoted in Curiger, *Looks et tenebrae*, p. 152.

26 In 1969 Borofsky began to count to infinity, a task that occupied him exclusively for some years. In more recent years his counting marks time and ticks off objects completed; like edition numbers, it ties things together while differentiating them.

27 Clifford S. Ackley sees *Double Standard* (1984) as an allusion to the print's affinity with drawing. Clifford S. Ackley, "Double Standard: the Prints of Terry Winters," *The Print Collector's Newsletter*, Vol. XVIII, No. 4, September–October 1987, p. 123.

28 Dunham in Elizabeth Armstrong and Sheila McGuire, *First Impressions: Early Prints by Forty-six Contemporary Artists*, New York: Hudson Hills Press, and Minneapolis: Walker Art Center, 1989, p. 134.

29 Fischl in Curiger, *Looks et Tenebrae*, p. 172.

30 In addition to the 11 regular editions, there were a number of HC variants, some of them printed as HC editions; also, *Untitled 1992*, used plates from *The Seasons*.

31 In other versions the plates are printed four-up or in pinwheel formation.

32 Johns in Peter Fuller, "Jasper Johns Interviewed," Parts 1, 2. *Art Monthly 18*, July–August and September 1978, quoted in Riva Castleman, *Jasper Johns: A Print Retrospective*, New York: the Museum of Modern Art, 1986, p. 46.

33 Lisa Liebman has pointed out how many of Bourgeois's sculptural forms reflect the aesthetic of Atelier 17, where "the master printmaker and his apprentices quested for archetypal resonance using primary forms and an unadorned semi-automatic line." Lisa Liebman, "Louise Bourgeois, At Last," *The Print Collector's Newsletter*, Vol. XXIV, No. 1, March–April 1993, p. 7.

34 Zen calligraphy has been a recurrent inspiration in postwar art, especially prints, and is visible in the work of Mark Tobey, Henri Michaux, and Sam Francis.

35 Johns in Christian Geelhaar, *Jasper Johns Working Proofs*, New York and London: Petersburg Press, 1980, p. 38.

8 THE ETHOS OF THE EDITION

1 Roni Feinstein, *Robert Rauschenberg: The Silkscreen Paintings 1962–64*, New York: Whitney Museum of American Art, in association with Boston, Toronto, London: Bulfinch Press, Little, Brown and Company, 1990, p. 22.

2 Coosje van Bruggen, *John Baldessari*, Los Angeles: The Museum of Contemporary Art, and New York: Rizzoli, 1990, p. 16.

3 Baldessari in interview with Nancy Drew, *John Baldessari*, New York: the New Museum, 1981, p. 63. Cited in Bice Curiger, *Looks et Tenebrae*, New York and Zurich: Peter Blum Edition, 1984, p. 168.

4 Baldessari does not go to photo files in search of particular subjects or connections, but collects pictures that interest him and allows the connections to assert themselves over time.

5 Matt Mullican in "Multiples and Objects and Books", *The Print Collector's Newsletter*, Vol. XXII, No. 3, July–August 1991, p. 99. Mullican has also made his paintings by rubbing paintstick on canvas through cardboard and masonite stencils.

6 K.O.S. was formed when Rollins was teaching a class in a New York City public school in the Bronx. The K.O.S. members who worked on the *St Antony* prints were: Richard Cruz, George Garces, Carlos Rivera, and Nelson Savignon.

7 Holzer in interview with Bruce Ferguson in *Jenny Holzer: Signs*, Des Moines: Des Moines Art Center, 1986, p. 67. Cited in Elizabeth Armstrong and Sheila McGuire, *First Impressions: Early Prints by Forty-six Contemporary Artists*, New York: Hudson Hills Press, and Minneapolis: Walker Art Center, 1989, p. 100.

8 Holzer in Nancy Prinsenthal, "Political Prints: An Opinion Poll," *The Print Collector's Newsletter*, Vol. XIX, No. 2, May–June 1988, p. 45.

9 Though Kruger's images are necessarily printed, she has only occasionally indulged in limited edition, handmade prints. Her *Untitled* (1985) portfolio, and her benefit print for the artists' bookshop Printed Matter, *Read Between the Lines* (1989), are two important exceptions. Another major limited edition work was her *livre d'artiste* with Stephen King, *My Pretty Pony* (1988). In general however, she has preferred installations of large-scale works; populist collectibles such as books, T-shirts, and matchbooks; or public forms, such as billboards and posters, which do not aspire to be owned at all.

10 The Guerilla Girls is an anonymous organization of women in the art world. The anonymity is strictly maintained: they only appear in public in gorilla masks, all correspondence is through PO boxes, and all telephone contact is via an answering service.

11 In 1991 the Guerilla Girls responded to several museum requests and put together a portfolio of collected works from 1985–90. The portfolio is made up partly of surplus originals, and partly of reprints (the reprints were done on archival paper). All were numbered with a banana rubber stamp and "signed" with a lipstick kiss.

12 Co-Lab (Collaborative Laboratories, Inc.) was founded in 1978 with the aims of collaborative creation, social involvement, cheap production and distribution of art. It had a core membership of about fifty artists who produced paintings, drawings, film, video, and a cable television series, in addition to large numbers of inexpensive prints and multiples. Smith's first screenprints were artist's T-shirts made for "A More Store," a kind of seasonal shop for multiples that was run by Co-Lab.

13 Printed on the tie is the following: "I saw him for the first time in December 1985, at a lecture he was giving. I found him attractive, but one thing bothered me: he was wearing an ugly tie. The next day I anonymously sent him a thin brown tie. Later, I saw him in a restaurant; he was wearing it. Unfortunately, it clashed with his shirt. It was then I decided to take on the task of dressing him from head to toe: I would send him one article of clothing every year at Christmas. In 1986, he received a pair of silk grey socks; in 1987, a black alpaca sweater; in 1988, a white shirt; in 1989 a pair of gold-plated cuff links; in 1990 a pair of boxer shorts with a Christmas tree pattern; nothing in 1991; and in 1992, a pair of grey trousers. Some day, when he is fully dressed by me, I would like to be introduced to him."

14 Bloom is expert at soliciting from the viewer behavior that reflects the content of the piece: the pages of her book *Never Odd or Even*, about secrecy and symmetry, had to be slit open by the viewer in order to be seen.

15 There was also a Broodthaers precedent for this in *Paysage d'Automne* 1973, an edition of 140 sold and numbered as a single work.

16 Dye sublimation printing, commonly used for commercial color proofing, is not yet commonly used in art production.

17 Baldessari in van Bruggen, *John Baldessari*, p. 11.

NOTES ON THE PRINTS

Printers are listed when the information is available. When using commercial rather than art printers, records were often not kept of who the printer was, particularly with European prints in the 1960s.

References to catalogue raisonnés and proofs are also given. The following abbreviations are used: AP (artist's proof); PP (printer's proof); TP, CTP (trial proof, colour trial proof); WP (working proof); HC (hors de commerce); BAT (bon à tirer); RTP (right to print), A (archive copy); C (cancellation proof).

1 Jean Dubuffet. *L'Enfle-Chique I*, 1961, color lithograph, 58 × 35 cm ($22\frac{3}{4} \times 13\frac{3}{4}$ in.), edition of 20. Photograph courtesy Philadelphia Museum of Art, gift of the Friends of the Philadelphia Museum of Art. © ADAGP Paris and DACS London 1996.
Paper: Arches Raisin. Proofs: 5 HCs, 4 working proofs. There were six variant editions of *l'Enfle-Chique*.

2 Stanley William Hayter. Page from *21 Etchings and Poems*, with poem by Jacques-Henri Levesque, 1960, engraving, 29.1 × 19.3 cm ($11\frac{7}{16} \times 7\frac{9}{16}$ in.), edition of 80. Printed by the artist. Published by Morris Gallery, New York. Photograph courtesy The Museum of Modern Art, New York. Gift of Mrs Jacquelynn Shlaes.

3 Willem de Kooning. *Landscape at Stanton Street*, 1971, lithograph, 75.9 × 56.5 cm ($29\frac{7}{8} \times 22\frac{1}{4}$ in.), edition of 60. Printed by Hollander Workshop. Published by Hollander Workshop/M. Knoedler & Co., New York. Photograph courtesy Collection Walker Art Center, Minneapolis. Gift of Xavier Fourcade, New York, 1974. © ARS New York and DACS London 1996.

4 Grace Hartigan. *The Hero Leaves His Ship I*, 1960, lithograph, 75.5 × 53.5 cm ($29\frac{3}{4} \times 21\frac{1}{8}$ in.), edition of 27. Printed and published by Universal Limited Art Editions. Photograph courtesy The Art Institute of Chicago, ULAE Collection, challenge grant of Mr and Mrs Thomas Dittmer; restricted gift of supporters of the Department of Prints and Drawings; Centennial Endowment, 1982.503.
Paper: German Copperplate, handmade. Printer: Robert Blackburn.

5 Larry Rivers. *Stones: US*, 1957, lithograph, 48.2 × 59 cm ($19 \times 23\frac{1}{4}$ in.), edition of 25. Printed and published by Universal Limited Art Editions. Photograph courtesy Universal Limited Art Editions.
Paper: Douglas Howell handmade. Proofs: 5 APs.

6 Robert Motherwell. *A la pintura: Black 1–3*, 1968, letterpress, lift-ground etching, and aquatint, 65.5 × 97 cm ($25\frac{3}{4} \times 38\frac{3}{16}$ in.), edition of 40. Printed and published by Universal Limited Art Editions. Photograph courtesy The Museum of Modern Art, New York. Gift of Celeste Bartos.
Belknap 86. Paper: J. B. Green mold-made. Proofs: 8 APs, 2 PPs, 1 poet's proof, 1 translator's proof, 172 TPs, 141 WPs, 2 "trial sets," 21 practice trial proofs, 2 sets cancellation proofs, 17 single dedication proofs. Printers: Donn Steward, Juda Rosenberg, Esther Pullman.

7 Robert Motherwell. *Gauloises Bleues (White)*, 1970, aquatint and linecut, 57.6 × 39.3 cm ($22\frac{3}{4} \times 15\frac{1}{2}$ in.), edition of 40. Printed and published by Universal Limited Art Editions. Photograph courtesy The Art Institute of Chicago, ULAE Collection, challenge grant of Mr and Mrs Thomas Dittmer; restricted gift of supporters of the Department of Prints and Drawings; Centennial Endowment, 1982.854.
Belknap 37. Paper: Auvergne à la Main, Richard de Bas. Proofs: 4 APs, 1 PP, 4 TPs, 1 WP. Printer: Donn Steward.

8 Robert Motherwell. *Automatism B*, 1965–66, lithograph, 76.2 × 52.7 cm ($30 \times 20\frac{3}{4}$ in.), edition of 100. Printed and published by Hollander Workshop. Photograph courtesy Brooke Alexander Editions.
Belknap 7. Paper: Rives BFK (varies). Proofs: artist's proofs. Printer: Irwin Hollander.

9 Barnett Newman. *Untitled*, 1961, lithograph, 76.4 × 56.2 cm ($30\frac{1}{16} \times 22\frac{1}{8}$ in.), edition of 30. Printed at Pratt Graphic Arts Center. Published by the artist. Photograph courtesy Susan Sheehan Gallery, New York. Reproduced courtesy Annalee Newman insofar as her rights are concerned.
Yard p. 96. Paper: Arches.

10 Helen Frankenthaler. *Persian Garden*, 1965–66, color lithograph, 65.5 × 51 cm ($25\frac{3}{4} \times 20$ in.), edition of 24. Printed and published by Universal Limited Art Editions. Photograph courtesy Brooke Alexander Editions.
Williams 8. Paper: Auvergne à la Main, Richard de Bas. Printer: Ben Burns. Proofs: 5.

11 Lee Bontecou. *Fifth Stone*, 1964, lithograph, 105.1 × 75.5 cm ($41\frac{3}{4} \times 29\frac{1}{8}$ in.), edition of 27. Printed and published by Universal Limited Art Editions. Photograph courtesy Art Institute of Chicago, ULAE Collection, challenge grant of Mr and Mrs Thomas Dittmer; restricted gift of supporters of the Department of Prints and Drawings; Centennial Endowment, 1982.97.
Field 5. Paper: Rives BFK. Proofs: 7 APs, 7 TPs, 1 WP, 3 HCs. Printer: Zigmunds Priede.

12 Cy Twombly. *Untitled II*, 1967–74, etching, open bite and aquatint, 69.5 × 102.5 cm ($27\frac{1}{2} \times 40\frac{1}{2}$ in.), edition of 23. Printed and published by Universal Limited Art Editions. Photograph courtesy Brooke Alexander Editions.
Bastian 11. Paper: J. Green. Proofs: 5 APs, 1 PP. Printer: Donn Steward.

13 Mark Tobey. *Ground of Confidence*, 1972, drypoint and color aquatint, 51 × 33.8 cm ($20 \times 13\frac{1}{4}$ in.), edition of 55. Printed by Austel & Fischer, Hanau. Published by Edition de Beauclair, Frankfurt am Main and the Kunstverein für die Rheinlande und Westfahlen, Düsseldorf. Photo courtesy Kupferstichkabinett, Staatliche Museen zu Berlin, Preußischer Kulturbesitz. © DACS 1996.
Heidenheim 36. Proofs: 4 HCs, 6 APs.

14 Richard Diebenkorn. *#11 from 41 Etchings Drypoints*, 1965, etching and aquatint, 45 × 37.5 cm ($17\frac{3}{4} \times 14\frac{3}{4}$ in.), edition of 25. Printed and published by Crown Point Press. Photograph courtesy Brooke Alexander Editions.
Guillemin p. 117. Paper: Rives BFK. Proofs: 10 APs.

15 Pablo Picasso. *1.6.68* from the "347" engravings, 1968, aquatint, 53.5 × 65.5 cm ($21 \times 25\frac{3}{4}$ in.), edition of 50. Printed by Atelier Crommelynck, Paris. Photograph courtesy Alan Cristea Gallery. © DACS 1996.

16 Ben Nicholson. *Tesserete*, 1966, etching and india ink, 19 × 23 cm ($7\frac{1}{2} \times 9$ in.), edition of 50. Printed by François Lafranca, Locarno. Published by Galerie Beyeler, Basel. Photograph courtesy Ikeda and Lokker, Tokyo. © Angela Verren-Taunt 1996. All rights reserved DACS.
Lafranca 29b. Proofs: 6 APs.

17 Antoni Tàpies. *Untitled*, 1962, lithograph and collagraph with flocking, 56 × 76.2 cm ($22\frac{1}{16} \times 30$ in.), edition of 50. Printed by Damià Caus at Foto-Repro, Barcelona. Published by Sala Gaspar, Barcelona. © 1993, Fundació Antoni Tàpies, Barcelona. Galfetti 43.

18 Antoni Tàpies. Plate 2 from the *Suite Catalana*, 1972, intaglio, 76.2 × 101.5 cm ($30 \times 39\frac{15}{16}$ in.), edition of 75. Printed by Joan Barbarà, Barcelona. Published by Editorial Gustavo Gili, Barcelona. © 1993, Fundació Antoni Tàpies, Barcelona. Galfetti 303.

19 Henri Michaux. Plate 2 from the portfolio *Parcours*, 1965, etching, 52.8×40.8 cm (20¾ × 16 in.), edition of 60. Photograph courtesy National Gallery of Australia, Canberra. © ADAGP Paris and DACS London 1996.

20 Anton Heyboer. *de Geniale Psyche*, 1966, color etching, 100×65 cm (39½ × 25½ in.), edition of 9. Printed and published by the artist. Photograph courtesy Galerie Espace, Amsterdam. NB Heyboer usually numbers his prints as editions of 9, though this is not always not the case.

21 Jean Dubuffet. *Scintillement* from *Géographie*, the fourth color album of *Les Phénomènes*, 1959–60, color lithograph, 63.5×45 cm (25 × 17¾ in.), edition of 23. Photograph courtesy Philadelphia Museum of Art, gift of Ralph F. Colin. © ADAGP Paris and DACS London 1996. Paper: Arches. Edition: 20 numbered copies, and three marked A, B, and C.

22 Robert Rauschenberg. *Accident*, 1963, lithograph, 104.8×75 cm (41¼ × 29½ in.), edition of 29. Printed and published by Universal Limited Art Editions. Photograph courtesy Universal Limited Art Editions. © Robert Rauschenberg/DACS London, VAGA New York 1996. Foster 12. Paper: Rives BFK; 3 APs of State 1 (unbroken) and 1 AP of State II. Printers: Robert Blackburn and Zigmunds Priede.

23 Robert Rauschenberg. *Merger*, 1962, lithograph, 57.1×44.5 cm (22½ × 17½ in.), edition of 16. Printed and published by Universal Limited Art Editions. Photograph courtesy Brooke Alexander Editions. © Robert Rauschenberg/ DACS London, VAGA New York 1996. Foster 5. Paper: Japan. Proofs: APs and TPs. Printer: Robert Blackburn.

24 John Cage and Calvin Sumsion. *Not Wanting to Say Anything About Marcel*, 1969, plexigram (eight screenprinted plexiglass sheets in a wooden base; the sheets of the plexigram may be rearranged at will) from the portfolio of one lithograph and one plexigram. Plexiglass sheets: 35.5×50.8 cm (14×20 in.) each, edition of 125. Printed by Hollander Workshop. Published by Eye Editions, Cincinnati. Photograph courtesy Philadelphia Museum of Art: Purchase of the Lola Dowin Peck Fund. Proofs: 18 APs.

25 John Cage and Calvin Sumsion. *Not Wanting to Say Anything About Marcel*, 1969, lithograph from the portfolio of one lithograph and one "plexigram", 69.8×101.6 cm (27½ × 40 in.), edition of 125. Printed by Hollander Workshop. Published by Eye Editions, Cincinnati. Photograph courtesy Philadelphia Museum of Art. Purchase of the Lola Dowin Peck Fund. Proofs: 18 APs.

26 Jasper Johns. *Target*, 1960, lithograph, 57.5×44.7 cm (22⅛ × 17⅛ in.), edition of 30. Printed and published by Universal Limited Art Editions. Photograph courtesy Universal Limited Art Editions. © Jasper Johns/DACS London, VAGA New York 1996. Field 1. Paper: Japan. Proofs: 3 APs and TPs. Printer: Robert Blackburn.

27 Jasper Johns, *0–9*: Edition A/C, page 5, 1960–63, lithograph, 52.1×39.4 cm (20½ × 15½ in.), edition of 10. Printed and published by Universal Limited Art Editions. Photograph courtesy The Art Institute of Chicago, ULAE Collection, challenge grant of Mr and Mrs Thomas Dittmer; restricted gift of the supporters of the Department of Prints and Drawings; Centennial Endowment, 1982.945. © Jasper Johns/DACS London, VAGA New York 1996. Field 22. Paper: cream laid Angounois à la main. Proofs: 3 APs, 9 TPs, 4 HCs, 3 others.

28 Barnett Newman. *Canto VII* from *18 Cantos*, 1963, lithograph, 76.4×56.2 cm (30¹/₁₆ × 22⅛ in.), edition of 18. Printed and published by Universal Limited Art Editions. Photograph courtesy The Museum of Modern Art, New York. Gift of the Celeste and Armand Bartos Foundation. Reproduced courtesy of Annalee Newman insofar as her rights are concerned. Yard p. 47. Paper: Angoumois à la main. Proofs: 6 APs, 22 TPs, 10 WPs (for full set). Printer: Zigmunds Priede.

29 Sam Francis. *The White Line*, 1960, color lithograph, 90.5×63.3 cm (35½ × 25 in.), edition of 75. Printed by Emil Matthieu, Zurich. Published by Klipstein & Kornfeld. Photograph courtesy Galerie Kornfeld, Bern/Zurich. Paper: Rives BFK. Proofs: artists proofs.

30 Antoni Tàpies. *Ditades damunt diari*, 1974, etching and aquatint, 65.5×50.2 cm (25¾ × 19¾ in.), edition of 100. Printed by Joan Barbarà, Barcelona. Published by Sala Pelaires, Palma de Mallorca. Photograph © 1993 Fundació Antoni Tàpies, Barcelona. Galfetti 505.

31 Pierre Soulages. *Eau-forte XVI*, 1961, etching, 76×56 cm (30×22 in.), edition of 100. Printed and published by Lacourière, Paris. Photograph courtesy the artist. Paper: Arches-Velin.

32 Pierre Alechinsky. *Prisma*, 1988, color etching and aquatint, 191×90.5 cm (75¼ × 35½ in.), edition of 70. Printed by Vigna Antoniniana, Stamperie d'Arte. Published by 2RC. Photograph courtesy Galerie Espace, Amsterdam.

33 Pierre Alechinsky. *Panoplie*, 1967, color lithograph, 54×53 cm (21¼ × 20¾ in.), edition of 100. Printed by Imprimerie Clot, Bramsen et Georges, Paris. Published by Van de Loo, Munich. Photograph courtesy Otto van de Loo, Munich. Rivière 331. Proofs: 5 APs. There were also 1000 offset examples cut in two to accompany the catalogue *Pierre Alechinsky: 20 Jahre Impressionen, œuvre-katalog Druckgraphik.*

34 Corneille. *Enchantement de l'été*, 1962, color lithograph, 56.2×76 cm (22⅛ × 30 in.), edition of 120. Printed by Michel Cassé, Paris. Published by L'Œuvre Gravée, Paris/Zurich/ Locarno. Photograph courtesy Stede146lijk Museum Amsterdam. © ADAGP Paris and DACS London 1996. Donkersloot-van den Berghe 116.

35 Jasper Johns. *Four Panels from Untitled 1972*, 1973–74, lithograph, embossing and debossing on four sheets, 101.6×72.4 cm (40×28½ in.) each sheet, edition of 45. Printed and published by Gemini GEL. Photograph courtesy Gemini GEL. © Jasper Johns/DACS London, VAGA New York 1996. Field 194–197. Paper: Laurence Barker Grey handmade. Proofs: 10 APs, and 11 other proofs of Panel A/D, 9 other proofs of panel B/D, 16 other proofs of Panel C/D, and 32 other proofs of Panel D/D. Printers: Ron McPherson, Serve Lozingot, Charly Ritt, James L. Webb.

36 Jasper Johns. *Usuyuki*, 1979–81, color screenprint, 74.9×120.6 cm (29½ × 47¼ in.), edition of 85. Printed by Simca Print Artists. Published by the artist and Simca Print Artists. Photograph © 1989 Sotheby's, Inc. © Jasper Johns/DACS London, VAGA New York 1996. Segal 35. Paper: Japanese handmade paper. Proofs: 15 APs.

37 Jasper Johns. *Flags 1*, 1973, color screenprint, 69.9×88.9 cm (27½ × 35 in.), edition of 65. Printed by Simca Print Artists. Published by the artist and Simca Print Artists. Photograph © 1989 Sotheby's, Inc. © Jasper Johns/DACS London, VAGA New York 1996. Field 173. Proofs: 7 APs. Printers: Takeshi Shimada, Kenjiro Nonaka, Hiroshi Kawanishi.

38 Jasper Johns. *Decoy*, 1971, color lithograph, 104.1×73.6 cm (41×29 in.), edition of 55. Printed and published by Universal Limited Art Editions. Photograph courtesy Universal Limited Art Editions. © Jasper Johns/DACS London, VAGA New York 1996. Field 134. Paper: Rives BFK. Proofs: 4 APs.

39 Robert Rauschenberg. *Booster*, 1967, color lithograph and screenprint, 182.8×90.2 cm (72×35½ in.), edition of 38. Printed and published by Gemini GEL. Photo courtesy Gemini GEL. © Robert Rauschenberg/DACS London, VAGA New York 1996. Foster 47. Paper: Curtis Rag.

40 Jim Dine. *Eleven Part Self-Portrait (Red Pony)*, 1964–65, lithograph, 104.8×75.2 cm

(41¼ × 29⅝ in.), edition of 13. Printed and published by Universal Limited Art Editions. Photograph courtesy The Art Institute of Chicago, ULAE Collection, challenge grant of Mr and Mrs Thomas Dittmer; restricted gift of supporters of the Department of Prints and Drawings; Centennial Endowment, 1982.227.
Mikro 27. Paper: BFK Rives. Proofs: 2 APs. Printer: Ben Berns.

41 Jim Dine. *The Crash #2*, 1960, lithograph from the set of five, 81.3 × 50.8 cm (32 × 20 in.), edition of 33. Printed by Emiliano Sorini at Pratt Graphic Art Workshop. Published by Martha Jackson Gallery, New York. Photograph courtesy Print Collection, Miriam and Ira D. Wallach Division of Art, Prints and Photographs, The New York Public Library, Astor, Lenox and Tilden Foundations.
Mikro 2. Paper: Rives BFK.

42 Claes Oldenburg. *Orpheum Sign*, 1961, etching and aquatint, 29.8 × 23.8 cm (11¾ × 9⅜ in.), edition of 60. Plate prepared at Pratt Graphic Art Workshop and editioned by Georges Leblanc, Paris. Published by Arturo Schwarz, Milan. Photograph courtesy Brooke Alexander Editions.

43 Jim Dine. *Toothbrushes #1*, 1962, lithograph, 64.2 × 51.7 cm ($25\frac{3}{16}$ × 20½ in.), edition of 16. Printed and published by Universal Limited Art Editions. Photograph courtesy Brooke Alexander Editions.
Mikro 13. Paper: Chatham British handmade. Proofs: 1 AP. Printer: Zigmunds Priede.

44 Jim Dine. *Braid State II*, 1972, etching, 97 × 63 cm (38 × 25 in.), edition of 50. Printed and published by Petersburg Press. Photograph courtesy Brooke Alexander Editions.
Williams 149. Paper: Nideggen German Buff. Proofs: 14 APs. Printers: Maurice Payne, Alan Uglow, Winston Roeth.

45 Wayne Thiebaud. *Lunch Counter* from the portfolio *Delights*, 1964, etching, 38.1 × 27.9 cm (15 × 11 in.), edition of 100. Printed and published by Crown Point Press. Photograph courtesy Brooke Alexander Editions.

46 Wayne Thiebaud. *Dispensers* from the portfolio *Delights*, 1964, etching, 38.1 × 27.9 cm (15 × 11 in.), edition of 100. Printed and published by Crown Point Press. Photograph courtesy Brooke Alexander Editions.

47 Wayne Thiebaud. *Big Suckers*, 1971, color aquatint, 55.9 × 74.9 cm (22 × 29½ in.), edition of 50. Printed by Crown Point Press. Published by Parasol Press, Ltd. Photograph courtesy Brooke Alexander Editions.

48 Roy Lichtenstein. *Brushstroke*, 1965, color screenprint, 58.4 × 73.6 cm (23 × 29 in.), edition of 280. Published by Leo Castelli. © Roy Lichtenstein. Photograph courtesy Brooke Alexander Editions.
Bianchini 14. Cartridge paper.

49 James Rosenquist. *Marilyn*, 1975, color lithograph, 106 × 75 cm (41¾ × 29½ in.), edition of 75. Printed and published by Petersburg Press, Ltd. Photograph courtesy Brooke Alexander Editions. © James Rosenquist/DACS London, VAGA New York 1996.
Paper: Arches Cover.

50 Claes Oldenburg. *Tea Bag*, 1966, screenprint on felt, plexiglass, and plastic, 99.8 × 71.4 × 7.6 cm ($39\frac{1}{16}$ × $28\frac{1}{16}$ × 3 in.), edition of 125. Printed by Knickerbocker Machine and Foundary, Inc., New York. Published by Multiples, Inc. Photograph courtesy Susan Sheehan Gallery, New York.

51 Robert Indiana. *Love*, 1967, color screenprint, 91.4 × 91.4 cm (36 × 36 in.), edition of 250. Printed by Sirocco Screenprinters, New Haven. Published by Multiples, Inc. Photograph courtesy The Museum of Modern Art, New York. Riva Castleman Fund.
Sheehan 39. There was also an edition of 2275 and a second edition of 250, both printed by Maurel Studios, New York, and published by Mass Originals and Multiples, New York; these were printed on different paper, without margins, and are unsigned (with a handful of exceptions).

52 Andy Warhol. *Self-Portrait*, 1967, screenprint on silver coated paper, 58.4 × 58.4 cm (23 × 23 in.), edition of 300. Printed by Total Color, New York. Published by Leo Castelli Gallery, New York. Photograph courtesy Susan Sheehan Gallery, New York. © ARS New York and DACS London 1996.
Feldman/Schellmann 16. Published to announce a Warhol exhibition at Castelli; some prints are signed verso, some are signed recto.

53 Andy Warhol. *Jackie II*, 1966, color screenprint from the *Eleven Pop Artists II* portfolio, 61 × 76.2 cm (24 × 30 in.), edition of 200. Printed by KMF, Inc., New York. Published by Original Editions, New York. Photograph courtesy Edition Schellmann. © ARS New York and DACS London 1996.
Feldman/Schellmann 14.

54 Allen Jones. *Life Class*, 1968, book in the form of seven two-part, recombinable lithographs, upper: 34.3 × 56.5 cm (13½ × 22¼ in.); lower: 46.3 × 56.5 cm (18¼ × 22¼ in.), edition of 75. Printed by Emil Matthieu (hand lithography) and Beck & Partridge, Ltd. (photolithography). Published by Ars Moderna, Basel and Editions Alecto, London. Photograph courtesy Kupferstichkabinett, Staatliche Museen zu Berlin, Preußischer Kulturbesitz.
Stünke 66–74. Proofs: 15 APs.

55 R. B. Kitaj. *The Flood of Laymen* from *Mahler Becomes Politics, Beisbol*, 1965, color screenprint, 76.2 × 50.8 cm (30 × 20 in.), edition of 70. Printed by Kelpra Studio. Published by Marlborough Graphics. Photograph courtesy Marlborough Graphics.

56 R. B. Kitaj. *Partisan Review* from *In Our Time*, 1970, screenprint, 78.7 × 57.2 cm (31 × 22½ in.), edition of 150. Printed by Kelpra Studio. Published by Marlborough Graphics. Photograph courtesy Marlborough Graphics.

57 Peter Blake. *Tattooed Man* from *Side-Show*, 1974–78, wood engraving from the set of five, 26.7 × 21 cm (10½ x 8¼ in.), edition of 100. Printed by White Ink Studios, London. Published by Waddington Graphics. Photograph courtesy Alan Cristea Gallery.
Paper: Tonosawa, Japanese handmade. Proofs: 30 APs, 1 HC.

58 David Hockney. *Paris, 27 rue de Seine*, 1971, etching and aquatint, 89.5 × 71.1 cm (35¼ × 28 in.), edition of 150. Printed and published by Petersburg Press. Photograph courtesy Brooke Alexander Editions.
Paper: J. B. Green moldmade.

59 Fluxus (George Brecht, Joe Jones, Ay-O, Takehisa Kosugi, Ben Vautier, George Maciunas, etc.). *Fluxkit*, 1964 (this example 1966), vinyl case with mixed media, 30.5 × 43.2 × 12.7 cm (12 × 17½ × 5 in.) overall. Published by Fluxus. The Gilbert and Lila Silverman Fluxus Collection, Detroit. Photograph courtesy The Walker Art Center, Minneapolis.

60 Fritz Glarner. *Point Center 1941*, page 2 of *Recollection*, 1964–68, lithograph, 36.5 × 57.2 cm (14¾ × 22¾ in.), edition of 30. Printed and published by Universal Limited Art Editions. Photograph courtesy The Art Institute of Chicago, ULAE Collection, challenge grant of Mr and Mrs Thomas Dittmer; restricted gift of supporters of the Department of Prints and Drawings; Centennial Endowment, 1982.1772.
Paper: Angoumois à la main, with artist's signature in watermark. Proofs: 6 APs 2 PPs, trial proofs and working proofs.

61 Bridget Riley. *19 Greys A*, 1968, screenprint, 76.2 × 76.2 cm (30 × 30 in.), edition of 75. Printed by Kelpra Studio. Published by Rowan Gallery. Photograph courtesy the artist.

62 Bridget Riley. *19 Greys C*, 1968, screenprint, 76.2 × 76.2 cm (30 × 30 in.); edition of 75. Printed by Kelpra Studio. Published by Rowan Gallery. Photograph courtesy the artist.

63 Robert Watts. *Fingerprint*, *c.* 1965, plastic box, offset on paper, plaster, ink, 10.2 × 12 × 2.5 cm (4 × 4¾ × 1 in.); edition unknown. Published by Fluxus. Photograph courtesy Walker Art Center, Minneapolis.

64 Richard Artschwager. *Locations*, 1969, box (formica on wood) and five objects of wood, glass, formica, plexiglass, and rubberized horsehair, 38.1 × 27.3 × 12.7 cm (15 × 10¾ × 5 in.),

edition of 90. Published by Brooke Alexander, Inc. Photograph courtesy Brooke Alexander Editions.

65 Bernhard Luginbühl. *Grosser Zyklop II*, 1967–70, copper engraving, 85.7 × 105.7 cm ($33\frac{3}{4} \times 41\frac{1}{2}$ in.), edition of 50. Photograph courtesy Stedelijk Museum Amsterdam.

66 Lucio Fontana. *Plate 5* from *Sei Acquaforti Originali*, 1964, etching, printed in yellow-white, 44.1 × 33.2 cm ($17\frac{3}{8} \times 13\frac{1}{16}$ in.), edition of 50. Printed by 2RC. Published by Marlborough, Rome. Photograph courtesy The Museum of Modern Art, Abby Alrich Rockefeller Fund.

67 Diter Rot (Dieter Roth). *Bok 3b* and *Bok 3d: Reconstruction*, 1961–74, reconstruction of two books, originally published in 1961 by Forlag editions (Reykjavik), made from perforated comics and coloring books, 23 × 17 cm ($9 \times 6\frac{1}{2}$ in.), edition of 1000. Published by Hansjorg Mayer, Stuttgart. Photograph courtesy Print Collection, Miriam and Ira D. Wallach Division of Art, Prints and Photographs, The New York Public Library, Astor, Lenox and Tilden Foundations.
Issued as Volume 7 of Rot's *Gesammelte Werk*. Reconstructions of the two earlier books were issued bound together. Of the edition of 1000, 100 were signed and numbered.

68 Wolff Vostell. *Starfighter*, 1967, screenprint with glitter from the *Graphik des kapitalistischen Realismus* portfolio, 53 × 81.5 cm ($20\frac{3}{4} \times 32$ in.), edition of 80. Printed by Birkle + Thomer + Co., Berlin. Published by René Block, Berlin. Photograph courtesy Print Collection, Miriam and Ira D. Wallach Division of Art, Prints and Photographs, The New York Public Library, Astor, Lenox and Tilden Foundations.
Block V.14. Proofs: 40 HCs.

69 Sigmar Polke. *Freundinnen*, 1967, offset lithograph on cardboard, 48 × 61 cm (19 × 24 in.), edition of 150. Published by Edition h, Hanover. Photograph courtesy Susan Sheehan Gallery, New York.
Block P1; 25 proofs; some members of the edition and some proofs were handcolored in 1968.

70 Gerhard Richter. *9 Objekte*, 1969, offset lithograph from the set of nine, 45 × 45 cm ($17\frac{3}{4} \times 17\frac{3}{4}$ in.), edition of 80. Published by Edition der Galerie Heiner Friedrich and v. Pape, Munich. Photograph courtesy Brooke Alexander Editions.

71 Öyvind Fahlström. *Sketch for "World Map" Part I (Americas, Pacific)*, 1972, offset lithograph, 86.5 × 101.5 cm (34 × 40 in.), edition of 7,000 or more. Printed by Triggs Color Printing Corporation, New York. Published by the artist and distributed as the centerfold in the *Liberated Guardian*, Vol. 3, No. 1 (May 1972). Photograph courtesy Feigen, Inc., Chicago and Sharon Avery Fahlström. © DACS 1996.
Avery 7. Of the original edition of 7000 or so, only about 300 copies, unfolded and kept by the artist, remain.

72 Ed Ruscha. *Standard Station*, 1966, color screenprint, 65.4 × 101.9 cm ($25\frac{3}{4} \times 40\frac{1}{8}$ in.), edition of 50. Printed by Art Krebs, Los Angeles. Published by Audrey Sabol, Villanova. Photograph courtesy Brooke Alexander Editions.

73 Ed Ruscha. *OOO*, 1970, color lithograph, 50.8 × 71.1 cm (20 × 28 in.), edition of 90. Printed by Cirrus Editions. Co-published by Cirrus Editions and Brooke Alexander, Inc. Photograph courtesy Brooke Alexander Editions. Paper: Arches white. Proofs: 16 APs, 11 other proofs.

74 Sam Francis with text by Walasse Ting. From *1¢ Life*, 1964, color lithograph with type, 40.2 × 57.8 cm ($16 \times 22\frac{3}{4}$ in.), edition of 100. Printed by Maurice Beaudet, Paris, typography by Georges Girard, Paris. Published by E. W. Kornfeld, Bern. Photograph courtesy Galerie Kornfeld, Bern.
There was also an unsigned edition of 2000. The signed and numbered "special" edition of 100 was broken up as follows: 20 New York Edition; 20 Paris Edition; 20 Rest of the world; 40 for artists and collaborators.

75 Roy Lichtenstein with text by Walasse Ting. *Girl* and *Spray Can* from *1¢ Life*, 1964, color lithograph with type, 40.2 × 57.8 cm ($16 \times 22\frac{3}{4}$ in.), edition of 100. Printed by Maurice Beaudet, Paris, typography by Georges Girard, Paris. Published by E. W. Kornfeld, Bern. Photograph courtesy Galerie Kornfeld, Bern. © Roy Lichtenstein.
There was also an unsigned edition of 2000. The signed and numbered "special" edition of 100 was broken up as follows: 20 New York Edition; 20 Paris Edition; 20 Rest of the world; 40 for artists and collaborators.

76 Roy Lichtenstein. *Sweet Dreams, Baby!*, 1965, color screenprint from the *11 Pop Artists III* portfolio, 95.6 × 70.2 cm ($37\frac{1}{2} \times 27\frac{1}{2}$ in.), edition of 200. Printed by Knickerbocker Machine and Foundry, Inc., New York. Published by Original Editions, New York. © Roy Lichtenstein. Photograph © 1991 Sotheby's, Inc.
Bianchini 11. Proofs: 20 proofs reserved for Philip Morris, Inc.

77 Joe Goode. *Untitled*, 1971, lithograph and screenprint, 35.6 × 58.4 cm (14 × 23 in.), edition of 50. Printed and published by Cirrus Editions Ltd. Photograph courtesy Cirrus Editions Ltd. Paper: Copperplate Deluxe. Proofs: 14 APs; 6 other proofs.

78 James Rosenquist. *Dusting Off Roses*, 1965, color lithograph, 78.1 × 55.1 cm ($30\frac{3}{4} \times 21\frac{11}{16}$ in.), edition of 35. Printed and published by Universal Limited Art Editions. Photograph courtesy Universal Limited Art Editions. © James Rosenquist/DACS London, VAGA New York 1996.
Varian 2. Paper: Italia handmade. Proofs: artist's proofs, trial proofs, working proofs.

79 Andy Warhol. *Tomato* from *Campbell's Soup I*, 1968, screenprint from the portfolio of ten, 88.9 × 58.4 cm (35 × 23 in.), edition of 250. Printed by Salvatore Silkscreen Co., Inc., New York. Published by Factory Additions, New York. Photograph courtesy Susan Sheehan Gallery, New York. © ARS New York and DACS London 1996.
Feldman/Schellman 46. Proofs: 26 APs lettered A–Z on verso.

80 Andy Warhol. *Marilyn*, 1967, color screenprint from the set of ten, 91.5 × 91.5 cm (36 × 36 in.), edition of 250. Printed by Aetna Silkscreen Products, Inc./Du-Art Displays. Published by Factory Additions, New York. © ARS New York and DACS London 1996. Photograph © 1989 Sotheby's, Inc.
Feldman/Schellmann 31. Proofs: 26 APs, signed and lettered A–Z on verso.

81 Andy Warhol. *Cow*, 1966, screenprinted wallpaper, 115.5 × 75.5 cm ($45\frac{1}{2} \times 29\frac{3}{4}$ in.); unlimited edition. Printed by Bill Miller's Wallpaper Studio, Inc., New York. Published by Factory Additions, New York. Photograph courtesy Edition Schellmann. © ARS New York and DACS London 1996.
Feldman/Schellmann 11. Though the edition was unlimited, 100 were rubber stamp signed and numbered.

82 Richard Hamilton. *My Marilyn (a)*, 1965, color screenprint, 69 × 102 cm ($27\frac{1}{4} \times 40\frac{1}{4}$ in.), edition of 17 varied proofs. Printed by the artist at the University of Newcastle upon Tyne. Published by Robert Fraser Gallery, London. Photograph courtesy Alan Cristea Gallery.
Waddington 58. There is also a regular edition of *My Marilyn* 1965 printed at Kelpra Studio in an edition of 75 and published by Editions Alecto.

83 Richard Hamilton. *I'm Dreaming of a Black Christmas*, 1971, screenprint on collotype with collage, 74.7 × 100 cm ($29\frac{1}{2} \times 39\frac{3}{8}$ in.), edition of 150. Printed by collotype printed at E. Schreiber, Stuttgart, screenprinted at H. P. Haas, Stuttgart and Dietz Offizen, Lengmoos (Germany). Published by Petersburg Press. Photograph courtesy Alan Cristea Gallery.
Waddington 80. Paper: Schoeller Elfenbein-Karton. Proofs: 15 APs.

84 Richard Hamilton. *Kent State*, 1970, color screenprint, 73 × 102 cm (28 × 40 in.), edition of 5000. Printed by Dietz Offizin, Lengmoos (Germany). Published by Dorothea Leonhart, Munich. Photograph courtesy Walker Art

Center, Minneapolis. Gift of Mr and Mrs Russell Cowles, II, 1979.
Waddington 75. Paper: Schoeller Durex. Proofs: 50 APs and two complete sets of 14 state proofs.

85 Peter Blake. *Beach Boys*, 1964, color screenprint from the Institute of Contemporary Arts portfolio, 75.6 × 51 cm (30⅛ × 20⅛ in.), edition of 40. Printed by Kelpra Studio. Published by Institute of Contemporary Arts, London. Photograph courtesy Tate Gallery.

86 Eduardo Paolozzi. *As Is When: Tortured Life*, 1965, color screenprint, 96.5 × 66 cm (38 × 26 in.), edition of 65. Printed by Kelpra Studio. Published by Editions Alecto. Photograph courtesy Tate Gallery.

87 Patrick Caulfield. *Ah! storm clouds rushed from the Channel coasts* from *The Poems of Jules Laforgue*, 1973, book of 22 screenprint illustrations for 12 poems, accompanied by a slipcase of loose prints, 40.5 × 35.5 cm (16 × 14 in.); three separate editions: two of 200 each and one of 100. Printed by Advanced Graphics, London. Published by Petersburg Press in collaboration with Waddington Graphics. Photograph courtesy Alan Cristea Gallery.
Waddington 38t. Edition A: book in English, with a slip case of 6 loose prints; Edition B: book in French with a slip case of a different 6 loose prints; Edition C: book in English with a portfolio of 22 prints with wider margins. Each of the three editions has an extra 20 proofs.

88 Patrick Caulfield. *Ruins*, 1964, color screenprint from the Institute of Contemporary Arts portfolio, 50.8 × 76.2 cm (20 × 30 in.), edition of 40. Printed by Kelpra Studio. Published by the Institute of Contemporary Arts (London). Photograph courtesy Alan Cristea Gallery. Waddington 1; 10 proofs.

89 Joe Tilson. *Transparency Vallegrande Bolivia, October 10th*, 1969, screenprint on rigid PVC, lumiline and paper, collaged, 71 × 51 cm (28 × 20 in.), edition of 70. Printed by Kelpra Studio. Published by Marlborough Graphics. Photograph courtesy Alan Cristea Gallery. Vancouver 20.

90 Joe Tilson. *Sky One*, 1967, three-dimensional screenprint with vacuum-formed and vacuum-metallized objects, 124 × 69 cm (48¾ × 27⅛ in.), edition of 70. Printed by Kelpra Studio. Published by Marlborough Fine Art. Photograph courtesy Alan Cristea Gallery. Vancouver 12. Paper: J. Green Double Elephant.

91 Joe Tilson. *Earth Mantra*, 1977, soft-ground etching and aquatint, 106 × 76 cm (41¾ × 30 in.), edition of 70. Printed by Grafica Uno. Published by Waddington Graphics. Photograph courtesy Alan Cristea Gallery.
Vancouver 42. Some prints were dated.

92 David Hockney. *The Start of the Spending Spree and the Door Opening for a Blonde* from *A Rake's Progress*, 1961–63, etching from the set of 16, 50.8 × 61.6 cm (20 × 24¼ in.), edition of 50. Printed at the Royal College of Art. Published by Editions Alecto. Photograph courtesy the artist.

93 Karl Gerstner. *Diagon 31²*, 1956–67, alterable object made of screenprint on plastic bars, 62 × 62 cm (24½ × 24½ in.), edition of 125. Published by Galerie der Spiegel, Cologne. Photograph courtesy the artist.

94 Richard Paul Lohse. *Zentrum aus vier Quadraten als Ergebnis der vier Kreuzflächen*, 1976, screenprint, 58 × 58 cm (22¾ × 22¾ in.). Photograph courtesy Richard Paul Lohse-Stiftung, Zurich.

95 Joseph Albers. *White Line Square VIII*, 1966, lithograph, 53.3 × 53.3 cm (21 × 21 in.), edition of 125. Printed and published by Gemini GEL. Photograph courtesy Gemini GEL. © DACS 1996.

96 Dieter Roth. *In Oelper scheperts (Braunschweiger Landschaft mit Käsebäumen*, 1973, soft cheese on hand-printed offset lithograph in plastic, 32 × 49 cm (12½ × 19 in.), edition of 100. Printed by Karl Schulz, Braunschweig. Published by Kunstverein Rheinland-Westfalen. Photograph courtesy Edition Schellmann.
Proofs: 25 APs.

97 Öyvind Fahlström. *Elements from "Masses,"* 1976, baked enamel on metal with magnets, 70 × 70 cm (27½ × 27½ in.), edition of 50. Printed by Multirevol, Milan. Published by Multhipla, Milan (this illustration represents the maquette, made of acrylic and ink on vinyl and ragboard, 49.5 × 49.5 cm [19½ × 19½ in.]). Photograph courtesy Feigen Inc., Chicago and Sharon Avery Fahlström. © DACS 1996.
Avery 27. Proofs: 7 APs. Printer: Renato Volpini.

98 Enrico Baj. *Generale Urlante*, 1966, color lithograph, 100 × 70 (39½ × 27½ in.), edition of 60. Printed and published by Sergio Tosi and Paolo Bellasich, Milan. Photograph courtesy the artist.
Petit 135. Originally part of a portfolio including works by Bury, Crippa, Fontana, Hains, Soto and Spoerri. The "portfolio" was a solid box in which the lithographs were rolled.

99 Joseph Beuys. *Erdtelephon*, 1973, screenprint on felt board, 99 × 60 cm (39 × 23½ in.), edition of 100. Published by Edition Schellmann. Photograph courtesy Edition Schellmann. © DACS 1996.
Schellmann 79.

100 Joseph Beuys. *Minneapolis-Fragments*, 1977, lithograph printed in white on black printed surface, with pencil line from set of six (alternate version of edition printed in black on white), 64 × 89 cm (25½ × 35 in.), edition of VI,

stamped Free International University. Printed by Karl Imhof, Munich. Published by Edition Schellmann & Klüser. Photograph courtesy Edition Schellmann
Schellmann #233–38. © DACS 1996.

101 Sigmar Polke. *Untitled*, 1988, screenprint and offset lithograph, 98.5 × 69 cm (38½ × 27 in.), edition of 450 (approximate). Published by Griffelkunst, Hamburg. Photograph courtesy Edition Schellmann.

102 Gerhard Richter. *Schiff*, 1972, color offset lithograph, 50 × 65 cm (19½ × 25½ in.), edition of 250. Printed by Richard Bacht, Essen. Published by Kultursministerium Nordrhein-Westfalen, Dusseldorf. Photograph courtesy Edition Schellmann.
Block R35.

103 Gerhard Richter. *Farbfelder: 6 Anordnungen von 1260 Farben*, 1974, offset lithograph from a portfolio of six, 64.4 × 79.2 cm (25¼ × 31 in.), edition of 32. Printed by Kischbaum KG, Dusseldorf. Published by Edition der Galerie Heiner Friedrich, Munich. Photograph courtesy Edition Schellman.
Block R38.

104 Jannis Kounellis. *Untitled*, 1975, offset lithograph with embossing and preserved butterfly, in galvanized iron case, 57 × 42 cm (22½ × 16½ in.), edition of 90. Printed by Studio Bulla, Rome. Published by Mario Pieroni, Pescara. Photograph courtesy Edition Schellmann.
Schellmann 7. Paper: Magnani rag.

105 Ellsworth Kelly. *Calla Lilly 3*, 1983, lithograph, 91.4 × 63.5 cm (36 × 25 in.), edition of 30. Printed and published by Gemini GEL. Photograph courtesy Gemini GEL.

106 Ellsworth Kelly. *Large Grey Curve*, 1974, screenprint with embossing, 62.3 × 213.7 cm (24⅛ × 84⅛ in.), edition of 30. Printed and published by Gemini GEL. Photograph courtesy Gemini GEL.

107 Ellsworth Kelly. *Wall*, 1979, etching and aquatint, 80 × 71.1 cm (31½ × 28 in.), edition of 50. Printed and published by Tyler Graphics Ltd. Photograph courtesy Tyler Graphics Ltd.

108 Frank Stella. *Marriage of Reason and Squalor*, 1967, lithograph, 38.1 × 55.9 cm (15 × 22 in.), edition of 100. Printed and published by Gemini GEL. Photograph courtesy Gemini GEL. © ARS New York and DACS London 1996.
Axsome 7. Paper: Barcham Green. Proofs 9 APs, 6 other proofs. Printer: Ken Tyler.

109 Agnes Martin. *On a Clear Day*, 1973, screenprint from the set of thirty, 30.8 × 30.5 cm (12⅛ × 12 in. each), edition of 50. Printed by Editions Domberger, Stuttgart. Published by Parasol Press, Ltd. Photograph courtesy Susan Sheehan Gallery, New York.

110 Brice Marden. *Adriatics*, 1973, etching from the set of seven, 82.8 × 92.4 cm (32⁹⁄₁₆ × 36⅜ in.),

edition of 35. Printed by Crown Point Press. Published by Parasol Press, Ltd. Photograph courtesy Susan Sheehan Gallery, New York. Tate 22f. Paper: Rives BKF. Proofs: 12 APs; 5 of the 7 prints in the set were printed in editions of 40, this and one other were printed in editions of 35.

111 Brice Marden. *Adriatics*, 1973, etching and aquatint from the set of seven, 82.8 × 56.5 cm ($32\frac{9}{16}$ × $22\frac{1}{4}$ in.), edition of 40. Printed by Crown Point Press. Published by Parasol Press, Ltd. Photograph courtesy Susan Sheehan Gallery, New York. © ARS New York and DACS London 1996.
Tate 22a. Paper: Rives BFK. Proofs: 12 APs.

112 Brice Marden. *Tiles*, 1979, etching and sugarlift aquatint from the set of four, 75.5 × 57.2 cm ($29\frac{3}{4}$ × $22\frac{1}{4}$ in.), edition of 30. Printed and published by Crown Point Press. Photograph courtesy Tate Gallery. © ARS New York and DACS London 1996.
Tate 31c. Paper: Somerset satin. Proofs: 12 APs and 1 BAT. Printers: Stephen Thomas, Nancy Anello.

113 Mel Bochner. *Rules of Inference*, 1974–77, etching and aquatint, 75.6 × 99 cm ($29\frac{3}{4}$ × 39 in.), edition of 35. Printed by Crown Point Press. Published by Parasol Press, Ltd. Photograph courtesy Susan Sheehan Gallery, New York. Proofs: 10 APs.

114 Sol Lewitt. *Squares with a Different Line Direction in Each Half Square*, 1971, four from the set of ten etchings, 36.8 × 36.8 cm ($14\frac{1}{2}$ × $14\frac{1}{2}$ in.) each, edition of 25. Printed by Crown Point Press. Published by Parasol Press, Ltd. Photograph courtesy Susan Sheehan Gallery, New York.
Tate E1.

115 Sol Lewitt. *A Square Divided Horizontally and Vertically into Four Equal Parts, Each with a Different Direction of Alternating Parallel Bands of Lines*, 1982, woodcut, 76.2 × 76.2 cm (30 × 30 in.), edition of 60. Printed by Michael Berdan, Boston. Published by Multiples, Inc. Photograph courtesy Brooke Alexander Editions.
Tate W2.

116 Sol Lewitt. *Lines In Color On Color From Corners Sides and Centers to Specific Points on a Grid*, 1978, color screenprint from the set of seven, 76.2 × 76.2 cm (30 × 30 in.), edition of 25. Printed by Jo Watanabe, New York. Published by Multiples, Inc. Photograph courtesy Brooke Alexander Editions.

117 Richard Long. From *Nile: Papers of River Muds*, 1990, book of paper handmade from the muds of 14 rivers and screenprinted with the name of each river, 22 leaves, each leaf 38 × 31 cm (15 × $12\frac{1}{4}$ in.), edition of 88. Paper made by Madeleine Pestiaux, typography by Les Ferriss, screenprinting by Jeff Wasserman. Published by Lapis Press, Los Angeles. Photograph courtesy Spencer Collection, The New York Public Library, Astor, Lenox and Tilden Foundations. Paper technician: Wally Dawes; binding by Klaus Ullrich Rötzscher.

118 Claes Oldenburg. *Print IV* from *Notes*, 1968, color lithograph with embossing from the portfolio, 57.6 × 40 cm ($22\frac{11}{16}$ × $15\frac{3}{4}$ in.), edition of 100. Printed and published by Gemini GEL. Photograph courtesy Gemini GEL.

119 Claes Oldenburg. *Screwarch Bridge (State II)*, 1980, etching (hard ground, spitbite and aquatint), 80 × 147.3 cm ($31\frac{1}{2}$ × 58 in.); edition of 35. Printed by Aeropress, New York. Published by Multiples, Inc. Photograph courtesy Sotheby's. © 1987 Sotheby's, Inc.
Paper: Arches Roll. Printers: Pat Branstead and Young Soon Min.

120 Gilbert and George. *The Sadness in Our Art*, 1970, offset lithograph on charred paper, 37.4 × 25.4 cm ($14\frac{3}{4}$ × 10 in.). Photograph courtesy The Sol Lewitt Collection and the Wadsworth Athaneum, Hartford.

121 Eleanor Antin. *100 Boots on the Way to Church, Solana Beach, California, Feb. 9, 1971 11:30 AM*, 1971, postcard mailed April 15, 1971. One of a series of 51 postcards sent from 1971 to 1973, 11.4 × 17.8 cm ($4\frac{1}{2}$ × 7 in.), edition of 1000. Published by artist. Photograph courtesy Ronald Feldman Fine Arts, New York.

122 Giovanni Anselmo. *Verticale*, 1966–73, color photograph, 83 × 56.5 cm ($32\frac{1}{2}$ × $22\frac{1}{4}$ in.), edition of 17. Published by Giorgio Persano, Milan/Turin. Photograph courtesy Baron/Boisanté, New York.

123 Marcus Raetz. *Schatten*, 1991, photogram-gravure and aquatint, 176.5 × 67.3 cm ($69\frac{1}{2}$ × $26\frac{1}{2}$ in.), edition of 35. Printed and published by Crown Point Press. Photograph courtesy Crown Point Press.
Paper: Somerset Textured White.

124 Joseph Kosuth. One from *Ten Unnumbered Corrections*, 1991, a suite of ten relief-printed photoengravings, 25.4 × 25.4 cm (10 × 10 in.), edition of 25. Printed by Purgatory Pie Press, New York. Published by Ruth Benzacar Editions, Buenos Aires. Photograph courtesy Leo Castelli, New York. © ARS New York and DACS London 1996.
Paper: Johannot rag. Proofs: 5 APs. Printer: Dikko Faust.

125 Shusaku Arakawa. *Untitled 5* from *No! Says the Signified*, 1973–74, color lithograph with screenprint, 57.2 × 76.4 cm ($22\frac{1}{2}$ × $30\frac{1}{16}$ in.), edition of 60. Printed by Graphicstudio. Published by Graphicstudio and Multiples, Inc. Photograph courtesy National Gallery of Art, Washington. Gift of Graphicstudio/University of South Florida and the artist. B.97.

126 Bruce Nauman. *Studies for Holograms*, 1970, screenprint from the portfolio of five, 66 × 66 cm (26 × 26 in.), edition of 150. Printed by Aetna Studios, New York. Published by Castelli Graphics, New York. Photograph courtesy Sotheby's. © 1990 Sotheby's, Inc.
Cordes 1–5. Paper: 100 lb Kromecote. Proofs: 10 APs.

127 Bruce Nauman. *TV Clown*, 1982–85, lithograph, 76.2 × 111.8 cm (30 × 44 in.), edition of 35. Printed by Arber and Son Editions, Alameda, New Mexico. Published by Brooke Alexander Editions. Photograph courtesy Brooke Alexander Editions.
Cordes 55. Paper: Transpagra. Proofs: 9 APs, 6 other proofs.

128 Bruce Nauman. *Violins/Violence*, 1982–83, drypoint, 71.1 × 99.4 cm (28 × $39\frac{1}{8}$ in.), edition of 23. Printed and published by Gemini GEL. Photograph courtesy Gemini GEL.
Cordes 47. Paper: Fabriano Rosapina. Proofs: 7 APs, 7 other proofs. Printer: Ken Farley.

129 Vito Acconci. *Stones for a Wall #7*, 1977–79, lithograph from the set of ten, 76.2 × 59 cm (30 × $23\frac{1}{4}$ in.), edition of 10. Printed and published by Landfall Press. Photograph courtesy Landfall Press.
Paper: HMP. Proofs: 1 AP, 9 other proofs. Printers: Jack Lemon, Milan Milojevic.

130 Daniel Buren. *Framed/Exploded/Defaced*, 1979, color aquatint in 25 individually framed fragments, each fragment 20.3 × 20.3 cm (8 × 8 in.), edition of 46 color variants. Printed and published by Crown Point Press. Photograph of installation at Galerie Paul Maenz, Cologne, 1980, courtesy Crown Point Press.
Paper: Roll BFK.

131 Hans Haacke. *Tiffany Cares*, 1978, photo-etching, 73.6 × 104.1 cm (29 × 41 in.), edition of 35. Printed and published by Crown Point Press. Photograph courtesy Crown Point Press.
Paper: Twinrocker.

132 Hanne Darboven. *Wende "80,"* 1980, portfolio of 416 offset lithographs and six records, 58.4 × 43.2 cm (23 × 17 in.) each sheet, edition of 250. Printed by Sost and Co., Hamburg. Published by the artist. Photograph courtesy Edition Schellmann.

133 Vija Celmins. *Concentric Bearings B*, 1983, aquatint, drypoint and mezzotint, 43.2 × 38.1 cm (17 × 15 in.), edition of 35. Printed and published by Gemini GEL. Photograph courtesy Gemini GEL.

134 Chuck Close. *Keith*, 1972, mezzotint, 132.1 × 106.7 cm (52 × 42 in.), edition of 10. Printed by Crown Point Press. Published by Parasol Press, Ltd. Photograph courtesy The Museum of Modern Art, New York. John B. Turner Fund.

135 Chuck Close. *Phil Manipulated*, 1982, handmade paper, 177.8 × 137.2 cm (70 × 53½ in.), edition of 20. Printed by Joe Wilfer, New York. Published by Pace Editions. Photograph courtesy Pace Prints.

136 Vija Celmins. *Ocean*, 1992, woodcut, 49.5 × 39.4 cm (19½ × 15½ in.), edition of 50. Printed and published by Grenfell Press. Photograph courtesy Grenfell Press. Paper: Whatman 1953.

137 Robert Cottingham. *Hot*, 1973, color lithograph, 58.4 × 58.4 cm (23 × 23 in.), edition of 100. Printed and published by Landfall Press. Photograph courtesy Landfall Press.

138 Richard Estes. *Ten Doors* from the *Urban Landscape Portfolio*, 1972, color screenprint, 50 × 70 cm (19¹⁵⁄₁₆ × 27⅛ in.), edition of 100. Printed by Domberger. Published by Parasol Press, Ltd. Photograph courtesy Brooke Alexander Editions.

139 Sylvia Plimack Mangold. *Flexible and Stainless*, 1975, color lithograph, 53.3 × 74.3 cm (21 × 29¼ in.). Printed by Paul Narkiewicz. Published by Brooke Alexander, Inc. Photograph courtesy Brooke Alexander Editions.

140 Alex Katz. *The Swimmer*, 1974, aquatint, 71.4 × 91.1 cm (28⅛ × 35⅞ in.), edition of 84. Published by co-published by Brooke Alexander, Inc., and Marlborough Graphics, Inc., New York. Photograph courtesy Brooke Alexander Editions. Maravell 75.

141–143 Jennifer Bartlett. *Day and Night*, 1978, set of three: one etching and two drypoints, 38.1 × 27.9 cm (15 × 11 in.) each, edition of 35. Printed by Aeropress, New York. Published by Multiples, Inc. Photograph courtesy Brooke Alexander Editions.

144–146 Pat Steir. *Drawing Lesson, Part I, Line*, 1978, three etchings from the set of seven, 30.5 × 30.5 cm (12 × 12 in.), edition of 25. Printed and published by Crown Point Press. Photograph courtesy Crown Point Press. Paper: Arches Satine.

147 Richard Hamilton. *Picasso's Meninas*, 1973, etching (hard- and soft-ground, stipple, open-bite and lift-ground aquatint, engraving, drypoint, burnishing) from the portfolio *Hommage à Picasso*, 75 × 50.5 cm (29½ × 20 in.), edition of 150. Printed by Atelier Crommelynck. Published by Propylaen Verlag, Berlin. Photograph courtesy Alan Cristea Gallery. Waddington 88. Paper: Rives. Proofs: 15 APs and 15 PPs.

148 Robert Kushner. *Music*, 1981, color lithograph with sequins, feathers, and bronze painted crowns, 58.4 × 76.8 cm (22⅛ × 30¼ in.), edition of 25. Printed and published by Solo Press. Photograph courtesy Solo Impressions.

149 Michelle Stuart. *Tsikupuming*, 1974–75, embossed lithograph on paper mounted on cheesecloth, 34.9 × 28 cm (13¾ × 11 in.), edition of 24. Printed and published by the Tamarind Institute. Photograph courtesy the Tamarind Institute. Paper: Arjomari Arches. Proofs: 5 APs, 19 other proofs.

150 David Hockney. *Celia in an Armchair*, 1981, lithograph, 101.5 × 121.9 cm (40 × 48 in.), edition of 74. Printed and published by Gemini GEL. Photograph courtesy Gemini GEL.

151 Robert Motherwell. *The Stoneness of the Stone*, 1974, lithograph, 104.1 × 76.2 cm (41 × 30 in.), edition of 75. Printed by Tyler Graphics Ltd. Published by Brooke Alexander, Inc. Photograph courtesy Tyler Graphics Ltd. Belknap 136. Paper: light grey Twinrocker laminated to medium gray Twinrocker paper. Proofs: 8 APs (I–VIII).

152 Eduardo Chillida. *Eldu*, 1971, etching, 12.9 × 9.8 cm (5 × 3¾ in.), edition of 60. Printed and published by Maeght. Photograph courtesy Ikeda and Lokker, Tokyo. Michelin 108.

153 Eduardo Chillida. *Euzkadi IV*, 1976, etching, 159.5 × 115 cm (62¾ × 45¼ in.), edition of 50. Printed by Atelier Morsang. Published by Maeght. Photograph courtesy Ikeda and Lokker, Tokyo. Michelin 189. Proofs: 3 APs.

154 Carel Visser. *Composition*, 1961, woodcut, 61 × 85 cm (24 × 33½ in.). Printed by the artist. Photograph courtesy Stedelijk Museum Amsterdam. © DACS 1996.

155 Mel Kendrick. *Untitled (B)*, 1990, woodcut from the set of eight, 152 × 119.3 cm (60 × 47 in.), edition of 10. Printed by Grenfell Press. Published by Editions Ilene Kurtz. Photograph courtesy Betsy Senior Contemporary Prints, New York.

156 Martin Puryear. *Dark Loop*, 1982, woodcut, 57.8 × 76.2 cm (22¾ × 30 in.), edition of 35. Printed and published by Landfall Press. Photograph courtesy Landfall Press.

157 Richard Serra. *Videy Afangar #5*, 1991, etching, 24.5 × 30.5 cm (10 × 12 in.), edition of 75. Printed and published by Gemini GEL. Photograph courtesy Gemini GEL.

158 Joel Shapiro. *Untitled*, 1989, woodcut, 53.3 × 43.8 cm (21 × 17¼ in.); edition of 21. Printed and published by Grenfell Press, New York. Photograph courtesy Grenfell Press, New York. Paper: Whatman 1958. Proofs: 6 APs.

159 Richard Deacon. *Muzot*, 1987, etching on oilcloth from a portfolio of four prints, 64 × 64 cm (25³⁄₁₆ × 25³⁄₁₆ in.), edition of 25. Printed by Peter Kneuhühler, Zurich. Published by Margarete Roeder Editions, New York.

Photograph courtesy Brooke Alexander Editions. Of the edition of 25, 1–15 were printed on oilcloth, 16–25 were printed on paper. Proofs: 2 PPs 2 APs.

160 Not Vital. *Tongue*, 1990, lift-ground aquatint made from a cow tongue, 107.9 × 107.9 cm (42½ × 42½ in.), edition of 18. Printed by Harlan-Weaver Intaglio, New York. Published by Baron/Boisanté Editions, New York. Photograph courtesy Baron/Boisanté Editions, New York. Paper: Somerset Satin. Proofs: 5 APs, 1 HC, 1 PP, 1 BAT, 1 dedication print.

161 Richard Artschwager. *Interior*, 1972, screenprint, 83.2 × 116.8 cm (32¾ × 46 in.), edition of 68. Printed by Heinrici Silkscreen, New York. Published by Brooke Alexander, Inc. Photograph courtesy Brooke Alexander Editions.

162 Richard Artschwager. *Sailors*, 1972, screenprint, 62.9 × 45.1 cm (24¾ × 17¾), edition of 180. Printed by Styria Studios. Published by the Cologne Art Fair. Photograph courtesy Brooke Alexander Editions.

163 David Reed. *For Francesco de Cairo*, 1987, monotype, 71.1 × 233.7 cm (28 × 92 in.). Printed and published by Garner Tullis Workshop. Photograph courtesy Garner Tullis Workshop. Paper: Rives BFK.

164 David Storey. *Untitled* (series X, impression II), 1988, monotype, 94 × 59.7 cm (37 × 26 in.). Printed and published by Derrière l'Etoile Studios. Photograph courtesy the artist.

165–167 Oleg Kudryashov. *Composition (triptych) no. 284*, 1982, set of three: drypoint uninked with monotype watercolor; drypoint with additional lines incised after inking; and drypoint with monotype watercolor and additional lines incised after inking, 72.4 × 121.3 cm (28½ × 47¾ in.) each sheet. Printed and published by the artist. Photo courtesy Museum of Fine Arts, Boston. Gift of Mrs Frederick B. Deknatel.

168 Richard Tuttle. *In Praise of Historical Determinism I, II, and III*, 1974, two lithographs and one screenprint, 76.2 × 55.9 cm (30 × 22 in.) each, edition of 50. Screenprinting by Maurel Studios, New York. Lithography by George C. Miller & Son, New York. Published by Brooke Alexander, Inc. Photograph courtesy Brooke Alexander Editions.

169 Ellsworth Kelly. *Colors on a Grid, Screenprint*, 1976, screenprint and lithograph, 122.6 × 122.6 cm (48¼ × 48¼ in.), edition of 46. Printed and published by Tyler Graphics Ltd. Photograph courtesy Tyler Graphics Ltd.

170 Ellsworth Kelly. *18 Colors (Cincinnati)*, 1981, 18 color lithograph, 40.6 × 229.9 cm (16 × 90½ in.), edition of 57. Printed and published by Gemini GEL. Photograph courtesy Gemini GEL.

171 Donald Judd. *Untitled*, 1988, set of ten woodcuts, 60 × 80 cm (23 1/8 × 31 1/2 in.) each, edition of 25. Printed by Derrière l'Etoile Studios. Published by Brooke Alexander, Inc. Photograph courtesy Brooke Alexander Editions. Paper: Okawara. Blocks cut by Jim Cooper. Printer: Maurice Sanchez.

172 Donald Judd. *Untitled*, 1961–79, woodcut printed in oilpaint on Japanese paper, from the set of two, 53.3 × 73.7 cm (21 × 29 in.), edition of 25. Published by Edition der Galerie Heiner Friedrich, Munich. Photograph courtesy Edition Schellmann.

173 Frank Stella. *Double Grey Scramble*, 1972–73, 50-color screenprint, 73.6 × 128.9 cm (29 × 50 3/4 in.), edition of 100. Printed and published by Gemini GEL. Photograph courtesy Gemini GEL. © ARS New York and DACS London 1996.
Axsome 93. Paper: Arches moldmade. Printers: Kenneth Tyler, Jeffrey Wasserman, assisted by Marie Porter; 25 APs, 7 other proofs.

174–178 Robert Mangold. *Five Aquatints*, 1975, portfolio of five color aquatints and soft-ground etchings, 22.9 × 22.9 cm (9 × 9 in.) each, edition of 50. Printed by Crown Point Press. Published by Parasol Press, Ltd. Photograph courtesy Susan Sheehan Gallery, New York. Proofs: 15 APs.

179 Robert Ryman. *Seven Aquatints*, 1972, aquatint from the set of seven, 61 × 61 cm (24 × 24 in.), edition of 50. Printed by Crown Point Press. Published by Parasol Press, Ltd. Photograph courtesy Susan Sheehan Gallery, New York. Proofs: 10 APs.

180 Mel Bochner. *Second Color Quartet*, 1990, color lithograph on four sheets, 88.9 × 114.3 cm (35 × 45 in.) overall, edition of 35. Printed by Derrière l'Etoile Studios. Published by Diane Villani, New York. Photograph courtesy Diane Villani, New York.

181 Dorothea Rockburne. *Radiance*, 1983, color lithograph printed on both sides, cut and folded, 101.6 × 81.3 cm (40 × 32 in.), edition of 37. Printed and published by Gemini GEL. Photograph courtesy Gemini GEL.
Paper: Transpagra vellum.

182 Sandy Gellis. *Spring 1987: In the Northern Hemisphere*, 1987–88, twelve color photo-etchings, 30.5 × 30.5 cm (12 × 12 in.) each, edition of 12. Printed at the Printmaking Workshop, New York. Published by the artist. Photograph courtesy the artist.
Paper: Fabriano and Prans Praga. Printer: Julie D'Amato.

183 Blinky Palermo. *Flipper*, 1970, screenprint on two sheets, 85.5 × 66 cm (33 1/2 × 26 in.) each sheet, edition of 90. Printed by Atelier Laube, Munich. Published by Edition der Galerie Heiner Friedrich, Munich. Photograph courtesy Daniel Newburg, New York. © DACS 1996.
Jahn 8. Paper: offsetkarton. Proofs: 10 APs (signed, but unnumbered), 3–4 trial proofs.

184–189 Tom Phillips. *The Birth of Art*, 1973, zinc stencil progressively eroded and relief printed, six from the set of ten, 26.4 × 58.4 cm (10 3/8 × 23 in.), edition of 5. Printed by the artist at Croydon College of Art. Published by Tetrad Press. Photograph courtesy the artist and Alan Cristea Gallery.

190 Tom Phillips. *Sixty-four Stopcock Box Lids*, 1976, screenprint, 101.3 × 71.1 cm (39 7/8 × 28 in.), edition of 50. Printed by Bernard Cook. Published by Waddington Graphics. Photograph courtesy Alan Cristea Gallery.

191 Christo. *(Some) Not Realized Projects: Whitney Museum of American Art, Packed, Project for New York*, 1971, color lithograph with collage, 71.1 × 55.9 cm (28 × 22 in.), edition of 100. Printed and published by Landfall Press. Photograph courtesy Landfall Press.
Schellmann 35. Paper: Arjomari.

192 Jan Dibbets. *Untitled*, 1974, collotype and screenprint from the portfolio *Landscape*, 33 × 40 cm (13 × 15 3/4 in.), edition of 55. Screenprinting by Domberger, collotype printing by E. Schreiber, Stuttgart. Published by Edition Schellmann. Photograph courtesy Edition Schellmann.

193 Pieter Holstein. *Dog Watching Omnipresence*, 1975, hand colored etching, 50 × 65 cm (19 3/4 × 25 1/2 in.), edition of 40. Printed and published by the artist. Photograph courtesy the artist.

194 Bruce Nauman. *Oiled Dead*, 1975, lithograph and screenprint, 115.6 × 125.7 cm (45 1/2 × 49 1/2 in.), edition of 10. Printed and published by Gemini GEL. Photo courtesy Gemini GEL.
Cordes 33. Paper: Arches. Proofs: 3 TPs. Lithograph printed by Charly Ritt and Jim Webb, screenprinting by Robert Knisel and Richard Ewen; there was a second state of the print published in an edition of 14 with 7 APs and 6 other proofs.

195 Vito Acconci. *3 Flags for 1 Space and 6 Regions*, 1979–81, color photo-etching in six parts, 182.9 × 162.5 cm (72 × 64 in.) overall, edition of 25. Printed and published by Crown Point Press. Photograph courtesy Crown Point Press. Paper: Rives BFK.

196 Marcel Broodthaers. *La Signature Série 1 Tirage illimité*, 1969, black and red screenprint on tracing paper, 54.5 × 73.8 cm (21 1/2 × 29 in.), "unlimited" edition of 60. Published by the artist. Photograph courtesy Michael Werner Gallery, New York and Cologne.

197 Marcel Broodthaers. *Museum-Museum*, 1972, color screenprint on black, two parts, 83.9 × 59.1 cm (33 × 23 1/4 in.) each sheet, edition of 100. Published by Editions Staeck, Heidelberg. Photograph courtesy Michael Werner Gallery, New York and Cologne.

198 Chris Burden. *Diecemila*, 1977, color photo-etching printed on both sides of the paper, 25.4 × 35.5 cm (10 × 14 in.), edition of 35. Printed and published by Crown Point Press. Photograph courtesy Crown Point Press.
Paper: handmade (Don Farnsworth).

199 Mario Merz. *Da un Erbario Raccolto nel 1979 Woga-Woga, Australië*, 1989, color lithograph from the set of 14, 46 × 34 cm (18 1/8 × 13 1/2 in.), edition of 120. Photograph courtesy Stedelijk Museum Amsterdam.

200 Jannis Kounellis. *Untitled*, 1979, aquatint and photo-etching, 114.3 × 91.4 cm (45 × 36 in.), edition of 21. Printed and published by Crown Point Press. Photograph courtesy Crown Point Press.
Schellmann 10. Paper: Rives BFK.
Proofs: 10 APs.

201 Franz Gertsch. *Schwarzwasser*, 1990–91, woodcut, 274 × 217 cm (108 1/4 × 85 1/2 in.), edition of 33 color variants. Printed by the artist and Nik Hausmann. Published by the artist and Turske & Turske, Zurich. Photograph courtesy the artist.
Mason 12. Paper: Japon Heizoburo. The edition of 33 consists of: 3 APs, 20 impressions in different colors (1/20–20/20), and 10 impressions in different colors (I/X–X/X). There were some color trial proofs as well.

202 Alex Katz. *Black Shoes*, 1987, color etching and aquatint, 57.2 × 73.7 cm (22 1/8 × 29 in.), edition of 60. Printed and published by Crown Point Press. Photograph courtesy Crown Point Press.
Paper: Somerset. Printers: Doris Simmelink and Chris Sukimoto.

203 David Hockney. *What Is This Picasso?* from *The Blue Guitar*, 1976–77, color etching and aquatint from the set of 20, 45.7 × 52 cm (18 × 20 1/2 in.), edition of 200. Printed by Maurice Payne. Published by Petersburg Press. Photograph courtesy the artist.
Paper: Inveresk. Proofs: 35 (I–XXXV).

204 Philip Pearlstein. *Models with Mirror*, 1983–85, color etching and aquatint, 90.5 × 137.2 cm (35 5/8 × 53 3/4 in.), edition of 60. Printed by Graphicstudio. Published by Graphicstudio and 724 Prints, New York. Photograph courtesy Graphicstudio.
20 proofs.

205 Roy Lichtenstein. *Bull Profile Series: Bull II*, 1973, lithograph and linecut from the series of six, 68.6 × 88.9 cm (27 × 35 in.), edition of 100. Printed and published by Gemini GEL. © Roy Lichtenstein. Photo courtesy Gemini GEL.
Proofs: 13 APs, 10 other proofs. Printers: Kenneth Tyler, Ron McPherson, Bruce Porter, assisted by Ron Olds.

206 Roy Lichtenstein. *Bull Profile Series: Bull IV*, 1973, lithograph, screenprint and linecut from the series of six, 68.6 × 88.9 cm (27 × 35 in.), edition of 100. Printed and published by Gemini GEL. © Roy Lichtenstein. Photograph courtesy Gemini GEL.
Proofs: 13 APs, 8 other proofs. Printers: Kenneth Tyler, Ron Olds, Ron McPherson, assisted by Bruce Porter.

207 Roy Lichtenstein. *Goldfish Bowl*, 1981, woodcut, 63.5 × 46.3 cm (25 × 18¼ in.), edition of 30. Printed and published by Tyler Graphics Ltd. © Roy Lichtenstein. Photograph courtesy Tyler Graphics Ltd.
Paper: natural Okawara handmade.
Proofs: 10 AP, 6 other proofs.

208 Helen Frankenthaler. *Essence Mulberry, State I*, 1977, eight color woodcut, 100.3 × 47 cm (39½ × 18½ in.), edition of 10. Printed and published by Tyler Graphics Ltd. Photograph courtesy Tyler Graphics Ltd.
Krens 63. Paper: handmade gray Maniai.
Proofs: 2 TP, C.

209 Barry Flanagan. *Killary Harbour 1979*, 1980, linocut, 38.5 × 57 cm (15¼ × 22½ in.), edition of 30. Printed by Carol Docherty at the artist's studio, London. Published by Waddington Graphics. Photograph courtesy Alan Cristea Gallery.
Paper: Vélin d'Arches crème.

210 Robert Rauschenberg. *Hoarfrost Editions: Plus Fours*, 1974, transfer and collage on silk, 170.2 × 241.3 cm (67 × 95 in.), edition of 28. Printed and published by Gemini GEL. Photograph courtesy Gemini GEL. © Robert Rauschenberg/DACS London, VAGA New York 1996.

211 David Hockney. *Le Plongeur, Paper Pool 18*, 1978, colored, pressed paper pulp in twelve sheets, together: 182.9 × 217.2 cm (72 × 171 in.). Printed and published by Tyler Graphics Ltd. Photograph courtesy Tyler Graphics Ltd.

212 Alan Shields. *Odd-Job*, 1984, woodcut, etching, stitching, and collage on handmade papers, 106.7 × 106.7 cm (42 × 42 in.), edition of 46. Printed and published by Tyler Graphics Ltd. © Alan Shields/Tyler Graphics, Ltd. Photograph courtesy Tyler Graphics Ltd.
Proofs: 17 APs, 5 other proofs.

213 Frank Stella. *Noguchi's Okinawa Woodpecker* from the *Exotic Bird Series*, 1977, color lithograph and screenprint, 86 × 116.5 cm (33⅞ × 45⅞ in.), edition of 50. Printed and published by Tyler Graphics Ltd. Photograph courtesy Tyler Graphics Ltd. © ARS New York and DACS London 1996.
Axsome 109.

214 Frank Stella. *Pergusa Three, State I*, 1983, relief print in 40 colors from magnesium plates and woodblocks on handmade dyed paper, 167.6 × 132 cm (66 × 52 in.), edition of 10. Printed and published by Tyler Graphics Ltd. Photograph courtesy Tyler Graphics Ltd. © ARS New York and DACS London 1996.
Axsome 143a.

215 Joel Shapiro. *Untitled*, 1990, color aquatint from a portfolio of four, 94.9 × 69.2 cm (37⅜ × 27¼ in.), edition of 60. Printed and published by Aldo Crommelynck. Photograph courtesy Pace Prints.

216 Nathan Oliveira. *London Site 8–11*, 1984, monotype with hand painting, 66 × 55.9 cm (26 × 22 in.). Printed and published by the artist. Photograph courtesy the artist.

217 Judy Pfaff. *Manzanas Y Naranjas* from *Six of One...*, 1987, color woodcut, 149.9 × 177.8 cm (59 × 70 in.), edition of 15. Printed and published by Crown Point Press. Photograph courtesy Crown Point Press.
Paper: Hosho.

218 Michael Mazur. *Wakeby Day II*, 1983, pastel and monotype, 182.9 × 365.8 cm (72 × 144 in.). Printed by Robert Townsend at Impressions Workshop, Boston. Published by the artist. Photograph courtesy the artist. Collection Brooklyn Museum.

219 Therese Oulton. *Untitled*, 1989, monotype, 97.1 × 66 cm (38¼ × 26 in.). Printed and published by Garner Tullis Workshop. Photograph courtesy Garner Tullis Workshop.

220 Nancy Graves. *Ngetal*, 1977, hand-colored etching with aquatint, engraving and drypoint, 80 × 90.2 cm (31½ × 35½ in.), edition of 33. Printed and published by Tyler Graphics Ltd. Photograph courtesy Tyler Graphics Ltd.
Paper: Arches cover. Proofs: 9 APs, 3 TPs, 3 CTPs, SP, 2 WPs, RTP, PP 1, A, C.

221 John Cage. *The Missing Stone*, 1989, color spitbite and aquatint etching on smoked paper, 137.2 × 104.1 cm (54 × 41 in.), edition of 25. Printed and published by Crown Point Press. Photograph courtesy Crown Point Press.
Paper: smoked Somerset White Textured.

222 Howard Hodgkin. *Monsoon*, 1987, lithograph, watercolor and gouache, 107.5 × 135 cm (42⅜ × 53⅛ in.), edition of 85. Printed by Solo Press. Published by Waddington Graphics. Photograph courtesy Ikeda and Lokker, Tokyo.
Proofs: 11 APs. Printers: Judith Solodkin and Arnold Brooks, hand-coloring by Cinda Sparling.

223 Howard Hodgkin. *Black Monsoon*, 1987, lithograph and gouache, 107.5 × 135 cm (42⅜ × 53⅛ in.), edition of 40. Printed by Solo Press. Published by Waddington Graphics. Photograph courtesy Ikeda and Lokker, Tokyo.
Proofs: 11 APs. Printers: Arnold Brooks, hand coloring by Cinda Sparling.

224 Howard Hodgkin. *In an Empty Room*, 1990, etching with carborundum and gouache, 120 × 150 cm (47¼ × 59 in.), edition of 55. Printed by 107 Workshop, Wiltshire. Published by Waddington Graphics. Photograph courtesy Ikeda and Lokker, Tokyo.
Proofs: 15 APs. Printed and hand-colored by Jack Shirreff.

225 Georg Baselitz. *LR*, 1966, chiaroscuro woodcut from three blocks, approximately 45 × 35 cm (17¾ × 13¾ in.), edition of about 20 variants. Printed and published by the artist. Photograph courtesy Maximilian Verlag/Sabine Knust, Munich.
Jahn 49. The edition varies in paper, in inking color, and in the number of blocks used.

226 Arnulf Rainer and Gunter Brus. *Depth Obscured*, 1985–86, etching, photoetching and drypoint, 45.2 × 31.2 (17 13/16 × 12 7/16). Photograph courtesy The Museum of Modern Art, New York.

227 Georg Baselitz. *Adler*, 1981, woodcut from the portfolio *Erste Konzentration II*, 65 × 50 cm (25½ × 19¾ in.), edition of 50. Printed by Elke Baselitz. Published by Maximilian Verlag/Sabine Knust, Munich. Photograph courtesy Maximilian Verlag/Sabine Knust, Munich.

228 Markus Lüpertz. *Flasche II*, 1980, lithograph, 95.5 × 65.5 cm (37½ × 25¾ in.), edition of 40. Printed by Clot Bramsen et Georges, Paris. Published by Edition der Galerie Heiner Friedrich, Munich. Photograph courtesy Maximilian Verlag/Sabine Knust.
Cantz 170. A reworking of *Flasche I*.
Paper: Arches-Velin.

229 Anselm Kiefer. *Wege der Weltweisheit: Hermannsschlacht*, 1980, woodcut with painted additions in acrylic and shellac, 344.8 × 528.3 cm (135¾ × 208 in.). Printed by the artist. Photograph courtesy The Art Institute of Chicago, restricted gift of Mr and Mrs Noel Rothman, Mr and Mrs Douglas Cohen, Mr and Mrs Thomas Dittmer, Mr and Mrs Ralph Goldenberg, Mr and Mrs Lewis Manilow, and Mr and Mrs Joseph R Shapiro; Wirt D Walker Fund, 1986.112. Photograph by courtesy of the artist.

230 A. R. Penck. *Acht Erfahrungen*, 1982, woodcut from the set of eight, 80 × 60 cm (31½ × 23½ in.), edition of 50. Printed by François Lafranca, La Collinasca, Ticino (Switzerland). Published by Peter Blum Edition. Photograph courtesy Peter Blum Edition.
Paper: handmade by Lafranca; 10 additional proofs.

231 Enzo Cucchi. *La Mano di Pietra*, 1982, etching and aquatint, 85 × 60 cm (33 × 23½ in.), edition of 50. Printed by Stamperia Grafica del Colle, Ancône. Published by Edition Schellmann and Klüser. Photo courtesy Edition Schellmann.
Paper: Fabriano.

232 Enzo Cucchi. *Un'Immagine Oscura...*, 1982, color etching, 120 × 176 cm (47¼ × 69¼ in.), edition of 30. Printed by Vigna Antoniniana

Stamperia d'Arte, Rome. Published by Peter Blum Edition. Photograph courtesy Peter Blum Edition.
Paper: Fabriano Rosaspina. Proofs: 6.

233 Francesco Clemente. *Self Portrait No. 2*, 1981, etching, 40.6 × 52 cm (16 × 20½ in.), edition of 10. Printed and published by Crown Point Press. Photograph courtesy Crown Point Press. Paper: Arches Satinée.

234 Stephen Ellis. *Plate VI* from *Escorial*, 1991, drypoint and aquatint from the set of eight, 32 × 24 cm (12½ × 9¼ in.), edition of 15. Printed by Niels Borch Jensen. Published by the artist and Elizabeth Koury, New York. Photograph courtesy Betsy Senior Contemporary Prints, New York.

235 Troels Wörsel. *The Spanish Set*, 1990, etching and aquatint from the set of 25 etchings and one screenprint on plexiglass, 76.2 × 55.9 cm (30 × 22 in.), edition of 15. Printed and published by Dan Albert Benvenista, Madrid. Photograph courtesy Print Collection, Miriam and Ira D. Wallach Division of Art, Prints and Photographs, The New York Public Library, Astor, Lenox and Tilden Foundations. Paper: Zerkall-Butten.

236 Philip Guston. *Pile Up*, 1979, lithograph, 50.8 × 76.2 cm (20 × 30 in.), edition of 50. Printed and published by Gemini GEL. Photograph courtesy Gemini GEL.

237 H. C. Westermann. *The Human Fly*, 1971, woodcut, 62.5 × 46 (24⅛ × 18¹/₁₆ in.), edition of 21. Printed and published by the artist. Photograph courtesy Milwaukee Art Museum, Gift of Quad/Graphics, Inc., Pewaukee, with National Endowment for the Arts Matching Funds. © Estate of H. C. Westermann/DACS London, VAGA New York 1996.

238 Roger Brown. *Standing While All Around Are Sinking*, 1977, aquatint, 61 × 50.8 cm (24 × 20 in.), edition of 50. Printed by Timothy Berry, Chicago. Published by Teaberry Press, Chicago. Photograph courtesy Phyllis Kind Gallery, Chicago/New York.
Paper: Rives BFK. Proofs: 4.

239 Donald Baechler. *Increments*, 1987, etching and aquatint from the set of five, 90.1 × 69.8 cm (35½ × 27½ in.), edition of 17. Printed by Donna Shulman, Brooklyn. Published by Baron/Boisanté Editions, New York. Photograph courtesy Baron/Boisanté Editions, New York.

240 George Condo. *Clown*, 1989, color aquatint, 62.9 × 54 cm (24¾ × 21¼ in.), edition of 55. Printed and published by Aldo Crommelynck. Photograph courtesy Pace Prints.

241 Keith Haring. *Untitled #1*, 1982, lithograph from the group of six, 61 × 91.4 cm (24 × 36 in.), edition of 40. Printed by Maurice Sanchez. Published by Barbara Gladstone Gallery, New

York. © 1983 The Estate of Keith Haring. Photograph courtesy Barbara Gladstone Gallery, New York.
Paper: Arches 88.

242 Terry Winters. *Double Standard*, 1984, lithograph, 198.1 × 108 cm (78 × 42½ in.), edition of 40. Printed and published by Universal Limited Art Editions. Photograph courtesy Collection Walker Art Center, Minneapolis. Walker Special Purchase Fund, 1986.
Proofs: 8. Printers: John Lund, Douglas Volle.

243 Jonathan Borofsky. *274075*, 1982, etching from the portfolio of six etchings and seven screenprints, 76 × 56 cm (30 × 22 in.), edition of 50. Printed by Robert Aull and Leslie Sutcliffe, Los Angeles. Published by Peter Blum Edition. Photograph courtesy Peter Blum Edition.
Paper: Velin d'Arches. Proofs: 10.

244 Jonathan Borofsky. *274075*, 1982, screenprint from the portfolio of six etchings and seven screenprints, 76 × 56 cm (30 × 22 in.), edition of 50. Printed by H. M. Büchi, Basel. Published by Peter Blum Edition. Photograph courtesy Peter Blum Edition.
Paper: Velin d'Arches. Proofs: 10.

245 Jonathan Borofsky. *Berlin Dream Stamp*, 1986, black and white photo print with perforations, 33 × 49.5 cm (13 × 19½ in.), edition of 100. Printed and published by Gemini GEL. Photograph courtesy Gemini GEL.
Paper: Kodak RC.

246 Susan Rothenberg. *Pinks*, 1980, hand-inked woodcut in two colors, 48.3 × 68.6 cm (19 × 27 in.), edition of 20 variants. Printed by Aeropress, New York. Published by Multiples, Inc. Photograph © 1991 Sotheby's, Inc. Maxwell 7. Paper: impressions 1–17 printed on Umbria, impressions 18–20 printed on Rives Lightweight. Proofs: 12 APs, 1 exhibition proof; each impression is unique.

247 Elizabeth Murray. *Untitled State I*, 1980, lithograph from a set of five, 57.8 × 45.7 cm (22¾ × 18 in.), edition of 35. Printed by Derrière l'Etoile Studios. Published by Brooke Alexander, Inc. and Paula Cooper Gallery, New York. Photograph courtesy Brooke Alexander Editions.

248 Elizabeth Murray. *Untitled State IV*, 1980, lithograph from a set of five, 57.8 × 45.7 cm (22¾ × 18 in.), edition of 35. Printed by Derrière l'Etoile Studios. Published by Brooke Alexander, Inc. and Paula Cooper Gallery, New York. Photograph courtesy Brooke Alexander Editions.

249 Carroll Dunham. *Untitled*, 1984–85, two-color lithograph, 71 × 48.5 cm (28 × 19 in.), edition of 42. Printed and published by Universal Limited Art Editions. Photo courtesy Collection Walker Art Center, Walker Special Purchase Fund.
Paper: handmade J. Whatman. Proofs: 6 APs, 1 PP.

250 Jane Kent. *Untitled*, 1990, aquatint and mezzotint, 66 × 55.9 cm (26 × 22 in.), edition of 20. Printed by Cindy Ettinger at the artist's studio, New York. Published by Dolan/Maxwell, Philadelphia. Photograph courtesy the artist.
Paper: Rives BFK. Proofs: 1 AP.

251 Jasper Johns. *The Seasons*, 1989, etching and aquatint, 48.6 × 129.9 cm (19⅛ × 51⅛ in.), edition of 54. Printed and published by Universal Limited Art Editions. Photograph courtesy Universal Limited Art Editions. © Jasper Johns/DACS London, VAGA New York 1996.

252 Louise Bourgeois. *Untitled*, 1989–91, drypoint, 49 × 56 cm (19¼ × 22 in.), edition of 50. Printed by Harlan and Weaver Intaglio, New York. Published by Peter Blum Edition. Photograph courtesy Peter Blum Edition.

253 Louise Bourgeois. *Quarantania (II)*, 1947–90, etching, 47.5 × 32.5 cm (18½ × 13 in.), edition of 50. Published by Galerie Lelong, New York. Photograph courtesy Galerie Lelong, New York.

254 Richard Diebenkorn. *#5* from *Five Aquatints with Drypoint*, 1978, aquatint and drypoint, 48.3 × 33.6 cm (19 × 13¼ in.), edition of 35. Printed and published by Crown Point Press. Photograph courtesy Brooke Alexander Editions.
Guillemin p. 113. Paper: Rives Heavyweight Buff. Proofs: 10 APs, 1 TP. Printers: Lilah Toland, David Kelso.

255 Richard Diebenkorn. *Passage 1*, 1990, etching and aquatint, 74.9 × 50.8 cm (29½ × 20¼ in.), edition of 35. Printed and published by Crown Point Press. Photograph courtesy Crown Point Press.
Paper: Rives Heavyweight White.

256 Brice Marden. *Etchings to Rexroth #9*, 1986, etching from the set of 25, 50 × 41 cm (19½ × 16 in.), edition of 45. Printed by Jennifer Melby, New York. Published by Peter Blum Edition. Photograph courtesy the artist. © ARS New York and DACS London 1996. Tate 40/9. Paper: Rives BFK. Proofs: 10 APs.

257 Lesley Dill. *The Poetic Body: Poem Gloves*, 1992, letterpress and collage, 45.7 × 33.02 cm (18 × 13 in.), edition of 20. Printed and published by Solo Impression Inc. Photograph courtesy Solo Impression Inc.
Letterpress printed onto silk tissue, which is sewn into the shape of gloves, mounted on Richard de Bas paper. Proofs: 10 APs, 5 other.

258 Richard Prince. *"(no title),"* 1991, lithograph from the set of twelve, 38.1 × 27.94 cm (15 × 11 in.), edition of 26. Printed by Robert Arber and Son, New Mexico. Published by I. C. Editions, New York. Photograph courtesy I. C. Editions, New York.
Proofs: 6 APs, 3 PPs, 1 ICE Edition.

259 Ed Ruscha. *Rooster*, 1988, etching, 111.8 × 77.5 cm (44 × $30\frac{1}{2}$ in.), edition of 50. Printed and published by Crown Point Press. Photograph courtesy Crown Point Press.
Paper: Somerset White.

260 Tim Rollins + K.O.S. *The Temptation of St Antony XXV – the Solitaires*, 1990, aquatint with photogravure and chine collé, 41.3 × 29.8 cm ($16\frac{1}{4}$ × $11\frac{11}{16}$ in.), edition of 15. Printed and published by Crown Point Press. Photograph courtesy Crown Point Press.
Paper: Lana Gravure White, and Whatman's Laid White (chine collé).

261 Tim Rollins + K.O.S. *The Temptation of St Antony XVI – the Solitaires*, 1990, aquatint with photogravure and chine collé, 41.3 × 29.8 cm ($16\frac{1}{4}$ × $11\frac{11}{16}$ in.), edition of 15.
Printed and published by Crown Point Press. Photograph courtesy Crown Point Press.
Paper: Lana Gravure White, and Whatman's Laid White (chine collé).

262 Jenny Holzer. *Truisms*, 1978, poster installation (photostats). Photograph courtesy Barbara Gladstone Gallery, New York.

263 Barbara Kruger. *Your Body Is a Battleground*, 1989, offset lithograph poster, Polish edition. Photograph courtesy the artist.

264 Guerilla Girls. *Women In America...*, 1988, offset lithograph poster, unlimited edition. Photograph courtesy New York Public Library.

265 Art Spiegelman. *Mickey, Mouse & Maus*, 1992, three color lithograph, from the set *4 Mice*, 20.3 × 15.2 cm (8 × 6 in.), edition of 30. Printed by Corridor Press, Otego, New York. Published by Raw Graphics, New York. © 1992 Art Spiegelman. Photograph courtesy Galerie St Etienne, New York.
Paper: Rives BFK. Printer: Timothy Sheesley. The same image was also released in two-color edition of 75 inserted into a special hardcover edition of *Maus*.

266 Sue Coe. *The Selection*, 1991, lithograph, 76.2 × 55.9 cm (30 × 22 in.), edition of 20. Printed and published by the Washington University School of Fine Arts Printmaking Workshop, St Louis. © 1991 Sue Coe. Photo courtesy Galerie St Etienne, New York.

267 Christopher Wool. *Untitled*, 1989, monotype, 187 × 94 cm ($73\frac{1}{8}$ × 37 in.). Printed by Derrière l'Etoile Studios. Published by Edition Julie Sylvester, New York. Photograph courtesy Edition Julie Sylvester, New York.
Paper: handmade Suzuki.

268 Matthew Lawrence. *The Cleansing*, 1992, woodcut, 304.8 × 121.9 cm (120 × 48 in.), open edition. Printed and published by the artist. Photograph courtesy the artist.
Printed on mulberry rice paper, mounted on canvas.

269 Kiki Smith. *All Souls*, 1988, screenprint on fifteen attached sheets, 228.6 × 156.2 cm (90 × $60\frac{1}{2}$ in.). Printed by the artist. Photograph courtesy Fawbush Gallery, New York. Collection Brooklyn Museum.
Paper: Thai tissue. There are several examples of this subject; each is unique.

270 Christian Marclay. *Untitled*, 1990, surface monotype from phonograph records, 114.3 × 114.3 cm (45 × 45 in.). Printed and published by Solo Impression, Inc. Photograph courtesy Solo Impression, Inc.

271 Barbara Bloom. *Signature Lettraset* from *The Reign of Narcissism*, 1989, lettraset sheet, 33 × 25.4 cm (13 × 10 in.), unlimited edition. Published by artist. Photograph courtesy Jay Gorney Modern Art, New York.

272 Christian Boltanski. *Gymnasium Chases*, 1991, portfolio of 24 photogravures and colophon, 52.3 × 41.9 cm ($23\frac{1}{4}$ × $16\frac{1}{2}$ in.) each, edition of 15. Printed and published by Crown Point Press. Photograph courtesy Crown Point Press.

273 Victor Burgin. *Fiction Film*, 1991, duotone screenprint with varnish from the set of nine, 76.2 × 95.3 cm (30 × $37\frac{1}{2}$ in.), edition of 35. Printed by Coriander Studio, London. Published by Paragon Press, London. Photograph courtesy Paragon Press, London.

274 Arnulf Rainer. *Dornenkreuz*, 1990–91, drypoint on shaped plate, 65 × 50 cm ($25\frac{1}{2}$ × $19\frac{3}{4}$ in.), edition of 35. Printed by Karl Imhof, Munich. Published by Maximilian Verlag/Sabine Knust, Munich, and Galerie Heike Curtze, Vienna. Photo courtesy Galerie Heike Curtze, Vienna.
Paper: Rives BFK.

275 Jörg Immendorff. *Erbe* from the *Café Deutschland Gut* series, 1982, color linocut, 180 × 230 cm ($70\frac{3}{4}$ × $90\frac{1}{2}$ in.), edition of 10. Printed by the artist. Published by Maximilian Verlag/Sabine Knust, Munich. Photo courtesy Maximilian Verlag/Sabine Knust, Munich.

276–279 A. R. Penck. *Ur End Standart*, 1972, four screenprints from the portfolio of 15, 70 × 70 cm ($27\frac{1}{2}$ × $27\frac{1}{2}$ in.) each, edition of 75. Printed by H. G. Shultz and U. Seifeneder, Munich. Published by Edition der Galerie Heiner Friedrich, edition × Verlag Gernot v. Pape, Fred Jahn, Munich, and Michael Werner, Cologne. Photograph courtesy Maximilian Verlag/Sabine Knust, Munich.
Braunschweig 73. Paper: Primula-Umschlag-Karton.

280 Per Kirkeby. *Untitled*, 1987, color woodcut, 69.5 × 64.5 cm ($27\frac{3}{8}$ × $25\frac{3}{8}$ in.), edition of 20. Printed by Niels Borch Jensen, Copenhagen. Published by Maximilian Verlag/Sabine Knust, Munich. Photograph courtesy Maximilian Verlag/Sabine Knust, Munich.
Paper: 40 gr. Japan.

281 Francesco Clemente. *Untitled*, 1984, color woodblock print, 42.7 × 57.2 cm ($16\frac{13}{16}$ x $22\frac{1}{2}$ in.), edition of 200. Printed by Tadashi Toda, Shi-un-do Print Shop, Kyoto. Published by Crown Point Press. Photograph courtesy Crown Point Press.
Paper: Tosa Kozo; 27 proofs.

282 Sandro Chia. *Figure Looking Out*, 1983, etching, 75.5 × 56 cm ($29\frac{3}{4}$ × 22 in.), edition of 25. Printed by Sarah Feigenbaum and Michele Pisa, New York. Published by Edition Schellmann and Klüser. Photograph courtesy Edition Schellmann.

283 Mimmo Paladino. *Muto*, 1985, color etching and aquatint with fur collage, 156.5 × 88 cm ($61\frac{1}{2}$ × $34\frac{1}{2}$ in.), edition of 35. Printed by Harlan-Weaver Intaglio, New York. Published by Edition Schellmann. Photograph courtesy Edition Schellmann.

284 Mimmo Paladino. *Sirene*, *Vespero*, *Poeta Occidentale*, 1986, three-part etching, aquatint, and drypoint with gold leaf, 199.5 × 98.5 cm ($78\frac{1}{2}$ × $38\frac{3}{4}$ in.) each sheet, edition of 28. Printed by Grafica Uno. Published by Waddington Graphics. Photograph courtesy Alan Cristea Gallery.
Paper: Magnani, edition of 28 with 10 APs.

285 René Daniëls. *Lland Stival*, 1985, color screenprint, 115.5 × 85.5 cm ($45\frac{1}{2}$ × $33\frac{1}{2}$ in.), edition of 120. Photograph courtesy Galerie de Expeditie, Amsterdam.

286 Günther Förg. *Krefeld Suite*, 1987, one bronze relief and four two-color lithographs, bronze: 77 × 49 × 5 cm ($30\frac{1}{2}$ × $19\frac{1}{2}$ in.), lithographs: 69 × 53 cm ($27\frac{1}{2}$ × 21 in.), edition of 12. Bronze cast by Hans Mayr, Munich; lithographs printed by Karl Imhof, Munich. Published by Edition Julie Sylvester, New York. Photograph courtesy Edition Julie Sylvester, New York.

287 Eric Fischl. *Year of the Drowned Dog*, 1983, set of six color etchings, 58.5 × 175.3 cm (23 × 69 in.) overall, edition of 35. Printed by Peter Kneubühler, Zurich. Published by Peter Blum Edition. Photo courtesy Peter Blum Edition.
Paper: Zerkall; 10 additional proofs.

288 Wayne Thiebaud. *Candy Apples*, 1987, color woodblock print, 59.7 × 61.6 cm ($23\frac{1}{2}$ × $24\frac{1}{4}$ in.), edition of 200. Printed and published by Crown Point Press. Photograph courtesy Crown Point Press. Paper: Tosa-kozo.

289 Richard Bosman. *Man Overboard*, 1981, color woodcut from one block, 72.4 × 48.3 cm ($28\frac{1}{2}$ × 19 in.), edition of 17. Printed by Chip Elwell and Ted Warner, New York. Published by Brooke Alexander, Inc. Photograph courtesy Diane Villani, New York.
Paper: oriental DDE-4. Proofs: 9 APs, 3 PPs.

290 David Wojnarowicz. *Four Elements: Earth, Wind, Fire and Water*, 1990, color lithograph in two parts, 62.9 × 76.2 cm ($24\frac{3}{4}$ × 30 in.) each sheet. Printed and published by Normal Editions

Workshop, Normal, Illinois. Photograph courtesy University Galleries, Normal, Illinois.

291 Robin Winters. *Fiddleback Fleamarket*, 1987, sixteen woodcuts on wood veneer, mounted and framed, 118.1 × 85 cm (46½ × 33½ in.) overall, edition of 5. Printed and published by Experimental Workshop, San Francisco. Photograph courtesy Betsy Senior Contemporary Prints, New York.
Printed on maplewood veneer hinged to ragboard. Proofs: 1 AP, 1 EXP. Printers: John Stemmer, David Crook.

292 Joan Mitchell. *Sunflowers II*, 1992, lithograph on two sheets, 145.4 × 104.1 cm (57¼ × 41 in. each), edition of 3. Printed and published by Tyler Graphics Ltd. Photograph courtesy Tyler Graphics Ltd.

293 Sam Francis. *Green Buddha*, 1982, color lithograph, 149.8 × 127 cm (59 × 50 in.), edition of 20. Printed and published by Gemini GEL. Photograph courtesy Gemini GEL.

294 Susan Rothenberg. *Between the Eyes*, 1983–84, handpainted lithograph and woodcut with collage, 146 × 86.4 cm (57½ × 34 in.), edition of 36. Printed and published by Universal Limited Art Editions. Photograph courtesy Collection Walker Art Center, Minneapolis, Butler Family Fund, 1984.
Maxwell #21; printed by Keith Brintzenhofe.

295 Richard Diebenkorn. *Large Bright Blue*, 1980, etching and aquatint, 101.6 × 66 cm (40 × 26 in.), edition of 35. Printed and published by Crown Point Press. Photo courtesy Crown Point Press. Guillemin p. 111. Paper: Rives heavyweight. Printers: Lilah Toland, Nancy Aniello. Proofs: 10 APs, 7 TPs. The companion print, *Large Light Blue*, 1980, uses one of the same plates, printed as a "ghost."

296 Richard Hamilton. *The Apprentice Boy*, 1988, dye-transfer of an electronically collaged image, 64 × 63 cm (25⅛ × 24¾ in.), edition of 12. Printed by Simon Bell Associates, London. Published by Waddington Graphics. Photograph courtesy Alan Cristea Gallery. Waddington 145. Electronic collage done with Martin Holbrook at Harmer Holbrook Limited, London, on a Quantel Graphic Paintbox. Print retouched by Allan Eayres. Printed on dye-transfer paper, mounted on Archivart board. Proofs: 2 APs.

297 Robert Rauschenberg. *Bellini #4*, 1988, color intaglio, 152.4 × 97.8 cm (60 × 38½ in.), edition of 47. Printed and published by Universal Limited Art Editions. Photo courtesy Universal Limited Art Editions. © Robert Rauschenberg/DACS London, VAGA New York 1996.

298 Robert Mapplethorpe. *Ken Moody (Untitled #1)*, 1985, color gravure and screenprint, 76.9 × 63.2 cm (30¼ × 24⅞ in.), edition of 60. Printed by Graphicstudio. Published by Graphicstudio.

Photograph courtesy Graphicstudio. © The Estate of Robert Mapplethorpe. 18 proofs.

299 John Baldessari. *Fallen Easel*, 1988, nine-part color lithograph and screenprint on paper and photo-sensitized aluminum, 188 × 241.3 cm (74 × 95 in.) overall, edition of 35. Printed by Cirrus Editions, Ltd. Co-published by Multiples, Inc. and Cirrus Editions, Ltd. Photograph courtesy Brooke Alexander Editions. Proofs: 15 APs, 7 others. Printers: Francesco Siqueiros, Robert Dansby, Richard Hammond.

300–308 John Baldessari. *Black Dice*, 1982, nine color etchings (aquatint, photo etching, soft ground and sugar lift) with accompanying photograph, 42 × 50 cm (16½ × 19¾) each, edition of 35. Printed by Peter Kneubühler, Zurich. Published by Peter Blum Edition. Photograph courtesy Peter Blum Edition. Paper: Velin d'Arches; 10 additional proofs.

309 John Baldessari. *Two Sets (One With Bench)*, 1989–90, photogravure with color aquatint, 120.6 × 75.6 cm (47½ × 29¾ in.); edition of 45. Printed by Patricia Branstead. Published by Brooke Alexander. Photograph courtesy Brooke Alexander Editions.

310 Ger van Elk. *Roquebrun II*, 1980, screenprint and photolithograph, 56 × 103 cm (22 × 40½ in.), edition of 20. Published by Multiples, Inc. Photograph courtesy Galerie de Expeditie, Amsterdam.

311 Laurie Simmons. *Ventriloquism*, 1986, color lithograph from the portfolio of two photogravures and one photolithograph, 85 × 67.6 cm (33½ × 26⅛ in.), edition of 40. Printed by Derrière l'Etoile Studios. Published by Editions Ilene Kurtz, New York. Photograph courtesy Editions Ilene Kurtz, New York. Paper: Rives. Other proofs: 13

312 Sarah Charlesworth. *Tartan Sets*, 1986, photolithograph from the set of three, 81.3 × 61 cm (32 × 24 in.), edition of 60. Printed by Derrière l'Etoile Studios. Published by Editions Ilene Kurtz, New York. Photograph courtesy Editions Ilene Kurtz, New York. Paper: Ragcote. Proofs: 13.

313 Thomas Ruff. *C-Prints*, 1991, C-prints in translucent paper wrappers, screenprinted both sides with astronomic data, 49.5 × 49.5 cm (19½ × 19½ in.), edition of 50. Printed by Theo Kneubühler, Zurich. Published by Parkett. Photograph courtesy Parkett.

314 Sherrie Levine. Untitled from *Meltdown* ("After Kirschner"), 1989, color woodblock print, 92.7 × 65.4 cm (36½ × 25¾ in.), edition of 35. Printed by Derrière l'Etoile Studios. Published by Peter Blum Edition. Photograph courtesy Peter Blum Edition.

315 Joan Nelson. *Untitled*, 1990, lithograph and screenprint, 40.6 × 40.6 cm (16 × 16 in.), edition of 45. Printed and published by Cirrus

Editions, Ltd. Photo courtesy Cirrus Editions. Paper: Rives BFK. Printers: Francesco Siqueiros, Robert Dansby, Jeff Decoster. Proofs: 12 APs, 19 other proofs.

316 Matt Mullican. *Untitled*, 1990–91, wooden cabinet containing 449 oilstick rubbings from magnesium relief plates, the plates produced photographically from a 19th-century encyclopedia, cabinet: 144 × 77.5 cm (56¾ × 30½ in.), paper: 66 × 48.3 and 66 × 96.5 cm (26 × 19 and 26 × 38 in.), edition of 10. Published by Brooke Alexander, Inc. and Michael Klein, Inc., New York. Photograph courtesy Brooke Alexander, Inc. and Michael Klein, Inc., New York.

317 Mike Kelley. *Goethe Quote*, 1992, photograph with screenprinted mat, 63.5 × 44.5 cm (25 × 17½ in.), edition of 60. Printed by Birchler Siebdruck, Zurich. Published by Parkett. Photograph courtesy Parkett.

318 Barbara Kruger. *Read Between the Lines*, 1989, offset lithograph with engraving, 63 × 58 cm (25 × 23 in.), edition of 50. Printed by Derrière l'Etoile Studios. Published by Printed Matter, New York. Photograph courtesy Printed Matter, New York.
Paper: Rives BFK. Proofs: 10 APs, 2 Workshop proofs, 1 BAT. Printers: D. Schulman, J. Petruzzell, M. Sanchez, J. Miller.

319 Randy Bolton. *Seeing and Believing*, 1990, three-panel screenprint, 151.1 × 81.3 cm (59½ × 32 in.), edition of 7. Printed and published by the artist. Photograph courtesy the artist.

320 Ed Ruscha. *Tails* from *Cameo Cuts*, 1992, suite of six two-color lithographs with title page and colophon designed by the artist, 30.5 × 30.5 cm (12 × 12 in.), edition of 28. Printed by Hamilton Press, Venice, California. Published by Edition Julie Sylvester, New York. Photograph courtesy Edition Julie Sylvester.

321 Ed Ruscha. *World Series: Girls*, 1982, color lithograph, 63.5 × 86.36 cm (25 × 34 in.), edition of 40. Printed and published by Gemini GEL. Photograph courtesy Gemini GEL.

322 Sophie Calle. *The Tie*, 1993, screenprint on silk tie, edition of 150. Printed by Fabric Frontline, Zurich. Published by Parkett. Photograph courtesy Parkett.

323 Felix Gonzalez-Torres. *Untitled (The End)*, 1990, stack of offset lithographs, 55.9 × 71.1 × 59.7 cm (22 × 28 × 23½ in.), endless copies. Photograph courtesy Andrea Rosen Gallery, New York. Collection of Cynthia Plehn.

324 General Idea. *AIDS Stamps*, 1988, offset lithograph on perforated paper, 25.4 × 20.3 cm (10 × 8 in.), edition of 200. Published by Parkett. Photograph courtesy S. L. Simpson Gallery, Toronto.

The following titles appear in abbreviated form:

Elizabeth Armstrong and Sheila McGuire, *First Impressions: Early Prints by Forty-six Contemporary Artists*, New York: Hudson Hills Press in association with Walker Art Center, Minneapolis, 1989.

Ruth E. Fine, *Gemini GEL: Art and Collaboration*. Washington: National Gallery of Art, and New York: Abbeville Press, 1984.

Richard S. Field and Ruth E. Fine, *A Graphic Muse, Prints by Contemporary American Women*, South Hadley, Mass.: Mount Holyoke College Art Museum, 1987.

Ruth E. Fine and Mary Lee Corlett, *Graphicstudio: Contemporary Art from the Collaborative Workshop at the University of South Florida* (exhibition catalogue), Washington: National Gallery of Art, 1991.

Edition Schellmann 1969–1989: Catalogue Raisonné. Munich and New York: Edition Schellmann, 1989.

Kenneth E. Tyler, *Tyler Graphics: Catalogue Raisonné, 1974–1985*, New York: Abbeville Press, and Minneapolis: Walker Art Center. With a foreword by Elizabeth Armstrong and essay by Pat Gilmour.

Esther Sparks, *Universal Limited Art Editions: A History and Catalogue: The First Twenty-Five Years.* Chicago: the Art Institute of Chicago, and New York: Harry N. Abrams, Inc., 1989.

Where an artist may be known by another name, this is given in brackets.

Vito Acconci

b. New York, New York 1940. Acconci became known in the late 1960s and early 1970s for his visceral performance works, most of which centered on manipulations of his own body. His first prints, done at the Lithography Workshop of the Nova Scotia College of Art and Design in 1971–72, were literally "performances on stone," employing marks made by kissing the stone, or biting his flesh then pressing it against the stone. In his later sculptures and installations, Acconci concentrated on the social, political, and architectural structures that are used to intimidate and exert power, and his prints echo these concerns. They often bear images of violence or confrontation, and many are multipartite works that constitute portable architectural installations. Acconci has worked extensively with Crown Point Press and Landfall Press.

Vito Acconci, interview with Robin White, *View*, Vol. II, No. 5–6, October–November 1979.
Armstrong and McGuire, *First Impressions*
Deborah Wye, *Committed to Print: Social and Political Themes in Recent American Printed Art*, New York: the Museum of Modern Art, 1988.

Josef Albers

b. Bottrop Germany 1888 – *d.* New Haven, Connecticut 1976. After studying and working at the Bauhaus, in the 1930s Albers moved to the US, where he became an influential teacher at Black Mountain College and Yale University. The works for which he is best known are those in which he used concentric squares to explore "the interaction of color" (the title of his 1963 book on color theory). He made prints throughout his life, including some interesting and austere geometric woodcuts in the 1940s, but the vast bulk of his printed work lies in the numerous portfolios of etchings and screenprints produced in the 1960s and 1970s by Tamarind, Gemini GEL, Tyler Graphics, and Ives-Stillman, Inc. (New Haven). Many of Albers's theories were adopted and exploited by Op artists such as Richard Anuszkiewicz.

Josef Albers, *The Interaction of Color*, New Haven: Yale University Press, 1963.

François Bucher, *Josef Albers: Despite Straight Lines: An Analysis of His Graphic Constructions*, Cambridge, Massachusetts: MIT Press, 1977.
Jo Miller, *Josef Albers: Prints 1915–1970*, Brooklyn: the Brooklyn Museum, 1973.
Margit Staber (ed.), *Josef Albers: Graphic Tectonic; ein Zyklus von acht Lithographien aus dem Jahr 1942*, German, English, French, and Italian editions. Cologne: Galerie Der Spiegel, 1968.
Sam Hunter (ed.), *Josef Albers: Paintings and Graphics 1917–1970*, Princeton: The Art Museum, Princeton University, 1971. With essays by Hugh M. Davies, Peter Morrin, and Mary Gibbs.
Gerald Nordland and Kenneth E. Tyler, *Josef Albers: White Embossings on Gray* (brochure), Los Angeles: Gemini GEL, 1971.
Kenneth E. Tyler, Josef Albers, and Henry T. Hopkins, *Josef Albers: White Line Squares* (exhibition catalogue), Los Angeles: Los Angeles County Museum of Art and Gemini GEL, 1966.
Nicholas Fox Weber, *Josef Albers, Never Before* (brochure), Bedford Village, New York: Tyler Graphics Ltd.

Pierre Alechinsky

b. Brussels 1927. A founding member of CoBrA in 1949, Alechinsky has since the 1940s made paintings, drawings, collages, and prints that are characterized by the confluence of calligraphic grace and a nimble imagination. He studied both book illustration and typography in Brussels and later worked extensively with Hayter (and even titled a 1968 portfolio *Hayterophilies*) and prints form an essential part of his activities. They range from the flung-ink abstractions of *Communication* (1967), to figurative, multi-panel images that read like storyboards for the subconscious. Alechinsky has made many *livres d'artiste*, and his portfolios are often accompanied by literary texts. He has collaborated with many printers and publishers, including 2RC and Clot, Bramsen et Georges, but most of Alechinsky's work has been printed in his studio in Bougival by Jean Clerté. He has won many graphics awards, including those of the Belgian Graphics Triennial and the Cracow Biennial.

Pierre Alechinsky: 20 Jahre Impressionen: Oeuvre-Katalog Druckgraphik, Munich: Galerie van de Loo, 1967.
Michel Butor and Michel Sicard, *Alechinsky: Travaux d'Impression* (includes a catalogue of book works 1946–92), Paris: Éditions Galilée, 1992.

Yves Rivière, *Pierre Alechinsky: Les Estampes de 1946 à 1972*, Paris: Yves Rivière, 1973.

Shusaku Arakawa

b. Nagoya City, Japan 1936. A painter, filmmaker, and printmaker, who studied medicine and mathematics as well as art, Arakawa has been primarily concerned with "the mechanisms of meaning" (the title of his ongoing collaboration with philosopher Madeleine Gins). He often expresses semiotic perplexities in combinations of found images and printed words. Arakawa has employed screenprint, lithography, etching and embossing, often mixing trompe-l'œil illusionism with unexpected elements of physical reality. The printshops with whom he has collaborated include Graphicstudio, Aeropress, Handworks, Maurel Studios, Styria Studios, and Vermillion Editions. Many of his prints were published by Multiples, Inc. In 1986 Arakawa was made "Chevalier des arts et des lettres" by the government of France.

Arakawa: Print Works, 1965–1979, Kitakyushu, Japan: Kitakyushu City Museum of Art, 1979.
The Prints of Arakawa (exhibition catalogue), Williamstown, Massachusetts: Williams College Museum of Art, 1979.
Philip Larson, "Words in Print," *The Print Collector's Newsletter*, Vol. V, No. 3, July–August 1974, pp. 53–56.
Fine and Corlett, *Graphicstudio*.

Richard Artschwager

b. Washington D.C., 1923. Since the early 1960s Artschwager has produced furniture-like sculptures covered in formica, in which the apparent function of the objects is negated, and grisaille paintings on heavily textured materials, such as celotex, in which photographic images break down into pointillist spots. Since the early 1970s Artschwager has also produced multiples that correspond to his sculptural interests, and etchings, lithographs, and screenprints that reflect the paintings' fascination with the dimensional qualities of objects and the flatness of photographic or painted imagery.
In his later etchings Artschwager has exploited the specific textural properties of intaglio to provoke the tension between image and object that is at the heart of all his work.

Gene Baro, *Twenty-Second National Print Exhibition* (exhibition catalogue), Brooklyn: the Brooklyn Museum, 1981.
Richard Artschwager: Complete Multiples (exhibition catalogue), New York: Brooke Alexander Editions, 1991. Includes interview between Brooke Alexander and Richard Artschwager.

Seventeenth National Print Exhibition (exhibition catalogue), Brooklyn: the Brooklyn Museum, 1970.

Enrico Baj

b. Milan, 1924. Baj's use of found objects in his paintings, assemblages, and prints has often caused his work to be seen in the context of Pop, though its roots are in the older European traditions of Expressionism, Surrealism, and the black comedy of the absurd. His "Generals" and "Dames" are combinations of the grotesque and the decorative. Baj has been associated with various self-defined "movements," including the International Movement for an Imaginary Bauhaus (with Asger Jorn), and the Milanese Nouveaux Realistes. Embracing the principle of multiplicity, Baj has produced "Generals" of polyester, as well as many lithographs, etchings, and books. He has worked extensively at Grafica Uno in Milan.

Roberta Baj and Enrico Crispolti, *Enrico Baj: Catalogue of his Works*, Turin: Bolaffi Arte, 1974.
Jean Petit, *Enrico Baj: Catalogue de l'œuvre gravé et lithographié 1952–1970*, Geneva: Editions Rousseau, 1970.
———, *Enrico Baj: Catalogue de l'œuvre graphique et de multiples*, Geneva: Editions Rousseau, 1973.
———, *Enrico Baj: Catalogue de l'œuvre gravé et lithographié 1970–73*, Geneva: Editions Rousseau, 1975.
Roberto Sanesi, Jan van der Marck, Giorgio Upiglio, Jean Petit, *Baj: catalogo generale delle stampe originali*, Milan: Electa, 1986.
John L. Tancock, *Multiples: the First Decade*, Philadelphia: Philadelphia Museum of Art, 1971.

John Baldessari

b. National City, California, 1931. Baldessari explores the essential ambiguities of narrative and human communication through suggestive combinations of both his own photographs and found photographs, such as film stills. Though he made occasional prints in the 1970s – most notably the lithograph *I Will Not Make Any More Boring Art* (1971) – it was in the 1980s that Baldessari became a prolific and committed printmaker, producing lithographs, etchings, and screenprints in which the found photographs and his manipulations of them merge into a physical unit. He has worked with Crown Point Press, Peter Blum Edition, and Brooke Alexander Editions. Baldessari has also produced numerous artist's books, films, and videotapes, and with Arion Press in San Francisco, an illustrated edition of Lawrence Sterne's *Tristam Shandy*, itself an early example of duplicitous and convoluted narrative.

John Baldessari, untitled statement in "White in Art is White?", *The Print Collector's Newsletter* 8,

March–April 1977.
John Baldessari, interview, *View*, Vol. VIII, 1992–93.
Coosje van Bruggen, *John Baldessari*, Los Angeles: The Museum of Contemporary Art, and New York: Rizzoli, 1990.
Bice Curiger, *Looks et tenebrae*, New York and Zurich: Peter Blum Edition, 1984.

Jennifer Bartlett

b. Long Beach, California 1941. As a painter, Bartlett has made great use of serial variation to examine the fundaments of pictorial style, a practice carried over into her prints. In the five-part *Graceland Mansion* (1978–79) Bartlett systematically varied the medium, chromatic tone, manual stroke, and vantage point of her simple house forms. Beginning with simple black-and-white etchings in 1978, Bartlett quickly expanded her understanding of print media, employing lithography, Japanese woodblock, Western woodblock, screenprint, and all manner of intaglio processes, often in exotic combinations. Many of her prints are regarded as *tours de force* of printerly technique. She has worked with Aeropress, Simca Print Artists, and Harlan Weaver (New York).

Armstrong and McGuire, *First Impressions*.
Richard S. Field, "Jennifer Bartlett: Prints, 1978–1983," *The Print Collector's Newsletter*, Vol. XV, No. 1, March–April 1984.
Field and Fine, *A Graphic Muse*.
Sue Scott, *Jennifer Bartlett: A Print Retrospective*, Orlando: Orlando Museum of Art, 1994. With an interview with the artist, and essay by Richard S. Field.

Georg Baselitz (Hans-Georg Kern)

b. Deutschbaselitz, Saxony 1938. Baselitz achieved international recognition in the early 1980s with the rise of the new German figurative art, but he had been practicing his own mode of expressive figuration in painting and in print from the early 1960s. Baselitz moved to West Germany in 1958 after being expelled from art school in East Berlin. His early prints were etchings and remarkable chiaroscuro woodcuts of figures, heads, and landscapes. Baselitz's signature device of composing his work upside down developed in the late 1960s, and in 1974 he began the monumental wood and linocuts which established his renown as a printmaker. In the subsequent twenty years, his prints, like his paintings, have become increasingly loose and expressive, and recognizable subjects have receded into a flurry of forceful strokes. With occasional exceptions, the linocuts and woodcuts are printed by the artist and his wife,

Elke Baselitz. His recent etchings have been printed with Niels Borch Jensen (Copenhagen) and Till Verclas (Hamburg).

Carmen Alborch, Rainer Michael Mason and Nicholas Serota, *Georg Baselitz Prints/Grabados/Gravures 1964–1990*, London: the Tate Gallery, 1991.

Georg Baselitz, Siegfried Gohr, and Rainer Michael Mason, *Georg Baselitz: Gravures 1963–1983* (exhibition catalogue), Geneva: Cabinet des Estampes, Musée d'Art et d'Histoire, 1984.

Dorothea Dietrich-Boorsch, "The Prints of Georg Baselitz," *The Print Collector's Newsletter*, Vol. XII, No. 6, January–February 1982.

Georg Baselitz: Druckgraphik 1985–1990 (exhibition catalogue), Munich: Bayerische Vereinsbank, 1991. With essay by Rainer Michael Mason.

Georg Baselitz: Radierungen 1989, Munich: Maximilian Verlag/Sabine Knust, n.d. with a text by Joseph Brodsky.

Georg Baselitz: Sculptures et Gravures Monumentales, with foreword by Françoise Woimant, Paris: Bibliothèque Nationale, 1985.

Günther Gercken, "Renaissance der Druckgraphik: Georg Baselitz, Jörg Immendorff, Markus Lüpertz, A. R. Penck," in Peter Pakesch (ed.), *Druckgraphik 1970–85*, Graz: Künstlerhaus Graz, Grazer Kunstverein, 1986.

Siegfried Gohr, D. Koepplin, Franz Dahlem, *Georg Baselitz: Gemälde, Handzeichnungen und Druckgraphik*, Cologne: Kunsthalle Köln, 1976.

Siegfried Gohr and D. Kuhrman, *Georg Baselitz: Druckgraphik/Prints/Estampes 1963–1983* (exhibition catalogue), Munich: Staatliche Graphische Sammlung and Prestel-Verlag, 1984.

Siegfried Gohr, *Georg Baselitz: Radierungen und Holzschnitte 1991/92*, Munich: Maximilian Verlag/Sabine Knust, 1992.

Fred Jahn, *Baselitz: peintre-graveur. Band I: Werkverzeichnis der Druckgraphik 1963–1974 – Band II: Werkverzeichnis der Druckgrafik 1974–1982*, Bern: Gachnang and Springer, 1983–87.

L'Italie & l'Allemagne – nouvelles sensibilités, nouveaux marchés, Geneva: Cabinet des Estampes, Musée d'Art et d'Histoire, 1983. Essays by Maurice Besset, Peter Blum, Johannes Gachnang, Sabine Knust, Rainer Michael Mason, et al.

Rainer Michael Mason, "Baselitz peintre-graveur," *Art Press* 91 (1985).

R. Wedewer, Fred Jahn, Mircea Eliade, Six Friedrich, *Georg Baselitz: Radierungen 1963–74, Holzschnitte 1966–67*, Leverkusen: Städtisches Museum Leverkusen, Schloß Morsbroich, 1974.

R. Wedewer, G. Reinhardt, and G. Baselitz, *Georg Baselitz: Druckgraphik 1963–1988: Radierungen, Holzschnitte, Linolschnitte*, Leverkusen: Museum Morsbroich Leverkusen, 1989.

Françoise Woimant, "Georg Baselitz: Gravures et sculptures," *Nouvelles de l'estampe* 79, 1985.

Joseph Beuys

b. Krefeld 1921 – *d.* Düsseldorf 1986. The most influential artist of postwar Germany, Beuys viewed art as a catalyst for spiritual regeneration, and included teaching, political actions, and performances in his definition of art activities. Most of the objects Beuys made were regarded by him as relics or "waste products" of the actual, transitory, art event. Thus he did not particularly esteem unique works over editioned ones, and prints and multiples were an essential part of his work. Between 1965 and 1986 he produced hundreds of editions of films, felt suits, offset posters, xeroxes, postcards, as well as woodcuts, etchings, and lithographs. These editions ranged from the casual to the luxurious, from the unlimited to the limited, from in-house productions to formal publications, many of them with Editions Schellmann.

Willi Bongard, *Joseph Beuys: Multiplizierte Kunst 1965–1980*, Düsseldorf, 1980.

Ursula Meyer and Ingrid Krupka, "Joseph Beuys: I Speak for the Hares," *The Print Collector's Newsletter*, Vol. IV, No. 4, September–October 1973.

Jörg Schellmann and Bernd Klüser, *Joseph Beuys: Multiples*, Munich: Editions Jörg Schellmann, 1972.

———, *Joseph Beuys: Multiples und Graphik*, Munich: Schellmann und Klüser, 1974.

———, *Joseph Beuys: Multiples – catalogue raisonné*, Bonn: Verlag Schellmann and Klüser, 1977.

Jörg Schellmann (ed.), *Joseph Beuys: die Multiples: Catalogue Raisonné 1965–1986*, New York and Munich: Edition Schellmann, 1991.

Max Bill

b. Winterthur 1908 – *d.* 1994. A painter, designer, sculptor, printmaker, and writer, Bill has been a stalwart proponent of a rational, mathematically based abstract art. He studied at the Bauhaus in 1927–29, and was a member of the Abstraction-Création group in the 1930s. His clean-edged geometries enjoyed a surge of popularity and influence in the 1950s and 1960s. Throughout his career Bill has produced lithographs and screenprints, often serial variations within given geometric or chromatic parameters.

Max Bill: Das druckgraphische Werk bis 1968, Nürnberg: Albrecht Dürer Gesellschaft, 1968.

Peter Blake

b. Dartford, Kent 1932. Blake's inventive collages of photographic nostalgia made him one of the most visible young British artists of the 1960s, whose design for the cover of the Beatles' "Sgt Pepper" album was known to millions. In the 1970s Blake moved from London to the countryside, formed the Brotherhood of Ruralists, and began working in a more handmade figurative mode. His print work has been sporadic: his screenprint editions of the 1960s and early 1970s were followed by a remarkable portfolio of wood-engravings, *Side Show* (1974–78), and some years later by his etchings of *James Joyce in Paris*, printed with Aldo Crommelynck. Recently, Blake has returned to screenprint with his twenty-six print set, *Alphabet* (1991). Since the 1970s his works have been published by Waddington Graphics.

Peter Blake: Drawings and Prints Catalogue, Turin: Galleria Documenta, 1980.

Anne Kirker, *Prints of the 70s by 6 British Artists* (exhibition catalogue), Wellington, 1980.

Six British Artists: Prints 1974–1981, London: Waddington Galleries, 1981.

Mel Bochner

b. Pittsburgh, 1940. Bochner's drawings, photographs, books, and prints explore the linguistic and logical structures used to produce meaning. Bochner's early works consisted of numerical configurations – immaterial explorations of the abstract relationship of elements. He then progressed to the expression of these relationships through hand-drawn dots. In the aquatints he began making in the 1970s, Bochner endowed these cerebral structures with an intense physical presence. In the 1980s Bochner made richly drawn etchings and lithographs in which multiple sheets come together to display a cogent composition of tumbling blocks. Bochner has worked with Crown Point Press, Maurice Payne, and Derrière l'Etoile, and his prints have been published by Parasol Press and Diane Villani.

Paul Cummings, "Interview: Mel Bochner Talks with Paul Cummings," *Drawing 10*, May–June 1988.

Minimalist Prints (exhibition catalogue), New York: Susan Sheehan Gallery, 1990.

Nancy Tousley, *Prints: Bochner, LeWitt, Mangold, Marden, Martin, Renouf, Rockburne, Ryman*, Toronto: Art Gallery of Ontario, 1975.

Jonathan Borofsky

b. Boston 1942. Borofsky's cacophonous installations of paintings, wall-drawings, and mechanized sculptures derive largely from dream imagery, and represent an attempt to find spiritual agreement between interior "brain chatter" and the exterior pressures of the world. In 1969 Borofsky began counting to infinity, a project that has remained a consistent element of his work. He has produced many prints and sculptural editions, recording numbers, dream narratives, and Persian incantations. Many of Borofsky's prints contain numbers that count up with each impression. Almost all of his editions have been produced with Gemini GEL; the most important exception being the screenprint and etching portfolio, *274075* (1982), published by Peter Blum.

James Cuno, *Subject(s): Prints and Multiples by Jonathan Borofsky 1982–1991* (exhibition catalogue), Hanover, New Hampshire: Hood Museum of Art, Dartmouth College, 1992. With an essay by Ruth Fine.

Michael Klein, "Jonathan Borofsky: Private & Public," *The Print Collector's Newsletter*, Vol. XIV, No. 2, May–June 1983.

Suzanne Volmer, "Drawings and Prints: As the Twain Meet," *Arts Magazine* 57, February 1983.

Richard Bosman

b. Madras, India 1944. Bosman's cliché melodramas were among the most visible manifestations of Neo-Expressionism in America in the early 1980s. The woodcuts he made with printer Chip Elwell were executed with a maximum of slash and swagger, yet retained a cool detachment that caused his work to be described as "expressionless Expressionism." Though he is also a painter, Bosman is, unusually, best known for his prints. In addition to woodcut, he has worked in etching and lithography, often creating a sense of impending menace through the use of multiple frames.

Elizabeth Armstrong and Marge Goldwater, *Images and Impression: Painters Who Print* (exhibition catalogue), Minneapolis: Walker Art Center, 1984.

Andrew Stevens, *Prints by Richard Bosman: 1978–1988*, Madison: Elvehjem Museum of Art, University of Wisconsin, 1989.

Susan Tallman, "High Tide, Low Tide: the Unsettling Work of Richard Bosman," *Arts Magazine,* February 1991.

Marcel Broodthaers

b. Brussels 1924 – *d.* Cologne 1976. A Belgian poet and bookseller who turned to art in his forties, Broodthaers became one of the most influential European artists of the 1960s and 1970s. His canny, visually elegant work took the form of films, paintings, sculptures, vacuum-formed plastic reliefs, books, and prints. Broodthaers was fascinated by the way context constructs meaning for works of art, and was more interested in the social effects of replication than in the niceties of etching or lithography technique. Most of his editions

were printed by letterpress, screenprint, or offset lithographs, and many of them intentionally twisted the conventions of the limited-edition, signed and numbered, fine-art print.

Todd Aldgren, "Marcel Broodthaers: On the Tautology of Art & Merchandise," *The Print Collector's Newsletter*, Vol. XXIII, No. 1, March–April 1992.

Marcel Broodthaers: The Complete Prints, New York: Michael Werner, 1991.

V. Bacchetta and P. Cuenat, *Marcel Broodthaers: l'Œuvre Graphique*, Geneva, 1991.

Johannes Gachnang, "Broodthaers/Roth/Johns/Rainer/Lewitt/Kirkeby," in Peter Pakesch (ed.), *Druckgraphik 1970–85*, Graz: Künstlerhaus Graz, Grazer Kunstverein, 1986.

Pat Gilmour. "The Prints of Marcel Broodthaers." *The Print Collector's Newsletter*, Vol. VII, No. 2, May–June 1976.

Daniel Buren

b. Boulogne-Billancourt, France 1938. Since 1965 Buren has made his works in situ, designing installations of his signature stripes that defy the expectation of art as a discrete object and draw attention to the architectural, social, and economic structures that surround it. In his prints Buren has tried various strategies for bringing this sense of site specificity into an editionable form: in *Framed/Exploded/Defaced* (1979), made with Crown Point Press, he cut a large striped aquatint into twenty-five framed fragments, which were sold with a certificate requiring that the prints be installed in an even grid, occupying the full expanse of any given wall, and making allowance for any pre-existing features; *Three Light Boxes for One Wall* (1989), published by Schellmann, shrinks or stretches to accommodate the height of the space; his lithographs with Gemini GEL were designed to appear compositionally incomplete without an architectural context. In Buren's editions, the color of the stripes changes from impression to impression so that each example is chromatically unique.

Daniel Buren, interview with Robin White, *View*, Vol. I, February 1979.

Edition Schellmann 1969–1989: Catalogue Raisonné.

John Cage

b. Los Angeles 1912 – *d.* New York 1992. One of the most important composers of the twentieth century, Cage also exerted an enormous influence on the visual arts. His belief in an art that was not structured by personal taste, and that could incorporate all manner of events, materials, and experiences,

was of critical importance to Johns and Rauschenberg, as well as Pop and Fluxus artists. In the late 1960s Cage made his first prints, whose structure was derived, as his musical compositions were, through chance methods, primarily the throwing of the I-Ching. From 1977 until his death, Cage made an annual visit to Crown Point Press, producing a body of delicate and evanescent images in etching and monotype. Many incorporate chance and elements of nature: stones, fire, and smoke.

Anne d'Harnoncourt, *John Cage: Scores and Prints*, New York: the Whitney Museum of American Art, Buffalo: the Albright-Knox Art Gallery, and Philadelphia: the Philadelphia Museum of Art, 1982.

John Cage Etchings 1978–1982, San Francisco: Point Publications, 1982.

John Cage, interview with Robin White, *View*, Vol. I, 1979.

Patrick Caulfield

b. London 1936. Patrick Caulfield belongs to the generation of British artists who made their painting debut in the "New Generation" exhibitions in the early 1960s, and their print debut in the ICA portfolio put together by Richard Hamilton in 1964. A realist rather than a Pop artist, Caulfield portrays the world as if reduced to flawless design elements: thick black lines and brilliant blocks of color, elements perfectly suited to screenprint reproduction. With their clean edges and flat surfaces, his paintings have much the appearance of screenprints, but he has used the intimacy of the print to present small details and quiet still lifes, rather than the large vistas that often appear in his painting. Most of his screenprints have been printed at Kelpra Studio or at Advanced Graphics. They have been published by Waddington Graphics, Bernard Jacobson, Editions Alecto, and Petersberg Press.

Patrick Caulfield: Prints 1964–81, London: Waddington Galleries, 1981. Essay by Bryan Robertson.

Patrick Caulfield Print Retrospective: Complete Works 1964–1976 (exhibition catalogue), Santa Monica: 1977.

Mark Glazebrook, "Why Do Artists Make Prints?," *Studio International*, June 1967.

Norbert Lynton, *Patrick Caulfield: Paintings and Prints* (exhibition catalogue), Edinburgh, 1975.

Vija Celmins

b. Riga, Latvia 1939. Celmins's meticulous grisaille renderings of expansive night skies, desert floors, and ocean surfaces are based on photographs, and grew out of the artist's desire to remove the obvious subjectivity of formal invention and composition while maintaining the mysterious transcendence of art. As well as paintings, occasional sculptures, and drawings, Celmins has produced many prints. Her mezzotints and woodcuts are among her strongest works, endowing her incremental marks with a substantive physical presence. Celmins has made lithographs with Cirrus and with Tamarind; mezzotints with Gemini GEL, and woodcuts with Grenfell Press.

Carter Ratcliff, "Vija Celmins: An Art of Reclamation." *The Print Collector's Newsletter*, Vol. XIV, No. 6, January–February 1984.

Field and Fine, *A Graphic Muse*.

Fine, *Gemini GEL*.

Sandro Chia

b. Florence 1946. One of the young Italian painters identified in the early 1980s as the "Transavantgarde," Chia was celebrated for his winsome, lighter-than-air figures floating through landscapes rife with mythological suggestion and art-historical borrowings. A *peintre-graveur* in the European tradition, Chia has made prints throughout his career, and is an accomplished etcher. Chia has maintained an etching press in his studio, and has also worked at Graphicstudio, Stamperie d'Arte Grafica/Studio S. Reparata (Florence), Aeropress, and Harlan Weaver (New York).

Danny Berger, "Sandro Chia in His Studio: an Interview," *The Print Collector's Newsletter*, Vol. XII, No. 6, January–February 1982.

Bice Curiger, *Looks et tenebrae*, New York and Zurich: Peter Blum Edition, 1984. Preface by Jean-Christophe Ammann.

Don Hawthorne, "Prints from the Alchemist's Laboratory," *ARTnews* 85, February 1986.

Sandro Chia Prints 1973–1984 (exhibition catalogue), New York: The Metropolitan Museum of Art, Mezzanine Gallery, 1984.

Edition Schellmann 1969–1989: Catalogue Raisonné.

Eduardo Chillida

b. San Sebastiàn, Spain 1924. An eminent Spanish sculptor, Chillida is also a distinguished printmaker whose etchings, lithographs, and woodcuts echo the interlocking volumes of his sculpture as well as his agile line drawings of hands. His early aquatints were composed of thick linear shapes that collected as if by gravity. He often uses shaped plates or blocks, transforming the paper support from a background for imagery to an active element, equal in presence to the printed form. In addition to a large number of single prints, many of which have been published by Maeght, Chillida has illustrated literary works,
including Heidegger's *Die Kunst und der Raum*, produced with Erker Verlag.

J. Carrete, J. Vega, V. Bozal, and F. Fontbana, *El grabado en España S. XIX–XX*, Madrid: Espana Calpe, 1988. (Volume XXXII of *Summa Artis: Historia General del Arte.*)

Gabriel Celaya and Santiago Amon, "Chillida," *Derrière le Miroir* 1973.

Julien Clay, *Œuvre Graphique*, Paris: 1978.

Eduardo Chillida: Das graphische Werk 1959–1972, Radierungen – Holzschnitte – Lithographien, Ulm: Ulmer Museum, 1973. Introduction by Gisèle Michelin.

Juan D. Fullando, "Chillida," *Derrière le Miroir* 174 1968.

Richard Harprath, Wolfgang Holler, *Eduardo Chillida: Druckgraphik und Zeichnungen* (exhibition catalogue), Munich: Staatliche Graphische Sammlung, Neue Pinakothek, 1990.

Gisèle Michelin, *Chillida: L'Œuvre Graphique*, Paris: Maeght Editeur, 1978.

Carmen Lizariturry and José Bakedano, *Chillida: l'Œuvre Graphique 1977–1985*, Bilbao: Museo de Bellas Artes, 1985.

Christo (Christo Javacheff) and Jeanne-Claude

b. Gabrovo, Bulgaria 1935. Christo first began wrapping consumer items in 1958, when associated with the Nouveau Réalistes group in Paris. The wrapping served to emphasize commodification, and also to make the commonplace appear mysterious and unknowable. In 1968 Christo, with wife and collaborator Jeanne-Claude, began wrapping public buildings, and has gone on to wrap notable geological features. In addition to producing multiples of his wrapped objects, Christo has used printmaking as a means of documenting and popularizing his visionary proposals. His lithographs, like his drawings, often employ collaged fabric. He has worked extensively with Landfall Press.

Jörg Schellmann and Joséphine Benecke, *Christo: Prints and Objects*, English Edition: New York: Edition Schellmann and Abbeville Press, 1988. English/German Edition: Munich: Edition Schellmann and Schirmer/Mosel Verlag. Introduction by Werner Spies.

Edition Schellmann 1969–1989: Catalogue Raisonné.

Francesco Clemente

b. Naples 1952. Clemente, whose incessant series of self-portraits and provocative mix of mysticism and scatology made him the most visible artist of the "Transavantgarde," is also recognized as one of his generation's finest printmakers. His eloquent line, and his gift for inventing evocative pictorial motifs, can be seen in his first prints, such as the *Febbre Alta*
portfolio of woodcuts (1982), and in most of his subsequent printed work. An artist of great technical versatility, Clemente has made etchings with Crown Point Press and Maurice Payne (for Raymond Foye Editions); woodcuts with François Lafranca (for Peter Blum Edition); Japanese woodblock prints with Tadashi Toda (for Crown Point Press). With Petersburg Press Clemente produced an illustrated version of Alberto Savinio's *The Departure of the Argonaut* (1986).

Elizabeth Armstrong and Marge Goldwater, *Images and Impressions: Painters Who Print* (exhibition catalogue), Minneapolis: Walker Art Center, 1984.

Danny Berger, "Francesco Clemente at the Metropolitan: An Interview," *The Print Collector's Newsletter*, Vol. XIII, No. 1, March–April 1982.

Bice Curiger, *Looks et tenebrae*, New York and Zurich: Peter Blum Edition, 1984. Preface by Jean-Christophe Ammann.

Francesco Clemente: Prints 1981–85 (exhibition catalogue), New York: Metropolitan Museum of Art, 1985.

Francesco Clemente, interview with Robin White, *View* No. 3, November 1981.

Don Hawthorne, "Prints from the Alchemist's Laboratory," *ARTnews* 85, February 1986.

Edition Schellmann 1969–1989: Catalogue Raisonné.

Chuck Close

b. Monroe, Washington 1940. Close is well known for his enormously enlarged portrait heads, hand-painted and executed from photographs. For Close, the photograph represents both a way of gaining distance from the subject and a way to escape the expressive tyranny of invented compositions. His first professional print was *Keith* (1972), a giant mezzotint in which Close for the first time revealed the grid that underlay all his work. In subsequent prints, Close has emphasized the status of individual marks as discrete material bodies in etching, Japanese woodblock, lithography, and manipulated paper-pulp. He has worked with Crown Point Press, Landfall, Graphicstudio, Vermillion, and Joe Wilfer (for Pace Editions).

Chuck Close: editions: a catalog raisonné and exhibition, Youngstown, Ohio: The Butler Institute of American Art, 1989.

Chuck Close: Handmade Paper Editions, New York: Pace Editions, 1983.

Verna Posever Curtis, *The Photograph and the Grid: Chuck Close Handmade Paper Editions, David Hockney Photo Composites* (exhibition catalogue), Milwaukee: Milwaukee Art Museum, 1984.

Michael Shapiro, "Changing Variables: Chuck Close and His Prints," *The Print Collector's Newsletter*, Vol. IX, No. 3, July–August 1978.

Corneille (Cornelis van Beverloo)

b. Liège, Belgium 1922. A founding member of CoBrA, Corneille was originally trained as an etcher and is a self-taught painter. In 1949 he moved to Paris where he worked with S. W. Hayter at Atelier 17. He has contributed prints to a large number of books, and has produced many portfolios of prints that are accompanied by his own verse, and by the works of poets ranging from Charles Baudelaire to Octavio Paz. Though he has made occasional screenprints, etchings and relief prints, most of his printed work has been lithographic, and has been printed by Michel Cassé (Paris).

Graham Birtwistle and Patricia Donkersloot-Van den Berghe, *Corneille: Het Complete Grafische Werk 1948–1975*, Amsterdam: Meulenhoff, 1992.

Robert Cottingham

b. Brooklyn 1935. A former commercial artist and art director, Cottingham is one of the best-known photorealist painters to have emerged in the 1970s. His depictions of American cityscapes, with their fondness for brash signage and raking light, are particularly well suited to graphic media. He has made intense and polished etchings and lithographs with Landfall Press and Tandem Press (Madison, Wisconsin).

William C. Landwehr, *Robert Cottingham: A Print Retrospective 1972–86*, Springfield, Missouri: Springfield Art Museum, 1986.

Enzo Cucchi

b. Morro d'Alba, Italy 1950. Cucchi's allusive and often lugubrious landscape paintings were part of the return to allegory and figuration in Italian art of the late 1970s. Cucchi's prints have ranged from small, concise, black-and-white etchings to the enormous, dramatically embossed intaglio triptych, *La Lupa di Roma*. They have been printed at Stamperie Grafica del Colle (Ancona) and 2RC, and have been published by Peter Blum Edition and Edition Schellmann & Klüser.

Danny Berger, "Enzo Cucchi: An Interview," *The Print Collector's Newsletter*, Vol. XIII, No. 5, October–November 1982.
Enzo Cucchi: Etchings and Lithographs 1979–85, Munich and New York: Edition Schellmann, 1985.
Bice Curiger, *Looks et tenebrae*, New York and Zurich: Peter Blum Edition, 1984. Preface by Jean-Christophe Ammann.
Monica Faber, "Über Francesco Clemente und Enzo Cucchi," in Peter Pakesch, ed. *Druckgraphik 1970–1985* (exhibition catalogue), Graz: Künstlerhaus Graz, Grazer Kunstverein, 1986.

Don Hawthorne, "Prints from the Alchemist's Laboratory," *ARTnews 85*, February 1986.
Edition Schellmann 1969–1989: Catalogue Raisonné.

Hanne Darboven

b. Munich, 1941. Since 1968 Darboven has practiced her own hermetic calendrical writing system, filling reams of paper with a rhythmic scrawl of numeric calculations and commentary, interspersed with photographs, clippings, and other ephemera denoting the passage of time. These appear most often in the form of massive wall-works, but Darboven has also released numerous artist's books, single prints, and boxed print sets, which allow the opportunity for intimate perusal that the work solicits.

Edition Schellmann 1969–1989: Catalogue Raisonné.

Richard Diebenkorn

b. Portland, Oregon 1922 – *d.* Berkeley, California 1993. Throughout his career, Diebenkorn oscillated between figuration and abstraction. His painting in both modes was characterized by a visible struggle for resolution, but also by its serene and limpid light, and its elegant structural foundations. In the early 1960s, he began the collaboration with Crown Point Press that was to continue until his death. Between 1962 and 1965 Diebenkorn etched more than 100 plates, mainly of quiet domestic scenes or local landscapes. After a hiatus of twelve years, Diebenkorn returned to intaglio, with spare, linear etchings and drypoints, and then with increasing subtlety and richness. The 1980s saw Diebenkorn's most prolific and masterful period as a printmaker. He began employing this washes of intense color in aquatint, and expanded his scale dramatically in works such as *Green* (1986). He also travelled to Kyoto to produce luminous Japanese woodblock prints. Although he produced a handful of lithographs with Gemini GEL and Tamarind, and monotypes with Garner Tullis, Diebenkorn was always more comfortable with the procedural and material obstinacy of etching.

Mark Stevens, Phyllis Plous, Chantal Guillemin, *Richard Diebenkorn: Etchings and Drypoints 1949–1980*, Houston: Houston Fine Arts Press, 1981.
Richard Diebenkorn: Monotypes (exhibition catalogue), New York: Pamela Auchincloss Gallery, 1988.
Gerald Nordland, *Richard Diebenkorn: Graphics 1981–1985*, Billings, Montana: Yellowstone Art Center, 1989.

Jim Dine

b. Cincinnati, Ohio 1935. Dine is one of the most prolific and popular painter/printmakers of his generation. He attained early success

with his "Happenings" and with paintings that incorporated common household objects. Often grouped with Pop, Dine's interests were always more personal and emotive: the objects that formed his early vocabulary – tools, palettes, bathrobes – were stand-ins for the figure of the artist. An avid printmaker from art school days, Dine made his first prints at Pratt Graphics Center before beginning to work at ULAE. In 1966 Dine moved to London and gave up painting for three years in order to concentrate on writing and printmaking, working primarily with Petersburg Press. Dine has collaborated with many of the most eminent printers of our time, including Chris Prater at Kelpra Studio, Aldo Crommelynck, Graphicstudio, Mitchell Friedman (Vermont) and Toby Michel (Los Angeles). Prints are a central part of his activity. Later motifs have included hearts, the *Venus de Milo*, and portraits of his wife, Nancy.

Jim Dine: Complete Graphics, Berlin: Galerie Mikro and London: Petersburg Press, 1970.
Jim Dine, "Prints: Another Thing," *Artist's Proof* 6 1966.
Jim Dine's Etchings, New York: The Museum of Modern Art, 1978.
Ellen G. D'Oench and Jean E. Feinberg, *Jim Dine Prints: 1977–1985*, New York: Harper and Row, 1986.
J. Dumouchel, "Gravures de Jim Dine, ou mieux connaître ce qui est inconnu," *Ateliers* 3 1974.
Thomas Krens (ed.), *Jim Dine Prints: 1970–1977*, New York: Harper and Row, in association with Williams College, 1977.
Konrad Oberhuber and Donald Saff, *Jim Dine: Youth and the Maiden*, Vienna: Graphische Sammlung Albertina, 1990.
Sparks, *Universal Limited Art Editions.*

Jean Dubuffet

b. Le Havre 1901 – *d.* Paris 1985. A major figure in French postwar art, Dubuffet reacted against the refinement and restraint of fine art, and he sought in his own work the emotional directness he perceived in the art of children and the insane. He began making prints with Mourlot in 1945, and in the late 1950s began his extraordinary *Phenomena* lithographs, in which he explored hundreds of techniques for generating images without drawing. He rubbed or impressed materials against the stone, and experimented with the chemical solutions on which lithography depends. Some of these were re-used as elements in his figurative prints of the early 1960s. In his last decades, Dubuffet worked mainly in his abstract "Hourloup" style of interlocking red and black lines.

Noël Arnaud, *Jean Dubuffet: gravures et lithographies*, Silkeborg, Denmark: Silkeborg Museum, 1961.

Audry Isselbacher, *Dubuffet Prints at the Museum of Modern Art*, New York: the Museum of Modern Art and Fort Worth: Modern Art Museum of Fort Worth, 1989. With essays by Susan J. Cokke, James L. Fisher, E. A. Carmean.

Elaine Johnson, "The 'Phenomena' of Jean Dubuffet." *Artist's Proof* 3 1962.

Max Loreau, *Catalogue des travaux de Jean Dubuffet*, Paris: J. J. Pauvert, Editeur. (Vol. XXVI, *Les Phénomènes*).

Kneeland McNulty, et al., *The Lithographs of Jean Dubuffet*. Philadelphia: Philadelphia Museum of Art, 1964.

Ursula Schmitt, *Supplément au catalogue des gravures et lithographies de Jean Dubuffet*, Paris: C. Bernart, 1966.

Sophie Webel (ed.), *L'Œuvre gravé et les livres illustrés par Jean Dubuffet: Catalogue raisonné*, Paris: Baudoin Lebon, 1991. Preface by Daniel Abadie.

Marcel Duchamp

b. Blainville, France 1887 – *d.* 1968. Duchamp's radical redefinition of art, proposed in the early years of the century, has been of critical importance to the development of art since 1960. Arguably Duchamp's greatest influence was on artists' perceptions of "originality" and reproduction. His most famous works – the "Large Glass" and the "readymades" – had all been completed by 1923, and his subsequent art production consists largely of reproductions and glosses on these earlier works, and includes etchings and facsimile lithographs as well as many less conventional editions. Duchamp's ideas were admired by Cage, Johns, Rauschenberg, and Hamilton, who transmitted them to yet another generation. Though Duchamp himself was not a particularly devoted printmaker, his impact on the production of prints and other editions has been incalculable.

Arturo Schwarz, *The Complete Works of Marcel Duchamp*, New York: Abrams, 1970.

Hellmut Wohl, "Duchamp's Etchings of *the Large Glass* and *The Lovers*," *Dada/Surrealism*, No. 16, 1987.

Richard Estes

b. Kewanee, Illinois 1936. Estes's photorealist painting of American cityscapes depict a world of clean edges, sharp light and shallow reflection, free of human incident. In 1972 Estes produced the first of his *Urban Landscape* portfolios for Parasol Press, in which these images were given form in screenprints of astonishing precision and complexity, printed by Domberger.

John Arthur, "Richard Estes: The Urban Landscape in Print" (interview), *The Print Collector's Newsletter*, Vol. X, No. 1, March–April 1979.

Öyvind Fahlström

b. Saõ Paulo 1928 – *d.* New York 1976. A politically committed, formally innovative artist, Fahlström made paintings, sculptures, and prints as well as writing plays and poetry, and conducting "Happenings." Born in Brazil, he was educated in Sweden, and subsequently lived in America, Italy, and Scandinavia. Most of his works deal with global politics, as represented through the graphic devices of cartoons, maps, and game boards. Fahlström developed the "variable" picture, in which the pictorial elements are not fixed and can be rearranged by the viewer. Some of his print editions were made in the image of games to be cut up and played, while others used magnets and enamelled metal to create moveable parts.

Susan Tallman, "Pop Politics: Öyvind Fahlström's Variables," *Arts Magazine*, December 1990.

Eric Fischl

b. New York, New York 1948. Fischl's poignantly painted depictions of pathological middle-class family life made him one of the most successful artists of the 1980s. In his early etchings Fischl suggested the contingency of human interaction by isolating the various figures in a scene within their own plate marks, and, in the small masterpiece, *Year of the Drowned Dog* (1983), within their own sheets. Fischl has also worked in Japanese woodcut, and extensively in monotype. His editions have been published by Peter Blum Edition, Crown Point Press, and Getler/Pall (New York) and printed with Tadashi Toda (Kyoto), Peter Kneubühler (Zurich) and Maurice Sanchez at Derrière l'Etoile.

Kenneth Baker, "Eric Fischl: 'Year of the Drowned Dog,' *The Print Collector's Newsletter*, Vol. XV, No. 3, July–August 1984.

Lucinda Barnes, *Eric Fischl: Scenes Before the Eye – the Evolution of "Year of the Drowned Dog" and "Floating Islands,"* Long Beach: University Art Museum, California State University; Berkeley: University Art Museum; Honolulu: Contemporary Arts Center, 1986.

Bice Curiger, *Looks et tenebrae*, New York and Zurich: Peter Blum Edition, 1984. Preface by Jean-Christophe Ammann.

Eric Fischl, interview with Tazmi Shinoda and Constance Lewallen, *View*, Vol. 5, Fall 1988.

Scenes and Sequences: Recent Monotypes by Eric Fischl, Text by E. L. Doctorow, Hanover, New Hampshire: Hood Museum of Art, 1990. Essays by Elizabeth Armstrong, James Cuno, Richard S. Field, and Carol Zemel.

Barry Flanagan

b. Prestatyn, North Wales 1941. Known primarily for his work as a sculptor, Flanagan made his first etchings in 1970. While his sculptural work has ranged from hessian sacks filled with sand in the 1960s to carved stone works in the 1970s to his famous cast bronze hares of the 1980s, Flanagan's prints have tended to be swift and lyrical evocations of everyday life. Ever conscious of the "personality" of different materials, Flanagan deftly manipulated the robust linearity of etching and the pliable grain of linocut. Waddington Graphics has published most of his prints.

Catherine Lampert, *1960s and 1970s, Prints and Drawings by Barry Flanagan*, Llandudno: Mostyn Art Gallery, 1981.

David Brown, *Barry Flanagan: Etchings and Linocuts*, Waddington Graphics, 1984.

Fluxus

Fluxus was a loose gathering of artists, composers, and poets, who in the early 1960s found a shared aesthetic of "insignificance." This aesthetic initially found expression in small, casual performances, and later in mass-produced objects, games, and performance scores. Its perfunctory approach to production and to objects precluded any serious involvement in traditional print media, but Fluxus is important to the subsequent history of prints in its assertion of multiplicity as an end in itself. It leads directly to print-based movements such as mail art and artist's books. George Maciunas was the central figure of Fluxus, responsible for both the administration and the design of Fluxus publications (which some-times meant the redesign of other artists' works). Other artists involved included Nam June Paik, Yoko Ono, Wolf Vostell, and Robert Watts.

In the Spirit of Fluxus, essays by Simon Anderson, Elizabeth Armstrong, Andreas Huyssen, Bruce Jenkins, Douglas Kahn, Owen F. Smith, and Kristine Stiles, Minneapolis: Walker Art Center, 1993.

Jon Hendricks (ed.), *Fluxus Codex*, Detroit: The Gilbert and Lila Silverman Fluxus Collection and New York: Harry N. Abrams, 1988.

Lucio Fontana

b. Rosario di Santa Fé, Argentina 1899 – *d.* Comabbio 1968. The painter Lucio Fontana is best known for the slashed and punctured canvases that were the ultimate realizations of his theory of "Spatialism." In the last decade of his life, Fontana produced a handful of prints and multiples which were also characterized by perforated forms. The most interesting of these are the aquatints, made with 2RC in Rome, in which the paper is allowed to rupture under the extreme pressure of printing.

Lucio Fontana et al, *Lucio Fontana* 2 vols, Brussels: Edition de la Connaissance, 1974.

Günther Förg

b. Füssen, Germany 1952. Förg works simultaneously in several very different modes: enormous photographs of faces and of architecture, site-specific wall paintings, and geometric abstractions that are often produced in series, and given form in paint, in cast bronze, and in print. The tension between clear formal structures and the turbulent unpredictability of the real world is evident in all these works, and has been used to great effect in Förg's etchings, woodcuts, lithographs, and monotypes, in which his sensuous handling is balanced against classical geometric forms. One of the most important printmakers among younger European artists, Förg has worked with Karl Imhof (Munich), Mary McLaughlin (Munich), Artelier (Graz), Thomas Sebening (Munich), and Derrière l'Etoile (New York). His works are published by Gisela Capitain (Cologne) and Julie Sylvester (New York).

Dorothea Dietrich, "An Interview with Günther Förg," *The Print Collector's Newsletter*, Vol. XX, No. 3, July–August 1989.

Helmut Draxler, "The Apollonian Moment: The Art of Günther Förg," *The Print Collector's Newsletter*, Vol. XX, No. 3, July–August 1989.

Günther Förg: Stations of the Cross, New York: Edition Julie Sylvester, 1990. With an essay by Rainer Speck.

Günther Förg: gesamte editionen/ the complete editions 1974–1988, Rotterdam: Museum Boymans van Beuningen, and Cologne: Galerie Gisela Capitain, 1989. With essays by Luise Horn and Karel Schampers.

Sam Francis

b. San Mateo, California 1923 – *d.* 1994. An eminent Abstract Expressionist painter of the "Second Generation," Francis grew up in California, and lived in Paris, Switzerland, Japan and America. His colorful paintings, based on controlled accident, are characterized by a structured splash and splatter. Francis began making prints seriously in 1960, and within three years had completed hundreds of prints with Emil Matthieu (Zurich) and with Tamarind. With strategic recombinations of color plates, Francis was able to exploit printmaking's discontinuous stages as compositional tools. Though most of his printed work was lithographic, he also made screenprints, etchings, and monotypes. In 1962 Francis won the International Print Biennial in Tokyo. In addition to Matthieu and Tamarind, he collaborated with Gemini GEL and Garner Tullis, and in 1973 established The Litho Shop in Santa Monica.

Ebria Feinblatt and Jan Butterfield, *Sam Francis Monotypes* (exhibition catalogue), Los Angeles: Los Angeles County Museum of Art, 1980.

Fine, *Gemini GEL*.

Sam Francis and George Page, *Sam Francis: The Litho Shop, 1970–79* (exhibition catalogue), New York: Brooke Alexander Gallery, 1979.

Sam Francis: Exhibition of Drawings and Lithographs (exhibition catalogue), San Francisco: San Francisco Museum of Modern Art, 1967.

Manuel Gasser, "Sam Francis: Lithographs by an Action Painter," *Graphis* November/December 1962.

Connie W. Lembark, *The Prints of Sam Francis: A Catalogue Raisonné 1960–1990*, New York: Hudson Hills Press, 1992.

Peter Selz, *Sam Francis*, New York: Harry N. Abrams, Inc., 1982. With essays on his prints by Susan Einstein and Jan Butterfield.

Helen Frankenthaler

b. New York, New York 1928. Frankenthaler's lyrical abstractions, made by staining the canvas so that the object and the image are indivisible, made her one of the best known of the second-generation Abstract Expressionist painters. She was first invited to ULAE in 1960, but for a long time felt that lithographs were too small in scale and too indirect in execution to capture the intensity of her painting. With the creation of her important woodcuts in the 1970s, Frankenthaler found a direct and expressive voice in print, and has since devoted considerable energy to etching, lithograph, and monotypes. She has worked with ULAE, Tyler Graphics, Crown Point Press and Garner Tullis, in the USA, and at 2RC in Rome and Ediciones Poligrafa in Barcelona.

Thomas Krens, *Helen Frankenthaler: Prints 1961–1979*, New York: Harper and Row, 1979.

Helen Frankenthaler Prints: 1985–87, Mount Kisco, New York: Tyler Graphics Ltd., 1987.

Karl Gerstner

b. Basel 1930. Gerstner, an artist, designer, and principal of an important advertising agency, has been an important advocate of mass-produced, user-manipulable artworks. With Daniel Spoerri and Galerie Der Spiegel, Gerstner revived the multiples publishing program MAT in 1960s. His own works are mathematically determined abstractions, whose elements can often be rearranged by the owner.

Karl Gerstner, "Was darf Kunst kosten?" in *Ars Multiplicata: Vervielfältigte Kunst seit 1945*, Cologne: Wallraf-Richartz-Museum, 1968. Reprinted in English, "What should Art cost?," in *New Multiple Art*, London: Arts Council of Great Britain, 1970.

Karl Gerstner: Ideenskizzen und Bilder/Color Fractals (exhibition catalogue), Basel: Museum für Gegenwartskunst and Galerie Littmann, 1992. With essays by Gerstner and Sabine Fehlemann; interview with Gerstner by Dieter Koepplin.

Franz Gertsch

b. Möringen, Bern, Switzerland 1930. The most prominent European proponent of photorealism, Gertsch began to make paintings from projected slides in 1969. Though these enormous portrait heads appear to have been airbrushed, they were painted meticulously with tiny brushes. Gertsch made a few lithographs in this style, but his reputation as a printmaker rests on the enormous woodcut portraits and landscapes he began in 1986. In these monochrome works, Gertsch cuts tiny notches of light to mimic the shimmer of photography in the stiffness of wood. The blocks are often used to print several editions in different colors.

Michael Danoff, "Franz Gertsch," *Parkett* 28, June 1991.

Franz Gertsch: Farbholzschnitte 1986 bis 1988 (exhibition catalogue), Berlin: Galerie Michael Haas, 1989.

Helmut Friedel, "Wirkliche, monochrome Bilder/ Real Monochrome Images," *Parkett* 28, June 1991.

Ulrich Loock, "Die Zeit der Malerei, die Zeit der Repräsentation/Time of Painting, Time of Representation," *Parkett* 28, June 1991.

Rainer Michael Mason, *Franz Gertsch: Bois Gravés Monumentaux/Grossformatige Holzschnitte/Large-scale Woodcuts*, Geneva: Cabinet des Estampes and Zurich: Turske and Turske, 1989. With an essay by Dieter Ronte. Republished, with an additional essay by Riva Castleman, as *Franz Gertsch: Large-scale Woodcuts/Xilografías Monumentales*, Geneva: Cabinet des Estampes, 1990. Third edition, with essays by Riva Castleman, Helmut Friedel and Ulrich Loock, published as *Franz Gertsch: Holzschnitte*, Munich: Städtische Galerie im Lenbachhaus, 1991.

Rainer Michael Mason, "Die Holzschnitte: Ein Prozess der Läuterung/The Woodcuts: A Process of Purification," *Parkett* 28, June 1991.

Amei Wallach, "How can you tell a Franz Gertsch from a Chuck Close?/Wie kann man einen Franz Gertsch von einem Chuck Close unterscheiden?," *Parkett* 28, June 1991.

Fritz Glarner

b. Zurich 1899 – *d.* Locarno 1972. Glarner's principle of "Relational Painting" derived from the lessons of Suprematism and de Stijl, and like those earlier utopian movements, sought a cosmic harmony in dynamically balanced, abstract forms. A close friend of Tatyana and Maurice Grosman, he was the second artist to work at ULAE after Rivers. His most important work there was *Recollection* (1958–64), an artistic autobiography in fourteen lithographs, which exhibits an uncharacteristic quickness and spontaneity.

Riva Castleman, "Fritz Glarner's Recollection," *Art International* 13, November 1969.
Sparks, *Universal Limited Art Editions.*

Nancy Graves

b. Pittsfield, Massachusetts, 1940 – *d.* New York, 1995. Though best known for her shamanistic camel sculptures and her gregarious, polychrome bronzes, Graves made paintings, films, dance sets, and costumes, as well as etchings, lithographs, monotypes, and screenprints. All these works combine a wildly decorative imagination with elements of art history or natural history. Graves studied lithography while in graduate school, and briefly worked at Mourlot in the early 1960s. Her first professional prints, made with Landfall in 1972, were lithographs that used geological surveys of the moon to structure pointillist patterns of dots. Subsequent prints with Tyler Graphics and 2RC were more elaborately embellished, and often employ hand-painting and monotype.

Armstrong and McGuire, *First Impressions.*
Field and Fine, *A Graphic Muse.*
Diane Kelder, "New Editions by Nancy Graves," *Arts Magazine* October 1988.
Patrick O'Connor, *Nancy Graves: Prints 1972–1988* (exhibition catalogue), New York: Associated American Artists, 1988.
Tyler Graphics: Catalogue Raisonné, 1974–1985.

Philip Guston

b. Montreal 1913 – *d.* Woodstock, New York 1980. A figurative painter in the 1930s, Guston turned to lyrical abstraction in the 1950s and 1960s, and then to a vocabulary of cartoon-like figures and forms. These later works, in which urgent emotion meets with rough pictographic invention, were very influential on younger American painters in the late 1970s. Guston made some abstract lithographs with Hollander and Tamarind, but his best known prints are those made at Gemini shortly before his death.

John Coplans, *Philip Guston I* (brochure), Los Angeles: Gemini GEL, 1980.
Philip Guston II (brochure), Los Angeles: Gemini GEL, 1981.
Philip Guston III (brochure), Los Angeles: Gemini GEL, 1983.

Hans Haacke

b. Cologne, 1936. In the early 1960s, Haacke made works that demonstrated natural systems such as condensation and evaporation. He exhibited with the Zero Group, and produced multiples such as *Condensation Cube*. In the 1970s, Haacke turned his attention to political and economic systems, scrutinizing the symbiotic relationship between large corporations and the art world. He released several editions of prints that reproduce and recontextualize corporate statements. Though Haacke had briefly studied intaglio technique at Atelier 17 in 1960–61, his choice of medium in later works has been parasitic, adopting the look and feel of the subject being addressed: "luxurious" etching for *Tiffany Cares* (1978), and slickly impersonal screenprint for works about the Mobil Oil Company.

Hans Haacke, interview with Robin White, *View* 1, November 1978.
John L. Tancock, *Multiples: the First Decade*, Philadelphia: Philadelphia Museum of Art, 1971.

Richard Hamilton

b. London 1922. The most famous of British Pop artists, Hamilton was a core member of the ICA group in London in the 1950s, and helped set the ideological groundwork for an art that took the fabulous richness of media culture as its subject. Since that time his art has been deeply involved with mechanisms of reproduction. In screenprints of the 1960s and 1970s Hamilton borrowed images from newsprint, film, and television, and modified them through printerly interference. Ever fascinated by the possibility of true mass production, Hamilton produced the screenprint *Kent State* (1971) in an edition of 5,000, and designed the so-called "White Album" for the Beatles. Hamilton has sought out printers for such rare specialties as collotype, and has collaborated with many of the most eminent printers of the day, including Chris Prater at Kelpra and Ken Tyler. With Aldo Crommelynck he produced his masterpiece of pastiche and printerly technique, *Picasso's Meninas* (1973), as well as the etchings for James Joyce's *Ulysses* which have occupied him since 1980. Most recently, Hamilton has become involved in digital image manipulation with computers.

Stephen Coppel, "Richard Hamilton's Ulysses Etchings: an examination of work in progress," *Print Quarterly*, Vol. 6, No. 1, March 1989.
Richard S. Field, *The Prints of Richard Hamilton*, Middletown, Connecticut: Davison Art Center, Wesleyan University, 1973.
Richard Hamilton and Richard S. Field, *Richard Hamilton: Image and Process: Studies, stage and final

proofs from the graphic works 1952–82, London: the Tate Gallery and Stuttgart: Edition Hansjörg Mayer, 1983.
Richard Hamilton, *Collected Words*, London: Thames and Hudson, 1983.
Richard Hamilton: Prints 1939–83, London: Waddington Graphics and Stuttgart: Edition Hansjörg Mayer, 1984.
Richard Hamilton: Prints 1984–91, Stuttgart and London: Edition Hansjörg Mayer in association with Waddington Graphics, 1992.
Susan Tallman, "Richard Hamilton's Ulysses," *Arts Magazine*, September 1988.

Grace Hartigan

b. Newark, New Jersey, 1922. As a painter, Hartigan was hailed in 1959 as "one of the prime, gifted swashbucklers of the Second Generation" of Abstract Expressionism. Avidly involved in literature as well as art, Hartigan has collaborated on several *livres d'artistes* with contemporary poets such as James Schuyler. Though printmaking has not been central to her concerns, the lithographs she made at ULAE to accompany Barbara Guest's poetry are powerful statement of expressionism in print.

Sparks, *Universal Limited Art Editions.*

Stanley William Hayter

b. London 1901 – *d.* Paris 1988. Hayter was one of the few specialist printmakers to have exerted an influence on the broader course of art history. In 1927 Hayter, who had started out as a chemist and later learned engraving from Joseph Hecht in Paris, founded Atelier 17, where many important artists were first exposed to intaglio printing. In the 1940s, Hayter relocated the Atelier in New York, where it became a hub of the exiled European art community, and a place where younger American artists, such as Robert Motherwell and Jackson Pollock, encountered the great Surrealists. Hayter's own work was influenced by Surrealism, and involved a semi-automatist engraving and elaborate color printing techniques. His fascination with intricate intaglio color printing was carried on in America by artists such as Gabor Peterdi and Mauricio Lasansky. Many other artists who did not choose to follow the burin nonetheless understood and expanded upon his philosophy of collaborating with materials. Hayter was the recipient of numerous prizes and awards for his prints, and was made a Chevalier, Legion d'Honneur in 1951; a Chevalier de l'Ordre des Arts et Lettres in 1968; and a Commander of the British Empire in 1967.

Peter Black and Desirée Moorhead (ed.), *The Prints of Stanley William Hayter: a Complete Catalogue,*

London: Phaidon, and Mount Kisco: Moyer, Bell Ltd. 1992. With essay by Jacob Kainen.

P. M. S. Hacker (ed.), *The Renaissance of Gravure: The Art of S. W. Hayter* (exhibition catalogue), Oxford: Oxford University Press, 1988.

P. M. S. Hacker, "The Color Prints of Stanley William Hayter," *The Tamarind Papers* 14, 1991–92.

Stanley William Hayter, *New Ways of Gravure*, London: Routledge and Kegan Paul, 1949. Rev. edn: New York: Watson-Guptill, 1981.

Hayter et l'Atelier 17, Gravelines, France: Musée du Dessin et de l'Estampe Originale, Arsenal de Gravelines, 1993. With essays by Dominique Tonneau-Ryckelynck, Carla Esposito, Duncan Scott, and Peter Hacker.

Graham Reynolds, *The Engravings of S. W. Hayter* (exhibition catalogue), London: Victoria and Albert Museum, 1967.

Anton Heyboer

b. Indonesia 1924. Heyboer, who lives in primitive conditions in the marshes of northern Holland, makes rough, symbological etchings as a way of structuring his day-to-day life. His traumatic early life included internship in a Nazi work camp, and he began etching while institutionalized in the 1950s. With increased interest in the emotional quality of the art of children and the insane (Art Brut) during the late 1950s and early 1960s, Heyboer's idiosyncratic etchings found a serious audience. His prints, which are made from roofing zinc and printed by the artist and the female companions who live with him, are usually numbered, though not always printed, as an edition of nine.

J. L. Locher, *Anton Heyboer*, Amsterdam, 1976.

David Hockney

b. Bradford, Yorkshire 1937. Hockney is an unusual figure in contemporary art, beloved by the broad, art-going public and respected by the critical establishment, and as well known for his books, prints, and stage designs as he is for his paintings. Though his early, quixotic figurative works were often considered a manifestation of British Pop, Hockney was always more interested in story-telling, personality, and the evocation of autobiographical experience than in the effects and processes of mass-media. He also preferred drawing to photographic appropriation and manipulation. His important print cycles of the 1960s and early 1970s were done as etchings, a process he learned while in art school and continued subsequently with printers Maurice Payne and Aldo Crommelynck. In the 1970s, Hockney began

working regularly at Gemini GEL in his adopted city of Los Angeles, producing lithographic cycles such as the *Weather Series*, and a large number of portraits and interiors. Later in the decade, Hockney's enormous "paper pools," made of dyed and manipulated paper pulp, helped to establish handmade paper as a serious art medium. In recent years he has adopted the copying machine, the fax machine, and the digital paintbox as printmaking tools. Hockey has won numerous awards for his printed work, including those at the Biennale de Paris (1963); the Eighth International Drawings and Engravings Biennale in Lugano (1964); the Sixth International Graphics Exhibition in Ljubljana (1965); and the First International Print Biennale in Krakow (1966).

Mario Amaya, *Exhibition of Paintings and Prints by David Hockney* (exhibition catalogue), Manchester: Whitworth Art Gallery, University of Manchester, 1969.

Wilke von Bonin, *David Hockney: Œuvrekatalog-Graphik*, Berlin and London: Galerie Mikro and Petersburg Press, 1968.

Andrew Brighton, *David Hockney: Prints 1954–77*, London: Petersburg Press for the Midland Group and the Scottish Arts Council, 1979.

Marc Fumaroli, *David Hockney: Dessins et Gravures*, Paris: Galerie Claude Bernard, 1975.

Günther Gercken, *David Hockney: Zeichnungen, Grafik, Gemälde* (exhibition catalogue), Bielefeld, 1971.

Mark Glazebrook and David Hockney, *David Hockney : paintings, prints and drawings 1960–1970*, London: Whitechapel Art Gallery, 1970.

Marco Livingstone, *David Hockney, etchings and lithographs*, London: Thames and Hudson and Waddington Graphics, 1988.

Felix H. Man, ed. *Europäische Graphik* Vol. 7, Munich: Galerie Wolfgang Ketterer, 1971.

Barbara Mathes, *David Hockney: Print Retrospective*, New York: M. Knoedler and Co., 1973.

Peter Plagens, "David Hockney's New Prints," *Print Review* 2, 1973.

Nikos Stangos (ed.), *David Hockney: Paper Pools*, London: Thames and Hudson, and New York: Abrams, 1980.

Howard Hodgkin

b. London 1932. Admired for his small, densely layered works on wood, Hodgkin is also the creator of large, translucent prints, which have, since 1977, been composed of interleaved passages of printing and hand-coloring. Hodgkin's subject is the recollection of emotion, and his use of layering parallels the accretions and alterations that memory imposes on experience. In making prints Hodgkin will often use the same printing plates to produce two editions, distinguished by different inkings and by

radically different hand-coloring. (The hand-coloring is done by a technician following the artist's example, and provides an intriguing mixture of personal and impersonal touch.) Hodgkin has made lithographs with Solo Press; etchings with Aldo Crommelynck, Ken Farley, Maurice Payne, and 107 Workshop (Wiltshire); and screenprints (without hand-coloring) at Kelpra Studio. They have been published by Petersburg Press, Bernard Jacobson and Waddington Graphics.

Elizabeth Knowles, *Howard Hodgkin: Prints 1977–83*, London: Tate Gallery, 1985.

Yoko Ikeda and Raymond Lokker, *Howard Hodgkin*, London and Tokyo: Ikeda and Lokker, 1991.

Antony Peattie, *Howard Hodgkin: Hand Coloured Prints 1986–1991*, London: Waddington Graphics, 1991.

John Russell, *Howard Hodgkin: Graphic Work: Fourteen Hand-Coloured Lithographs and Etchings*, London: Lumley Cazalet, 1990.

Robert Indiana (Robert Clark)

b. New Castle, Indiana 1928. Indiana studied painting and graphics at the School of the Art Institute of Chicago before coming to New York in the 1950s, and his compact compositions of letters and symbols owe as much to product-oriented graphic design as they do to earlier American painters such as Hartley and Demuth. His flat colors and sharply defined edges were perfect for screenprint, and many of his paintings were reproduced in this way. By far his best-known work is *LOVE* (1964) versions of which have occupied him for nearly three decades.

Susan Sheehan and Catherine Mennenga, *Robert Indiana Prints: A Catalogue Raisonné 1951–1991*, New York: Susan Sheehan Gallery, 1991. Introduction and interview by Poppy Gandler Orchier.

William Katz, *Robert Indiana: The Prints and Posters, 1961–1971*, Stuttgart and New York: Edition Domberger, 1971.

Jasper Johns

b. Augusta, Georgia 1930. One of the most important painters of the century, Johns is also widely acknowledged as the greatest printmaker of our time. Since he made his first lithograph at the fledgling ULAE in 1960, the course of his career and of the American print renaissance have seemed to be fundamentally linked. Johns's eloquent lithographs of the 1960s helped to establish the reputation of both ULAE as a shop and lithography as a medium. (Even the controversy over originality that erupted as a result of Johns's constant reuse of his earlier work was necessary to the establishment of the print as a serious form.) The etchings he produced when ULAE added intaglio facilities in 1967 are now seen as instrumental in the subsequent revival of etching. At the end of the decade, Johns participated in the technological expansion of lithography, working at Gemini on large-scale lithographs that were "cooler" than those he made at ULAE, and on novel forms such as the lead reliefs of 1969–70. With Petersburg Press and printer Aldo Crommelynck, Johns returned to etching in the mid-1970s, producing the masterful *livre d'artiste Fizzles/ Foirades* with Samuel Beckett. Johns's "Savarin" monotypes heralded the popular rediscovery of that medium, and although the extraordinarily elaborate screenprints Johns began with Simca Print Artists in 1972 did not initiate a broad-based screenprinting revival, they did redefine it as a technique capable of powerful nuance. In the late 1980s, Johns returned to ULAE, producing an extended series of etching variations on his painting cycle, *The Seasons*. Almost all Johns's prints restate the motifs and images of his paintings, but such restatement is an essential feature of Johns's art, and can be found in his paintings and drawings as well. Johns has discovered, in the reversals, transfers, and repetitions of printmaking, mechanical devices for articulating his fascination with forms of difference and identity.

The Prints of Jasper Johns 1960–1993: A Catalogue Raisonné, with an essay by Richard S. Field. West Islip: Universal Limited Art Editions, 1993.

Roberta Bernstein, "Johns and Beckett: Foirades/Fizzles," *The Print Collector's Newsletter*, Vol. VII, No. 5, November–December 1976.

————, "Jasper Johns and the Figure: Part One – Body Imprints," *Arts Magazine* 52, October 1977.

Michael Blackwood (dir. and prod.), *Jasper Johns: Decoy* (film), 1972.

Riva Castleman, *Jasper Johns: A Print Retrospective* (exhibition catalogue), New York: The Museum of Modern Art, 1986.

————, *Jasper Johns: Lithographs* (exhibition catalogue), New York: the Museum of Modern Art, 1970.

Richard S. Field, "The Making of 'Souvenir'", *The Print Collector's Newsletter*, Vol. I, No. 2, May–June 1970.

————, "Jasper Johns's Flags," *Print Collector's Newsletter*, Vol. VII, No. 3, July–August 1976.

————, *Jasper Johns: prints 1960–1970*, Philadelphia: the Philadelphia Museum of Art, and New York: Praeger Publishers, 1970.

————, *Jasper Johns: 1st Etchings, 2nd State* (exhibition catalogue), Los Angeles: Betty Gold Fine Modern Prints, 1971.

————, *Jasper Johns/Screenprints* (exhibition catalogue with original screenprint cover), New York: Brooke Alexander Gallery, 1977.

————, *Jasper Johns: Prints 1970–1977* (exhibition catalogue), Middletown, Connecticut: Wesleyan University Press, 1978.

Christian Geelhaar, *Jasper Johns Working Proofs*, New York and London: Petersburg Press, 1980.

Judith Goldman, *Jasper Johns: Prints 1977–81* (exhibition catalogue), Boston: Thomas Segal Gallery, 1981.

Judith Goldman, *Foirades/Fizzles* (exhibition catalogue), New York: The Whitney Museum of American Art, 1977.

————, *Jasper Johns: 17 Monotypes*, West Islip, New York: Universal Limited Art Editions, 1982.

Henry Hopkins, *Jasper Johns: Figures 0–9*, Los Angeles: Gemini GEL, 1968.

Walter Hopps, *Jasper Johns: Fragments – According to What/Six Lithographs*. Los Angeles: Gemini GEL, 1971.

Carlo Huber (ed.), *Jasper Johns Graphik* (exhibition catalogue) Bern: Verlag Kornfeld & Klipstein, 1970.

Jasper Johns: Drawings and Prints 1975–1979 (exhibition catalogue) Houston: Janie C. Lee Gallery, 1979.

Jasper Johns: Lithographs 1973–1975, Los Angeles: Gemini GEL, 1975.

Jasper Johns: Printed Symbols. Minneapolis: Walker Art Center, 1990. Introduction by Elizabeth Armstrong. Essays by James Cuno, Charles W. Haxthausen, Robert Rosenblum, and John Yau. Interview with Jasper Johns by Katrina Martin.

Jasper Johns: The Seasons, New York: Brooke Alexander Gallery, 1991. Essay by Roberta Bernstein.

John Palmer Leeper, *Jasper Johns: The Graphic Work* (exhibition catalogue), San Antonio: Marion Koogler McNay Art Institute, 1969.

Katrina Martin (dir. and prod.), *Hanafuda/Jasper Johns* (film), 1980.

Annette Michelson, "The Imaginary Object: Recent Prints by Jasper Johns," *Artist's Proof* 8, 1968.

Barbara Rose, "The Graphic Work of Jasper Johns," Parts 1, 2, *Artforum* 8, March and September 1970.

————, "Decoys and Doubles: Jasper Johns and the Modernist Mind," *Arts Magazine* 50, May 1976.

————, *Jasper Johns: 6 Lithographs (after "Untitled 1975") 1976*, Los Angeles: Gemini GEL, 1976.

Alan Shestack, "Jasper Johns: Reflections," *The Print Collector's Newsletter*, Vol. VIII, No. 6, January–February 1978.

Alan R. Solomon, *Jasper Johns: Lead Reliefs*, Los Angeles: Gemini GEL, 1969.

Susan Tallman, "Jasper Johns," *Arts Magazine*, September 1990.

Joseph E. Young, "Jasper Johns' Lead-Relief Prints," *Artist's Proof* 10, 1971.

Asger Jorn (Asger Oluf Jorgensen)

b. Vegrur, Denmark 1914 – *d.* Aarhus 1973. An indefatigable artist and theorist, Jorn was a founding member of CoBrA (1948–51); of the Situationist International (1953–57); of the Movement for an Imaginary Bauhaus, with Enrico Baj (1954–61); and of the Scandinavian Institute for Comparative Vandalism (1962–75). In the 1930s he worked with Leger and Le Corbusier, but his own work hovers between the whimsicality of Paul Klee and the darker psychoses of Ensor. He made experimental films and music (with Dubuffet), and was, throughout his career, a masterful printmaker. Many of his etchings, woodcuts and lithographs are classics of European expressionism.

Asger Jorn: die gesamte Druckgrafik, Munich: Galerie van de Loo, 1973.

Asger Jorn, Rene Bertele, Christian Dotrement, *Jorn: Œuvre Gravé*, Paris: Centre National d'Art Contemporain, 1973.

Alex Katz

b. New York 1927. Since the 1950s, Katz has pursued his highly reductive, stylized realism, in which people and places are rendered in carefully articulated blocks of flat color. It is a particularly graphic manner and Katz has transformed many of his painted images into printed ones. He has worked in direct and offset lithography; in etching and drypoint; in screenprint; and in Japanese and Western woodcut. He has collaborated with many printers, including Aldo Crommelynck, Crown Point Press, Chip Elwell, and Simca Print Artists.

Gerrit Henry, "Alex Katz: from Theater to Poetry," *The Print Collector's Newsletter*, Vol. XXIII, No. 4, September–October 1992.

Alex Katz/Face of the Poet (exhibition catalogue), New York: Brooke Alexander, Inc., 1979.

Alex Katz, interview, *View*, Vol. VII, 1990–91.

Nicholas P. Maravell, *Alex Katz: the Complete Prints*, New York: Alpine Fine Arts Collection, 1983. Interview with Carter Ratcliff.

Elke M. Solomon and Richard S. Field, *Alex Katz: prints* (exhibition catalogue), New York: Whitney Museum of American Art, 1974.

Barry Walker, *Alex Katz: A Print Retrospective* (exhibition catalogue), New York: the Brooklyn Museum in association with Burton Skira, 1987.

Ellsworth Kelly

b. Newburgh, New York 1923. Though he has been labeled both a Minimalist and a painter of "post-painterly abstraction," Kelly has always stood apart from any larger movements. His pristine, flatly colored forms are not derived from pure geometry, but distilled from scenes observed in the real world. Kelly lived in Paris through the 1950s, and his first set of prints, the *Suite of Twenty-Seven Color Lithographs*, were made there with Macght. With Gemini GEL Kelly has produced many lithographs of often extravagant proportion, as well as numerous sculptural editions. He has also made lithographs of his guileless, graceful drawings of plants. At Tyler Graphics, Kelly has worked in screenprint, lithography, and handmade paper.

Richard H. Axsome, *The Prints of Ellsworth Kelly: a catalogue raisonné, 1949–1985*, New York: Hudson Hills Press in association with the American Federation of the Arts, 1987.
Fine, *Gemini GEL*.
Ellsworth Kelly: the Paris Prints 1964–65, New York: Susan Sheehan Gallery, 1992. With an interview and essay by Henry Geldzahler.
Tyler Graphics: Catalogue Raisonné, 1974–1985.
Diane Waldman, *Ellsworth Kelly: drawings, collages, prints 1950–1970*, Greenwich: New York Graphic Society, 1971.

R. B. Kitaj

b. Cleveland, 1932. In 1958 Kitaj moved from America to London, where he became associated with the British Pop painters who, like Kitaj, appropriated media images for creative re-use. Kitaj collaged photographs, text, and other pictorial elements into compositions whose density was a visual manifestation of the density of meaning he intended them to carry. Kitaj worked with Kelpra Studio from 1962 to 1972, completing two important series of screenprints, *Mahler Becomes Politics: Beisbol* (1965) and *In Our Time* (1969). In the 1980s, Kitaj abandoned photomechanical techniques and reproduction in favor of more traditional drawing and painting.

Pat Gilmour, "R. B. Kitaj and Chris Prater," *Print Quarterly*, June 1994.
Mark Glazebrook, "Why Do Artists Make Prints?," *Studio International*, June 1967.
Werner Haftman and R. B. Kitaj, *R. B. Kitaj: Complete Graphics 1963–1969*, Berlin: Galerie Mikro, 1969.
R. B. Kitaj and Wieland Schmied, *R. B. Kitaj*, Rotterdam: Museum Boymans-van Beuningen, 1970. Foreword by R. Hammacher-van den Brande.
Ron B. Kitaj: Complete Graphics, Hanover: Kestner-Gesellschaft, 1970.
R. B. Kitaj: The Complete Graphic Works 1963–1970, London: Marlborough Fine Art, Ltd., 1971.
Maurice Tuchman, *R. B. Kitaj Paintings and Prints*, Los Angeles: the Los Angeles County Museum of Art, 1965.

Willem de Kooning

b. Rotterdam 1904. De Kooning was, along with Pollock and Rothko, one of the great heroes of Abstract Expressionism, though from the 1950s his paintings included tell-tale figurative elements, often grotesquely distorted. Never really captivated by the process of printmaking, his activity in the area was sporadic, though his best lithographs are extraordinary encapsulations of action painting on stone. His participation in *21 Etchings and Poems* (1960) was followed by two lithographs in 1960. In 1970–71 de Kooning produced several important lithographs at Hollander's Workshop, some of which were published by Knoedler Gallery.

John Ashbery, "Willem de Kooning: A Suite of New Lithographs," *ArtNews Annual* 37, 1971.
Lanier Graham, *The Prints of Willem de Kooning: a Catalogue Raisonné 1957–71 Vol. 1*, Paris: Baudoin Lebon, 1991.
Lanier Graham, Dan Budnik, *Willem de Kooning: Printer's Proofs from the Collection of Irwin Hollander, Master Printer*, New York: Meredith Long Contemporary/Salander-O'Reilly Galleries, 1991.
Philip Larson, "Willem de Kooning: The Lithographs," *The Print Collector's Newsletter*, Vol. V, 1974.

Jannis Kounellis

b. Piraeus, Greece 1936. A sculptor often associated with Arte Povera, Kounellis is concerned with the interaction of nature and artifice. His works often employ natural forces, such as the four elements or examples of animal or plant life, and link them to man-made relics through poetic gestures. His prints have taken traditional forms, such as photo-etchings of wild flowers arrayed around a dense black square, and well as more radical ones, as in a 1974 "print" of asbestos, glassine, and phosphorus, meant to be ignited. Most have been commercially printed or fabricated, but Kounellis has worked with Crown Point Press and Max Dunkes (Munich). Many of his prints and multiples have been published by Editions Schellmann.

Jannis Kounellis, interview with Robin White, *View*, Vol. I, March 1979.
Jörg Schellmann, *Jannis Kounellis: Editions 1972–1990*, Munich and New York: Editions Schellmann, 1991.
Edition Schellmann 1969–1989: Catalogue Raisonné.

Sol LeWitt

b. Hartford, Connecticut 1928. A critical figure in the development of Conceptual art, LeWitt has, since the 1960s, made art by defining a given set of conditions, and methodically demonstrating all possible permutations of those conditions. The serialism endemic in this practice was naturally suited to the serial permutational nature of the print, and LeWitt has been a sensitive and prolific printmaker. While his early etchings and screenprints minimized physicality in order to emphasize the process over the object, LeWitt's prints have grown increasingly sensuous over the years, incorporating the subtle textures of Japanese woodblock prints and the chromatic intensity of color aquatints. In addition to limited edition prints with Crown Point Press, Multiples, Inc., Parasol Press, and other publishers, LeWitt has also produced many inexpensive artist's books.

Jeremy Lewison, *Sol LeWitt: Prints, 1970–1986*, London: Tate Gallery, 1986.
Norbert Lynton, *Order and Experience: Prints by Agnes Martin, Sol LeWitt, Robert Ryman, Robert Mangold, Brice Marden, Edda Renouf*, Arts Council of Great Britain, 1975.
Minimalist Prints (exhibition catalogue), New York: Susan Sheehan Gallery, 1990.
Sol LeWitt: Books 1966–1990, Frankfurt: Portikus, 1990.
Sol LeWitt: Graphik, 1970–75, Katalog der Siebdrucke, Lithographien, Radierungen Bücher, Basel: Kunsthalle and Bern: Verlag Kornfeld & Cie, 1975.
Nancy Tousley, *Prints: Bochner, LeWitt, Mangold, Marden, Martin, Renouf, Rockburne, Ryman*, Toronto: Art Gallery of Ontario, 1975.
Edition Schellmann 1969–1989: Catalogue Raisonné.

Roy Lichtenstein

b. New York City, 1923. A seminal figure in American Pop painting, Lichtenstein has also been an active printmaker for most of his career. In the early 1950s Lichtenstein won an award for a woodcut at the Brooklyn Museum National print exhibition. Later, he began transporting the thick black lines and assertive dot screens of cheap print into painting, and hit upon both a startling merger of "high" and "low" culture, and a brilliant design conceit that was predisposed to printed replication. Lichtenstein's early prints based on his comic-strip paintings and drawings of the early 1960s were offset lithographs and screenprints in large editions. With the *Haystack* and *Cathedral* series of lithographs in 1969, Lichtenstein became more directly involved with printmaking processes, and began to draw increasingly on art history for his imagery. His *Mirrors* series has been regarded as a brilliant analysis of optical observation and representational convention. For several years in the 1980s Lichtenstein concentrated on woodcut, in prints that roamed from German

Expressionism to Cézanne's apples to Matisse's goldfish. Lichtenstein has remained open to new techniques and technologies, employing elaborate combinations of lithography, woodcut, screenprint, and screened wax on paper, and using mylar, foil, and plastics in addition to paper. He has also made editions of sculptures, of bronze and wood furniture, enamel jewelry, banners, and ceramics. He has worked with Gemini GEL, Graphicstudio, Mourlot, and Styria Studios.

American Prints from the Sixties (exhibition catalogue), New York: Susan Sheehan Gallery, 1989.
Sidney Chafetz, "Four Early Lichtenstein Prints," *Artist's Proof* 10, 1970.
John Coplans, *Roy Lichtenstein: Graphics, Reliefs and Sculpture 1969–1970*, Irvine: Art Gallery, University of Southern California, 1970.
Ruth Fine and Mary Lee Corlett, *The Prints of Roy Lichtenstein* (catalogue raisonné), Washington: The National Gallery of Art and New York: Hudson Hills Press, 1994.
Philip Larson, *Johns, Kelly, Lichtenstein, Motherwell, Nauman, Rauschenberg, Serra, Stella: Prints from Gemini GEL*, Minneapolis: Walker Art Center, 1974.
Barbara Rose, *Roy Lichtenstein, Entablature Series*, Bedford Village NY: Tyler Graphics Ltd., 1976.
Roy Lichtenstein: A Retrospective of Prints, 1962–1971 (exhibition catalogue), San Francisco: John Berggruen Gallery, 1971.
Roy Lichtenstein: New Prints and Sculptures from Graphicstudio (exhibition catalogue), Gotheborg, Sweden: Weterling Gallery, 1989.
The Graphic Art of Roy Lichtenstein (exhibition catalogue), Cambridge: The Fogg Art Museum, 1975.
Diane Waldman, *Roy Lichtenstein: Drawings and Prints 1962–1969*, New York: Chelsea House, 1969; London: Thames and Hudson, 1970.

Richard Long

b. Bristol 1945. Long uses art to mark the interaction of the artist and the landscape. In the late 1960s Long began documenting his walks through the countryside using maps, photographs, and strings of words. He released many print editions and artist's books, recording the artist's direct manipulations of natural materials. Later Long began to retrieve elements from nature into gallery spaces – stone, wood, pine needles, mud – a change reflected in editions like the *Papers of River Muds* (1990) in which the paper incorporates mud from the rivers whose names are printed in its surface. Long's prints have been published by Edition Schellmann and by Brooke Alexander, Inc., The printers he has worked with include Matthieu (Zurich) and Domberger (Stuttgart).

Edition Schellmann 1969–1989: Catalogue Raisonné.

Robert Mangold

b. North Tonawanda, NY 1937. Mangold's works consist of simple linear (and sometimes physical) divisions of the pictorial surface, paired with a delicate chromatic touch. He has described his work as being about "fitting and not fitting," and there is often a discernable quality of tension or compression between the edges of the work and the line within. In his early aquatints Mangold employed the expanded form of the series to elucidate further the subtleties of geometric section and color on which his work depends. His later woodcuts are somewhat looser and more substantial in their appearance. Mangold has worked with Crown Point Press, and has been published by Parasol Press, Brooke Alexander Editions, and Paula Cooper Gallery.

Norbert Lynton, *Order and Experience: Prints by Agnes Martin, Sol LeWitt, Robert Ryman, Robert Mangold, Brice Marden, Edda Renouf*, Arts Council of Great Britain, 1975.
Robert Mangold, interview with Robin White, *View* 1, December 1978.
Minimalist Prints (exhibition catalogue), New York: Susan Sheehan Gallery, 1990.
Donna M. Stein. "New Editions: Robert Mangold, Seven Aquatints," *ARTnews* 73, March 1974.
Nancy Tousley, *Prints: Bochner, LeWitt, Mangold, Marden, Martin, Renouf, Rockburne, Ryman,* Toronto: Art Gallery of Ontario, 1975.

Robert Mapplethorpe

b. Floral Park, New York 1946 – *d.* New York, New York 1989. Robert Mapplethorpe's elegantly stylized photographs of flowers, faces, and naked figures are charged with a combination of sexuality and artificiality. A connoisseur of physical textures, Mapplethorpe sought various ways of expanding the limited surface texture of the photograph: in two series of works at Graphicstudio he employed photogravure, enhanced by hand-coloring, flocking, screenprint, and silk collé. He also made prints with Editions Schellmann.

Fine and Corlett, *Graphicstudio.*
Edition Schellmann 1969–1989: Catalogue Raisonné.

Brice Marden

b. Bronxville, New York 1938. One of the most important abstract painters of his generation, Marden first became known for his architectonic canvases, with their solid panels of muted encaustic colors. Though often described as a Minimalist, Marden's aesthetic is closer to the restrained Abstract Expressionism of Barnett Newman. And like Newman, Marden became an exquisite printmaker. In the 1960s, while working at Chiron Press, Marden made a number of screenprints, but it was in working at Crown Point Press on prints for Parasol Press in 1971 that Marden became seriously involved in the process. He has made occasional lithographs, but intaglio has been the medium of his major works. In the mid-1980s, Marden abandoned rectilinear geometry, turning toward the vocabulary of calligraphic glyphs and linear networks that first appeared in the portfolio, *Etchings to Rexroth.* The printers with whom Marden has collaborated include Crown Point Press, Jennifer Melby, Simca Print Artists, and Untitled Press. His prints have been published by Parasol Press, Peter Blum Edition, and the artist himself.

Pat Gilmour, "The Prints of Brice Marden," *The Print Collector's Newsletter*, Vol. XXII, No. 2, May–June 1992.
Norbert Lynton, *Order and Experience: Prints by Agnes Martin, Sol LeWitt, Robert Ryman, Robert Mangold, Brice Marden, Edda Renouf*, Arts Council of Great Britain, 1975.
Brice Marden, interview with Robin White, *View*, Vol. III, June 1980.
Minimalist Prints (exhibition catalogue), New York: Susan Sheehan Gallery, 1990.
Parkett 7, January 1986. Includes *Etching for Parkett* (1986) reproduced as a foldout, and three articles on Marden's work: "Drawings/Brice Marden"; Lisa Liebmann, "Brice Marden: the Duse of Minimalism = die Duse der Minimal Art"; and Francesco Pellizzi, "For Brice Marden: Twelve Fragments on Surface."
Nicholas Serota, Roberta Smith, Stephen Bann, *Brice Marden: Paintings, Drawings, Etchings 1975–1980*, Amsterdam: Stedelijk Museum, and London: Whitechapel Art Gallery, 1981.
Nancy Tousley, *Prints: Bochner, LeWitt, Mangold, Marden, Martin, Renouf, Rockburne, Ryman,* Toronto: Art Gallery of Ontario, 1975.

Robert Motherwell

b. Aberdeen, Washington 1915 – *d.* 1991. A major figure in American painting, Motherwell was the only member of the first generation Abstract Expressionists to produce a large body of prints. He studied engraving with Kurt Seligman in 1941, and later worked briefly at Atelier 17 though he then abandoned print media for nearly twenty years. From the mid-1960s until his death Motherwell produced etchings and lithographs that reflected the essentially gestural nature of his art, his fascination with paper and with collage, and his passion for the written word. Motherwell produced several important *livres d'artistes*, including the famous *A la pintura* (1968–72). He worked with ULAE, Hollander's Workshop, Kelpra Studio and Tyler Graphics, Ltd., and in the mid-1970s he set up full etching and lithographic facilities at his studio in Greenwich, Connecticut.

Dorothy C. Belknap and Stephanie Terenzio, *The Prints of Robert Motherwell with a Catalogue Raisonné 1943–1990*, New York: Hudson Hills Press, in association with the American Federation of the Arts, 1980, 1984, 1991.

Arthur A. Cohen, *Robert Motherwell/Selected Prints 1961–1974* (exhibition catalogue) with original lithograph cover, New York: Brooke Alexander, Inc., 1974.

John J. McKendry, Diane Kelder, and Robert Motherwell, *Robert Motherwell's A la pintura: the Genesis of a Book* (exhibition catalogue), New York: the Metropolitan Museum of Art, 1972.

Robert Motherwell/Prints 1977–1979 (exhibition catalogue with original lithograph cover), New York: Brooke Alexander Inc., 1979.

Tyler Graphics: Catalogue Raisonné, 1974–1985.

Elizabeth Murray

b. Chicago 1940. Elizabeth Murray painted her first shaped canvases in 1975. Later she began to compose her exuberant, semi-abstract paintings out of multiple canvases, conveying even more dramatically a sense of forms come to life and leaping into the world. Murray's first professional print project, made at Derrière l'Etoile and inspired by Picasso, was a five-part sequential reworking of the same lithographic stone, and captured both the inventiveness of her drawing and the changeability that characterizes her art. Murray has also worked with ULAE and with Simca Print Artists.

Armstrong and McGuire, *First Impressions.*

David P. Becker, *Elizabeth Murray Prints 1979–1990*, Boston: Barbara Krakow, and West Islip: Universal Limited Art Editions, 1990.

Jacqueline Brody, "Elizabeth Murray: Thinking in Print" (interview), *The Print Collector's Newsletter*, Vol. XXIII, No. 3, July–August 1982.

Field and Fine, *A Graphic Muse.*

Bruce Nauman

b. Fort Wayne, Indiana, 1941. Nauman's idiosyncratic and powerful art has taken the form of architectural installations, sculpture, video, holograms, neon signs, photographs, and prints. Just as his interest in the manipulation of the body found expression in three-dimensional works, his interest in the manipulation of language found a natural form in his word prints, which often use the printerly devices of reversal, inversion, and recombination to convolute meaning. Nauman has also made eloquent drypoint and lithographic renderings of his sculptures and video installations, as well as photographic editions, artists books, and sculptural editions. The printers with whom he has collaborated include Cirrus, Gemini, Simmelink/Sukimoto Editions (Marina del Rey, California), and Robert Arber and Son Editions (Alameda, New Mexico).

Armstrong and McGuire, *First Impressions.*

Christopher Cordes, *Bruce Nauman: Prints 1970–89* (catalogue raisonné), New York: Castelli Graphics and Lorence-Monk Gallery and Chicago: Donald Young Gallery, 1989. Essay by John Yau.

Gail Stavitsky, "California in Print-1, A Series: Bruce Nauman, Charles Christopher Hill, Kenneth Price," *Artweek* 10, April 21, 1979.

Susan Tallman, "Clear Vision: the Prints of Bruce Nauman," *Arts Magazine* November 1989.

Barnett Newman

b. New York 1905 – *d.* New York 1970. "The outstanding metaphysical painter of the postwar era," Newman achieved critical success late in life. His monumental, monochrome paintings, divided by one or more vertical "zips," were too austere for most other artists and critics of the 1950s. Newman did not begin making prints until 1961, and his print output was small – just five projects and a total of forty-two prints. But many, such as the *18 Cantos*, are lithographic masterpieces. His last etchings shown an unprecedented austerity and rigor, and were influential on younger artists, such as Marden. With the exception of his first three lithographs, which were printed at Pratt Graphics Center and published by the artist, and one etching published by Abrams, Newman's prints were printed and published by ULAE.

Hugh M. Davies, *The Prints of Barnett Newman*, New York: the Barnett Newman Foundation, 1983. With an essay by Riva Castleman.

Franz Meyer, *Barnett Newman: Notes.* Amsterdam: Stedelijk Museum, 1993.

Claes Oldenburg

b. Stockholm 1929. Oldenburg, whose monumental sculptures of humble consumer pleasures are famous the world over, has throughout his career been fascinated with the implications of mass production and reproduction, and has created large numbers of prints and multiples. After moving to New York in 1956, Oldenburg became involved in the creation and production of "Happenings" and environmental installations, but gradually moved from emphasizing performance to emphasizing objects as carriers of meaning. In 1965 Oldenburg made his first proposals for monuments and his first sculptural editions. (In Oldenburg's work, the distinction between prints and multiples is often fuzzy, as many works contain elements of both.) The lithographic portfolio *Notes* (1968) records the serendipity of observation and associations whence they spring. Subsequently, Oldenburg has often used prints as a vehicle for his project proposals, ranging from the sumptuous hand-colored etching *Screwarch Bridge State III* (1981) to inexpensive, high-quality offset lithographs. He has worked with many printers and fabricators including Aeropress, Aldo Crommelynck, Crown Point Press, Gemini GEL, and Landfall Press, and his works have been published by Editions Alecto, Multiples, Inc., and Original Edition.

Gene Baro, *Claes Oldenburg: Drawings and Prints,* New York: Paul Bianchini; and London and New York: Chelsea House, 1969. Reprinted Secaucus, New Jersey: Wellfleet Books, 1988.

Claes Oldenburg: Recent Prints (exhibition catalogue), New York: Knoedler Gallery, 1973.

Claes Oldenburg: Multiples in Retrospect 1964–1990, New York: Rizzoli, 1991. Foreword by Arthur Solway. Introduction by Thomas Lawson.

Claes Oldenburg: Drawings, Watercolors and Prints (exhibition catalogue), Stockholm: Moderna Museet, 1977. Essays by Bjorn Springfeldt and Coosje van Bruggen.

Oldenburg: Works in Edition, Los Angeles: Margo Leavin Gallery, 1971.

Judith Goldman, "The Case of the Baked Potatoes," *The Print Collector's Newsletter*, Vol. III, No. 2, May–June 1972.

———, "Sort of a Commercial for Objects," *The Print Collector's Newsletter*, Vol. II, No. 6, January–February 1972.

John Loring, "Oldenburg on Multiples" (interview), *Arts Magazine*, Vol. 48, No. 8, May 1974.

Joseph E. Young, "Claes Oldenburg at Gemini." *Artist's Proof* 9, 1969.

Mimmo Paladino

b. Paduli, Italy 1948. A painter often associated with the "Transavantgarde," Paladino first came to international attention in the early 1980s with his paintings of solemn figures and wistful animals. From the time of his first professional etchings in 1980 Paladino has been recognized as a dynamic printmaker with a particular affinity for the sinuous, incisive line of etching and linocut. He often uses the two in combination to provoke unexpected collisions of texture and tone. In recent works he has combined traditional etching techniques with woodcut, screenprinting, embossing, and photo-etching. He has worked with Aeropress (for Multiples, Inc.), Harlan and Weaver, Grafica Uno, and Arte 3 (Milan). His prints have been published by Multiples, Inc., Editions Schellmann, and Waddington Graphics.

Danny Berger, "Mimmo Paladino: an Interview," *The Print Collector's Newsletter*, Vol. 14, No. 2, May–June 1983.
Michael Desmond, *Memories and Voices: the Art of Mimmo Paladino*, Canberra: the Australian National Gallery, 1990.
Edition Schellmann 1969–1989: Catalogue Raisonné.
Mimmo Paladino: Etchings, Woodcuts and Linocuts 1983–86 (exhibition catalogue), London: Waddington Graphics, and Philadelphia: Dolan/Maxwell Gallery, 1986.
Mimmo Paladino: Prints 1987–1991 (exhibition catalogue), London: Waddington Graphics, 1991.

Blinky Palermo (Peter Schwarze Heisterkamp)

b. Leipzig 1943 – *d.* Sri Lanka 1977. Palermo's quixotic abstraction has only gained in influence and respect in the years after his death. From 1966 to 1975 Palermo made prints that echoed many aspects of his varied production: editioned versions of his roughly geometric "Prototypes," documents of his site-specific (and temporary) wall drawings, printed versions of his rigorous, graceful abstract paintings. The collaboration between form, color, and physical circumstance that gave Palermo's work its idiosyncratic beauty was extended in the prints, where images reappeared, severed from their original context, as inexplicable geometric designs. Most of his editions were commercially printed screenprints or lithographs published by Galerie Heiner Friedrich in Munich, though several were done in conjunction with museum exhibitions.

Walter Ehrmann, *Palermo Druckgraphik 1970–74*, Leverkusen: Städisches Museum Leverkusen, 1975.
Erich Maas and Delano Greenidge (ed.), *Blinky Palermo 1943–1977*, New York: Delano Greenidge Editions, 1989. Essays by Franz Dahlem, Evelyn Weiss and Max Wechsler. Exhibition history and bibliography by Aurel Scheibler.
Fred Jahn, *Palermo: die gesamte Grafik und alle Auflagenobjekte 1966 bis 1975* (catalogue raisonné), Munich: Fred Jahn, 1983. Essays by Rudi Fuchs and Johannes Cladders.
Susan Tallman, "Blinky Palermo, After the Fact," *Arts Magazine*, Vol. 63, No. 10, Summer 1989.

Eduardo Paolozzi

b. Leith, Scotland 1924. A member of the Independent Group at the London ICA, Paolozzi was, along with Richard Hamilton, one of the first artists to employ images lifted from advertising with a Pop sensibility, and one of the first to begin making screenprints with Chris Prater at Kelpra Studios. His suite *As Is When* (1965), based on the life of Ludwig Wittgenstein, is considered a masterpiece of screenprint. Most of Paolozzi's screenprints were reproductions executed by the printer of collages made for the purpose. In printing the editions, Paolozzi would vary the inking from one impression to the next, wreaking havoc with both traditional definitions of originality, and the traditional uniformity of the edition. Primarily a sculptor, Paolozzi has also made editions of ceramics, textiles, and jewelry.

Eduardo Paolozzi – Complete Graphics, Berlin: Galerie Mikro, 1967 and London: Petersburg Press, 1969.
Rosemary Miles, *The complete prints of Eduardo Paolozzi: prints, drawings, collages 1944–77*, London: Victoria & Albert Museum, 1977.
Peter Selz and Christopher Finch, *Eduardo Paolozzi: A Print Retrospective* (exhibition catalogue), Berkeley: University of California and London: Editions Alecto, 1968.

Phillip Pearlstein

b. Pittsburgh 1924. Pearlstein is one of America's most respected Realists, best known for his paintings and prints of nude figures arranged around decorative surfaces and presented with meticulous dispassion. Pearlstein's early lithographs were clean, draftsmanly images that emphasized the sharp linearity of his drawing. In his later color aquatints, the supple surfaces of skin, fabrics, and floor are composed into flat graphic patterns of intense color. Pearlstein has also turned his cool eye on landscapes, producing large aquatints and woodcuts of natural sites and historically important panoramas such as Rome, Jerusalem, Stonehenge and Macchu Picchu. Pearlstein has worked extensively with Graphic-studio and Landfall Press, as well as with Tamarind and the Printmaking Workshop (New York).

Dennis Adrian, "The Prints of Phillip Pearlstein", *The Print Collector's Newsletter*, Vol. IV, No. 3, July–August 1973.
Alexander Dückers, *Zeichnungen und Aquarelle, die Druckgraphik* (exhibition catalogue), Berlin: Staatliche Museen Preussischer Kulturbesitz, 1972.
Richard S. Field, *Philip Pearlstein: Prints, Drawings Paintings* (exhibition catalogue), Middletown, Connecticut: Davison Art Center, Wesleyan University, 1979.
Judith Goldman, "The Proof is in the Process: Painters as Printmakers," *ARTnews* 80, September 1981.
William C. Landwehr, *The Lithographs and Etchings of Philip Pearlstein*, Springfield: Springfield Art Museum, 1978. Essay by Richard S. Field.

Philip Pearlstein: Landscape Aquatints 1978–1980 (exhibition catalogue with original lithograph cover), New York: Brooke Alexander Gallery, 1981. With an essay by Jerome Viola.

A. R. Penck (Ralf Winkler)

b. Dresden 1939. Poet, jazz musician and self-taught artist, Penck developed his pictographic vocabulary of stick-figures, "standards," and mathematical symbols, in East Germany during the early 1970s (he emigrated to the West in 1980). The runic primitivism of his work is an attempt to initiate direct communication. He has made etchings, woodcuts, lithographs, and screenprints throughout his career. Those made in the East were usually private notes, rarely printed in any sizable editions, while those made in the West have received far wider distribution. The printers with whom he worked most in Dresden were D. Pfeiler and J. Lorenz. Since 1980 Penck has printed with Aldo Crommelynck, Karl Imhof (Munich), François Lafranca, Valter Rossi at 2RC, Jack Shirreff (England), and Kurt Zein (Vienna). Most of these works have been published by Maximilian Verlag/Sabine Knust.

A. R. Penck: Editionen 1989, Munich: Maximilian Verlag, Sabine Knust, 1989.
A. R. Penck: Graphik Ost/West, Braunschweig: Kunstverein Braunschweig, 1986.
Bice Curiger, *Looks et tenebrae*, New York and Zurich: Peter Blum Edition, 1984. Preface by Jean-Christophe Ammann.
Dorothea Dietrich, "A Talk with A. R. Penck" (interview), *The Print Collector's Newsletter*, Vol. XIV, No. 3, July–August 1983.
Günther Gercken, "Renaissance der Druckgraphik: Georg Baselitz, Jörg Immendorff, Markus Lüpertz, A. R. Penck," in Peter Pakesch (ed.), *Druckgraphik 1970–85*, Graz: Künstlerhaus Graz, Grazer Kunstverein, 1986.

Tom Phillips

b. London 1937. A painter, poet, composer, and printmaker, Phillips is best known for his ongoing project, *A Humument*, in which the pages of a mediocre Victorian novel (chosen at random) have been reworked and overpainted, while key words have been selected out to form a second, and quite independent narrative. The interaction of visual and literary content is a persistent feature of Phillips's art, and much of his printed work has played the two against each other, as in the sequential state etchings *The Birth of Art* (1973). Phillips has also made a series of thirty-eight lithographic portraits, all sequential revisions of the same stone. A second magnum opus took the form of his translation and illustrations of Dante's *Inferno* (1979–83).

Tom Phillips, J.-Y. Bosseur, *Tom Phillips: œuvre gravé*, London: the British Council, 1979.

Tom Phillips, *A Humument* (trade edition), London: Thames and Hudson, 1980.

Tom Phillips, *Dante's Inferno* (trade edition), London: Thames and Hudson, 1985.

Tom Phillips, *Works/Texts to 1974*, Stuttgart: Edition Hansjörg Mayer, 1975.

Tom Phillips, *Works and Texts*, London: Thames and Hudson, and the Royal Academy, 1992.

Tom Phillips: Prints and Graphics (exhibition catalogue), Leigh: Turnpike Gallery, 1987.

Pablo Picasso

b. Málaga 1881 – *d*. Mougins, France 1973. The most famous artist of the century, Picasso took to printmaking with the same instant mastery and formal inventiveness he displayed in painting, sculpture, drawing, and collage. As in his other media he was almost unimaginably prolific, producing some 2200 prints over a period of nearly seventy years. In the 1920s and 1930s Picasso worked with etching, and in the fifteen years following the war, he entered into an extremely fruitful collaboration with Imprimerie Mourlot Frères, which did much to ennoble both lithographic technique and the opinion of it held by the art public. In the late 1950s, Picasso tired of the logistical difficulties of working with printers in Paris, and began collaboration with a local printer of linocut. Later, the Crommelynck brothers set up an etching studio near Picasso's home, and in 1968 Picasso completed the famous *347* etchings. Though the "contemporary" period can be defined to some extent by the waning influence of Picasso and the School of Paris, the artist's technical proficiency and indefatigable visual imagination were inspirational to many artists in the 1960s and 1970s. Hockney, Hamilton, and Johns are among those who paid homage to Picasso in their prints.

George Bloch, *Picasso: Catalogue de l'œuvre gravé et lithographié*, vols I–IV, Berne: Kornefeld and Klipstein, 1979.

Donald H. Karshan, *Picasso Linocuts: 1958–1963*, New York: Tudor Publishing Co., 1968.

William Lieberman and L. Donald McVinney, *Picasso Linoleum Cuts: the Mr and Mrs Charles Kramer Collection in the Metropolitan Museum of Art*, New York: the Metropolitan Museum of Art and Random House, 1985.

Picasso – Sixty Years of Graphic Works, Los Angeles: Los Angeles County Museum of Art, 1966. Preface by E. Feinblatt. Essays by D. Kahnweiler and B. Geiser.

Picasso, 347 Gravures, Chicago: Art Institute of Chicago, 1968. Introduction by Aldo and Piero Crommelynck.

Sylvia Plimack Mangold

b. New York, New York 1938. Plimack Mangold's works are realistic, conceptually rich, and lyrical. Her paintings and prints of the 1970s were startlingly accurate depictions of floorboards and measuring devices. These gave way to pictures of pictures, in which loosely rendered landscapes were edged by deceptively realistic, hand-drawn strips of masking tape. In recent works these landscapes have broken free of their trompe l'œil housings to stand on their own.

19th National Print Exhibition (exhibition catalogue), Brooklyn: the Brooklyn Museum, 1975.

Ellen G. D'Oench and Hilarie Faberman, *Sylvia Plimack Mangold: Works on Paper, 1968–1991; with a Catalogue Raisonné of the Prints*, Middletown, Connecticut: Davison Art Center, Wesleyan University, 1992.

Sigmar Polke

b. Oels, Germany 1941. Polke's work of the early 1960s used both media imagery and printing conventions such as overblown dot screens, but his concerns were far more convoluted than mere Pop appropriation, and his subsequent work has proved him to be a singularly difficult artist to categorize. His paintings regularly employ seemingly preposterous combinations of borrowed printed imagery, elegant and expressive drawing, fabric patterns, and evocative materials like gold flakes and liquid varnish. His prints are similarly mystifying and mystical: he made some Pop-ish screenprints in the early 1960s, followed by many inexpensive photo-offset productions of baffling or distorted imagery. More recently he has produced numerous offset lithographs based on his loose, improvisatory drawings.

René Block, *Grafik des Kapitalistischen Realismus*, Berlin: Edition René Block, 1971.

————, *K. P. Brehmer, K. H. Hödicke, Sigmar Polke, Gerhard Richter, Wolf Vostell: Werkverzeichnisse der Druckgrafik Band II: 1971–1976*, Berlin: Edition René Block, 1976.

John T. Paoletti. "Higher Beings Command: the Prints of Sigmar Polke," *The Print Collector's Newsletter*, Vol. XXII, No. 2, May–June 1991.

Marcus Raetz

b. Berne, 1941. Raetz has been scrutinizing questions of vision and illusion for more than three decades, in anamorphic installations, "drawings" arranged from natural debris (a handful of eucalyptus leaves that describe a face), and cartoon-like reductions of the phenomena of perception. An avid and prolific printmaker, Raetz has produced hundreds of etchings, lithographs, woodcuts, and heliogravures, which range from Cozens-like blotted landscapes to precise linear drawings that expose the tenuous and negotiable relationship between the eye and its object.

Markus Raetz, interview, *View* Vol. VIII, 1992–93.

Juliane Willi-Cosandier, Josef Helfenstein, Rainer Michael Mason, *Markus Raetz: Les Estampes 1958–1991* (catalogue raisonné), Zurich: Galerie & Edition Stähle, 1991.

Arnulf Rainer

b. Baden, Austria 1929. Rainer's practice of obliterating images with agitated strokes was developed by the artist in the 1950s as a form of psychic exploration and expression far removed from the compositional niceties of Informel. His prodigious print production includes lithographs of dense, surrealist-inflected figuration, abstract linear tangles, and the hallucinogen-inspired *Wahnfall* offset lithographs of 1967, but the vast majority of his prints are the "Überdeckungen" – drypoints in which repeated scratches come together to form an impenetrable mass. In the mid-1970s, Rainer used these scratches to obliterate photogravures of grimacing faces; in his other works the scratches form their own, thicket-like composition. Rainer often uses cruciform plates, and the rhythmic stroke and intense color of these prints appears both frenetic and serene. Rainer has collaborated on editions with Dieter Roth and Günter Brus. His drypoints have been printed by Rudolph Lauterbach, Robert Finger, and Kurt Zein in Vienna, and by Karl Imhof in Munich.

Otto Breicha, *Arnulf Rainer: Überdeckungen. Mit einem Werkkatalog sämtlicher Radierungen, Lithographien und Siebdrucke 1950–1971* (catalogue raisonné), Österreichische Graphiker der Gegenwart, Vol. 7, Vienna: Edition Tusch, 1972.

Johannes Gachnang, "Broodthaers/Roth/Johns/Rainer/Lewitt/Kirkeby," in Peter Pakesch (ed.), *Druckgraphik 1970–85*, Graz: Künstlerhaus Graz, Grazer Kunstverein, 1986.

Werner Hoffman, *Arnulf Rainer*, Vienna: Museum des 20. Jahrhunderts, 1968.

John T. Paoletti, "Arnulf Rainer: Prints as Encounter and Event," *The Print Collector's Newsletter*, Vol. XVIII No. 1, March–April 1987.

Arnulf Rainer: Graphik-übermalungen: Handüberarbeitete Druckgraphik von 1961 bis 1980 (exhibition catalogue), Munich: Galerie Sigrid Friedrich/Sabine Knust, 1981.

Robert Rauschenberg

b. Port Arthur, Texas 1925. One of the most important American artists of the century, Robert Rauschenberg is also one of its great printmakers, and has had a profound influence on the aesthetics, technical innovations, and critical standing of the print. Rauschenberg briefly attended Black Mountain College where he studied with Albers and formed a lasting friendship with John Cage and Merce Cunningham. Rauschenberg shared Cage's disinterest in subjective expression, and his openness to the world outside "art." Throughout the 1950s Rauschenberg engaged in a variety of informal print processes, such as blueprint, in an effort to break down the barriers between life and art, but it was in 1962, the year that he first made lithographs at ULAE and that he began to use photographic silkscreens in his paintings, that Rauschenberg was able to give these ideas graphic form. His early lithographs, like his paintings of the time, were heavily overworked melanges of found photographic material. In the late 1960s and early 1970s, Rauschenberg sought out technological adventure, co-founding Experiments in Art and Technology with engineer Billy Klüver in 1966, and collaborating with Gemini on prints of unprecedented scale. Later, Rauschenberg was the first major artist to create works of handmade paper, contributing to the emergence of paper works as an art form. In addition to ULAE and Gemini, Rauschenberg has worked with Graphicstudio and Styria, and in 1971 Rauschenberg and Robert Petersen established the Untitled Press on Captiva Island in Florida. Rauschenberg has always been an enormously productive artist, and in the early 1980s his reputation as a printmaker suffered as a result of overexposure. However, in editions such as the *Bellini* photogravures of the 1980s, Rauschenberg has demonstrated once again his brilliant eye for juxtaposition and graphic form.

Armstrong and McGuire, *First Impressions*.
Jack Cowart and James Elliott, *Prints from the Untitled Press*, Hartford, Connecticut: the Wadsworth Athaneum, 1973.
Suzanne Delehanty, Dwight Daman, Lawrence Alloway, *Rauschenberg: Graphic Art* (exhibition catalogue), Philadelphia: Institute of Contemporary Art, University of Pennsylvania, 1970.
W. H. Evans, "Printmaking Ensuite with Rauschenberg, Rockburne and LeWitt." *Print Review* 14, 1981.
Fine, *Gemini GEL*.
Fine and Corlett, *Graphicstudio*.
Edward A. Foster, *Robert Rauschenberg: Prints, 1948–1970*, Minneapolis: the Minneapolis Institute of Arts, 1970.
Philip Larson, *Johns, Kelly, Lichtenstein, Motherwell, Nauman, Rauschenberg, Serra, Stella: Prints from Gemini GEL*, Minneapolis: Walker Art Center, 1974.

Brian O'Doherty, "Rauschenberg," introduction to *International Print Biennale Catalogue*, Ljubljana, 1965.
Carter Ratcliff, "Rauschenberg's Solvent-Transfer Drawings," *The Print Collector's Newsletter*, Vol. XVIII, No. 2, May–June 1987.
Rauschenberg at Graphicstudio (exhibition catalogue), Tampa: Library Gallery, University of South Florida, 1974.
Robert Rauschenberg Graphik (exhibition catalogue), Karlsruhe: Kunstverein, 1971.
Robert Rauschenberg, "Work Notes on Lithography," (1962) published in *Rauschenberg: XXXIV Drawings for Dante's Inferno* (exhibition catalogue), Geneva: Galerie Gérald Cramer, 1968.
Mark Lesly Smith, "Suspended Shadows: the Miniature Blueprints of Rauschenberg & Weil," *The Print Collector's Newsletter*, Vol. XXIV, No. 4, September–October 1993.
Sparks, *Universal Limited Art Editions*.
Calvin Tompkins, *The Bride and the Bachelors*, New York: The Viking Press, 1965.
———, *Off the Wall: Robert Rauschenberg and the Art World of Our Time*, New York: Doubleday & Company, 1980.
Kenneth Tyler and Rosamund Felsen, "Two Rauschenberg Paper Projects," *Paper Art and Technology*, 1979.
Joseph E. Young, "Pages and Fuses: An Extended View of Robert Rauschenberg," *The Print Collector's Newsletter*, Vol. V, No. 2, May–June 1974.

Gerhard Richter

b. Dresden 1932. Shortly after moving from East to West Germany in 1961 Richter began painting fuzzy reproductions of photographs, which were initially seen as a Germanic manifestation of Pop art. Richter, however, cared less about the visual debris of popular culture than about the inherent complexities of representation. From 1965 to 1974 Richter produced offset lithographs, screenprints and photogravures, most of them blurred and not-quite-credible manipulations of photography. In the mid-1970s Richter began painting purely abstract works and produced the *Farbfelder* (1974) portfolio of methodical and meaningless color chips before largely abandoning the print.

René Block, *Grafik des Kapitalistischen Realismus*, Berlin: Edition René Block, 1971.
———, *K. P. Brehmer, K. H. Hödicke, Sigmar Polke, Gerhard Richter, Wolf Vostell: Werkverzeichnisse der Druckgrafik Band II: 1971–76*, Berlin: Edition René Block, 1976.
Hubertus Butin, *Gerhard Richter Editionen, 1965–1993*, Bremen: Kunsthalle Bremen, 1993.
Dorothea Dietrich, "Gerhard Richter: An Interview," *The Print Collector's Newsletter*, Vol. XVI, No. 4, September–October 1985.

Gerhard Richter: Graphik 1965–70, Essen: Museum Folkwang, 1970.
John T. Paoletti, "Gerhard Richter: Ambiguity as an Agent of Awareness," *The Print Collector's Newsletter*, Vol. XIX, No. 1, March–April 1988.

Larry Rivers

b. New York 1923. A former jazz musician turned painter, Rivers studied with two great painters of abstraction: Hans Hoffman and William Baziotes, but maintained his own urge toward representation. The first artist to work at ULAE, he was well attuned to the strengths of lithography, since he was a natural and elegant draftsman, who enjoyed leaving traces of half-completed events, erasures, and pentimenti. His prints at ULAE include the important collaboration with John O'Hara, *Stones* (1957–60), as well as many single lithographs such as *Lucky Strike In the Mirror* (1961).

Armstrong and McGuire, *First Impressions*.
W. K. Muller, "Prints and Multiples," *Arts Magazine*, Vol. 46, No. 4, December 1971.
Larry Rivers, "My Life Among the Stones," *Location* 1, Spring 1963.
Edition Schellmann 1969–1989: Catalogue Raisonné.
Sparks, *Universal Limited Art Editions*.

Dorothea Rockburne

b. Verdun, Quebec 1934. By folding, coloring, and scoring paper and fabric Rockburne articulates both the irreducible materiality of the art object and the myriad internal relationships that it can support. Rockburne has not made many prints, but the folded white-on-white aquatints of *Locus* (1975), made at Crown Point Press and published by Parasol Press, are among the great Minimalist prints of the 1970s. In the 1980s Rockburne worked with Gemini GEL on translucent paper works, folded and printed on both sides.

W. H. Evans, "Printmaking Ensuite with Rauschenberg, Rockburne and LeWitt."
Fine, *Gemini GEL*.
Minimalist Prints (exhibition catalogue), New York: Susan Sheehan Gallery, 1990.
Carter Ratcliff, "Dorothea Rockburne: New Prints," *The Print Collector's Newsletter*, Vol. V, No. 2, May–June 1974.
Nancy Tousley, *Prints: Bochner, LeWitt, Mangold, Marden, Martin, Renouf, Rockburne, Ryman*, Toronto: Art Gallery of Ontario, 1975.

James Rosenquist

b. Grand Forks, North Dakota 1933. One of the best known American Pop painters, Rosenquist developed his signature style while working as a billboard painter, and his fascination with enormous physical scale and with the intercutting of fragmentary images has remained a constant feature in his work. His prints have been characterized by technical audacity: in his first lithographs, done with ULAE in 1965, Rosenquist brought non-traditional tools to the job – airbrushes, stencils and paint rollers; *F-111* and *Horseblinders* were architecturally scaled, multi-panel prints that used futuristic materials like reflective mylar. In the late 1970s and early 1980s Rosenquist produced a great many etchings, some of whose publication rights were sold as a form of tax shelter. The resulting financial debacle somewhat tarnished Rosenquist's reputation as a printmaker, though many of his prints remain classics of the American Pop aesthetic. In 1983 Rosenquist received the World Print Award from the World Print Council at the San Francisco Museum of Modern Art. In the late 1980s, Rosenquist embarked on a series of ambitious works at Tyler Graphics, combined lithography and colored, pressed paper pulp. Rosenquist has also worked with Aeropress, Gemini GEL, Hollander's Workshop, Multiples Inc., Petersburg Press, and Styria Studios.

Roberta Bernstein, "Rosenquist Reflected: the Tampa Prints," *The Print Collector's Newsletter*, Vol. IV, No. 1, March–April 1973.
Fine and Corlett, *Graphicstudio*.
Constance W. Glenn, *Time Dust. James Rosenquist: Complete Graphics, 1962–1992*. New York: 1993.
James Rosenquist at USF (exhibition catalogue), Tampa: University of South Florida, 1988. With an essay by Donald Saff.
James Rosenquist: Gemälde, Räume, Graphik (exhibition catalogue), Cologne: Kunsthalle, 1972.
James Rosenquist: Nevermind, from Thought to Drawing (exhibition catalogue), New York: Universal Limited Art Editions, 1980.
James Rosenquist: Welcome to the Water Planet and House of Fire 1988–1989, Mount Kisco, New York: Tyler Graphics, Ltd. 1989. Essay by Judith Goldman.
James Rosenquist: Welcome to the Water Planet (videotape), Mount Kisco, New York: Tyler Graphics, Ltd. 1989.
Lithographs of James Rosenquist. Amsterdam: Stedelijk Museum, 1973.
Sparks, *Universal Limited Art Editions*.
Susan Tallman, "Big," *Arts Magazine*, Vol. 65, No. 7, March 1991.
Elayne H. Varian, *James Rosenquist: Graphics Retrospective* (exhibition catalogue), Sarasota, Florida: John and Mable Ringling Museum of Art, 1979.

Dieter Roth (Diter Rot)

b. Hanover 1930. In the course of his mercurial career Roth has produced films, sculptures of baked food, records, and vast numbers of books and print editions. He was trained as a graphic designer in Switzerland, and worked in the field for many years. While living in Iceland he became known (as "Diter Rot") for his highly original "Boks," in which he restructured the book form by reorganizing type into abstract patterns, punching holes, or slicing the pages. These were followed by even more extreme forms, like the *Literature Sausage* in which book pages were mulched into sausage casings. Roth's approach is persistently inventive and irreverent. In the 1960s, Roth produced a number of prints based on postcards of popular tourist attractions as well as plastic-encased editions in which food was allowed to putrefy. He has also produced many hand-drawn prints, which display almost psychedelic inventiveness and elaboration, and which brilliantly exploit the processes of their creation. He has collaborated with Richard Hamilton, Stefan Wewerka, and Arnulf Rainer. In 1973 Roth won the first prize of the International Print Biennale in Grenchen.

Richard Hamilton, "The Books of Diter Rot," *Typographica* 3, 1961. Reprinted in Hamilton, *Collected Words*.
Dieter Roth: Books and Graphics 1947–1971, Stuttgart, London and Reykjavik: edition Hansjörg Mayer, 1972.
Dieter Roth: Books and Graphics 1971–1979, Stuttgart, London and Reykjavik: edition Hansjörg Mayer, 1972.
Dieter Roth, *Gesammelte Werke, Band 20, Bücher und Grafik (1. Teil) aus den Jahren 1947 bis 1971*. London and Stuttgart: edition Hansjörg Mayer, 1972.
Dieter Roth, *Gesammelte Werke, Band 40, Bücher und Grafik (2. Teil) u.a.m. aus den Jahren 1971 bis 1979 (und Nachtrag zum 1. Teil)*. London and Stuttgart: edition Hansjörg Mayer, 1979.

Susan Rothenberg

b. Buffalo, NY 1945. A compelling and intuitive painter, whose works heralded the return of paint, canvas, and expressive imagery as artistic tools in the late 1970s, Rothenberg is also a masterful printmaker. Her 1980 woodcuts, printed by Aeropress and published by Multiples, Inc., were prominent examples of the woodcut revival, and her later lithographs, woodcuts, and etchings have eloquently embodied the tension between her energetic strokes, charismatic figures, and their material housing. She has worked with the most eminent of American printshops including ULAE, Gemini GEL, and Derrière l'Etoile. In 1985 she won the Grand Prix at the 16th International Biennial of Graphic Art, Ljubljana.

Rachel Robertson Maxwell, *Susan Rothenberg: The Prints* (catalogue raisonné to 1987), Philadelphia: Peter Maxwell, 1987. With essays by Jeremy Lewison, Wendy Weitman, and Keith Brintzenhofe.

Ed Ruscha

b. Omaha, Nebraska 1937. Since 1960 Ruscha has been occupied with essentially graphic questions about the provocative divergences that arise between words, images, and objects. In the late 1960s Ruscha gave up painting for some years to concentrate on prints, drawings, and books, which have always been an essential part of his work. The inexpensive, photo-offset books that Ruscha began making in 1963 were very influential on the subsequent development of the artists' book, and revealed a conceptual edge to his work, which had previously been considered Pop. Ruscha's early screenprints, such as *Standard Station* and *Hollywood* were comically heroic depictions of the language-filled American landscape. These were followed by lithographs in which words appeared to be spelled out by spilled liquids, or overrun by trompe l'œil bugs. In 1970 Ruscha further confused the distinction between subject and object by screenprinting with organic substances such as salmon roe, chocolate syrup, and caviar. Later in the decade he returned to hand-drawn lithographs of household objects floating through space, and of broad panoramas on which events or locations of significance are marked out. Ruscha's recent lithographs and etchings have, like his paintings, depicted grisaille silhouettes of common elements of the American dream: ranch houses, lawn jockeys, or the letters Q and A sitting on a small cusp of earth. Ruscha has been a peripatetic printmaker. He has made screenprints with Advanced Graphics Ltd. (London) and Styria Studio (New York); lithographs with Cirrus Editions Ltd., Gemini GEL, Graphicstudio, Ed Hamilton, Landfall Press, and Tamarind Lithography Workshop; and etchings with Crown Point Press. His editions have been published by Bernard Jacobson, Ltd., Multiples, Inc., and Editions Julie Sylvester, among others, as well as by the artist himself.

Armstrong and McGuire, *First Impressions*.
David Bourdon, "Ruscha as Publisher (or all booked up)," *ARTnews* 71, April 1972.
Reyner Banham, *Edward Ruscha: Prints and Publications, 1962–74* (exhibition catalogue), London: Arts Council of Great Britain, 1975.
John Coplans, "Concerning 'Various Small Fires': Edward Ruscha Discusses His Perplexing Publications," *Artforum* 3, February 1965.

Fine, *Gemini GEL.*

Fine and Corlett, *Graphicstudio.*

Christopher Fox, "Ed Ruscha Discusses His Latest Work," *Studio International*, June 1970.

Graphic works by Edward Ruscha (exhibition catalogue), Auckland: The Gallery, 1978.

Edward A. Foster, *Edward Ruscha: prints, drawings and books 1963–1971*, Minneapolis: Minneapolis Institute of Arts, 1972.

————, *Edward Ruscha (Ed-werd Rew-shay) Young Artist*, Minneapolis: Minneapolis Institute of Art, 1972.

Philip Larson, "Ruscha in Minneapolis," *The Print Collector's Newsletter*, Vol. III, No. 3, July–August 1972.

Philip Larson, "Words in Print," *The Print Collector's Newsletter*, Vol. V, No. 3, July–August 1974.

Howardena Pindell, "Words with Ruscha," *The Print Collector's Newsletter*, Vol. III, No. 6, January–February 1973. Interview reprinted in Dutch in *Edward Ruscha*, Amsterdam: Stedelijk Museum, 1976.

Antonio Saura

The Spanish painter and printmaker Saura has employed a wide variety of print processes – lithography, etching, aquatint, screenprint – in savage critiques of Spanish history, and of violence and oppression generally. His 1964 series *Historia de España* represented the great and powerful of Spanish history in grotesque caricature, while in later prints like *El Perro de Goya* (1972) and *Rembrandt* (1973) he has treated art historical subjects.

Mariuccia Galfetti, *Antonio Saura: l'œuvre imprimé/l'obra grafica 1958–84*, Madrid: Ministerio de Cultura, Dirección General de Bellas Artess y Archivos. 1985. With essays by Jean Frémon, Rainer Michael Mason; Antonio Saura.

Richard Serra

b. San Francisco, 1939. Best known for his site-specific sculptures, which use massive plates of Cor-ten steel to articulate subtleties of weight, balance, and the division of space, Serra is also a filmmaker and printmaker. In his prints Serra has explored the physical presence of black, which he sees as the essence of graphic media. His first richly drawn lithographs of 1972 have been seen as heralds of the subsequent flourishing of sculptors' prints. Later, with the staff of Gemini, Serra developed a method in which paintstick is pressed through a silkscreen to build up a dimensional mass of black on the paper surface, producing what are essentially large, repeatable drawings. Serra's *Afangar* series, based on his basalt sculptures for an Icelandic island, are deeply etched, thickly printed aquatints, in both minute and massive

sizes. Most of his prints have been made with Gemini GEL, but he has also worked with Item Editions in Paris.

Fine, *Gemini GEL.*

Philip Larson, *Johns, Kelly, Lichtenstein, Motherwell, Nauman, Rauschenberg, Serra, Stella: Prints from Gemini GEL*, Minneapolis: Walker Art Center, 1974.

Nancy Prinsenthal, "The 'Afangar Icelandic Series': Richard Serra's Recent Etchings", *The Print Collector's Newsletter*, Vol. XXII, No. 5, November–December 1991.

Richard Serra at Gemini 1983–1987, Los Angeles: Gemini GEL, 1987.

Richard Serra: Drawings and Etchings from Iceland (exhibition catalogue), New York: Matthew Marks Gallery, 1992. Interview with Mark Rosenthal.

Pierre Soulages

b. Rodez, France 1919. Soulages, probably the most eminent French painter of the "Informel" movement, began making prints in 1951 at Atelier Lacourière. In his etchings, as in his paintings, Soulages used the brush to construct abstract architectonic compositions of broad strokes. He works his paintings in broad impasto, and in the prints he allowed the acid to eat through the copper, perforating and shaping the plate so that it interacted with the paper much as sculpture interacts with the space around it. Soulages plays the subtle, glimmering light within the form off against the abrupt flashes where the image meets white paper. Soulages won the Grand Prize of the Ljubljana Print Biennale in 1959. In addition to Lacourière, Soulages has collaborated with printers 2RC and Alain Lambilliotte (Paris).

Georges Duby and Christian Labbaye, *Soulages: Eaux-Fortes, Lithographies*, Paris: Yves Rivière, 1974.

Dominique Ferriot, "Soulages et l'Eau-Forte," *L'Œil* no. 233, December 1974.

R. C. Kennedy, "Pierre Soulages: Prints," *Studio International*, April–May 1975.

Pierre Soulages: Eaux-Fortes 1952–1980, Association pour l'Animation des Musées, 1987.

Pat Steir

b. Newark, New Jersey 1940. In her paintings, drawings and prints Steir attempts to reconcile the intellectual curiosity of Conceptual art and the emotional immediacy of Abstract Expressionism. A former book designer and art director, Steir has a refined understanding of the interaction of image and language, and of image and reproduction. Her early lithographs commented on the nature of their manufacture, displaying test strokes and inking samples. In

later etchings and drypoints she has constructed lexicons of printerly markings, and has made direct allusion to the print's role as a vehicle for reproduction in works where she borrows from art history. Steir has worked with Landfall Press and Crown Point Press, and has participated in Crown Point's woodcut program in China.

Elizabeth Broun, *Form, Illusion, Myth: Prints and Drawings of Pat Steir*, Lawrence, Kansas: Spencer Museum of Art, 1983.

Pat Steir, interview with Robin White, *View*, Vol. I, June 1978.

Pat Steir, interview with Constance Llewellyn, *View*, Vol. VII, 1990–91.

Juliane Willi, Claude Ritschard, Jeremy Lewison, Rainer Michael Mason, *Pat Steir: Prints 1976–1988*. Geneva: Cabinet des Estampes, Musée d'Art et d'Histoire and London: Tate Gallery, 1988.

Frank Stella

b. Malden, Massachusetts, 1935. Since 1959 Frank Stella has evolved from the most radically reductive of painters to one of the most complex; at the same time his prints have gone from being concise restatements of his paintings to being elaborate cavalcades of formal and material invention. The stripe paintings that established his reputation as a Minimalist also provided the designs for his early lithographs, which were meant to be released as "albums" in which collectors could compile an entire series of works. At Gemini and Petersburg Press in the 1970s, Stella became more technically ambitious. As Stella's paintings came to employ increasingly complicated manipulations of space, both real and illusory, his prints followed suit. But it was not until the early 1980s when Stella began printing from the detritus of his metal wall reliefs that his prints took on a life of their own. The *Swan Engravings* and the *Circuits* of the 1980s were prints of enormous scale and complexity, produced with Tyler Graphics. Stella has also collaborated with Gemini GEL, and Petersburg Press.

Richard H. Axsome, *The Prints of Frank Stella: a catalogue raisonne, 1967–1982*, New York: Hudson Hills Press; Ann Arbor: University of Michigan Museum of Art, 1983.

Robert Hughes, *Frank Stella: the Swan Engravings*, Fort Worth: the Fort Worth Art Museum, 1984.

Frank Stella: The Circuit Prints (exhibition catalogue), Minneapolis: The Walker Art Center, 1988.

Antoni Tàpies

b. Barcelona 1923. As a painter, sculptor, and printmaker, Tàpies has been an important figure in postwar Spanish art. Initially associated with the abstract art of Informel, Tàpies had, by the early 1960s, developed his own distinctive mixture of matter painting, Expressionism, abstraction and figuration – a mixture that aimed at transcendence through the commonplace. Prints and books have been an important part of Tàpies's work since 1959, and he has created more that a thousand printed images. He has experimented with a wide variety of media, often applying unusual materials, such as flocking, or unusual techniques, such as carborundum printing, to achieve dramatic physical textures. A great lover of books, Tàpies has collaborated with many writers and poets, including Joan Brossa and Octavio Paz. He has earned awards for his graphic work at the Tokyo International Biennale of Prints (1960), the 7th International Biennale of Graphics (1967), the 4th British International Print Biennale, and the International Triennial of Original Graphic Prints in Grenchen (Switzerland). Tàpies has worked mainly with five publishers: Sala Gaspar (Barcelona), Erker (St Gallen), Maeght and Lelong, and Polìgrafa.

Antoni Tàpies: Das Gesamte Graphische Werk (exhibition catalogue), St Gallen: Kunstmuseum, 1967.
Antoni Tàpies: Das Gesamte Graphische Werk: Sammlung Dr Friedrich und Maria-Pilar Herlt (exhibition catalogue), Kassel: Kasseler Kunstverein.
Antoni Tàpies: Graphic Work 1947–1987 (exhibition catalogue), Portland, Maine: The Baxter Gallery, Portland School of Art, 1988.
Manuel Borja-Villel, "Antoni Tàpies on Prints: an Interview," *The Print Collector's Newsletter*, Vol. XXIII, No. 2, May–June 1992.
Mariuccia Galfetti, *Tàpies: Obra Grafica/Graphic Work 1947–1972* (catalogue raisonné), Barcelona: Editorial Gustavo Gili, S.A., 1973.
———, *Tàpies: Obra Grafica/Graphic Work 1973–1978* (catalogue raisonné), Barcelona: Editorial Gustavo Gili, S.A., 1980.
Deborah Wye, *Antoni Tàpies in Print* (exhibition catalogue), New York: the Museum of Modern Art and Harry N. Abrams, Inc., 1991.

Wayne Thiebaud

b. Mesa, Arizona 1920. A painter of life's small material joys, Thiebaud worked for many years as a commercial artist, a fact that may have contributed to the misreading of his carefully observed cakes, pies, and toys as examples of Pop art. Thiebaud's ordered and attentive vision is much closer to that of earlier artists such as Morandi. Prints have been an important part of Theibaud's work from the time of his *Delights*, a portfolio of tiny incisive etchings. Images of rabbits and lollipops have been followed by San Francisco cityscapes in which the city's verticality is extended into flat pattern. In his etchings, aquatints, and exceptional Japanese woodblock prints, Thiebaud gives weight and presence to passing pleasures and to ephemeral qualities of light and shadow. He has worked mainly with Crown Point Press, though many of his early prints were published by Parasol Press.

John Coplans, *Wayne Thiebaud: Graphics*, Pasadena: Pasadena Art Museum, 1968.
Wayne Thiebaud, interview with Constance Lewallen, *View*, Vol. VI, Winter 1990.
Wayne Thiebaud: Graphics 1964–1971, New York: Parasol Press, 1971.
Vision and Revision: Hand Colored Prints by Wayne Thiebaud (exhibition catalogue), San Francisco: California Palace of the Legion of Honor and Chronicle Books, 1991. With essays by Wayne Thiebaud, Bill Berkson, and Robert Flynn Johnson.

Joe Tilson

b. London, 1928. Tilson's scavenging of imagery, his "inspired carpentry," and his disregard for the two-dimensional norms of painting and printmaking made him one of the most visible British artists of the 1960s. His early screenprints often bore various addenda attached to the surface – plastic toys, cut-outs, glassine envelopes – and many were printed on plastic or other unlikely materials. In the 1970s Tilson left London and moved to the country, where he turned from screenprint to etching, and his subjects changed from media events to the more abiding rhythms of nature and mythology. He has continued to be deeply involved in print production and maintains etching facilities in his studio. Tilson has won numerous prizes for his prints, including the Grand Prizes of the Cracow Biennial, and of the Ljubljana Print Biennial of 1985. His early screenprints were printed mainly by Kelpra Studios; his later etchings have been made at 107 Workshop (Wiltshire), Grafica Uno, and 2RC.

Pat Gilmour, "A Linear Job on Ineffable Work of Paradoxical Complexity: Joe Tilson," *Vanguard* 8, October 1979.
———, "A Change of He(art) – the Prints of Joe Tilson," *The Print Collector's Newsletter*, Vol. XIII, No. 1, March–April 1982.
Joe Tilson: Graphics (exhibition catalogue), Vancouver: The Vancouver Art Gallery, 1979. With essay by Pat Gilmour.

Mark Tobey

b. Centerville, Wisconsin 1890 – *d*. Basel 1976. A painter of quiet abstractions, much influenced by Asian calligraphy, Tobey was recognized in Europe as an important painter before he achieved success in America, winning the painting prize of the Venice Biennale in 1958. In his seventieth year, Tobey moved to Switzerland and began a serious and prolonged involvement in printmaking. The over one hundred lithographs, etchings, screenprints and monotypes that he made in the last sixteen years of his life included works in a flung ink style derived from the Japanese Sumi drawings, semi-figurative compositions, and his more familiar, all-over webs of line and texture. Printers with whom Tobey often worked included Fred Genis and François Lafranca.

Hanns H. Heidenheim, *Mark Tobey: das Graphische Werk, Vol. I, Radierungen und Serigraphiën 1970–1975*, Düsseldorf, 1975.
Kristen Spangenberg, *Mark Tobey: A Decade of Printmaking*, Cincinnati: Cincinnati Art Museum, 1972.

Cy Twombly

b. Lexington, Virginia 1928. As a painter Twombly has employed the repetitive gestures of handwriting as an abstract vocabulary of form (in the manner of Abstract Expressionism), and as an iconography rich in commonplace associations (in the manner of Pop). He has been an occasional, but important, printmaker. Many of his etchings and aquatints of 1967–75, made at ULAE, repeat the loopy handwriting gestures of his paintings (though reversed, slanting from right to left). Twombly, who has lived in Rome since 1957, has also used prints to invoke the complexities of culture through acts of naming and writing: producing portfolios in which the prints bear only the scribbled names of Classical writers. Other prints have shared the character of his collages, combining pictorial clippings with his signature scrawl.

Heiner Bastian, *Cy Twombly: das grafische Werk, 1953–1984: a catalogue raisonné of the printed graphic work,* Munich and New York: Edition Schellmann, 1984.
Roberta Bernstein, "Cy Twombly: Recent Prints." *The Print Collector's Newsletter*, Vol. VI, No. 6, January–February 1976.

Wolff Vostell

b. Leverkusen, Germany 1932. A performance artist, painter, and printmaker, Vostell was a core member of Fluxus. Throughout the 1960s he used screenprinted images of the horrors of war and the excesses of consumer culture in his paintings and prints, often adorning them with glitter, lightbulbs, silk stockings, or other incongruous addenda. Later the prints took on a more documentary character, chronicling his performance works and unrealized visionary projects.

René Block, *Grafik des Kapitalistischen Realismus*, Berlin: Edition René Block, 1971.
————, *K. P. Brehmer, K. H. Hödicke, Sigmar Polke, Gerhard Richter, Wolf Vostell: Werkverzeichnisse der Druckgrafik* Band II: 1971–1976. Berlin: Edition René Block, 1976.

Andy Warhol (Andrew Warhola)

b. Pittsburgh, Pennsylvania 1928 – *d.* New York, 1987. The most famous of all Pop artists, Warhol was known as a painter, filmmaker, sculptor, publisher, printmaker, and general savant. A successful commercial artist and illustrator before he turned to painting, Warhol had an indisputable graphic touch and a thorough understanding of print media. After experimenting with various forms of mechanical repetition on canvas, he began screenprinting his paintings in 1962. With a single exception (a photoengraving done for the *International Avant-Garde*), all Warhol's prints were screenprinted. After participating in several group portfolios, Warhol established Factory Additions in 1967, which published his most important screenprint sets: the ten Marilyns (1967), the two sets of Campbell's soup cans (1969), and *Flowers* (1970). In the 1970s, Warhol's prints began to reveal more of the artist's "hand," culminating in a group of hand-colored screenprints after Warhol's drawings of flowers. Most of Warhol's later prints occur in the context of theme portfolios – "Jews of the Twentieth Century," "Reigning Queens," "Myths" – and combine photographic imagery with overlays of color block and line tracings. By the time of his death Warhol had produced more than 400 prints.

Frayda Feldman and Jörg Schellmann (ed.), *Andy Warhol Prints: A Catalogue Raisonné*, Munich and New York: Editions Schellmann; Munich: Schirmer/Mosel Verlag; New York: Ronald Feldman Fine Arts, Inc., 1989. With essays by Henry Geldzahler, Roberta Bernstein, and Rupert Smith.
Suzi Gablik, *Andy Warhol: Portrait Screenprints, 1965–1980*, London: Arts Council of Great Britain, 1981.
Gerard Malanga, "A Conversation with Andy Warhol," *The Print Collector's Newsletter*, Vol. 1, No. 6, January–February 1971.
Kynaston McShine (ed.), *Andy Warhol: A Retrospective*, New York: The Museum of Modern Art, 1989. With essays by Kynaston McShine, Robert Rosenblum, Benjamin H. D. Buchloh, and Marco Livingstone.
Hermann Wünsche, *Andy Warhol: Das grafische Werk, 1962–1980*, Bonn, 1981. With essays by Gerd Tuchel and Carl Vogel.

Editions Alecto (London)

The leading British publisher of Pop artists in the 1960s, Editions Alecto began as a student venture in nostalgic topographical prints. It expanded in 1962 and changed its focus to contemporary art. A great many of its publications were printed at Kelpra Studio, with whom Alecto had a close working relationship. In 1964 Alecto also established its own facilities for etching, lithography, and screenprinting, and was described by the London *Financial Times* as "the most ambitious organization in the field." Alecto published such important works as David Hockney's etching cycle *Rake's Progress* (1961–63) and Eduardo Paolozzi's screenprint portfolio *As Is When* (1965), as well as a set of Dubuffet playing cards, Claes Oldenburg's squeezable latex *London Knees* (1966), and other unconventional editions. In 1967 one of the firm's principals, Paul Cornwall-Jones, left to found Petersburg Press. Under the direction of Joe Studholme, for some years Editions Alecto continued to produce prints and multiples, including Ed Ruscha's *News, Mews, Brews* (1970), screenprinted with food and other organic matter. In addition to the artists mentioned above, Alecto published works by Josef Albers, Bernard Cohen, Alan Davie, Jim Dine, Richard Hamilton, and Allen Jones.

Atelier 17 (Paris/New York)

Atelier 17 was founded in 1927 by Stanley William Hayter to provide an open collaborative situation for artists to explore engraving and other intaglio techniques. Hayter, a chemist who had learned engraving from Joseph Hecht, emphasized the creative and unexpected aspects of interaction between artist and materials, and was very influenced by the Surrealists, many of whom worked at the atelier. In 1940 Hayter moved the atelier to New York, where it became a hub of the exiled European art community. It had a profound influence on American printmaking, leading to the adoption of intaglio as the virtuoso print medium most practiced in American universities. Hayter, who did not use aquatint, popularized the use of soft ground, and his deep understanding of the chemical behavior of intaglio inks resulted in refinements such as color viscosity printing. His best known followers in America were Gabor Peterdi and Mauricio Lasansky. Hayter's ethos also influenced many American painters, such as Pollock and Motherwell who worked at Atelier 17 in the 1940s. Following Hayter's return to Paris, the American Atelier 17 continued under the direction of Peter Grippe, and organized the publication of the important *21 Etchings and Poems* (1960). Among the hundreds of artists who worked at Atelier 17 have been some of the most famous names of modern and contemporary art: Pierre Alechinsky, Louise Bourgeois, Max Ernst, Hans Haacke, and Joan Miró are just a few.

Peter Black and Desirée Moorhead (ed.), *The Prints of Stanley William Hayter: a Complete Catalogue*, London: Phaidon, and Mount Kisco: Moyer, Bell Ltd. 1992. With an essay by Jacob Kainen.
P. M. S. Hacker (ed.), *The Renaissance of Gravure: The Art of S. W. Hayter*, Oxford: Clarendon Press, 1988.
Stanley William Hayter, *New Ways of Gravure*, London: Routledge and Kegan Paul, 1949. Revised edition: New York: Watson-Guptill, 1981.
Hayter et l'Atelier 17, Gravelines (France): Musée du Dessin et de l'Estampe Originale, Arsenal de Gravelines, 1993. With essays by Dominique Tonneau-Ryckelynck, Carla Esposito, Duncan Scott, and Peter Hacker.

Peter Blum Edition (New York)

Peter Blum began publishing prints in 1980, concentrating on the work of younger European and American painters, such as Enzo Cucchi, Francesco Clemente, and Eric Fischl. In contrast with the plethora of quickly produced, single prints that flooded the market in the late 1970s, Blum's editions are ambitious and beautifully presented portfolios. John Baldessari's *Black Dice* (1982), Eric Fischl's *Year of the Drowned Dog* (1983), and Brice Marden's *Etchings to Rexroth* (1986) rank among the artists' best works in any medium. Blum has matched an international array of artists with an equally international group of printers: Sherrie Levine with Derrière l'Etoile, A. R. Penck with Francois Lafranca (Locarno), and James Turrell with Peter Kneubühler (Zurich). Other artists who have produced portfolios with Blum are Jonathan Borofsky, Louise Bourgeois, Martin Disler, Helmut Federle, General Idea, Alex Katz, Barbara Kruger, Rosemary Trockel, and Terry Winters. Blum has also published books with many of these artists. He is one of the publishers of Parkett Magazine, which releases an edition with every issue.

Bice Curiger, *Looks et Tenebrae*: New York and Zurich: Peter Blum Edition, 1984.
Vincent Katz, "Interview with Peter Blum," *The Print Collector's Newsletter*, Vol. XXI, No. 4, September–October 1990.
L'Italie & l'Allemagne: Nouvelles Sensibilités, Nouveaux Marchés (exhibition catalogue), Geneva: Cabinet des Estampes, Musée d'Art et d'Histoire, 1983. With essays by Maurice Besset, Peter Blum, Johannes Gachnang, Nancy Gillespie, Sabine Knust, Rainer Michael Mason, Claude Ritschard, and Fulvio Salvadori.
Peter Blum Edition New York (exhibition catalogue), Groningen: Groninger Museum, 1985. With an essay by Steven Kolsteren.

Cirrus Editions (Los Angeles)

Cirrus Editions was founded in 1970 by Tamarind Master Printer Jean Milant, who was attracted to the less painterly, more conceptual art that was emerging in Southern California at the time. In print editions with John Baldessari, Chris Burden, Vija Celmins, Ed Moses, Bruce Nauman, and Ed Ruscha, Cirrus often extended the limits of conventional hand lithography. Joe Goode made ripped and gunshot-torn lithographs, William Wiley printed on chamois, and the shop has expanded to include relief printing, drypoint, screenprint, offset lithography, and monotype. In recent years, Cirrus has invited many younger artists, including Joan Nelson, Sabina Ott, Lari Pittman, and Sarah Seager. The Cirrus Editions archive is at the Los Angeles County Museum of Art.

Gus Foster, *Cirrus Editions, Ltd.*, Los Angeles: Cirrus Editions, 1973.
Joseph E. Young, *Cirrus Editions*, Los Angeles: Cirrus Editions, 1972.
Michael Knigin and Murray Zimiles, *The Contemporary Lithographic Workshop Around the World*, New York: Van Nostrand Reinhold Co., 1974.

Aldo Crommelynck (Paris and New York)
Piero Crommelynck (Paris)

After apprenticing with Fernand Lacourière, Piero and Aldo Crommelynck became known as the printers of Matisse, Miró, and most famously, of Picasso's etchings of the 1950s and 1960s. In 1973 Richard Hamilton and David Hockney went to the Crommelyncks' atelier to produce etchings for the *Hommage à Picasso* portfolio, which marked a new wave of appreciation for the subtle etching and almost ineffable aquatints that have become Crommelynck trademarks. In 1976 the Crommelyncks printed Jasper Johns's great *livre d'artiste* with Samuel Beckett, *Fizzles/Foirades*. In the mid-1980s the brothers parted ways. Piero Crommelynck went into semi-retirement in Paris, from which he has recently emerged, printing an edition with Swiss artist Not Vital. Aldo Crommelynck has continued as an active printer, and more recently, as a publisher, with ateliers in Paris and New York, where he has worked with established artists such as Dine and Oldenburg, and younger artists, such as Martin Disler, George Condo, and Terry Winters.

Aldo Crommelynck (exhibition catalogue), London: Waddington Graphics, 1987.
Adam Weinberg, *Aldo Crommelynck, Master Prints with American Artists* (exhibition catalogue), New York: Whitney Museum of American Art, Equitable Center, 1988.

Crown Point Press (Oakland/San Francisco)

Founded in 1962 by Kathan Brown, a young artist who had studied etching at the Central School of Arts and Crafts in London, Crown Point Press is the most prolific of the major American printshops, and the one most instrumental in the revival of etching as a medium of serious art. Brown's first editions, with Richard Diebenkorn and Wayne Thiebaud display a clarity and restraint quite unlike the expressive elaborations of intaglio printing characteristic of Hayter, Lasansky, and Peterdi. Brown's philosophy – emphasizing the process ("doing") over the object ("making") – fits the ethos of conceptual and minimalist art. In the 1970s Crown Point developed a close relationship with the publisher Parasol Press, printing its editions of Mel Bochner, Chuck Close, Sol LeWitt, Robert Mangold, Brice Marden, and Dorothea Rockburne. In the 1980s the press ceased contract printing to concentrate on its own publications. The Japanese woodblock program it established in 1982 with traditional woodblock printers in Kyoto has resulted in many highly acclaimed prints by Clemente, Close, Diebenkorn, Thiebaud, and others. In 1989 Crown Point established a similar program with printers in China. Other artists who have worked extensively with Crown Point include Vito Acconci, John Cage, Robert Kushner, Sherrie Levine, Tom Marioni, Tim Rollins + K.O.S., José Maria Sicilia, and Pat Steir.

Artist and Printer: Six American Print Studios (exhibition catalogue), Minneapolis: Walker Art Center, 1980. Introduction by Graham W. J. Beal.
Nancy Tousley, *Prints: Bochner, LeWitt, Mangold, Marden, Martin, Renouf, Rockburne, Ryman.* Toronto: Art Gallery of Ontario, 1975.
————, "In Conversation with Kathan Brown." *The Print Collector's Newsletter* Vol. VIII, No. 5, November–December 1977.
View (periodical published by Crown Point, featuring interviews with artists).

Derrière l'Etoile Studios (New York)

Founded by Maurice Sanchez, a Tamarind Master Printer who had previously worked for Petersburg Press, Derrière l'Etoile produced many of the best-known editions of the 1980s, including Donald Judd's 1988 woodcuts, and lithographs by Günter Förg, Elizabeth Murray, and Susan Rothenberg. Sanchez has made a specialty of monotype, perfecting a process somewhat related to dry lithography whereby a monotype can be printed in multiple impressions with relatively little attenuation. Robert Cumming, Eric Fischl, and David Storey are among the artists who have made protracted series of monotypes, revising and inventing on the same plate over a period of many months.

Edition Domberger (Stuttgart/Filderstadt)

Inspired by a US Information Service show he saw in 1950, Luitpold Domberger determined to take screenprint, which was a rather crude medium used mainly for printing milk bottles and packing crates, and to develop it as a sophisticated and exacting medium for artists. Along with Kelpra, Domberger was a vital force in the ascendancy of screenprint in the 1960s. But while Kelpra specialized in the photographic manipulations and dazzling hand-cutting required by Pop art, Domberger excelled in the subtle color rolls and impeccable precision essential to optical or hard-edged abstraction, or to the Pop of artists like Allan d'Archangelo. Domberger embraced the commercial potential of the medium, printing calendars, posters and limited edition prints in an endless stream of polished images. In addition to contract printing for publishers such as Parasol Press, Edition Domberger has run its own publishing operation, commissioning many theme portfolios, from "On the Bowery" (1969–71) to "Columbus: In Search of a New Tomorrow" (1992). It has printed or published works by, among others, Max Bill, Richard Estes, Ilya Kabakov, Robert Mangold, Agnes Martin, Nicholas Krushenick, and J. Raphael Soto.

Erker Presse (St Gallen)

A distinguished publisher of European prints, portfolios and *livres d'artiste*, Erker Presse was founded in 1963 by Franz Larese and Jürg Janett as an extension of Erker Gallery, and Erker Verlag, which publishes books by and about contemporary artists. The European fascination with graphics as a vehicle for the interaction of literature and art is conspicuously absent in most American shops, but is essential to the Erker enterprise, which has fostered many unexpected printed collaborations, such as those between sculptor Eduardo Chillida and philosopher Martin Heidegger, and between painter Antoni Tàpies and the psychoanalyst Alexander Mitscherlich. Erker also maintains an extensive documentation center and organizes lectures and symposia on issues of contemporary culture. The lithography workshop of Erker Presse has printed the work of Piero Dorazio, Asger Jorn, Mark Tobey, Günther Uecker, and many others.

Gesamtverzeichnis Erker, St Gallen: Erker Verlag, 1994.
Als Beispiel Erker: Galerie Verlag Presse (exhibition catalogue), Hagen, Germany: Karl Ernst Osthaus Museum, 1980.

Gemini GEL (Los Angeles)

In 1965 Kenneth Tyler, then Technical Director of Tamarind, left to set up his own contract printing firm, and a year later went into partnership with two art collectors, Sidney Felsen and Stanley Grinstein, establishing Gemini GEL (Graphic Editions Limited). The firm's initial aim was to publish prints by mature artists, and its first major project was with the septuagenarian Josef Albers. From the start Gemini was characterized by Tyler's penchant for technological innovation and his willingness to adapt industrial processes and industrial scale to the needs of contemporary artists. It was an approach that strongly appealed to younger artists in the 1960s, who became the mainstay of Gemini's publishing. Major early publications included Robert Rauschenberg's *Booster* (1967), then the largest lithograph ever produced, Jasper Johns's *Color Numeral Series* (1968–69), Roy Lichtenstein's *Cathedral Series* (1969), and Claes Oldenburg's *Profile Airflow* (1968), which marked the beginning of Gemini's involvement with sculpture and other non-traditional editions. With extensive facilities of its own, and a network of outside contractors, Gemini can accommodate almost any medium an artist wishes to explore. In 1974 Tyler left Gemini to start his own workshop, Tyler Graphics Ltd. He was succeeded as Master Printer by Serge Lozingot, who had worked with Dubuffet on the ground-breaking *Phenomena* lithographs in the late 1950s. Under the direction of Felsen and Grinstein, Gemini has continued to publish many of its early artists, including Ellsworth Kelly, David Hockney, and Claes Oldenburg, and has added new ones such as Jonathan Borofsky and Vija Celmins. The Gemini GEL Archive is at the National Gallery of Art, Washington.

Artist and Printer: Six American Print Studios (exhibition catalogue), Minneapolis: Walker Art Center, 1980. Introduction by Graham W. J. Beal.

Artists at Gemini GEL: Celebrating the 25th Year, New York: Harry N. Abrams, Inc., and Los Angeles: Gemini, GEL, 1992. Interviews by Mark Rosenthal. Introduction by Michael Botwinick. Photographs of the artists by Sidney B. Felsen.

Riva Castleman, *Technics and Creativity: Gemini GEL*, New York: Museum of Modern Art, 1971.

Ruth E. Fine, *Gemini GEL: Art and Collaboration*, Washington: National Gallery of Art, and New York: Abbeville Press, 1984.

Gemini GEL *Catalogue Raisonné*, Los Angeles: Gemini GEL, 1966–(continually updated).

Grafica Uno (Milan)

Founded in 1962 by master printer Giorgio Upiglio, Grafica Uno is one of the most respected contemporary European printshops, the source of numerous etchings, lithographs and relief prints by eminent artists of the pre-war period, including Giorgio de Chirico, Marcel Duchamp, and Wilfredo Lam; by later artists such as Alechinsky, Baj, and Dine; and by still younger painters like Mimmo Paladino. Upiglio is deeply interested in the art of the book, and has produced many remarkable *livres d'artiste* with Günter Grass, Man Ray and Duchamp, Enrico Baj, and others. Upiglio's editions often display the intensity and intimacy that have been the traditional strengths of the print, balanced by wholly contemporary irreverence and wit.

Giorgio Upiglio Stampatore in Milano: l'Opera Grafica, Milan: Giorgio Upiglio, 1975. Introduction by Leo Lioni.

Libricartelle 1962/1989, Milan: Giorgio Upiglio, 1989.

Graphicstudio (Tampa, Florida)

Graphicstudio is an independent division of the University of South Florida, established in 1968 by Donald Saff, an artist, professor, and author of the standard text, *Printmaking: History and Process* (see below). Saff's goal was to create a shop free of commercial considerations and open to technological challenges, which would act as an educational vehicle for students, printers, and artists. Graphicstudio has encouraged artists to propose difficult and unlikely ventures such as Robert Rauschenberg's trompe l'œil ceramics of 1972 or Roy Lichtenstein's laminated wood *Brushstroke Chair* (1986–88). In 1988 the workshop added the title "Institute for Research in Art" to its name. It has invented several new processes and procedures including "waxtype," a way of screenprinting that uses encaustic, and "helio-relief," a form of photomechanical woodcut made by sandblasting. Graphicstudio was shut down in 1976 due to financial problems within the university, but reopened in 1981. Other artists who have worked at Graphicstudio include Vito Acconci, Arakawa, Sandro Chia, Chuck Close, Robert Mapplethorpe, Philip Pearlstein, and James Rosenquist. The Graphicstudio archive is at the National Gallery of Art in Washington.

Gene Baro, *Graphicstudio U.S.F.: an Experiment in Art and Education* (exhibition catalogue), Brooklyn: Brooklyn Museum, 1978.

Ruth E. Fine and Mary Lee Corlett, *Graphicstudio: Contemporary Art from the Collaborative Workshop at the University of South Florida* (exhibition catalogue), Washington: National Gallery of Art, 1991.

Donald Saff and Deli Sacilotto, *Printmaking: History and Process*, New York: Holt, Rinehard and Winston, 1978.

Hollander's Workshop, Inc. (New York)

From the mid-1960s to the early 1970s Hollander's Workshop printed many extraordinary editions with the great American abstract painters, among them Sam Francis, Phillip Guston, Willem de Kooning, Robert Motherwell, and Jack Tworkov. Irwin Hollander had been Technical Director at Tamarind (1963–64) before moving to New York to establish his own workshop. Hollander was able to get remarkable prints from many artists who claimed to be uninterested in printmaking, and it was Motherwell's collaboration with Hollander in 1965 that aroused the artist's passion for graphic media. Hollander specialized in lithography, but hired outside printers for other media, as the artist desired. For several years before the shop shut down in the 1970s, Hollander was assisted by the Dutch master printer Fred Genis.

"Life and Work: Thoughts of an Artist-Printer: A Conversation with Irwin Hollander," *The Tamarind Papers* 8, 1985.

Niels Borch Jensen (Copenhagen)

Niels Borch Jensen trained as both a lithographer and etcher, working with Lakeside Studios (Michigan, USA), Grupo Quince (Madrid), and I. E. Grafik (Copenhagen), before establishing his own shop in 1979. Primarily an etching studio, renowned for its skill with drypoint, spit bite aquatint, and photogravure, the shop has also produced occasional relief prints and monotypes. Georg Baselitz, Jim Dine, Günther Förg, Per Kirkeby, Jörg Immendorff, and Antonio Saura have all made prints with Jensen. In addition to contract printing, the shop runs its own publishing program, concentrating on the work of younger artists such as Stephen Ellis and Al Taylor, and Scandinavian artists such as Erik A. Frandsen, Max M. Book, and Eva Löfdahl.

Kelpra Studio (London)

Kelpra, the screenprint studio that virtually defined the English Pop print, was founded by Christopher and Rose Prater in 1957. Early work with Gordon House, Richard Hamilton, and Eduardo Paolozzi led to a commission to print the famous ICA portfolio in 1963. This resulted in ongoing collaborations with many of the artists included in the portfolio, including R. B. Kitaj, Joe Tilson, and Patrick Caulfield. Throughout the 1960s, Kelpra did most of the printing for Editions Alecto and for Marlborough Graphics. Prater was an acknowledged virtuoso with the knife and he employed a talented cameraman, Dennis Francis, who helped develop techniques of posterization, polarization, and tri-chromatic printing, which allowed artists to manipulate and restructure borrowed photographic imagery with great inventiveness. Kelpra's productions often failed to satisfy rigid definitions of the "original print" since frequently the artist never touched the screen, but the relevance of this working method to the anti-expressionist content of the art was obvious to most discerning followers of contemporary art.

Pat Gilmour, Silvie Turner, *Kelpra Studio, An Exhibition to Commemorate the Rose and Chris Prater Gift*, London: Tate Gallery, 1980.

Christopher Prater, "Experiments in Screenprinting," *Art International*, December 1967.

Sabine Knust/Maximilian Verlag (Munich)

Sabine Knust was, along with Fred Jahn, Six Friedrich and Heiner Friedrich, one of the principals of Heiner Friedrich Edition, which throughout the 1970s published prints and multiples by Minimalist and Conceptual artists, including Donald Judd, Blinky Palermo, Gerhard Richter, and Fred Sandback. After the dissolution of the Friedrich Gallery, Knust began publishing on her own with the *Erste Konzentration* portfolios of 1982, which helped introduce Northern European artists Georg

Baselitz, Jörg Immendorff, Per Kirkeby, Markus Lüpertz, and A. R. Penck to an American audience. Knust has continued to publish these artists as well as other European painters such as Arnulf Rainer. She has worked with many printers, but most often with Karl Imhoff (Munich).

Landfall Press (Chicago)

Before founding Landfall Press in 1970, Tamarind Master Printer Jack Lemon had established lithographic workshops at the Kansas City Institute of Arts and at the Nova Scotia College of Art and Design. The first professional printshop in the American Midwest, Landfall has made prints with Chicago-based artists Ed Paschke and Roger Brown as well as with artists from further afield who share Lemon's fascination with the act of drawing. These range from Realists such as Philip Pearlstein and Robert Cottingham, to artists of more conceptual inclinations, such as Christo, Pat Steir, and Vito Acconci. The shop has printed both etchings and relief prints, but its primary focus remains on lithography. Landfall's archive is at the Milwaukee Art Museum.

Dennis Adrian, E. A. Maser, *Master Prints from Landfall Press: a Major Gift from an Alumnus*, Chicago: David and Alfred Smart Gallery, University of Chicago, 1980.
Artist and Printer: Six American Print Studios (exhibition catalogue), Minneapolis: Walker Art Center, 1980. Introduction by Graham W. J. Beal.
Landfall Press, Chicago: Landfall Press, 1971. Introduction by Harold Joachim.
Michael Knigen and Murray Zimiles, *The Contemporary Lithographic Workshop Around the World*, New York: Van Nostrand Reinholt Co., 1974.

Maeght/Lelong (Paris)

Maeght Editeur, the publishing arm of the influential Galerie Maeght, was an authoritative force in postwar European print production, especially in the 1950s and 1960s. Aimé Maeght, who had briefly run a printshop before opening his gallery in 1945, linked his exhibition program to the publication of catalogues, posters, *livres d'artiste*, print editions, and the distinguished periodical *Derrière le Miroir*, which made "original" lithographs broadly and inexpensively available. Maeght published many modern masters: Georges Braque, Pierre Bonnard, Marc Chagall, Henri Matisse, Joan Miró; as well as artists of subsequent generations: Pierre Alechinsky, Eduardo Chillida, and Antoni Tàpies. In 1965

the ARTE workshop was established, with facilities for lithography, etching, and offset, and staffed by printers René Lemoigne and Robert Dutrou. ARTE was directed by Maeght's son Adrien, and subsequently became an independent business. In 1977 a separate workshop, Atelier Maeght, was opened. Since Aimé Maeght's death in 1982, the gallery has been directed by Daniel Lelong, Jacques Dupin and Jean Frémon, and in 1987 its name was changed to Galerie Lelong. Atelier Maeght became Atelier Lelong in 1982. Lelong has added many younger artists to the roster, including James Brown, Ron Janowich, and Nicola de Maria.

Derrière le Miroir, Paris: 1946–82.
L'Univers d'Aimé et Marguerite Maeght, Saint Paul de Vence: Fondation Maeght, 1982.

MAT (Multiplication d'Art Transformable, Paris/Cologne)

MAT was founded by the artist Daniel Spoerri to produce editioned art objects that were not prints, were not reproductive, and that contained some kinetic or variable element. MAT's first collection, in 1959, is commonly accepted as the first formal publication of "multiples," but it attracted little market interest, and the idea was abandoned. In 1964 MAT was revived by Galerie Der Spiegel (Cologne), in collaboration with Spoerri and the artist Karl Gerstner, and became a conspicuous presence in the flourishing alternative editions market of the late 1960s. Among the artists who produced MAT editions are: Arman, Enrico Baj, Pol Bury, Christo, Marcel Duchamp, Robert Filliou, Roy Lichtenstein, Diter Rot, and Jesus Raphael Soto.

$1 \rightarrow \infty$: *New Multiple Art*, London: Arts Council of Great Britain, 1970.
ARS Multiplicata: vervielfältigte Kunst seit 1945. Cologne: Wallraff-Richartz-Museums, 1968.
John L. Tancock, *Multiples: the First Decade*, Philadelphia: the Philadelphia Museum of Art, 1971.

Marlborough Graphics (London/Rome/New York)

In 1963, largely at the instigation of its younger artists such as R. B. Kitaj and Joe Tilson, the Marlborough Gallery in London began publishing prints. Many were screenprints produced with Kelpra Studio, though many of the gallery's older artists preferred lithography and etching. Frank Auerbach, Lynn Chadwick, Barbara Hepworth, Gordon House, Oskar Kokoschka, Colin Lanceley, Henry Moore, Ben Nicholson, Victor Pasmore, John Piper, Ceri Richards, and Graham Sutherland were all published by Marlborough in London. When

Marlborough expanded with galleries in Rome and New York, these organizations pursued independent publishing ventures with local printers and local artists. Lucio Fontana's aquatints with 2RC were published by the Rome gallery; Marlborough Graphics (New York) published editions by Allan d'Archangelo, Adolph Gottlieb, Red Grooms, Phillip Guston, Alex Katz, Robert Motherwell, Larry Rivers, and J. Raphael Soto.

Mixografia (Mexico City/Los Angeles)

Mixografia is both the name of a workshop founded by Luis and Rea Remba in Mexico City, and the name of their proprietary method, developed in response to Rufino Tamayo's desire for "something new." The mixografia process, invented in 1973, involves three-dimensional cast plates, which print onto paper pulp that holds their shape. The firm also holds some thirty patents on various innovations in printing technology, and boasts the largest lithographic stone in the world (six by nine feet). In 1986 the shop relocated in Los Angeles. Artists who have experimented with the mixografia technique include Tamayo, Henry Moore, Jonathan Borofsky, Alberto Burri, Helen Frankenthaler, and Larry Rivers.

Estilo y materia: Mixografías y Múltiples de Maestros Contemporáneos (exhibition catalogue), Mexico City: Museo de Arte Moderno, 1991. Essays by T. del Conde, H. Hopkins, J. Butterfield.

Imprimerie Mourlot Frères (Paris)

One of the great names of twentieth-century printmaking, Mourlot was founded in the 1850s as a commercial lithographic shop. It became famous for its work with Chagall, Matisse, Miró, and especially Picasso. Mourlot employed several master chromolithographers who were capable of "translating" an artist's gouaches or watercolors into technically perfect lithographs. Mourlot's finesse and regulated methods of production, however, were less appealing to subsequent generations of artists, who preferred either the blatantly commercial and inexpensive offset or the flexibility of American shops. While it has worked with younger artists, the shop's fame still rests on its work with the School of Paris. A Mourlot shop was established in New York in 1967 with presses shipped from Paris, but closed in 1972.

Jean-Pierre Hammer, preface by Charles Sorlier, *Maurice Mourlot*, Marburg: Hitzeroth, 1987.

Multiples, Inc. (New York)

The publisher of some of the most famous images of the 1960s, including Claes Oldenburg's *Tea Bag* (1965) and Robert Indiana's *Love*

(1967), Multiples was organized with the intent of publishing non-traditional editions, working mainly with Pop artists and commercial fabricators. Its early publications included jewelry, banners, and even robots. Later it became involved in traditional printing as well, working with Crown Point Press, Aeropress, Derrière l'Etoile and others. Marian Goodman, who had been one of three founders, eventually became the sole principal, and in portfolios such as *Reality and Paradox* produced during the 1970s, continued to stress the conceptual edge that had long underlain Multiples publications. Among other artists, Multiples has published the work of Richard Artschwager, John Baldessari, Jennifer Bartlett, Mimmo Paladino, Susan Rothenberg, Ed Ruscha, Andy Warhol, and Robert Wilson.

Pace Editions (New York)

A division of Pace Gallery established to publish works by gallery artists, Pace Editions began in the 1960s with decorative productions by artists like Trova. In the mid-1970s, with the arrival of Jim Dine and Chuck Close, the organization shifted to the production of more serious and innovative art. Under the direction of Richard Solomon, it has published prints by John Chamberlain, Jean Dubuffet, Lucas Samaras and Julian Schnabel. Pace Editions is now closely associated with Aldo Crommelynck and with Joe Wilfer's Spring Street Workshop which was responsible for Chuck Close's important manipulated paper editions. Crommelynck and Wilfer both print and publish their own editions.

Parasol Press (New York)

Parasol Press was founded in 1970 by Robert Feldman, a former lawyer who had earlier published Mourlot lithographs by popular European artists. A publisher, not a printshop, Parasol quickly became known for its rigorous, sometimes difficult editions by younger artists of the 1970s, such as Mel Bochner, Chuck Close, Richard Estes, Sol LeWitt, Robert Mangold, Dorothea Rockburne, Robert Ryman, and Wayne Thiebaud. Most of these were intaglio works printed by Crown Point Press, or screenprints made by Domberger. In the 1980s, Parasol began working with artists such as Ida Applebroog, Christian Eckart, Tom Levine, and Donald Sultan. Crown Point ceased contract printing in the late 1970s, but Parasol continued to publish many intaglio editions, printed by Maurice Payne or Harlan/Weaver Intaglio. Parasol has also published a portfolio of rubber stamp prints, and has recently been researching the possibilities of the color copier.

J. Cladders and C. Weyergraf, *Mel Bochner, Sol LeWitt, Robert Mangold, Brice Marden, Agnes Martin, Edda Renouf, Dorothea Rockburne: Graphiken aus der Edition der Parasol Press, New York* (exhibition catalogue), Mönchengladbach: Städtisches Museum, 1975.

Lizbeth Marano, *Parasol and Simca: Two Presses/Two Processes*, Lewisburg PA: Bucknell University Press and Wilkes-Barre PA: Wilkes College Press, 1984.

Petersburg Press (London/New York)

After leaving Editions Alecto in 1967, Paul Cornwall-Jones established Petersburg Press, which became one of the most important publishers of younger American and European artists in the 1970s. It published several of Jim Dine's most eloquent portfolios; David Hockney's *Grimm's Fairy Tales* (1969) and *The Blue Guitar* (1972); James Rosenquist's monumental *F-111* (1974); Jasper Johns's *Foirades/Fizzles* (1976); and Frank Stella's *Polar Co-ordinates* (1980). Petersburg worked closely with Kelpra Studio, and with etchers Maurice Payne in London and Aldo Crommelynck in Paris, and at one point set up a printshop for Frank Stella in the painter's studio. In the 1980s the firm established a full printshop facility in New York. Always beset by financial difficulties, Petersburg has opened and closed its doors more than once, but with the collapse of the print market in the late 1980s, it ceased publishing. Its last important publication was Francesco Clemente's book illustrating Alberto Savinio's *The Departure of the Argonaut* (1986).

Ediciones Polìgrafa (Barcelona)

A commercial printshop established in 1914, Poligrafa began producing art books and prints in the early 1960s, under the directorship of Manuel de Muga. In 1976 his son, Joan de Muga opened Galeria Joan Prats, which has served as the primary distributor of Poligrafa prints. Poligrafa has done a great deal of printing with Antoni Tàpies, whose passion for unusual textures has inspired an abundance of technical experimentation and innovation. Other artists who have worked at Poligrafa include Pierre Alechinsky, Joan Brossa, Frederic Amat, George Condo, Eduardo Chillida, Helen Frankenthaler, Hans Hartung, Jaume Plensa, and Antonio Saura.

Ediciones Polìgrafa, London: Redfern Gallery, 1979.

Pratt Graphics (New York)

The Pratt Graphics Center was begun in 1956, with the aim of providing facilities (then virtually non-existent) for artists who wished to make prints. Co-founded by Margaret Lowengrund, an artist and gallery owner, and

Fritz Eichenberg, the Graphics Chairman at Pratt Institute, the center was funded by the Rockefeller Foundation, and was open to students and to professional artists, who could work on their own or hire a printer to assist them. Initially called Pratt Contemporaries, its name was changed quickly to Pratt Graphic Workshop, and then in the 1970s, Pratt Graphics Center. For many years, especially during the early 1960s, the workshop provided a critical service: Jim Dine and Barnett Newman made their first professional prints at Pratt, and the plates for David Hockney's *The Rake's Progress* (1961–63) and Claes Oldenburg's *Orpheum* (1962) were done there. But with the tremendous growth of printshops and publishing opportunities in the 1960s and 1970s the need for such an institution waned, and Pratt eventually left its Manhattan space and rejoined Pratt Institute in Brooklyn.

Artist's Proof, New York: the Pratt Graphics Center, 1961–71.

Print Review Magazine, New York: the Pratt Graphics Center 1973–1985

Clinton Adams, "Margaret Lowengrund and The Contemporaries," *Tamarind Papers*, Vol. 7, No. 1, Spring 1984.

Printmaking Workshop (New York)

The Printmaking Workshop was first established by the artist Robert Blackburn in 1948, as one of only a handful of printshops for artists at the time. Blackburn had first studied lithography at the Harlem Art Center in the 1930s, and later mastered the art in France. Blackburn was the first printer at ULAE, working there from 1957 to 1962, and collaborating on such influential works as Larry Rivers's and Frank O'Hara's *Stones* (1957–60) and the critical early prints of Jasper Johns and Robert Rauschenberg. In 1963 Blackburn returned to the Printmaking Workshop, which has endured as the most important public access workshop in America. The Workshop sponsors residencies for specialist printmakers and other artists wishing to make prints, as well as maintaining community outreach programs and Third World Fellowships. Will Barnett, Bernard Childs, and Michelle Stuart are among the notable artists who have worked there. Blackburn received a MacArthur Fellowship in acknowledgment of his contributions to American arts.

Harriet Green, Nina Parris, *Robert Blackburn: a Life's Work*, New York: The Alternative Museum, 1988.

Elizabeth Jones, "Robert Blackburn: An Investment in an Idea," *Tamarind Papers* 6, Winter 1982–83.

Galerie Denise René (Paris)

One of the foremost publishers of optical and kinetic prints and multiples, Galerie Denise René was founded on Vasarély's vision of a new world in which art objects were mass-produced and economically accessible, and in which the artist functioned as a designer of prototypes for replication. In 1953 the gallery began publishing screenprints by Sonia Delaunay, Auguste Herbin, Richard Mortensen, Vasarély and other abstract painters, most of which were printed by Ateliers Arcay in Paris. In 1963 Denise René began publishing multiples by kinetic artists such as Carlos Cruz-Diez, Julio Le Park, François Morrellet, and Jesus Raphael Soto.

Schellmann and Klüser/Editions Schellmann (Munich/New York/Cologne)

An important publisher of recent European and American art, Jörg Schellmann was inspired by Joseph Beuys and his embrace of the principle of multiplicity. Beginning in 1971, Schellmann was the primary publisher of Beuys's prints and multiples, and the author of three catalogues raisonnés of Beuys's editioned work. The firm has never maintained any kind of atelier, and its publications take a wide range of forms, from etchings and lithographs with painters such as Sandro Chia, Keith Haring, Mimmo Paladino, and David Salle, to lightboxes by Daniel Buren, a plastic-wrapped telephone by Christo, and a stone sculpture by Ulrich Rückheim. Schellmann also published several late portfolios by Andy Warhol. Founded as Edition Schellmann in 1969 in cooperation with Katia von den Velden and Bernd Klüser, it was known as Edition Schellmann and Klüser from 1975–89. In 1993 the firm moved its European headquarters to Cologne, and adopted the name Editions Schellmann.

Edition Schellmann 1969–1989 (catalogue raisonné), Munich and New York: Edition Schellmann, 1989.

Simca Print Artists (New York/Tokyo)

The remarkable specialty of Simca's printers Hiroshi Kawanishi, Takeshi Shimada, and Kenjiro Nomaka, is that of the painterly screenprint. Their reputation for virtuosity was established by the collaboration with Jasper Johns that began in 1972. It had been assumed in America and Europe that the strength of screenprint lay in its clean, flat boldness or in its adaptability to photographic manipulation, but works such as Johns's *Flags 1* (1973) or *Usuyuki* (1979–81) used subtle contrasts of transparency and opacity to produce unprecedented luminescence and depth. By painting directly on the screen rather than relying on the knife or the camera, and by printing the screens in multiple translucent layers, artists working with Simca have created a singularly rich form of screenprint. In addition to Johns, Jennifer Bartlett, Mel Bochner, Nancy Graves, Alex Katz, Brice Marden, Elizabeth Murray, Joel Shapiro, and Terry Winters have all worked with Simca.

Lizbeth Marano, *Parasol and Simca: Two Presses/Two Processes*, Lewisburg, Pennsylvania: Bucknell University Press and Wilkes-Barre, Pennsylvania: Wilkes College Press, 1984.

Katrina Martin (dir. and prod.), *Hanafuda/Jasper Johns* (film), 1980.

Solo Press/Solo Impression (New York)

Judith Solodkin, the first female Tamarind Master Printer, established Solo Press in New York in 1975, and by 1981 was employing six printers, and running projects with two or three artists simultaneously. Solo prints have often been characterized by ebullience rather than sobriety: Solodkin printed sequined and glittered prints with Robert Kushner, Joyce Kozloff's intricately decorative works, as well as Howard Hodgkin's intense hand-colored lithographs. With facilities for lithography, relief printing, and letterpress, Solo does both contract printing and publishing. Artists who have worked there include Ida Applebroog, Conrad Atkinson, Lynda Benglis, Komar & Melamid, Christian Marclay, and William Wegman.

Ruth E. Fine, "Judith Solodkin and Solo Press," *Tamarind Papers*, Vol. 13, No. 1, 1990.

Tamarind Lithography Workshop, Inc. (Los Angeles), Tamarind Institute (Albuquerque)

Tamarind Lithography Workshop, founded by June Wayne in 1960, was one of the cornerstones of the American print revival that began in the 1960s. A non-profit institution supported by the Ford Foundation, Tamarind established a training program for master printers; developed new lithographic materials and techniques; established a system of print documentation that has become the de facto standard among American publishers and galleries and a legal standard in many states; and exposed hundreds of artists to collaborative working methods. Among the more than two thousand lithographs printed there are those of Richard Diebenkorn, Sam Francis, Philip Guston, David Hockney, Allen Jones, and Louise Nevelson. Most of the major lithographic shops in America were founded by, or employ, Tamarind-trained printers. *The Tamarind Book of Lithography*, written by Clinton Adams and Garo Antreasian, is the standard text on technique. In 1970 Tamarind Lithography Workshop closed in Los Angeles, and the Tamarind Institute was formed as a division of the College of Fine Arts of the University of New Mexico, under the direction of Adams and Antreasian. In order to approach economic self-sufficiency, it inaugurated a contract printing program and a publishing program. It continues to train printers and print curators, and to sponsor artists' residencies.

Virginia Allen and William S. Lieberman, *Tamarind: Homage to Lithography*, New York: Museum of Modern Art, 1969.

Garo Z. Antreasian and Clinton Adams, *The Tamarind Book of Lithography: Art and Techniques*, New York: Harry N. Abrams, 1971.

E. Maurice Bloch, *Tamarind: A Renaissance of Lithography*, Washington D.C.: International Exhibitions Foundation, 1971.

Rebecca Schnelker and Judith Booth, *Tamarind Lithographs: a Complete Catalogue of Lithographs Printed at Tamarind Institute 1970–1979*, Albuquerque: Tamarind Institute, University of New Mexico, 1980.

Tamarind Lithography Workshop, Inc.: Catalogue Raisonné 1960–1970, Albuquerque: University of New Mexico Art Museum, 1989. Introduction by Marjorie Devon and Peter Walch.

Tamarind Technical Papers and *The Tamarind Papers*. Published twice yearly or yearly since 1974 by Tamarind Institute.

June Wayne, "The Tamarind Lithography Workshop," *Artist's Proof* 2, Spring 1962.

Garner Tullis Workshop (Santa Barbara)

Garner Tullis founded his first press, Experimental Impressions, in Philadelphia in 1962. In 1966 Tullis moved to California, where he began experimenting with radical new forms of handmade paper that were both sheets and objects. His Institute of Experimental Printmaking opened in Santa Cruz in 1972 and moved to San Francisco four years later. Like Ken Tyler, Tullis is fond of an engineering challenge, and has a passion for the expansive scale. Using massive hydraulic presses rather than conventional roll presses, Tullis has been able to achieve a tough, three-dimensional presence for works made on (or even made of) paper. His Institute pursued the possibilities of paper pulp and of monotype, which became the specialty of Garner Tullis Workshop, established in Santa Barbara in 1984. The workshop has branches in New York and in Italy, and has published monotypes by Charles Arnoldi, Jean-Charles Blais, Sam Francis, Therese Oulton, David Reed, Sean Scully, Emilio Vedova, John Walker, and others.

David Carrier, *History of Garner Tullis Workshop*, New York: Hudson Hills Press, 1995.

Phyllis Plous, *Collaborations in Monotype*, Santa Barbara: University Art Museum, 1988. Essay by Kenneth Baker.

2RC (Rome)

A virtuoso etcher, Valter Rossi of 2RC is one of the few European printers to have the facilities as well as the passion for the kind of expanded scale and inventiveness that has typified many American shops. From the time that he printed Lucio Fontana's radical, ruptured aquatints in 1964 Rossi has demonstrated a willingness to extend the boundaries of technique. Over the last thirty years he has printed the work of Pierre Alechinsky, Alberto Burri, Helen Frankenthaler, Henry Moore, Victor Pasmore, and Pierre Soulages, as well as younger artists such as Francesco Clemente, Enzo Cucchi, Carroll Dunham, and A. R. Penck.

Tyler Graphics Ltd.
(Bedford Village, New York)

In 1973 Ken Tyler left Gemini GEL and established Tyler Graphics in Westchester County outside New York. The new shop continued to emphasize the technological wizardry and ambitious scale that Tyler had exhibited at Gemini, but while Tyler's Gemini prints had a reputation for being "cool," masterful but somewhat mechanical, those of Tyler Graphics have been characterized by a tactile and visual warmth, intriguing textures, rich colors, and the discernible presence of the artist's hand. In the new workshop Tyler began experimenting with handmade paper pulp, eventually setting up his own paper mill, allowing Ellsworth Kelly, Kenneth Noland, and Frank Stella to work not simply on paper but in paper, and making possible the major achievement of Hockney's "Paper Pools." In the 1980s, fueled by a resurgent print market, Tyler's productions reached an unprecedented scale and complexity. Frank Stella's *Circuits* (1982–83) brought to printmaking the spacial intricacies of his enormous reliefs through combinations of relief printing, intaglio printing, and handmade paper of dyed pulps which would have been possible in no other shop in the world. The Tyler Graphics archive is at the Walker Art Center in Minneapolis.

Artist and Printer: Six American Print Studios (exhibition catalogue), Minneapolis: Walker Art Center, 1980. Introduction by Graham W. J. Beal.

Elizabeth Armstrong, et al, *Tyler Graphics: The Extended Image*, Minneapolis: Walker Art Center and New York: Abbeville Press, 1987.

Pat Gilmour, *Ken Tyler, Master Printer, and the American Print Renaissance*, New York: Hudson Hills Press and Canberra: Australian National Gallery, 1986.

Judith Goldman, *Art off the Picture Press: Tyler Graphics Ltd.*, Hempstead, NY: Emily Low Gallery, Hofstra University, 1977.

Amy Reigle Newland, *Paperworks from Tyler Graphics* (exhibition catalogue), Minneapolis: Walker Art Center, 1985.

Kenneth E. Tyler, *Tyler Graphics: Catalogue Raisonné, 1974–1985*, Minneapolis: Walker Art Center and New York: Abbeville Press, 1987. Foreword by Elizabeth Armstrong. Essay by Pat Gilmour.

Universal Limited Art Editions
(West Islip, New York)

One of America's most revered printshops, Universal Limited Art Editions (ULAE) was started in 1957 by Tatyana Grosman, a European emigrée with a love of printed matter, especially books. Through dogged persistence, she convinced many of the best young artists of the early 1960s to make lithographs. Major early works by Jasper Johns, Robert Rauschenberg, Larry Rivers, and Jim Dine helped to establish the reputation of the shop, and to inspire a new respect and interest in the print as an art form. Initially devoted to traditional stone lithography, ULAE gradually added new capabilities: etching, offset lithography, then facilities for photographic manipulations and relief printing. When Grosman died in 1982, the directorship of ULAE was assumed by printer Bill Goldston, who has expanded the publishing program to include younger artists such as Elizabeth Murray, Susan Rothenberg, Kiki Smith and Terry Winters. Other artists who have worked with ULAE include Lee Bontecou, Helen Frankenthaler, Fritz Glarner, Grace Hartigan, Robert Motherwell, Barnett Newman, and Jim Rosenquist. Its archives are at the Art Institute of Chicago.

E. Maurice Bloch, *Words and Images: Universal Limited Art Editions* (exhibition catalogue), Los Angeles: Frederick S. Wright Gallery, 1978.

Peter Gale and Tony Towle, *Contemporary American Prints from Universal Limited Art Editions/The Rapp Collection*, Toronto: Art Gallery of Ontario, 1979.

Esther Sparks, *Universal Limited Art Editions: A History and Catalogue: The First Twenty-Five Years*, Chicago: the Art Institute of Chicago, and New York: Harry N. Abrams, Inc., 1989.

Calvin Tompkins, "The Moods of a Stone," *New Yorker*, June 7, 1976.

————, "The Skin of the Stone," *The Scene: Reports on Post-Modern Art*, New York: The Viking Press, 1976.

Waddington Graphics (London)

Waddington Graphics began publishing prints in 1967, and initially confined itself to the work of painters represented by Waddington Gallery. Since 1973 it has been directed by Alan Cristea, previously at Marlborough Graphics, and has assembled a publishing program that includes many of Britain's most prominent artists: Peter Blake, Patrick Caulfield, Barry Flanagan, Richard Hamilton, Howard Hodgkin, John Hoyland, Allen Jones, and Joe Tilson, as well as non-Britons Jan Dibbets, Jim Dine, Mimmo Paladino, and Frank Stella. Waddington has no printing facilities, relying instead on the expertise of Aldo Crommelynck, Grafica Uno, and Kelpra Studio, among others. In 1995 Waddington Graphics became the Alan Cristea Gallery.

Waddington Graphics 1986 (exhibition catalogue), London: Waddington Graphics, 1986. Introduction by Alan Cristea.

GENERAL

Clifford S. Ackley, Thomas Krens, and Deborah Menaker, *The Modern Art of the Print: Selections from the Collection of Lois and Michael Torf*, Boston: The Museum of Fine Arts, 1984.

————, *70s into 80s: Printmaking Now*, Boston: Museum of Fine Arts, 1986.

————, Anne Havinga, Judy Weinland, *The Unique Print: 70s into 90s*, Boston: Museum of Fine Arts, 1990.

Jean Adhémar and Françoise Woimant, *L'estampe contemporaine à la Bibliothèque Nationale* (exhibition catalogue), Paris: Bibliothèque Nationale, 1973.

Amerikanische und Englische Graphik der Gegenwart, Hanover: Kestner Gesellschaft, 1974.

Garo Z. Antreasian, "Some thoughts about Printmaking and Print Collaborations," *Art Journal* 39, Spring 1980.

Elizabeth Armstrong, *Images and Impressions: Painters Who Print*, Minneapolis: The Walker Art Center, 1984.

———— and Sheila McGuire, *First Impressions: Early Prints by Forty-Six Contemporary Artists*, Minneapolis: The Walker Art Center in association with New York: Hudson Hills Press, 1989.

The Artist and the Printer: Lithographs 1966–1981: A Collection of Printer's Proofs (exhibition catalogue of proofs printed by Fred Genis), Melbourne: National Gallery of Victoria, 1982.

Paolo Bellini, *Histoire de gravure moderne*, Paris: Chez Jean de Bonnot, 1979.

Big Prints, essay by Frances Carey, London: Arts Council of Great Britain, 1982.

Black and White Since 1960: Prints from the Collection of Reba and Dave Williams, Raleigh: City Gallery of Contemporary Art, 1990.

Suzanne Boorsch, *Contemporary American Prints: Gifts from the Singer Collection* (exhibition catalogue), Los Angeles: Frederick S. Wight Art Gallery, University of California at Los Angeles, 1978.

Kathan Brown, *Ink, Paper, Metal, Wood: How to Recognize Contemporary Artists' Prints*, San Francisco: Point Publications, 1992.

Joshua Binion Cahn, *What is an Original Print?*, New York: Print Council of America, 1964.

Riva Castleman, *Contemporary Prints*, New York: Viking Press, 1973.

————, *Modern Art in Prints*, New York: The Museum of Modern Art, 1973.

————, *Prints of the Twentieth Century: A History*, New York: the Museum of Modern Art, 1976

and London: Thames and Hudson, 1988.

————, *Printed Art: a View of Two Decades*, New York: the Museum of Modern Art, 1980.

————, *Prints from Blocks: Gauguin to Now* (exhibition catalogue), New York: Museum of Modern Art, 1983.

————, *Seven Master Printmakers: Innovation in the Eighties*, (exhibition catalogue), New York: Museum of Modern Art, 1991. [Dine, Hockney, Johns, Lichtenstein, Rauschenberg, Rosenquist, Stella.]

Catalogue of the Print Collection, London: Tate Gallery, 1980.

R. H. Cohen, "Minimal Prints," *The Print Collector's Newsletter*, Vol. XXI, No. 2, May–June 1990.

Hanlyn Davies and Hiroshi Murata, *Art and Technology: Offset Prints* (exhibition catalogue), Bethlehem, Pennsylvania: Ralph Wilson Gallery, Lehigh University, 1983.

De Bonnard à Baselitz: Dix ans d'enrichissements du Cabinet des Estampes 1978–1988, Paris: Bibliothèque Nationale, 1992.

Theodore B. Donson, *Prints and the Print Market*, New York: Thomas Y. Crowell, 1977.

Alexander Dückers, *Druckgraphik der Gegenwart – 1960/1975 – im Berliner Kupferstichkabinett* (exhibition catalogue), Berlin: Kupferstichkabinett, SMPK, 1975.

————, *Druckgraphik: Wandlungen eines Mediums seit 1945* (exhibition catalogue) Berlin: Kupferstichkabinett, SMPK, 1981.

Fritz Eichenberg, *The Art of the Print*, New York: Abrams, 1976.

Richard S. Field and Louise Sperling, *Offset Lithography*, Middletown, Connecticut: Davison Art Center, Wesleyan University, 1973.

————, *Prints*, Geneva: Skira, 1981.

————, "Sentences on Printed Art," *The Print Collector's Newsletter*, Vol. XXV, No. 5, November–December 1994.

———— and Daniel Rosenfield, *Prints by Contemporary Sculptors*, New Haven: Yale University Art Gallery, 1982.

Ruth E. Fine, ed., *The 1980s: Prints from the Collection of Joshua P. Smith*, catalogue by Charles M. Ritchie with assistance from Thomas Coolsen, Washington D.C.: National Gallery of Art, 1990.

Pat Gilmour, *Modern Prints*, London: Studio Vista/Dutton, 1970.

————, *The Mechanized Image: An Historical Perspective on Twentieth Century Prints* (exhibition catalogue), London: Arts Council of Great Britain, 1978.

————, *Understanding Prints: A Contemporary Guide*, London: Waddington Graphics, 1979.

———— and Anne Willsford, *Paperwork* (exhibition catalogue), Canberra: Australian National Gallery, 1982.

————, ed., *Lasting Impressions: Lithography as Art*, London: Alexandria Press, 1988.

————, "'Originality' Circa 1960: A Time for Thinking Caps," *The Tamarind Papers* 13, 1990.

Mark Glazebrook, "Why Do Artists Make Prints? Answers of Printmakers to Questions Put by Mark Glazebrook," *Studio International* 173, June 1967.

Judith Goldman, "The Print Establishment," *Art in America* 61 July–August 1973 and "The Print Establishment II," *Art in America* 61, September–October 1973.

————, "Printmaking: the Medium Isn't the Message Any More," *ARTnews* 79, March 1980.

————, "The Proof Is In The Process: Painters as Printmakers," *ARTnews* 80, September 1981.

————, *The Pop Image: Prints and Multiples*, with essays by Ronny Cohen, Mignon Nixon, Hubetus Raben, and Christopher Sweet. New York: Marlborough Graphics, 1995.

Lanier Graham, *The Spontaneous Gesture: Prints and Book of the Abstract Expressionist Era*, Canberra: the Australian National Gallery, 1987, and Seattle: University of Washington Press, 1989.

————, "The Rise of the Livre d'Artiste in America: Reflections of *21 Etchings and Poems* and the Early 1960s," *The Tamarind Papers* 13, 1990.

Anthony Griffiths, *Prints and Printmaking: an Introduction to the History and Techniques*, London: British Museum, 1980.

Carol Hogben and Rowan Watson, *From Manet to Hockney: Modern Artists' Illustrated Books*, London: Victoria & Albert Museum, 1985.

"International List of Printmaking Workshops," *Print Review* 1, March 1973.

Colta Ives, et al, *The Painterly Print: Monotypes from the Seventeenth to the Twentieth Century* (exhibition catalogue), New York: the Metropolitan Museum of Art, 1980.

William M. Ivins, *How Prints Look*, New York: Metropolitan Museum of Art, 1943. Reprinted, Boston: Beacon Press, 1968.

————, *Prints and Visual Communication*, New York: 1953. Reprinted, Cambridge and London: The MIT Press, 1969.

Ellen S. Jacobowitz and Ann Percy, *New Art on Paper*, (exhibition catalogue), Philadelphia: Philadelphia Museum of Art, 1988.

Elaine L. Johnson, *Contemporary Painters and Sculptors as Printmakers*, New York: The Museum of Modern Art, 1966.

Diane Kelder, "Tradition and Craftsmanship in Modern Prints," *ARTnews* 70, January 1972.

————, "The Graphics Revival," *Art in America* 61, July–August 1973.

Michael Knigin and Murray Zimiles, *The Contemporary Lithographic Workshop Around the World*, New York: Reinhold, 1970.

Max Kozloff, "Three-Dimensional Prints and the Retreat from Originality," *Artforum* 4, December 1965.

Philip Larson, "Aquatints Again," *The Print Collector's Newsletter*, Vol. VIII, No. 3, July–August 1977.

L'Estampe aujourd'hui 1973–1978 (exhibition catalogue), Paris: Bibliothèque Nationale, 1978.

Norbert Lynton, *Order and Experience: Prints by Agnes Martin, Sol LeWitt, Robert Ryman, Robert Mangold, Brice Marden, Edda Renouf*, Arts Council of Great Britain, 1975.

————, Kathan Brown, Nancy Tousley, *Minimal Druckgraphik* (exhibition catalogue), Hanover: Kestner Gesellschaft, 1976.

Felix H. Man, introduction, *Homage to Senefelder*, London: Victoria and Albert Museum, 1971.

———— (ed.), *Europäisches Graphik, Vol. 6 and Vol. 7*, Munich: Galerie Wolfgang Ketterer, 1969 and 1971.

Michael Melot, *Prints*, Geneva: Editions d'Art Albert Skira, S.A., 1981.

Minimalist Prints (exhibition catalogue), New York: Susan Sheehan Gallery, 1990.

Charles Newton, *Photography in Printmaking* (exhibition catalogue), London: Victoria and Albert Museum, 1979.

Peter Pakesch (ed.), *Druckgraphik 1970–85* (exhibition catalogue), Graz: Künstlerhaus Graz, Grazer Kunstverein, 1986.

John T. Paoletti (ed.), *No Title: the Collection of Sol Lewitt* (exhibition catalogue), Middletown, Connecticut: Davison Art Center, Wesleyan University, 1981.

Deborah C. Phillips, "Looking for Relief? Woodcuts are Back," *ARTnews* 81, April 1982.

Elizabeth Phillips and Tony Zwicker, *The American Livre de Peintre*, introduction by Robert Rainwater, New York: The Grolier Club, 1993.

The Pop Art Print (exhibition catalogue), Fort Worth: The Fort Worth Art Museum, 1984.

Presswork: The Art of Women Printmakers, essays by Eleanor Hartney and Trudy Hansen, Washington: National Museum of Women in the Arts, 1991.

Projects and Editions 1984–87, New York: Delano Greenidge Editions, 1987.

Radierungen im 20. Jahrhundert (exhibition catalogue), Stuttgart: Staatsgalerie Stuttgart, 1987. With essays by Ulrike Gauss, Renate Hauff, Hans-Martin Kaulbach and Michael Scholz-Hänsel.

Retaining the Original: Multiple Originals, Copies, and Reproductions, Center for Advanced Study in the Visual Arts Symposium Papers VII, Studies in the History of Art: Vol. 20, Washington: National Gallery of Art, 1989. With essays by Rosalind E. Krauss, Brunhilde S. Ridgway, Miranda Marvin, Gary Vikan, Jonathan J. G. Alexander, Alan Gowans, Richard E. Spear, Caroline Karpinski, Beverly Louise Brown, Egon Verheyen, Jeffrey M. Muller, and Richard Schiff.

Dieter Ronte, "Amerikanische Druckgrafik nach 1945" in Dieter Honisch and Jens Christian Jensen (ed.), *Amerikanische Kunst von 1945 bis Heute*, Cologne: DuMont, 1976.

S. L. Sheridan, "Generative Systems Versus Copy Art: A Clarification of Terms and Ideas," *Leonardo* 16, Spring 1983.

Jiri Siblik, *Twentieth-Century Prints*, London and New York: Hamlyn, no date.

Wolfe Stubbe and Dietrich Mahlow, *Internationale Druckgraphik der letzten 25 Jahre* (exhibition catalogue), Nuremburg, 1971.

Craig A. Subler and Pinky Kase, *Cuts: An Exhibition of Woodcut and Relief Prints*, Kansas City: The University of Missouri and Kansas City Gallery of Art, 1982.

Susan Tallman, "The Woodcut in the Age of Mechanical Reproduction," *Arts Magazine*, January 1989.

Gunther Thiem, *Amerikanische und Englische Graphik der Gegenwart*, Stuttgart: Staatsgalerie, Graphische Sammlung, 1972.

Nancy Tousley, *Prints: Bochner, LeWitt, Mangold, Marden, Martin, Renouf, Rockburne, Ryman*, (exhibition catalogue with statements by the artists), Toronto: Art Gallery of Ontario, 1975.

Amei Wallach, "The Trouble with Prints: Abuses in Today's Market," *ARTnews* 80, May 1981.

Ruth Weisberg, "The Syntax of the Print: In Search of an Aesthetic Content," *The Tamarind Papers* 9, Fall 1986.

————, "The Absent Discourse: Critical Theories and Printmaking," *The Tamarind Papers* 13, 1990.

Paul Wember, *Blattkünste: International Druckgraphik seit 1945*, Krefeld: Scherpe Verlag, 1973.

Reba and Dave Williams, *The Later History of the Screenprint*, Print Quarterly 4, December 1987.

AMERICA

Dennis Adrian and Richard A. Born, *The Chicago Imagist Print: Ten Artists' Works, 1958–1987*, Chicago: The David and Alfred Smart Gallery, University of Chicago, 1987.

American Prints 1960–1985 in the Collection of The Museum of Modern Art, New York: the Museum of Modern Art, 1986.

American Prints of the Sixties, New York: Susan Sheehan Gallery, 1989.

Gene Baro, *30 Years of American Printmaking Including the 20th National Print Exhibition* (exhibition catalogue), Brooklyn: The Brooklyn Museum, 1976.

————, Michael Botwinick, *Twenty-first National Print Exhibition*, Brooklyn: The Brooklyn Museum, 1978.

————, *Twenty-second National Print Exhibition* (exhibition catalogue), Brooklyn: The Brooklyn Museum, 1981.

Mary Welsh Baskett, *American Graphic Workshops: 1968*, Cincinnati: Cincinnati Art Museum, 1968.

Graham W. J. Beal, *Artist and Printer: Six American Print Studios*, Minneapolis: Walker Art Center, 1980.

Karen F. Beall, et al., *American Prints in the Library of Congress*, Baltimore: Johns Hopkins Press, 1970.

Charles T. Butler and Marilyn Laufer, *Recent Graphics from American Print Shops* (exhibition catalogue), Mount Vernon, Illinois: Mitchell Museum, 1986.

Frances Carey and Antony Griffiths, *American Prints 1879–1979* (exhibition catalogue), London: the British Museum, 1980.

Riva Castleman, *American Impressions: Prints Since Pollock*, New York: Alfred A. Knopf, 1985.

Jack Cowart and James Elliott, *Prints from the Untitled Press*, Hartford, Connecticut: the Wadsworth Athaneum, 1973.

Ebria Feinblatt and Bruce Davis, *Los Angeles Prints: 1883–1980* (exhibition catalogue), Los Angeles: Los Angeles Museum of Art, 1981.

Richard S. Field, *Recent American Etching*, Middletown, Connecticut: Davison Art Center, Wesleyan University, 1975.

———— and Ruth E. Fine, *A Graphic Muse, Prints by Contemporary American Women* (exhibition catalogue), South Hadley, Mass.: Mount Holyoke College Art Museum, 1987.

Janet Flint, *Eight from California*, Washington D.C.: National Collection of Fine Arts, Smithsonian Institution, 1974.

Judith Goldman, *American Prints: Process and Proofs*, New York: Harper & Row, 1979.

————, *Print Publishing in America*, Washington D.C.: United States Communication Agency, 1980.

————, *Print Acquisitions 1974–1984*, New York: Whitney Museum of American Art, 1984.

The Innovators: Renaissance in American Printmaking, Washington D.C.: Jane Haslem Gallery, 1973.

Una E. Johnson, *American Prints and Printmakers*, New York: Doubleday, 1980.

Donald H. Karshan, "American Printmaking, 1670–1968," *Art in America* 56, July–August 1968.

John Loring, "American Prints from Fuses to Fizzles," *Art in America* 65, January–February, 1977.

Signe Mayfield, *Directions in Bay Area Printmaking: Three Decades*, Palo Alto: Palo Alto Cultural Center, 1992.

Elke Solomon, *Oversize Prints*, New York: Whitney Museum of American Art, 1971.

Andrew Stasik, Judith Goldman, Gabor Peterdi, Pat Gilmour, S. W. Hayter, *Prints USA 1982*, New York: Pratt Manhattan Center Gallery, 1982.

Andrew Stevens and James Watrous, *American Color Woodcuts: Bounty from the Block, 1890s–1990s*, Madison: University of Wisconsin, Elvehjem Museum of Art, 1994.

Vermillion Publications 1978–1983, Minneapolis: Vermillion Editions, 1983..

Barry Walker, *The American Artist As Printmaker* (exhibition catalogue), Brooklyn: the Brooklyn Museum, 1983.

————, *Public and Private: American Prints Today* (exhibition catalogue), Brooklyn: the Brooklyn Museum, 1986.

————, *Projects and Portfolios: The 25th National Print Exhibition* (exhibition catalogue), New York: Brooklyn Museum, 1989.

James Watrous, *A Century of American Printmaking, 1880–1980*, Madison: University of Wisconsin Press, 1984.

Deborah Wye, *Committed to Print: Social and Political Themes in Recent American Printed Art*, New York: the Museum of Modern Art, 1988.

EUROPE

Aspetti della grafica Europea, Venice: La Biennale di Venezia, 1971.

René Block, *Grafik der Kapitalistischen Realismus* (catalogue raisonné of K. P. Brehmer, K. H. Hödicke, Konrad Lueg, Sigmar Polke, Gerhard Richter, and Wolff Vostell), Berlin: Galerie René Block, 1971.

————, *Werkverzeichnisse der Druckgrafik, September 1971 bis Mai 1976, Vol. II* (catalogue raisonné of K. P. Brehmer, K. H. Hödicke, Sigmar Polke, Gerhard Richter, and Wolff Vostell), Berlin: Edition René Block, 1976.

J. Carrete, J. Vega, V. Bozal and F. Fontbona, *El Grabado en España: Siglos XIX y XX*, Madrid: Espasa Calpe, 1988.

Contemporary Spanish Prints, Madrid: Grupo Quince, 1979.

Antonio Gallego, *Historia del grabado en España*, Madrid: Ediciones Càtedra, S.A., 1979.

A. Kirker, *Prints of the 70s by Six British Artists*, Wellington (New Zealand): National Art Gallery, 1980. [Peter Blake, Patrick Caulfield, Richard Hamilton, Allen Jones, Tom Phillips, Joe Tilson]

Alfred Krens, "Aspects of German Prints After 1945," *The Print Collector's Newsletter*, Vol. XIV, No. 1, March–April 1983.

L'Italie & l'Allemagne: Nouvelles Sensibilités, Nouveaux Marchés (exhibition catalogue), Geneva: Cabinet des Estampes, Musée d'Art et d'Histoire, 1983. With essays by Maurice Besset, Peter Blum, Johannes Gachnung, Nancy Gillespie, Sabine Knust, Rainer Michael Mason, Claude Ritschard, Fulvio Salvadori.

Felix H. Man (ed.), *Europäische Graphik* Vol. 6, Munich: Galerie Wolfgang Ketterer, 1969.

Spanish Art Spanish Prints in the Eighties, Essays by Estrella de Diego, Juan Carrete Parrondo, Madrid: Ministerio de Asuntos Exteriores de España, 1991.

Recent European Prints, Cambridge: Massachusetts Institute of Technology, 1983.

Wolfgang Rothe, Herbert Bessel, and Heinz Neidel, *Druckgrafik des deutschen Informel 1951–1963*, Nuremberg: Albrecht Dürer Gesellschaft, 1975.

Gunther Thiem, *Der deutsche Holzschnitt im 20. Jahrhundert* (exhibition catalogue), Stuttgart: Instituts für Auslandsbeziehungen, 1984.

MULTIPLES

1→∞: New Multiple Art, London: Arts Council of Great Britain, 1970.

Ars Multiplicata: vervielfältigte Kunst seit 1945, Cologne: Wallraf-Richartz-Museums, 1968.

René Block, Marian Goodman, Arturo Schwarz, *Multiples, ein Versuch die Entwicklung des Auflagenobjektes darzustellen*, Berlin: Neuer Berliner Kunstverein, 1974.

Daniel Buchholz and Gregorio Magnani, *International Index of Multiples from Duchamp to the Present*, Tokyo: Wacoal Art Center of Spiral Garden, 1992.

John L. Tancock, *Multiples: the First Decade*, Philadelphia: the Philadelphia Museum of Art, 1971.

PERIODICALS

Arts Magazine, "Prints and Editions" column, 1988–92.

Artist's Proof, New York: Pratt Institute, Barre Publishers, and New York Graphic Society, 1961–71.

Nouvelles de l'Estampes.

Print Review, New York: Pratt Institute, Barre Publishers, and New York Graphic Society, 1972–1985.

Print Quarterly, 1984–

The Print Collector's Newsletter, 1970–

Tamarind Technical Papers and *The Tamarind Papers*, 1974–

View, Oakland and San Francisco: Crown Point Press, 1979–

TECHNIQUE

Garo Z. Antreasian and Clinton Adams, *The Tamarind Book of Lithography: Art and Techniques*, New York: Harry N. Abrams, 1971.

Jules Heller, *Printmaking Today*, New York: Holt, Rinehart and Winston, 1972.

————, *Papermaking*, New York: Watson, Guptill, 1978.

Gabor Peterdi, *Printmaking Methods Old and New*, New York: Macmillan, 1971.

John Ross, Clare Romano, and Tim Ross, *The Complete Printmaker: Techniques, Traditions, Innovations*, Free Press, 1972, 1989.

Donald Saff and Deli Sacilotto, *Printmaking: History and Process*, New York, etc.: Hold, Rinehard and Winston, 1978.

MONOGRAPHS
See also under Artists' Biographies, pp. 262–82.

Horst Antes
Günther Gercken, *Horst Antes: Catalog of Engravings 1962–1966*, Munich: Galerie Stangl, 1968.

Richard Anuszkiewicz
Stephen F. Eisenman, Nate Beckemeier, Cheryl Brutvan Edward Hawkins, *Richard Anuszkiewicz: Prints and Multiples, 1964–79*, Williamstown, Massachusetts: Sterling and Francine Clark Art Institute, and New York: Brooklyn Museum, 1979.

Arman
Jane Otmezguine and Marc Moreau, with Corice Arman, *Arman Estampes*, Paris, 1990.

Barbara Bloom
Kristin Brooke Schliefer, "Detective Stories: An Interview with Barbara Bloom," *The Print Collector's Newsletter*, Vol. XXI, No. 3, July–August 1990.
Susan Tallman, "Esprit de l'Escalier: Prints by Barbara Bloom," *Arts Magazine*, May 1988.

Christian Boltanski
Susan Tallman, "A Jewish High School in Vienna, 1931," *Arts Magazine*, October 1991.

Lee Bontecou
Richard S. Field, *Prints and Drawings by Lee Bontecou*, Middletown, Connecticut: Davison Art Center, Wesleyan University, 1975.

Louise Bourgeois
Lisa Liebman, "Louise Bourgeois, At Last," *The Print Collector's Newsletter*, Vol. XXIV, No. 1, March–April 1993.

Alberto Burri
Alberto Burri Prints 1959–1977, Rome: 2RC

Editrice, 1978. With essays by Vittorio Rubiu, Cesare Brandi, Maurizio Calvesi. Introduction by Paul Chadbourne Mills.

Pol Bury
Pol Bury: du Point à Ligne/van Punt tot Lijn, Brussels: Musées Royaux des Beaux-Arts de Belgique/Koninklijke Musea voor Schone Kunsten van Belgie, 1976.

Sue Coe
Susan Tallman, "Sue Coe and the Art of Abuse," *Arts Magazine*, April 1989.

Martin Disler
Martin Disler, Juliane Willi-Cosandier, *Martin Disler: the prints 1978–1988*, Geneva: Cabinet des Estampes, Musée d'Art et d'Histoire/St Gallen: Kunstverein St Gallen, 1989.

Carroll Dunham
Keith S. Brintzenhofe, "Carroll Dunham: In Progress to 'Red Shift'", *The Print Collector's Newsletter*, Vol. XIX, No. 6, January–February 1989.

Equipo Crónica
Equipo Crónica: *Obra Grafica y Multiples (1962–1982)*. Bilbao: Museo de Bellas Artes, 1988.

Günther Förg
Dorothea Dietrich, "An Interview with Günther Förg," *The Print Collector's Newsletter*, Vol. XX, No. 3, July–August 1989.
Helmut Draxler, "The Apollonian Moment: the Art of Günther Förg," *The Print Collector's Newsletter*, Vol. XX, No. 3, July–August 1989.
Günther Förg: Gesamte Editionen/The Complete Editions 1974–1988, Rotterdam: Museum Boymans-van Beuningen and Cologne: Galerie Gisela Capitain, 1989. With essays by Luise Horn and Karel Schampers.
Günther Förg: Stations of the Cross, New York: Edition Julie Sylvester, 1990. With essay by Rainer Speck.
Günther Förg: Acht Holzschnitte, Munich: Maximilian Verlag/Sabine Knust, 1990.

Lucian Freud
Lucian Freud: Recent Drawings and Etchings, New York: Matthew Marks Gallery, 1994. With an interview with the artist by Leigh Bowery, and text by Angus Cook.

General Idea
Sandra Simpson, *General Idea: Multiples*, Toronto: S. L. Simpson Gallery, 1993.
Susan Tallman, "General Idea," *Arts Magazine*, May 1990.

Felix Gonzalez-Torres
Susan Tallman, "The Ethos of the Edition: The Stacks of Felix Gonzalez-Torres," *Arts Magazine*, September 1991.
Deborah Wye, "'Untitled (Death by Gun)' by Felix Gonzalez-Torres," *The Print Collector's Newsletter* Vol. XXII, No. 4, September–October 1991.

Red Grooms
Paul Richard, *Red Grooms: a Catalogue Raisonné of his Graphic Work, 19)/–1981*, Nashville Tennessee: Fine Arts Center, 1981.

Hans Hartung
Hans Hartung and Rolf Schmücking, *Hans Hartung: Werkverzeichnis der Graphik, 1921–1965*, Braunschweig, 1965.

Hundertwasser
The Albertina Exhibition of Hundertwasser's Complete Graphic Work 1951–1975, Glarus, Switzerland: Gruener Janura AG, and New York: Art Center, New School for Social Research, 1975.

Jörg Immendorff
Jörg Immendorff: Café Deutschland Gut, Linolschnitte 82/83, Munich: Maximilian Verlag/Sabine Knust, 1983.

Alain Jacquet
Pierre Restany, *Alain Jacquet: Le Déjeuner sur l'herbe 1964–1989. 25e Anniversaire*, Paris 1989.

Allen Jones
Hein Stunke, *Allen Jones das grafische Werk*, Galerie der Spiegel, Cologne.

Donald Judd
John Loring, "Judding From Descartes, Sandbacking, and Several Tuttologies," *The Print Collector's Newsletter*, Vol. VII, No. 1, January–February 1977.

Jane Kent
Susan Tallman, "Prints and Prejudice," *Arts Magazine*, December 1989.

Joyce Kozloff
Interview with Robin White, *View*, Vol. III, 1980.

Robert Kushner
Roberta Bernstein, "The Joy of Ornament: The Prints of Robert Kushner," *The Print Collector's Newsletter*, Vol. XI, No. 1, January–February 1981.
Interview with Robin White, *View 2*, February–March 1980.

Maurício Lasansky
Phillip Lasansky and John Thein, *Lasansky: Printmaker*, Iowa City: University of Iowa Press, 1975.

Bernhard Luginbühl
Charles George and Renée Ziegler, *Bernhard Luginbühl, Oeuvre Gravé/Graphisches Werk*, Geneva: Musée d'Art et d'Histoire, Cabinet des Estampes, 1971.
Grafikkatalog 1974 von Bernhard Luginbühl, Geneva: Musée d'Art et d'Histoire, Cabinet des Estampes, 1974.

Markus Lüpertz
Dorothea Dietrich, "A Conversation with Markus Lüpertz," *The Print Collector's Newsletter*, Vol. XIV, No. 1, March–April 1983.
James Hofmaier (ed.), *Markus Lüpertz: Druckgraphik, Werkverzeichnis 1960–1990*, Stuttgart: Edition Cantz and Munich: Maximilian Verlag-Sabine Knust, 1991. With essays by James Hofmaier, Johann-Karl Schmidt, and Siegfried Gohr.
Günther Gercken, "Renaissance der Druckgraphik: Georg Baselitz, Jörg Immendorff, Markus Lüpertz, A. R. Penck," in Peter Pakesch (ed.)., *Druckgraphik 1970–85*, Graz: Künstlerhaus Graz, Grazer Kunstverein, 1986.

Michael Mazur
Michael Mazur, "Monotype: An Artist's View" in *The Painterly Print: Monotypes from the Seventeenth to the Twentieth Century*, New York: Metropolitan Museum of Art, 1980.
Amy Baker Sandback, "Not Fully Repeatable Information: Michael Mazur and Monotypes – an Interview," *The Print Collector's Newsletter*, Vol. XXI, No. 5, November–December 1990.

Matt Mullican
Nancy Princenthal, "Matt Mullican's Etchings: Rereading the Looking Glass," *The Print Collector's Newsletter*, Vol. XX, No. 5, November–December 1989.

Louise Nevelson
Gene Baro, *Nevelson: the Prints*, New York: Pace Editions, 1974.
Una E. Johnson, *Louise Nevelson: Prints and Drawings 1953–1966* (exhibition catalogue), New York, 1967.
Kristin L. Spangenberg, *Louise Nevelson as Printmaker* (exhibition catalogue), Cincinnati, 1974.

Ben Nicholson
Ben Nicholson – The Graphic Art Checklist and Biography, London: the Victoria and Albert Museum, 1975.
Carol Hogben, *Ben Nicholson: rétrospective de l'oeuvre graphique 1925–1969*, Les Sables-d'Olonne (France): Musée de l'Abbaye de Sainte-Croix, 1977.

Nathan Oliveira
Maudette Ball, *Nathan Oliveira: a Print Retrospective 1949–1980* (exhibition catalogue), Long Beach, California: California State University Art Museum and Galleries, 1980.

Thérèse Oulton
David Cohen, "Thérèse Oulton's Printmaking," *Print Quarterly* 6, December 1989.

Gabor Peterdi
Una E. Johnson, *Gabor Peterdi: 25 years of his prints, 1934–1959*, New York: Brooklyn Museum, 1959.
Gabor Peterdi, *Gabor Peterdi: Graphics 1934–1969*, New York: Touchstone Publishers, 1970.

Judy Pfaff
Judy Pfaff, interview with Constance Llewellyn, *View*, Vol. V, 1986–87.
Susan Tallman, "Six of One…: A Half-Dozen Woodcuts by Judy Pfaff," *Arts Magazine*, November 1988.

Richard Prince
Susan Tallman, "The Psychopathology of Everyday Life (Prince Prints)," *Arts Magazine*, March 1992.

Ceri Richards
Pat Gilmour, "Curiosity, trepidation, exasperation… salvation!" *The Tamarind Papers* 10, Spring 1987.
M. Gooding, S. Jones, *Ceri Richards: Graphic Reading*, Reading: Reading Museum and Art Gallery, and Cardiff: National Museum of Wales, 1979.

Bridget Riley
Bridget Riley: Silkscreen Prints, 1965–1978 (exhibition catalogue), London: Arts Council of Great Britain, 1979.

Tim Rollins + K.O.S.
"Tim Rollins + K.O.S.: Interview with Constance Lewallen," *View* 6, 1988–89.

Robert Ryman
Norbert Lynton, *Order and Experience: Prints by Agnes Martin, Sol LeWitt, Robert Ryman, Robert Mangold, Brice Marden, Edda Renouf*, Arts Council of Great Britain, 1975.
Amy Baker Sandback, *Robert Ryman: Prints 1969–1993*, New York: Parasol Press, 1994.
Naomi Spector, "Robert Ryman: Six Aquatints," *The Print Collector's Newsletter*, Vol. VIII, No. 1, March–April 1977.
Nancy Tousley, *Prints: Bochner, LeWitt, Mangold, Marden, Martin, Renouf, Rockburne, Ryman* (exhibition catalogue with statements by the artists), Toronto: Art Gallery of Ontario, 1975.

Fred Sandback
Fred Sandback: Werkverzeichnis der Druckgrafik 1970–1986, Munich: Galerie Fred Jahn, 1986.

Joel Shapiro
Joel Shapiro/Lithographs 1979–1980, New York: Brooke Alexander, Inc. and Paula Cooper Gallery.

Nancy Princenthal, "Against the Grain: Joel Shapiro's Prints," *The Print Collector's Newsletter*, Vol. XX, No. 4, September–October 1989.

Alan Shields
Howardena Pindell, "Tales of Brave Ulysses: Alan Shields Interviewed by Howardena Pindell," *The Print Collector's Newsletter*, Vol. V, No. 6, January–February 1975.

Kiki Smith
Kiki Smith: Prints and Multiples 1985–1993 (exhibition catalogue raisonné), essay by Nancy Stapen, Boston: Barbara Krakow Gallery, 1994.
Kristin Brooke Schleifer, "Inside & Out: an Interview with Kiki Smith," *The Print Collector's Newsletter*, Vol. XXII, No. 3, July–August 1991.
Susan Tallman, "The Skin of the Stone: Kiki Smith at ULAE," *Arts Magazine*, November 1990.

Richard Smith
Richard Smith, *Richard Smith: a Retrospective Exhibition of Graphics and Multiples*, London: The British Council, 1979. Includes essay originally published in *The Print Collector's Newsletter*, Vol. VI, No. 6, January–February 1976.

David Storey
Susan Tallman, "David Storey: Reductio ad Absurdum," *The Print Collector's Newsletter*, Vol. XXI, No. 3, July–August 1990.

Donald Sultan
Barry Walker, *Donald Sultan: A Print Retrospective*, New York: American Federation of the Arts, 1992.

Günter Uecker
Günter Uecker: Bilder und Objekte (exhibition catalogue), Stuttgart: Staatsgalerie Stuttgart, 1976.

Victor Vasarély
Marcel Joray (ed.), *Victor Vasarely* Vols I and II, Lucerne: Griffon, 1965 and 1970.
Helmut R. Leppien, "Multiples (Serigraphien, Lithographien, Kinetische Tiefenbilder, Reliefs, Dreidimensionale Objekte)" in *Vasarely*, Köln: Kunsthalle Köln, 1971.
Victor Vasarely: Serigrafieen 1949–1966, Amsterdam: Stedelijk Museum, 1967.

Emilio Vedova
Zeno Birolli and Antonello Negri, *Emilio Vedova: Grafica e didattica* (exhibition catalogue), Aosta: 1975.
Massimo Cacciari, "On the Engravings of Emilio Vedova," *Forum International* 12, March–April 1992.
Emilio Vedova: Monotypes from the Garner Tullis Workshop, New York: Pamela Auchincloss Gallery, 1990.

Bram van Velde
Hans-Herman Rief, *Das gesamte graphische Werk von Bram van Velde*, Worpswede: Worpsweder Kunsthalle, 1969.

Bram van Velde, Das graphische Werk, Band II, Worpswede: Worpsweder Kunsthalle, 1972.
Rainer Michael Mason, *Bram van Velde: Les Lithographies, 1923–1973*, Paris: Yves Rivière, 1973.
Bram van Velde: Les Lithographies: 1923–1973, Geneva: Cabinet des Estampes, 1974. With essays by Rainer Michael Mason and Jacques Putman, and preface by Charles Georg and Rudolph Koella.

Carel Visser
Carel Visser, Amsterdam: the Amsterdam Art Foundation, 1992.
Nicholas Serota, B. M. Reise, *Sculptor's Work by Carel Visser: Sculpture, Drawings, Prints and Jewellery 1952–1977*, London: Whitechapel Art Gallery, Bristol: Arnolfini Gallery, and Glasgow: Third Eye Center, 1978.

Not Vital
Robert Rainwater, "Signs of Life: Not Vital's Prints and Books," *The Print Collector's Newsletter*, Vol. XXIII, No. 2, May–June 1992.
Beat Stutzer, *Not Vital: Druckgrafik & Multiples*, Chur: Bündner Kunstmuseum, 1991.

June Wayne
Mary Welsh Baskett, *The Art of June Wayne*, New York: Harry N. Abrams, Inc. and Berlin: Gebrüder Mann Verlag, 1969.
June Wayne, "Broken Stones and Whooping Cranes: Thoughts of a Willful Artist," *The Tamarind Papers* 13 (1990).

Robin Winters
Holland Cotter, "Robin Winters: Performing in Print," *The Print Collector's Newsletter*, Vol. XIX, No. 4, September–October 1988.

aquatint: an intaglio process for creating an even tonal field. Particles of an acid-resistant material (powdered resin or asphaltum, spray lacquer, or spray paint) are deposited and fixed to the plate. When the plate is immersed in acid, only the interstices around the particles are bitten. When the particles are removed by a solvent, the surface of the plate exhibits a granular pattern of tiny pits and bumps. Depending on the size of the particles, the nature of their distribution, and the action of the acid, aquatint can produce an effect of velvety smoothness, or of rough stubble.

artist's book: though the term can apply to a broad range of works, it is usually reserved for books whose entire design is an expression of the artist's concept (as opposed to the *livre d'artiste*, in which the artist has provided isolated images to accompany a literary text). The form is generally dated from Dieter Roth's and Ed Ruscha's books of the late 1950s and early 1960s, and it blossomed in the 1970s with the rise of physically modest, conceptually rich art.

artist's proof (AP): a number of impressions pulled at the same time as the regular, numbered edition, traditionally set aside for the artist's use. Artist's proofs usually number no more than ten percent of the edition.

asphaltum: a bituminous compound that is acid-resistant and often used in etching grounds and aquatints. It can also be used in place of lithographic tusche.

BAT: the proof designated by the artist as the example that all impressions in the edition must match. Literally, "bon à tirer" – "good to print." Also called a "right to print" or RTP.

bleed: an image that runs to the edge of a sheet of paper, having no margins, is said to "bleed."

burin: a tool used for engraving, with a long metal shaft that ends in an angled lozenge-shaped tip. It carves a V-shaped groove in the metal, pushing the displaced metal before it, and creating a clean rich line. It is also called a "graver." (See **engraving**.)

cancellation proof: a proof pulled to demonstrate that a plate or stone has been defaced, and can therefore no longer yield an edition.

carborundum: an abrasive powder made of carbon and silicon. It is used for giving new grain to lithography stones, and has also been used in a form of intaglio printing invented by the artist Dox Thrash in the 1930s. The carborundum is fixed to a plate where its rough granular surface behaves much like aquatint.

cast paper: a form of paper made with a sculptural mold. The pulp dries on the form, assuming its three-dimensional shape.

chiaroscuro woodcut: a woodcut printed from multiple blocks, in which one block is used for line, while others are used for tone. A popular form of reproduction in the sixteenth century, it has been used most notably in the late twentieth century by Georg Baselitz.

chine collé: a method of attaching a thin piece of paper to the surface of a print with glue, in the process of printing. The paper used is often thin and smooth, and thus able to take a finer impression than the more substantial paper beneath. In contemporary prints, it is often used for purely aesthetic reasons, exploiting the visual qualities of the collé paper rather than its agility at reproducing printed line.

chop: a symbol embossed or blind-stamped in the margins of a print to indicate the printer, publisher, and sometimes the artist.

collagraph: a three-dimensional matrix that is usually built up by collaging elements with glue. It can be printed by intaglio and/or relief methods. An accessible craft method, it is rarely used in professional shops.

collotype: a photographic print method invented in the nineteenth century, which prints continuous tone rather than screened dots. A glass or zinc plate is coated with a light-sensitive gelatine, then exposed to light. Where the gelatine is hardened by light, more ink adheres, where the gelatine remains soft and moist less ink adheres. The image is fragile, and very long runs are difficult to maintain. Collotype is a rare printerly specialty, but can produce a remarkably subtle image. It has been used to great effect by Richard Hamilton in works such as *I'm Dreaming of a Black Christmas* (1971). The process is sometimes called "heliotype."

colophon: a page accompanying a portfolio or bound into a book, which gives essential information about how and by whom the work was made. The colophon commonly lists the printer, publisher, medium, paper, edition size, and in the case of typographic works, the typeface used.

debossing: an inverted form of embossing, in which a relief plate is placed *under* the sheet of paper run through a press.

deckle edge: the naturally irregular edge of a handmade sheet of paper. The deckle edge is formed where the paper pulp thins out to nothing at the edges (deckles) of a papermaking mould.

digigraph: an image designed or manipulated on a computer and printed by a computer printer, such as those using ink-jet, laser, or dye-sublimation technologies.

documentation: for technical, ethical, and (more recently) legal reasons, many printers and publishers have adopted a semi-standard practice of documenting their editions. A print's documentation should normally include: the name of the artist, the title, the paper type and size, the edition size, the number and nature of proofs outside the edition, the exact media used and the number of matrices and inking colors, the printer's names, the date of printing, where the image was signed and chopped, and whether or not the matrix was canceled.

dry lithography: a recently developed form of lithography which does not use the water/grease resistance of traditional lithography. Instead, the image is drawn with a solution of photocopier toner in water, and the non-printing part of the plate is sealed with silicon. Traditional grease pencils and inks can also be used, but this method is somewhat more complicated.

drypoint: an intaglio method that uses neither acid nor the specialized burin of engraving. The image is literally scratched into a bare plate with a needle, sending up rough burrs of metal on either side of the line. These burrs hold large amounts of ink, and provide drypoints with a characteristically fuzzy appearance. The burrs are also very delicate, and unless the plate is steel-faced, will collapse quickly under the pressures of intaglio presses, and drypoint editions therefore tend to be quite small.

edition: usually, a group of identical impressions, printed from the same matrices, and bearing the same title and date. Editions may be "limited" or "unlimited." The size of "limited" editions can vary from two to ten thousand or more. Sometimes the edition size is determined by the printing process itself, as when a stone breaks or a plate wears down; usually, however, the edition is artificially limited by the publisher or artist, and the stones or plates are destroyed or canceled after printing. The size of the edition is often indicated as the lower number in a fraction pencilled in the margin by the artist, while the upper number represents the single impression within the series (thus a print marked 3/35 is the third of thirty-five images in the edition). The upper number does *not* represent the order in which the impressions were printed. Commonly, the edition is accompanied by a number of proofs, pulled for the artist, the printers, or the publishers (see also **artist's proof**). Scrupulous publishers always disclose the number of proofs that exist outside the edition since deceptive marketers have sometimes released multiple "limited" editions of a single image (a regular edition, a roman numeral edition, and vast numbers of proofs). In the last thirty years artists have taken great delight in subverting the standard definition of the edition: in Paolozzi's and Daniel Buren's editions, for example, each impression is a unique color variant even though they are signed and numbered as an edition.

embossing: a form of pressurized printing without ink, such that the paper takes on the physical relief of the plate or block.

engraving: the oldest form of intaglio technique, in which grooves are cut into a bare plate with a burin. Any burrs that would catch ink are removed from the surface, and engraved lines are characteristically smooth and sinuous, with a distinctive tapering end. The standard method of reproducing art from the sixteenth into the nineteenth century, historic engravings have struck most twentieth-century eyes as stiff and formulaic, though the medium has had important champions, most notably Joseph Hecht and S. W. Hayter.

etching: an intaglio process, dating from the sixteenth century, in which the plate is covered with an acid-resistant ground through which lines are drawn with a sharp metal etching needle. When the plate is placed in acid, the exposed lines are bitten, while the protected surface of the plate is not. The strength of the line depends on the strength of the acid and the length of time the plate remains in it. It makes a rougher line than engraving, but allows much greater ease of drawing. Rembrandt was the first great master of the medium, and his experimental, spontaneous approach was a model for the late nineteenth-century painter/etchers such as Whistler, who touted

its "effects" rather than its reproductive capacity. The medium acquired a reputation for effeteness that it has taken much of this century to dispel.

foul biting: on an intaglio plate, any unintentional erosion that occurs when the acid-resistant ground is broken or scratched. Often used deliberately, as in Brice Marden's *Adriatics* (1973), to create subtle surface activity or tone.

ghost: an image pulled from a plate which has been already printed but not re-inked. Monotype plates often yield a succession of ever-fainter ghosts, which artists can use as departure points for further drawing. Ghosts can also be used in editions, as in Richard Diebenkorn's *Large Light Blue* (1980), which was printed as a ghost of *Large Bright Blue* (1980), then enhanced with the addition of secondary plates. Also called a "cognate."

ground: an acid-resistant compound of asphaltum, beeswax and rosin, used to coat etching plates. There are many different varieties. "Hard" grounds present a smooth surface that is easily drawn through with an etching needle, exposing the plate beneath to the acid. "Soft" grounds contain tallow in addition to the other ingredients and thus remain tacky. (See **soft ground** and **lift ground**.)

HC: a form of proof. HC stands for "hors de commerce," or outside of commerce. HC proofs may differ from the edition in some way: they may be printed on a different paper or use a slightly different inking, etc. They are often used by publishers as exhibition copies, enduring rougher treatment than the edition itself.

halftone: a process whereby a continuous tone image (a drawing, painting, photograph, etc.) is translated into small spots of black and white, by being photographed through a ruled glass or contact film screen. If the screen is fine enough (175–300 ruled lines to the inch) the individual dots are not easy to detect, while in coarser screens, such as those used in newspaper printing (about 70 lines to the inch), the dots are clearly visible.

heliogravure: a photographic intaglio process that is capable of printing continuous tone images. No halftone screen is used on the film. Instead, a gelatine tissue is photographically exposed, becoming harder in the lighter areas, softer in the darker, then fixed to a plate prepared with an aquatint ground, the aquatint grain acting in the place of the halftone screen to provide tone. The areas covered by soft tissue etch more quickly than those covered by harder tissue. Unlike photoetching or photoengraving,

where every dot is etched to the same depth, varying only in diameter, in heliogravure darker areas are etched more deeply. The result can be an unparalleled tonal richness and warmth. Long an obscure specialty, gravure became an increasingly popular medium with artists in the 1980s. Most gravures are black and white, but a handful of printshops have had success printing full-color photogravures.

heliorelief: a process invented at Graphicstudio in the 1980s for producing a photomechanical woodcut. A photo-sensitive emulsion is fixed to the wood, then exposed to light passing through a drawing on transparent mylar or some other form of transparent positive. The emulsion is thus hardened in some areas, but can be washed away in others. The block is then sandblasted, leaving the emulsion-covered areas in relief. The emulsion is then removed and the block can be printed.

intaglio: intaglio is a printing process in which ink is applied to a plate and then wiped from the surface, remaining only in the incisions or interstices. When passed through the rollers of the press, the ink is squeezed onto dampened paper. Intaglio prints are characterized by beveled plate marks, where the edges of the plate have embossed the paper, and by the distinctive way in which the ink sits up on the surface of the paper rather than soaking into it. **Aquatint, drypoint, engraving, etching**, and **mezzotint** are all intaglio processes.

letterpress: the relief printing of wooden or lead type using a platen press, in which a large flat plate is brought directly down onto paper, pressing it against the previously inked type, or a Vandercook press, in which rollers ink the type then press the paper over the surface of the type. The term is sometimes applied to other forms of relief printing that do not use type.

lift ground: an etching method whereby a sugar solution (hence the alternative term "sugar lift") is painted over an aquatint, then covered by asphaltum. When placed in warm water, the sugar solution swells and lifts up the asphaltum, exposing the aquatint below, so that only the painted areas are bitten when the plate is immersed in acid, while the rest of the metal surface remains covered with acid-resistant ground. It allows the artist to paint marks that print, rather than having to outline them negatively with a stop-out. The process is an old one, having been used by Gainsborough and later by Rouault, and enjoyed renewed attention as a result of Picasso's lift ground etchings of the 1960s.

linecut: a type of relief print block in which the areas that are not to be printed are removed by chemical or mechanical means. It was for many years a common form of newsprint illustration.

linocut: a relief print in which the design is carved into a sheet of linoleum fixed to a wooden block. Unlike wood, linoleum (which is made of oxidized linseed oil) has no grain, so it lends itself to more fluid carving and will print utterly flat tonal areas. The method was popularized in the 1930s by Matisse, and again by Picasso in the late 1950s.

lithography: a method of printing based on the chemical resistance of oil and water, invented by Aloïs Senefelder in 1798. The image is applied to a grained aluminum plate or to a naturally porous kind of Bavarian limestone using greasy ink ("tusche") or crayon. The plate or stone is then "etched" by a wash of acid and gum arabic, which fixes the image and makes the blank surfaces receptive to water. When tusche is rolled over the surface, it adheres to the artist's marks, but is repelled from the rest of the surface. Paper is then placed against its surface, and the stone or plate is run through a scraper-bar press. Lithographs often exhibit a very flat, polished surface. It is the most "painterly" of print media, both in terms of the artist's actions and the net result. Dismissed earlier in the century as too commercial (etching was considered more "artistic"), lithography was made respectable by the work of European artists such as Picasso. The European printers, like the Americans who emulated them, concentrated on antiquated stone methods that were no longer followed by commercial printers.

livre d'artiste: literally "artist's book," but the English and French terms are commonly used for rather different forms of the book. *Livre d'artiste* usually indicates a limited edition, finely printed volume including a poetic or literary text accompanied by handmade illustrations by one or more artists. Earlier in the century Parisian publishers, such as Vollard, presided over a period of great *livres d'artistes*, and the form has continued to enjoy more serious attention in Europe than in America, with artists such as Tàpies and Baj producing many fine volumes. Robert Motherwell's *A la pintura* (1968–72) and Jasper Johns's *Foirades/Fizzles* (1975–76) are rare examples of superb *livres d'artistes* by American artists.

magnesium plate: a type of matrix (often used by Tyler Graphics) to print both relief and intaglio. Magnesium plates are light and strong and can be printed in enormous sizes; they can either be painted on with an resistant liquid, or developed photochemically.

matrix: any surface which is used as the physical base from which images are printed. Etching plates, lithography stones, and woodblocks are all examples of matrices. Also called the "printing element."

mezzotint: from the Italian *mezzotinto*, "half tint." An intaglio process in which the entire surface of a metal plate is evenly pitted, usually by means of serrated tools called "rockers" or "roulettes," though it can also be done photomechanically. The artist works from dark to light by scraping and burnishing the rough surface to various degrees of smoothness. The rougher the surface, the more ink it holds, and the darker it will print. Mezzotint yields velvet blacks and soft gradations of tone. It was invented in 1642 and was a popular means of reproducing paintings in the eighteenth century.

mold: the device used for making paper, consisting of a mesh stretched tight in a wooden frame, which is dipped into a vat of paper pulp. The water drains through the mesh while the fibers collect on the surface, forming the sheet of paper.

monoprint: essentially a unique variant of a conventional print. The term can refer to etchings which are wiped in an expressive, not precisely repeatable manner; to prints made up of a variety of printing elements that change from one impression to the next; or to prints that are painted or otherwise reworked by hand either before or after printing. Simple hand-painting does not necessarily indicate a monoprint, since it can be repeated accurately enough to produce an edition (as in many of Howard Hodgkin's hand-painted etchings and lithographs).

monotype: a unique print made without the use of a fixed matrix, usually by painting or drawing on an unmarked metal or glass plate which is then run through the press. Though the process of printing transfers most of the ink from the plate to the paper, second impressions, called "ghosts" or "cognates," can be printed or used as the ground for further invention by the artist. The process was invented in the seventeenth century by Giovanni Benedetto Castiglione, a Genoese painter and etcher, and was later revived by Degas and others. A 1980 exhibition at the Metropolitan Museum of Art in New York, *The Painterly Print*, sparked new interest in the medium, particularly among American abstract painters.

multiple: a catch-all term used for editioned works of art that do not fit the traditional categories of print, cast sculpture, or tapestry. Multiples have been made throughout the twentieth

century, but the term came into popular usage in the 1960s, when there was a broad movement to produce inexpensive, mass-produced, works of art, many of which were motorized or had parts that could be altered by their owners.

offset lithograph: the process of almost all commercial printing, which was adapted by art printers in the 1960s. On an offset press the image is transferred from the lithographic plate to a cylindrical blanket, and then onto paper. Because of this double action, images do not appear reversed (as they do in etching, traditional lithography, or relief printing). Offset printing also works with thinner inks that dry more quickly, and can be used to lay down several transparent layers to attain subtle gradations of tone. Offset lithography often uses photomechanical processes.

open bite: an intaglio process in which unprotected areas of the plate are exposed to acid to produce a very light tone. The action of the acid lowers the surface of the plate around any stopped-out area, but since both areas remain smooth, ink will only be held around the periphery of the raised design. Open bite can also be used to lower the relief of an aquatint, eating down the raised bumps and thereby decreasing the depth of the ink-holding pits, causing it to print lighter.

original print: an artwork developed expressly for printed form (rather than a reproduction carried out without the involvement of the artist). The distinction originated at the time of Whistler, but it has proved notoriously difficult to define, and had occasioned more controversy among artists, publishers, curators, and collectors than any other issue of the contemporary print. As late as the 1960s it was assumed that the presence of photomechanical means obviated the presence of "originality" – an idea that had to be set aside in the face of the photomechanical painting of Rauschenberg and Warhol. Other definitions demanded that the artist work directly on the printing matrix, but the profusion of important prints, such as those by Paolozzi, in which the artist did not participate manually, dispelled that notion. It is now generally recognized that in prints, as in other forms of art, "originality" is a nebulous quality, whose presence or absence no rule can ensure.

paper: matted cellulose fibers; the material most commonly printed upon. Papermaking was invented in China some time in the first century BC, and appears to have arrived in Europe some 1500 years later. To create handmade paper, a two-part wooden frame with a mesh stretched across it (a mold), is lowered into a vat of slurry (fiber pulp and water), then lifted out, allowing the water to drain, and shaken to distribute the fibers evenly. The upper part of the frame is removed and the sheet is "couched" onto blankets where it dries. There is an almost infinite variety of papers: smooth, rough, handmade, machine-made, sized, unsized, coated, uncoated, laid, wove, and so on. Most Western art papers are "rag" papers made with cotton fibers, since the far cheaper woodpulp is highly acidic and produces unstable paper. The most commonly used papers for etchings and lithographs are Arches and Rives BFK (which both come in a variety of colors and weights.) The last three decades have seen a great resurgence of handmade papers. In the 1970s artists and printers in America became fascinated with the traditional Japanese handmade papers such as Gampi and Kozo (made from the strong sinewy fibers of mulberry bark), and began to view paper not simply as the support for artwork but as artwork in itself. Numerous methods were perfected that allowed artists to "paint," "draw," and "sculpt" with paper pulp. Rauschenberg's *Pages* and *Fuses* (1973–74), and Hockney's *Paper Pools* (1978) are highlights of these developments. (See also **cast paper**.)

photo-engraving: a way of making a photographic relief plate, using acid to eat away non-printing areas. It was widely used commercially earlier in this century, but is not often used in art.

photo-etching: an intaglio process in which the etching plate is coated with a light-sensitive acid-resistant ground and exposed, through a dot screen, to a photographic image. A "negative" resist dissolves in the areas that are exposed to light, while hardening in areas not exposed to light. Thus pits are etched and ink is held in the areas that appeared light in the photographic image. A positive resist dissolves where it is not exposed to light.

photogravure: a term used both generally, for any photographic intaglio process, and specifically, for the continuous-tone process also known as **heliogravure**. There is also, confusingly, a commercial intaglio photographic process called photogravure which employs halftone screens and a plate which is curled around a cylinder for "rotogravure" printing.

photolithography: a form of lithography in which light-sensitive plates are exposed to a photographic image, usually by means of a halftone screen. The vast majority of photolithographs are made on aluminum plates for offset presses, but it is possible to make photolithographs with stones as well.

photomechanical: a term referring to any process that allows a photographic image to be transferred to a mechanical matrix. This is usually done by means of a dot screen through which the continuous gradations of photography are translated into spots of black or white, or, in the case of color processes, the four "process" hues.

photoscreenprint: a form of screenprint in which a light-sensitive resist is applied to the screen and exposed to a photographic image that has been broken down by a dot screen. Areas exposed to light harden, while those unexposed do not and can be washed away, leaving an open mesh for the ink to pass through.

plate marks: the embossed ridge of paper left by the edge of a plate when printed under pressure.

plate tone: in intaglio printing, the surface of the plate may not be wiped entirely clean, continuing to bear a film of ink that prints on the paper as a pale tone. It was used extensively by Rembrandt and Whistler to produce misty effects and to heighten the drama of passages where pure white appears.

pochoir: French for "stencil." Stencils can be made from paper, film, plastic, or etched through thin metal. Color can be applied with dabbers, brushes, sprayguns, or other means. It has been used as a medium in its own right by artists from Matisse to Joel Shapiro, and it is a common way of "hand-coloring" an edition of prints consistently.

proof: any print that is not part of a regular edition. Trial proofs are pulled to check progress while a print is being made. Working proofs are trial proofs on which the artist has altered by hand – drawing, painting, etc. Other proofs may be indistinguishable from the print edition, but are not part of the regular numbering sequence, such as artist's proofs (APs) or printer's proofs (PPs; see also **artist's proof**).

publishing: print publishing can take many forms, and can encompass many different relationships between artist, printer, and dealer, but generally the publisher pays for the development and printing of the edition, in exchange for a percentage (usually 50 percent) of the profits. Although some publishers simply split the edition itself, giving the artist half of the prints, most maintain control of the entire edition, excepting the artist's proofs. Publishers may be identical with printshops (as in Tyler Graphics, Gemini, or ULAE) or they may exist independently, hiring printers as required (contract printing). Some publishers

are creatively involved in the development of the project, overseeing it on a daily basis, others simply fund the projects.

register, registration: the placement of sequentially printed plates so that everything lines up correctly in the final image.

RTP: see **BAT**

relief printing: any form of printing, such as woodcut or linocut, in which raised areas are inked and printed while recessed areas are not.

resist: any material applied to a surface to prevent the passage of another material. Most commonly, acid-resistant grounds or varnishes used to protect a plate in etching, or materials applied to a screen to prevent the passage of ink in screenprinting.

screenprint: a printing method invented at the beginning of the twentieth century, screenprinting is a variant on the ancient technique of the stencil. Ink is forced through stretched mesh fabric (traditionally silk, but now usually synthetic), parts of which have been blocked out. It differs fundamentally from other techniques in that the image is passed through the surface rather that being transferred from the surface. There is no mirror reversal. The block-out can be painted by hand with glue or lacquer; an adhesive film or tissue may be used which can be cut with a knife, then applied to the screen; or a light-sensitive resist may be painted on the screen and developed photographically. Screenprinting was used commercially since the 1920s on surfaces that were unprintable by other means: soda boxes, crates, etc. Its popularity as an art medium surged in the 1960s in part because of its commercial associations, and also because of its facility for hard-edged, flat patterns and for photographic manipulation.

serigraph: a name for screenprint coined in the 1930s, and later used in yet another attempt to distinguish artistic forms of printing from commercial ones. To make "serigraphs," the artist painted directly on the screen. Most contemporary screenprints have been made photomechanically or with knife-cut films instead, though Jasper Johns and other artists have made extraordinary, painterly, screenprints using "serigraphic" methods.

silkscreen: see screenprint.

soft ground: a non-drying etching ground used to produce soft lines and complex textures. Cloth and other objects can be pressed into the ground, leaving an impression that is transferred to the plate when it is bitten by acid. A piece of cloth or paper could also be laid on the soft ground and drawn on: when the cloth or paper is lifted from the surface, it pulls up some of the sticky ground with it, to give a broader, more granular line than that of an etching needle.

spit bite: an intaglio method in which the artist paints or splashes acid on a plate which has usually been prepared with an aquatint ground. The result can vary from a strong, painterly gesture to a delicate, translucent wash. The name derived from the fact that the brush used contains water or saliva.

siligraph: see **dry lithography**.

state: an intermediary stage in the development of a print. It is common for more than one edition to be printed from the same matrix in different states. Artists may choose to print the same plates or stones with two different inkings (as in Johns's *Fool's House*, 1972, and *Fool's House Black State*, 1972); or they may choose to rework a stone after an edition has been printed and print subsequent editions after each reworking (as in Picasso's famous *Bull* series, or Elizabeth Murray's *Untitled, States I–V*).

stereotype: a cast-metal relief printing surface. The term is often used to describe the type of photographic relief block commonly used for newspaper illustrations and advertisements. It has been used only occasionally by artists, most notably in the work of K. P. Brehmer in the 1960s.

stop-out: a means of shaping an aquatint field by painting the surface with an acid-resistant varnish before immersion in acid. The areas covered by the stop-out will not be bitten, while those left uncovered will. Stop-out varnish may also be used in line etching or soft ground etching to correct mistakes by covering accidentally exposed areas of the plate before it is put in acid.

sugar lift: see **lift ground**.

tusche: German for "ink," it is the name given to the greasy liquid used to make marks on a lithographic stone, plate, acetate, or Mylar. It can be thinned to the consistency of drawing ink or thickened into a solid form. Lithographic tusche can also be used to create hand-drawn stencils for screenprint.

Ukiyo-e: The great Japanese tradition of woodblock prints, celebrating the ephemeral pleasures of the world, that thrived from the seventeenth century into the nineteenth. Technically, the prints are distinguished from Western woodcuts by being made up of shaped blocks that are inked and then fit together (as opposed to blocks carved in relief to isolate a linear design). They are also printed with water-based rather than oil-based inks, and by careful hand-rubbing, rather than with a press. The result is a delicate, translucent image often deceptively akin to watercolors. When they were first seen in the West in the mid-nineteenth century, they started a tremendous fashion for Japanese decorative arts, and caused profound changes in the way European artists arranged and structured space (visible in the work of Gauguin, Toulouse-Lautrec, and Whistler). In the late 1970s a number of Western artists and printers became interested in the Ukiyo-e printing tradition, working with printers in Japan and in the United States.

waterless planography: see **dry lithography**.

watermark: an image formed in a sheet of paper when it is made, usually by sewing a wire or cast-metal design to the screen against which the paper pulp is drained. The paper is thinner where the wire sat, and will appear more translucent when held up to the light. Traditionally watermarks carried the name and device of the paper manufacturer, but handmade sheets can be made with watermarks in the form of an artist's signature or other designs. It is possible to make photographic watermarks, in which areas of light and dark are translated into areas of high and low relief in a wire mesh; where the relief is higher, the paper is thinner, and more light shines through, as seen in Barbara Bloom's *Esprit de l'Escalier* paper works (1988).

waxtype: a screenprinting method, developed at Graphicstudio, that uses wax-based pigments rather than conventional screenprint inks. The result is a surface with greater dimensional relief and tactile interest.

woodblock print: a relief print made from shaped blocks of wood that are not necessarily carved on the printing surface, as a woodcut is. Japanese Ukiyo-e prints are often described as woodblocks rather than woodcuts. But many relief prints combine both shaped blocks and incised blocks, and the terms are sometimes used interchangeably.

woodcut: the most ancient form of printing, dating back to the Chinese T'ang Dynasty (AD 618–906), and deriving from the practice of taking rubbings from stone inscriptions of famous writings. A block of wood is carved in relief, rolled with ink, and pressed against paper so that the raised portions print and the depressed portions do not. In the European woodcut tradition, the artist would draw a linear design on the block and the rest would be cut away, usually by artisans. In Europe, its greatest early exponent was Dürer; after the sixteenth century, engraving, which could provide much more detail, was favored over woodcut. Woodcut enjoyed a resurgence in the hands of Gauguin and Munch in the late nineteenth century, and again with the German Expressionists a few decades later. The Asian tradition of relief prints differs technically from that of Europe, employing water-based inks rather than oil-based ones, and hand-rubbing rather than presses (see **Ukiyo-e**), but twentieth-century artists have often employed elements of both.

wood engraving: a form of **relief print**, invented by Bewick in the late eighteenth century, in which the image is cut into the end-grain of a block of wood using engraving tools. It can produce extremely fine and stable lines that can provide an illusion of tonal change. It was the standard method of newspaper and magazine illustration throughout the nineteenth century. Enormously labor intensive, it has been used in recent years only rarely, most notably by Peter Blake.

ACKNOWLEDGMENTS

This book would not have been possible without the keen and congenial assistance of hundreds of artists, printers, curators, and print publishers. Foremost, I must thank Karen McCready, without whose enthusiasm and generosity this book would never have been written. Among the many others who have provided indispensable help and advice, Robert Monk was a font of useful fact and opinion from the earliest days of this project. In Amsterdam, Ad Petersen offered encyclopedic observations of European art of the 1960s and 1970s. Elizabeth Armstrong at the Walker Art Center in Minneapolis contributed her broad knowledge of print production throughout the United States, providing necessary correctives for New York provincialism, as did the staff of the Print Club of Philadelphia, which brought me into contact with hundreds of independent printmakers. Robert Rainwater and Roberta Waddell of the New York Public Library, and Jurrie Poot and Kick Splinter at the Stedelijk were all profoundly helpful in tracking down prints and publications that might otherwise have escaped my notice.

Among those who have given liberally of their time, records, and photographs are Mark Baron, Peter Blum, Gisela Capitain, Michael Domberger, Zsa-Zsa Eyck, Robert Feldman at Parasol Press, Delano Greenidge, Niels Borch Jensen, Sabine Knust, Franz Larese at Erke Verlag, Jack Lemon at Landfall Press, Jean Milant at Cirrus Editions, Leslie Miller at Grenfell Press, Denise René, Betsy Senior, Judy Solodkin at Solo Press, Linda Tyler at Tamarind Institute, Giorgio Upiglio at Grafica Uno, and Diane Villani. Sidney Felsen at Gemini GEL, Bill Goldston at ULAE, and Ken Tyler and Marabeth Cohen-Tyler at Tyler Graphics provided kilos of transparencies and archival information. Meg Malloy at Editions Schellmann in New York more than once stepped into the breach to supply vital materials. Alan Cristea and Paul Cornwall-Jones provided essential and entertaining accounts of British print activities of the 1960s and 1970s.

Many artists have also been generous with both time and materials, especially Pierre Alechinsky, Eleanor Antin, Enrico Baj, Mel Bochner, Pol Bury, Jeanne-Claude and Christo, Franz Gertsch, Karl Gerstner, Michael Mazur, Claes Oldenburg, Nathan Oliveira, Tom Phillips, Joe Tilson, Pierre Soulages, Michelle Stuart and Troels Wörsel. Sharon Avery-Fahlström was a great source of information and insight about the work of her late husband.

I have, throughout, depended upon an army of helpful and well informed gallery and museum staffs, who searched files, wrestled works out of storage, arranged photography sessions, cajoled artists, and arranged a mass of necessary details. In particular, I would like to thank Jil Weinberg Adams, Riva Blumenfeld, Sybille Boppart at Parkett, Pia Dornacher at Galerie van de Loo, Andy Ehrenworth at Susan Sheehan Gallery, Andrea Gayle and Elizabeth Sarnoff at Brooke Alexander Editions, Bryn James and Joanna Lohse James at the Richard Paul Lohse-Stiftung, Tom Jones and the late Joe Fawbush of Fawbush Gallery, Maura Marx at Galerie Heike Curtze, Cécile Panzieri at Galerie Lelong, Lieschen Potzunik at the Art Institute of Chicago, Anna Ramis at Fundació Antoni Tàpies, Joan Rothfuss and Siri Engberg at the Walker Art Center, Kim Schmidt at Crown Point Press, Anna Stein and Nina del Rio at Sotheby's, Tamantha Kuenz at the Philadelphia Museum, and Gordon Veneklasen at Michael Werner. Kathleen Dempsey at Waddington Graphics/Alan Cristea Gallery demonstrated both sublime patience and a near-miraculous ability to procure photographs and reference materials. Raymond Lokker in Tokyo provided perspicacious observations on the interweaving of print technique and art ideas. Karina Marotta in Madrid and Katerina Vatsella in Bremen were both generous with their expertise.

I must also acknowledge my debt to those earlier scholars and writers who demonstrated, at a time when it was not generally evident, the riches of printed art. The work of Riva Castleman, Richard S. Field, Ruth Fine, Pat Gilmour, Jeremy Lewison, Rainer Michael Mason, and Judith Goldberg provided the firm and necessary foundation upon which this book stands.

The final form of this text owes much to Nicolas Collins, Karen McCready, Jane Kent, and Wendy Monk, all of whom fought their way through the text in various less-than-sublime stages of its development. Finally, I must express my gratitude to my friends and family, who have been patient beyond expectation, supportive beyond measure, and cheerful beyond reason.